THE LEGACY OF HEGEL

THE LEGACY OF HEGEL

PROCEEDINGS OF THE
MARQUETTE HEGEL SYMPOSIUM
1970

EDITED BY

J. J. O'MALLEY, K. W. ALGOZIN,
H. P. KAINZ AND L. C. RICE

MARTINUS NIJHOFF / THE HAGUE / 1973

TABLE OF CONTENTS

Table of contents

EDITORS' PREFACE

The present volume represents the proceedings of the Marquette Hegel Symposium, held at Marquette University, Milwaukee, Wisconsin, on June 2-5, 1970. The Symposium, celebrating the two-hundredth anniversary of Hegel's birth, was presented under the combined sponsorship of the Philosophy Department of Marquette University, the American Council of Learned Societies, and the Johnson Foundation of Racine, Wisconsin. Its general theme embraced not only specific topics of interest in contemporary Hegel studies, but also the wider aspects of the influences and impact of Hegel's thought upon contemporary philosophical, political, and social problems. Principal contributors and panelists were selected for their scholarly achievements in Hegel studies and also in keeping with the broad view of the Hegelian legacy in current thought. All sessions of the Symposium were plenary, and designed for maximum discussion and interchange among participants. The Symposium Committee regrets that it has not been feasible to incorporate the transcript of the discussions (except for the round-table discussion on editing and translating Hegel) into this volume.

The papers presented in each day's sessions are published here with editorial changes and corrections made by their respective authors. The papers by Professors Otto Pöggeler and Eric Weil were originally translated by members of our Committee: the present versions incorporate many changes and corrections made by their authors. The comments on each paper were brought into their present form only after the Symposium, and in the light of the discussions which took place during it. The papers by Professors John Riedl and Nathan Rotenstreich were not delivered at the Symposium, and are thus included here as appendices. A bibliographical survey of recent Hegel scholarship by Professor Frederick Weiss was circulated among all the Symposium participants for comment: it appears here (as the third appendix) updated and with numerous revisions.

Lastly, the forward, "Thinking with Hegel," was prepared by Professor James Collins with the all-but-complete manuscript of this volume in hand.

The Symposium Committee would like to express its especial gratitude to Professor Paul Byrne, chairman of the Philosophy Department, and to the many other members of the Department whose planning and effort went into the Symposium. Thanks also are due to Professor James Collins, at Saint Louis University, for his many suggestions and useful comments along the way to our preparing the manuscript for publication. Preparation of the manuscript for this volume was supported by a grant from the Marquette University Committee on Research.

Joseph J. O'Malley
Keith W. Algozin
Howard P. Kainz
Lee C. Rice

THINKING WITH HEGEL

James Collins

We are inveterate commemorators, whether concerning our private lives or the common history of humanity. Especially when there looms upon the horizon a round-number anniversary of an outstanding political or religious figure, a poet or musician, a scientist or philosopher, we feel summoned to make some special response of celebration and interpretation. The quality of such a commemorative response is not measured by its lavish appearance, but rather by the range and perceptiveness of the effort to rethink a great man's accomplishments and his facets of significance for ourselves. The more we penetrate into his work and vision, taken in their own form as well as their shaping impact upon subsequent history, the more we enrich our sense of human resources to draw upon in meeting the problems of present existence. A commemoration signifies both that the source in question has an unsuspected fecundity, still to be realized, and that its realization comes about in the course of our active wrestling with issues rather than in the artificial calm of pure recall.

What are some of the appropriate kinds of questions to raise in an attempt to do commemorative justice to the bicentennial of Georg Wilhelm Friedrich Hegel's birth in 1770? I think it is essential to investigate at least five broad areas, upon which our understanding and use of his philosophy depend. They are: the state of the text, the progress of translation, internal problems of genesis-method-system, comparative relationships with other philosophers in the past, and critical points of connection with our contemporary modes of philosophizing. It is a measure of Hegel's extraordinary achievement that he should thus put our minds on the stretch, along all these approaches taken together. A quite definite functional meaning of his philosophical greatness is that he requires us to consider so wide a compass of issues, in order to assess his work and inter-workings with ourselves. Thinking philosophically with Hegel is a complex, always growing relationship which, at a fitting time of commemoration, we can seek to restate along at least these five main lines.

In studying most modern philosophers, we seldom encounter major questions about textual authenticity, such as frequently occur in ancient and medieval philosophy. But Hegel is an important exception to this rule, as we soon discover if we look for the original-language statement of some favorite quotation from him. Often a pithy expression will be found in the main text of an older edition of Hegel, but will be discreetly relegated to the section reserved for additions, conflations, and variant readings, in a critically edited version. Although some introductory expositions of his thought continue to ignore this change of textual status or treat it as philosophically insignificant, such practice is being more widely challenged. Sometimes, the findings of an advanced study of Hegel will turn precisely around the reservations which philosophical analysis must make in the use of some venerable, yet textually questionable, statements and entire sections.

A good function of a commemorative occasion is to pace ourselves on such improvements in textual presentation and historical practice. Using the 1931 centenary of Hegel's birth as a marker, we can observe the gradual formation of an attitude of increased sensitivity about the textual situation on the part of the worldwide community of Hegelian scholars, not just on the part of a few editors. Forty years ago, it was important to have the Jubilee Edition make more widely available the older collected edition of Hegel's writings, edited by his own students and followers. At the same time, it was clearly advantageous to have the textually reliable Meiner editions of the books published by Hegel himself. Especially in the case of the *Encyclopedia of the Philosophical Sciences* and the *Philosophy of Right*, however, there was a noticeable displacement of many familiar paragraphs. This called attention to the role of Hegel's first-generation editors in conflating their lecture notes and correcting even Hegel's own text, in accord with their philosophical and literary standards. If one then ventured into Hegel's posthumously published lecture courses, the discrepancies increased sharply between texts for which there is manuscript warrant from Hegel himself and the long-standard versions established by his early editors. For instance, there was a very sharp cutback of materials directly attributable to Hegel in the *Lectures on the Philosophy of Religion*, as well as a doctrinally significant reordering of the topics.

Such changes did not remove all value and authority from the Additions and previous versions of the Lectures, since something of Hegel's thought somehow suffused these records. But better controls were needed over the "something and somehow" factors. As the comparisons became available, they did generate in the wider company of Hegelian scholars a demand for a truly critical edition in which these kinds of texts would be clearly distinguished, providing a basis for determining their relationships and their roles in any subsequent historical interpretation of this philosophy. The story of the editorial plans and work, from Lasson and Hoffmeister to Pöggeler, is told authoritatively in the present volume by Pöggeler himself.

The crucial part played by translations is often unrealistically overlooked or downgraded. And yet the circulatory life of philosophy depends very considerably for its health upon the use of translations. Philosophy students in non-Germanic countries are usually eager to study the books of Hegel even before their command over the German language is sufficient to permit a reading of them in the original. This desire to move beyond lecture notes and secondary studies to a more direct engagement with the source philosopher deserves encouragement, even when the further acquaintance stops short with a translation. Students can make noticeable progress through this means, coming closer to grips with Hegel's modes of expression and argument. Some readers will then be motivated to read the original texts, but even those who never advance into the German works will have gained a foothold and made Hegel a permanent companion in their own philosophizing.

We are now in an exciting period when a new generation of Hegel translations is appearing. The pressures for such work come from many directions and are indicative of Hegel's surpassing stature as a philosopher. One demand is generated simply by the appearance of the critically edited German works, which expose the shortcomings of translations that were based upon the earlier collected works. It is likely that English readers will not be satisfied until all the Hegel translations match, in their own manner, the critical edition currently being published. T. M. Knox's rendition of the *Philosophy of Right* can serve as a model, and in the present volume Kenley Dove expresses the standard being observed for the *Phenomenology of Spirit*. A second source of discontent with older English versions lies in the general momentum of historical studies on Hegel. No matter what language is used for a truly pioneer and thorough study of some book of Hegel or problem in him, the consequence is likely to be a more careful understanding of central texts and a more rigorous, explicitly declared, policy in translating the key terms. Thus the looseness of previous English translations of *Geist* and *Vorstellung* is not tolerable under

present conditions of scholarship, which require that the defects be corrected and unnecessary obstacles removed.

Another reason for the retranslating of Hegel tells us a good deal about
ourselves, as well as about him. Our increased interest in the problem of
language is having a marked effect upon the quality demanded of translations. We want them to be sufficiently authentic and in the spirit of the
original to enable us to come close to Hegel's own use of language and concern for it. That concern expresses itself formally in a theory about language in general; it is also manifest in Hegel's many arguments probing
into the terms and constructions of the German language; and it under-
girds his constantly sensitive use of many stylistic modes of language, however difficult the actual text thus becomes for readers. All these qualities
have to be skillfully conveyed in translations that hope to function in today's linguistically oriented community of philosophers. It is perfectly legitimate to expect a basic linguistic faithfulness of this complex sort, so
that analyses of Hegel's concepts and arguments can be made on more
reliable grounds by philosophers who nevertheless do not intend to spend
additional effort in studying his original-language expressions. Particularly this consideration leads me to regard the problem of translating Hegel
as being crucial for his wider and more authentic inclusion in contemporary philosophical discussions.

At first acquaintance, the history of modern philosophy seems to be a
ponderous structure, wherein each system of thought occupies a fixed and
fully carved niche to be studied but in no way altered by ourselves. In order
to dispel this misleading impression, however, we have only to consider
Hegel from the genetic standpoint. It is only within our century that the
materials about his early development have become available, and only
within the past four decades that the theme of Young Hegel has been
intensively cultivated by historians. They have uncovered and emphasized
his early, foundational interest in economic and political affairs, literature
and the other arts, the inner conflicts among Greek-Jewish-Christian religious ideals and institutional expressions, and the specific philosophical
developments from Kant to Fichte and Schelling. Each of these facets
yields a new appreciation of Hegel's complex mind and comprehensive
aims in philosophy. Precisely how to correlate and emphasize the several
lines of his genetic thought presents a problem, as well as a real opportunity, for current researchers. That one's interpretation of the Young Hegel
affects many other issues in his later work can be verified – in the instance
of his theories of religion and social philosophy – by examining the essays

here contributed by Shlomo Avineri, Emil Fackenheim, and Kenneth Schmitz.

As the lineaments of Hegel's early reflections become more firmly drawn, we are beginning to reformulate some older questions concerning Hegelian method and system. The phenomenology of experience and the lifeworld of spirit no longer spring up mysteriously in the *Phenomenology of Spirit*, but can now be appreciated as constituting Hegel's first sustained, published effort at synthesizing the many elements of his initial inquiries. As Eric Weil testifies in this symposium, the dialectical-speculative method has to be reappraised in the light of developmental and comparative studies. It is not an artificial trichotomy imposed upon experience at all costs, and neither is it purely abstract and formal in significance. Historical studies are clarifying Hegel's intention of trying to develop a method that will join the concreteness and fluidity of human life with the philosopher's drive toward comprehensive thought. That we return constantly to a reading of this theory of social conflicts and the relations between conscience and the state, as well as to his reflections on the nature of tragedy and satire, attests his strength in these areas of interweaving descriptive richness and methodic criticism. It is frequently assumed, however, that Hegel's method and system produce but a grotesque failure in the philosophy of nature, and that such a defect dispenses us from weighing his more general claims to interpretive power. John Findlay's contribution challenges this assumption, and fortunately the translation of Hegel's writings on the *Philosophy of Nature* enables us to examine the question independently.

The quickening of interest in Hegel is largely fueled by comparative historical studies, relating him to other thinkers and to influential social tendencies. Sometimes, these paths of comparison establish a perspective coming from the past toward him as its culmination: "From Kant to Hegel" serving as a common rubric for developments in classical German philosophy. This retrospective view is by no means an extrinsic relationship and a luxury which the student of Hegel can readily forego. Although Hegel pronounces rather definitively upon Kant and Fichte, Jacobi and Schelling, in any particular context, it is significant that he never ceases to return to his Greek, German, and British sources when the context shifts and new problems arise. This is a sign that, for the interpreters of Hegel as well as for himself, his philosophy continues to receive fresh import from being considered in this relational spirit. What he teaches on the believing-knowing couplet, on the relation between substance and subject, on the problem of the absolute, on negativity and freedom in history, cannot be

properly grasped without taking into account his complex, lifelong struggles with other philosophers on these issues. He finds partial models in
Aristotle's self-thinking thought and Spinoza's *tractatus theologico-poli-
ticus*, in the Lockean descriptions of understanding and the Kantian antinomies of pure reason. The more capacious our understanding of previous
Western philosophies and cultural formations, the more advantageous is
our position for following Hegel's critical and consummative mind in its
comparative aspects.

The other major perspective regards his philosophy as a point of departure for later thinkers and movements, under the heading of "From
Hegel to Marx to Nietzsche to Heidegger." This is the approach represented here by the Marxian studies of Jean Calvez and James Doull. As an
initial inducement for reading Hegel, we are told that he constitutes an
important part of Marx's background. It is true enough that little sense
can be made of Feuerbach's *Principles of the Philosophy of the Future* or
of Marx's *Economic and Philosophic Manuscripts* and *German Ideology,*
without developing some frame of reference in Hegel and the Hegelian
Right and Left. Yet after this instrumental function is spelled out, there
still remains the challenge of a direct Philosophical study of Hegel, bearing these historical implications and criticisms in mind but not reducing
his philosophy to them. Just as an Aristotle and a Kant retain their philosophical integrity and distinctive methods, even when they are seen to
contribute something to Hegel's formation, so does the latter maintain his
own center of philosophizing with unique problems and insights for us.
The art of historical interpretation grows through our always renewed
modes of relating the comparative approaches to Hegel with the basic
internal analyses of his systemic concepts and reflections upon human experience.

Thinking *with* Hegel is a manner of philosophizing which regards his
work as being too valuable for us to ignore in our present inquiries, even
though we do not intend uncritically to espouse and repeat that work.
Such reflecting in critical openness to Hegel and his own conception of
"pure philosophical thinking" involves historical considerations, but it
cannot be confined to them. Just as Hegel is studied both in his original
German text and through translation into other languages, so his involvement in contemporary argument proceeds both through historical modes
and through direct theoretical analyses. These two sorts of inclusion of
Hegel in present inquiries are reflected in the discussions that occurred
during the present symposium. As the translating and historical interpreting situations improve, we can expect that there will be greater emphasis

in the English-speaking world upon Hegel as a regular component in alternative methodologies and concept constructions.

Especially since his theory of man is being recognized as more central than was previously supposed, he widens his ports of entry into present-day theorizing. Especially his *Science of Logic* has much to offer on such topics as the nature of language and conceptualization, the analysis and interrelation of different knowledge models, the construction of worlds and the achievement of identity through cross-world meanings, the relations between logic and ontology, and the whole process of systemic unification. What makes the Hegelian treatment of these topics so pertinent and demanding is its continuity with the phenomenology of experience, ethical-social relations, and history. Rather than fall on only one side of the great divide among the focal centers of contemporary philosophizing, Hegel's thought helps to uncover their binding problems and convergent goals.

There is one final sense of "thinking with Hegel" that emerges vividly from the present collection, as well as from other centennial meetings and joint publications. The study of Hegel flourishes only as a broadly based, cooperative activity on the part of the entire community of philosophers. Not only does it cut across linguistic barriers and cultural differences, but it also depends for its vitality and truthfulness upon the methods and judgments of diverse philosophical approaches. Whether or not Hegel succeeded in his own time in unifying various standpoints, it is undeniable that an adequate interpretation and use of his philosophy today require joint research and exchange of arguments, involving many philosophers who use different methods and conceptual frameworks. Hegelianism killed itself off in the last century by becoming a coterie possession of a few people, and nothing would be more swiftly fatal to Hegel studies in our century than to conduct them in a sectarian manner and in an esoteric atmosphere. Hegel the human philosopher belongs to humanity and stands open – both in his own intent and in principle – to our common inspection, criticism, and appreciation. The task of Hegelian scholars (like that of the centennial commemorators of Rembrandt and Beethoven) is to open up more routes for us to perceive and rework his contributions to mankind's self-exploration.

HEGEL EDITING AND HEGEL RESEARCH *

Otto Pöggeler

Today Hegel research and the editing of Hegel are pursued both intensively and extensively. Why this should be so is not immediately clear. The emergence of the complex "Hegel research" is certainly not to be explained merely by the fact that today scientific interest extends to all possible subjects. The attempt both to make Hegel's writings available in a complete edition and to research them with historical philology cannot have that relative indifference to the concerns of the present with which a germanist might edit a medieval text or an orientalist investigate an obscure language. (Though, to be sure, in this indifference or equanimity there can lie hidden a passionate commitment to the universal desire to know and an effort to preserve for it a free space not plotted and superintended by society.) Hegel research has participated directly in the attempt of our time to understand itself. For this has entailed philosophizing, and thus, the development of philosophy both with the aid of Hegel and in opposition to him. How is philosophy practiced in today's shrinking world? And what is Hegel's place in this philosophizing?

When we inquire about contemporary philosophy, we may perhaps distinguish – though with simplification – three geographical regions of philosophizing, three great spheres of influence which, to be sure, overlap and interpenetrate in many ways. There is continental Europe: the philosophy that has arisen here keeps alive its history, and at least some philosophical tendencies still consider justified the pursuit of the great fundamental questions of metaphysics, even if this be done by removing oneself from the classical tradition or, as in "hermeneutics," by stressing the historicity of all thinking. To the east (as seen from continental Europe) philosophy is bound to a politically instituted, marxist *Weltanschauung*. But this *Weltanschauung* has received a new stimulus with the announcement in the Soviet Union of the transition from socialism to ("more humanitar-

* Transl. Keith and Mary Algozin.

ian") communism, with the cultural revolution in China, and with the various neo-marxian revolutions in the European countries. To the west the English speaking world forms another independent sphere of influence. (The Scandanavian countries belong here, while South America and Japan appear more receptive at present to the influence of the continent.) English "common sense" (in conjunction with the old nominalistic and analytical traditions) has become highly stylized into a philosophizing which rejects all speculative thought as well as an immediate interrelation of theory and practice; it tends, rather, to a pragmatism which permits no questions other than those to which there are unequivocal answers. The three spheres of influence are, however, not as self-sufficient as they would have us believe. It is not just that they overlap (e.g. the influence of German idealism or of hermeneutic philosophy on American theology; the influence of neo-Marxism in the west; the strengthening of analytic philosophy in Germany). Rather, the situation is such that dialectical materialism can be just as foreign to a physicist in the Soviet Union as it is to a representative of logical positivism in the west; and a positivist just as little as a "metaphysician" can respond in an exclusively positivistic way to basic human questions (such as those about life and death and even the question about the meaning of scientific endeavor); and a philosopher whose interest is speculative metaphysics cannot in fact talk about the positive sciences in his work. What at first appears as a manifold of mutually exclusive philosophical "tendencies," could yet belong to a comprehensive philosophical effort, within which there is devotion to different tasks in momentarily one-sided ways.

The treatment of Hegel varies in each of the three geographical regions of contemporary philosophizing. To English analytic philosophy Hegel's thought is a pseudo-philosophy, which produced more unclarity than it eliminated, and which rendered itself politically suspect by its ambiguous relationship to that "open society" which today is felt worthy of support. Nevertheless, whoever inquires about the original philosophical meaning of American pragmatism and returns to the thought of Peirce, sees there a parallel to the starting point of Hegel (which Peirce himself stressed).[1] When, on the other hand, the socialist countries today seek a "more hu-

---

[1] Karl-Otto Apel, in his introduction to a German edition of Peirce, has stressed this parallelism and has described the roles played in modern society by the three schools of contemporary philosophizing. In other works Apel has shown that these three philosophies may be understood historically "as the continuation of Kant's primacy of practical reason and as the response to Hegel's completion of theoretical metaphysics as a metaphysics of history." Cf. *Charles Sanders Peirce: Schriften I; Zur Entstehung des Pragmatismus*, edited and introduced by Karl-Otto Apel, Frankfurt am Main, 1967, p. 14.

manitarian" socialism, the relation between Hegel and Marx becomes problematic in a new way: there is a positive turn toward the young Marx and, through him, toward Hegel. Further, in some eastern European countries, Hegel is the thinker who represents the philosophical tradition itself (insofar as it anticipated dialectical materialism). In continental Europe during the last two decades Hegel has been something like a *Klassiker vom Dienst*, that is, he has been that thinker treated most often in university seminars and lectures, his thought serving as that popular medium in which the various philosophical tendencies could be understood. But continental Europe's interest in Hegel has not meant "Hegelianism"; if Hegel's thought is taken as somehow the "completion of metaphysics," this is only in the sense that in him and with him "metaphysical" thinking in general is to be dismissed.

Meanwhile, seventy years of continuous Hegel research live on in contemporary Hegel scholarship. What different points of departure are present in the contemporary reception of Hegel is shown very concretely, for example, by some Japanese visitors. The older men, who studied in Europe during the first world war, take Hegel as the thinker who in the most far-reaching way – above all in the area of cultural philosophy – collected "experiences" and then with and against Kant broadened, or renewed as a problem, the starting point of transcendental philosophy. Others want to develop an authentic Japanese philosophy from within their own traditions, such as Zen-Buddhism, in dialogue with German idealism and perhaps with Heidegger. The younger men are already to some extent approaching Hegel from Marxism or from logical positivism, etc. At any rate, in seven decades, that complex "Hegel research" has been formed from the most various interpretive points of departure. This complex, to be sure, has arisen in a very random manner and is little organized; nevertheless, it both has, and more and more approaches, unity. At the present time there appear each year around eighty dependent works concerning Hegel (transactions of learned societies, chapters in books and anthologies); to this is to be added a scarcely surveyable wealth of autonomous writings.[2] Of course, it can also be pointed out how some themes of Hegel scholarship travel – how, for example, in the past years the theme "transcendental history in the late Hüsserl and in Hegel" travelled from France

---

[2] The *Hegel-Studien* (Bonn, 1961 ff.) attempts to give reports on all articles on Hegel, though as yet it has been unable to cover all of the articles which appear in the different languages. A bibliography of the Hegel writings which have appeared independently lists for a period of five years 280 titles of editions and new editions (*Hegel-Studien*, Vol. 5, Bonn, 1969).

to other Latin countries, and how today the theme "Hegel and Marx on alienation" travels from Europe to the USA, etc.

The Hegel scholarship of our century has from the beginning been linked with editorial concerns: Dilthey's discovery and presentation of the young Hegel went hand in hand with the editing of Hegel's early theological writings by Herman Nohl; the neo-Kantian and neo-Hegelian return to Hegel involved both a reworking of the hegelian texts, and the attempt to edit Hegel's lectures in new textual form. Kojève's's interpretation of the *Phänomenologie des Geistes* would not have been possible if Hegel's draft of his Jena system and Marx's parisian manuscripts had not been edited; and whoever relates Hegel and Hölderlin rests his case on documents previously little noticed. It is important therefore to discuss this relationship between Hegel scholarships and the editing of Hegel both with regard to its particular historical phases and its future possibilities.

I

During his lifetime, Hegel's publications were slow to win recognition. To the public his earliest writings, the critical works of his first years at Jena, stood in the shadow of his friend Schelling. Nor did the *Phänomenologie* bring the breakthrough Hegel had hoped for. Only after the silent Nürnberg years during which he taught at the *Gymnasium* and worked on the *Wissenschaft der Logik*, only in Heidelberg and then, especially, in Berlin, did Hegel display the power to form a widely recognized school of thought. In this he relied upon the outline of his thought, as presented in the *Enzyklopädie* and the *Rechtsphilosophie*, upon his critical reviews for the Heidelberg and the Berlin year-books, and, above all, upon his lectures. When he died suddenly in 1831 at just over sixty years of age, he was torn from the midst of his creative activity, leaving behind many projects and plans. His followers, who had become the most important philosophical school of the time, wanted to perpetuate his thought. So it was natural that immediately after Hegel's death his disciples and friends began an edition of his collected works. It was completed in 1845 and bears the stamp of the philosophical situation of its time: the conflict over the Hegelian system had already broken out and Hegel's followers wanted to erect as an insurmountable bulwark their edition of Hegel's works. Thus, they orientated themselves toward their teacher's finished system, expanding into three volumes that bare outline of Hegelian philosophy, the *Enzyklopädie*, using quotations hastily extracted from Hegel's manuscripts and from transcriptions of his lectures and then adding to this system his lectures themselves. Hegel's disciples tried to give their master's system the stamp of completion. Therefore, they had to overlook all documents which hinted at incompletions, tensions, and gaps in Hegel's thought, as well as the documents pertaining to his development. It did not at all occur to them that there could be serious interests in Hegel's development (aside from mere biographical interest and the question as to whether Hegel or Schelling played the leading role in the *Kritischen Journal*). Thus, the approach to the Hegelian manuscripts taken by the "friends of the departed" permitted the disappearance of important texts such as the early commentary on Kant's *Metaphysik der Sitten*, the commentary on Steuart's *Political Economy*, and also those Jena lectures which contained such important documents on the development of the system, especially of the *Phänomenologie*, documents such as the Jena notebook for the course in the history of philosophy and the Heidelberg notebook for the course in aesthetics. Those of Hegel's students who sought to carry on his thought in their own writings treated with great freedom even those texts printed during his lifetime. For stylistic and sometimes for doctrinal reasons they made countless textual changes, even rearranging and omitting texts. The idea of providing a critical edition in today's sense was completely foreign to them. Hegel himself had written to Daub, his friend at Heidelberg, when the latter was reading the revision of the second edition of the *Enzyklopädie*, "by the way, I give you complete freedom to correct, strike out, and insert entirely according to your judgment, wherever it appears obscure, incomprehensible, or repetitious." [3]

In 1870 one of Hegel's students, the disputatious and grandiloquent Karl Ludwig Michelet, expressed the slogan guiding the work of Hegel's followers when he entitled a work celebrating Hegel's one hundredth birthday: *Hegel, der unwiderlegte Weltphilosoph,* that is, "Hegel, the unrefuted world-philosopher." But how it really stood with Hegel at this time is shown clearly by the publisher's announcement which accompanied this volume: Hegel's works were now being sold at a lower price. At the time of Hegel's one hundredth birthday his philosophy was dead. The positive sciences – the historical as well as the natural sciences – had, it appeared, finally outgrown, as an outmoded fashion of human self-under-

---

[3] cf. *Briefe von und an Hegel,* edited by Johannes Hoffmeister, vol. III, Hamburg, 1954, p. 126. Herman Glockner reissued the old Hegel edition, with some changes, forty years ago as a "Jubilee Edition." As important as this edition has become for the study of Hegel, and indeed because of this, the use of it requires a critical attitude; cf. my review "Das Hegel Werk Hermann Glockners," *Philosophische Rundschau,* 8th series, Tübingen, 1960, 28-52.

standing, speculation in the style of German idealism. The liberation from Hegel seemed to be a liberation of science from philosophy altogether. In this vein the well-known physician and natural scientist Rudolf Virchow said in 1893 in his rectorial address in Berlin: "It is in any case certain that with the death of Hegel the university too was freed from the power of philosophical systems. No philosopher has since then assumed a position of similar control, and – we may say it with appreciation – none has laid claim to such a position." [4]

It was the rise of the sciences and the further development of political and religious life that led to the downfall of Hegelian philosophy. Yet it was soon necessary to inquire about the conditions which foster different scientific, political, moral and religious ways of relating to reality. This inquiry was developed philosophically as neo-Kantianism. Here Kant's critical philosophy was taken chiefly as a theory of knowledge, indeed, as a theory of the positive sciences. It was presupposed that there are sciences and that it is the sciences which decisively determine our comportment to that which is; on the basis of this presupposition philosophy was understood as the foundation of scientific comportment. Along with the task of grounding the natural sciences there arose that of grounding the cultural sciences. But when the search for foundations was extended to the cultural sciences, and when finally the question was asked, about the common root of both the cultural and the natural sciences – indeed, of nature and culture themselves – then one was approaching Hegel. Neo-Kantianism passed over into neo-Hegelianism. Wilhelm Dilthey, who was at first close to neo-Kantianism, later opposed it, orientating himself toward German romanticism and the historical school. He was suffused with the scientific approach, which was principally methodological in character. At first he referred the understanding operative in *Geisteswissenschaften*, not to a "bloodless" transcendental subject, but to concrete life and experience; then he referred it to the constellations of meaning constitutive of spiritual life, which develop historically and can be explained only "hermeneutically." As we know from Dilthey's famous Berlin Academy treatise, it was this approach that enabled him to discover the young Hegel. We may mention at this point the subsequent protest which spread in the universities against the neo-Kantian methodologism at the time of the first world war. In an academy address at Heidelberg Wilhelm Windelband confirmed – although not without a certain critical distance

---

[4] "Idee und Wirklichkeit einer Universität": *Gedenkschrift der Freien Universität Berlin*, in *Dokumente zur Geschichte der Friedrich-Wilhelms-Universität zu Berlin*, edited by W. Weischedel, Berlin, 1960, p. 422.

– the "renewal of Hegelianism." Here there gathered under the protection of Max Weber's liberality and tolerance, those minds which brought Hegel into the battle against the liberalism and methodologism which controlled Heidelberg and beyond. However, they (Julius Ebbinghaus, Hans Ehrenberg, Franz Rosenzweig, Georg Lukács, Ernst Bloch, and others) soon went beyond Hegel to a new (philosophical, religious, or political) orthodoxy. This laid the foundation for the fact that today's kinship with Hegel is not a Hegelianism, but bears in itself a protest against Hegel. It was Alexandre Kojève who used the Marxian protest against Hegel to discover a previously concealed vitality in Hegelian thought. He did this in such a way that through his Paris lectures on the *Phänomenologie des Geistes* he bound two decades of French philosophizing to Hegel and, in general, left a stronger mark on Hegel research than, for instance, Croce with his distinction between the living and the dead in Hegelian philosophy.

This renewal of Hegel, as achieved in Berlin, Heidelberg, and Paris, was (as I have already remarked) connected in the most diverse ways with the editorial work on the Hegelian texts. It almost seems as if in the first decades of our century there was felt again and again by the exponents of new intellectual tendencies the impulse, or the temptation, to make confrontation with Hegel possible by editing Hegelian texts. Fortunately, not everyone possessed that restraint displayed by Martin Buber when he rejected Dilthey's suggestion that he edit Hegel's early writings and, consistent with this, continued his studies outside of the Berlin privy councillor's sphere of influence. It was a group of important men who attempted the editing of Hegel and Hegel philology. For example, there was, along with Dilthey and his follower, the educator Herman Nohl, Franz Rosenzweig, who began as a historian and philosopher and then found his life's work in the renewal of Jewish religiosity; and Hans Ehrenberg, who came from the study of economics, by way of confrontation with Hegel, to Protestant theology. Georg Lasson, on the other hand, was immediately connected with the old Hegelian tradition through his father Adolf Lasson. Johannes Hoffmeister, a follower of Friedrich Gundolf and Richard Kroner, attempted to make clear that Hegel was a friend of Hölderlin, and sought again to free Hegel's philosophy from the bonds of overhasty systematization.

The confrontation with Hegel received a decisive stamp by the editing of Nohl, Rosenzweig, Ehrenberg, Lasson, and Hoffmeister. But although Lasson, along with his work as pastor, began to edit a "critical" edition of Hegel, and although the germanist Hoffmeister tried to continue this edition as a "new critical edition," this editorial work never got beyond its beginnings. It never produced a result comparable with the efforts of such scholars as Mommsen, Diels, or Bekker. It was apparent that the task demanded forms of organization quite different from those they had used, The participants, whether they withdrew from the enterprise or dedicated their lives to it, felt this and expressed it: only something like an academy of sciences, in an undertaking thoroughly planned and financed, would be able to produce a genuine critical edition of Hegel's work.

II

The interest in Hegel's work has steadily increased right up till today, the two hundredth anniversary of his birth. To be sure, typical Anglo-Saxon philosophizing does pass Hegel by; and French structuralism takes itself to be an opponent of Hegel's starting point; and in Germany those tendencies have grown stronger which oppose the attempts (whether metaphysical-historical, or hermaneutic and socio-historical, or linguistic) to see history and historical language as that founding element in which philosophy has always moved. But again and again, every philosophizing that tries to be more than methodology and theory of science finds itself referring to Hegel, whether positively, by studying with Hegel the problems of *philosophia perennis* or by taking his thought as a hermeneutic of the western world; or negatively, as in Marxism, where the relation to Hegel has become a matter of life and death since the political condemnation of the Hegelianizing tendencies of Lukács and Bloch. However, there still is not a sufficient textual foundation for the study of Hegel. Twelve years ago the *Deutsche Forschungsgemeinschaft* commissioned an edition of Hegel's works to rival the Academy Edition of Kant's works. The yield of more than fifty years of Hegel research and editorial activity was to be used in this critical edition, which was to collate the almost innumerable isolated and provisional editions of Hegelian texts. But unforseen difficulties stood in the way of this project; the first volume did not appear until 1968.[5] There were the following difficulties: when the work was begun there did not as yet exist established, adaptable methods for editing more recent philosophical writers. Because of the different conditions there could be no simple appropriation of the methods of the classical scholars. Only in the last decade did there begin a broader discussion by germanists of questions about the editing of more recent texts; and even today a germanist would scarcely be concerned philologically with Kant or Hegel (while the classical scholars work on Platonic texts without hesitation). So the principles of editing Hegel had to be worked out experimentally. For example, it was only in an advanced stage of the work that there was given up the normalization of the Hegelian spelling (that is the approximation of the old texts to the modern German spelling). Even later came the decision to deal with the volumes in chronological order.

The editorial work rests upon a complete collection of both the Hegelian manuscripts and the transcriptions of Hegel's lectures. But these manuscripts and transcripts are spread throughout the whole of Europe (including eastern Europe) and America. Searching and collecting (or photocopying) demand time and money. Yet, for example, only when the photocopies of all the Jena manuscripts are immediately at hand can one analyze the handwriting to work out a chronology of Hegel's Jena texts.

As the work proceeded it finally became evident that the Hegel scholarship of the first fifty years of this century had been unable to lay the foundation for a chronological Hegel edition, namely, a historical interpretation of the development of Hegel's thought. For example, the theory of the genesis of the *Phänomenologie* used by Haering, Hoffmeister, and Hyppolite to resolve an old conflict had to be given up as untenable. The chronology of Hegel's sketches of the Jena system has been overthrown; until now it was assumed that the *Logik, Metaphysik*, and *Naturphilosophie* were written in 1801, followed by *Realphilosophie I*, written in 1803/04, and *Realphilosophie II*, written in 1805/06. It was then asked how Hegel could fall from the high "dialectical" level of the *Logik, Metaphysik*, and *Naturphilosophie* of 1801 back into the Schelling-like forms of *Realphilosophie I* of 1803/04, only then to find his way back to his own starting point in *Realphilosophie II*. But this, the chief problem of interpretation, turned out to be a pseudo-problem, generated by a false chronology and incorrect editing. It was in 1804 that the *Logik, Metaphysik*, and *Naturphilosophie* were written; so Hegel's sketches of his system display a steady development. The manuscripts from 1803/04 are not a *Realphilosophie* at all; Hoffmeister only interpreted and edited them as such on the basis of the *Realphilosophie* of 1805/06. So while at the time of his death in 1955 Hoffmeister still believed that the Hegelian manuscripts and works were, in essence, sufficiently edited and that it was now time to undertake the editing of the lectures, it had to be recognized that there was lacking even the basic prerequisite for editing Hegel's manuscripts and works, namely, an adequate history of the development of Hegelian thought and a chronological arrangement of his manuscripts.

In order to facilitate the work of editing, the Hegel Archive was established in 1958. For the first ten years it was located in Bonn; in 1968 it became part of Ruhr University at Bochum; and in 1969 it was moved to this new university in Germany's largest industrial region. The Archive has the following tasks:

Above all it is to furnish the prerequisites necessary for a critical edition of Hegel's works. The concentration of labor at this one place is to guarantee continuity in the methodology, planning, and execution of the work.

The Archive collects all Hegel's publications, and photocopies of both his manuscripts and the transcriptions of his lectures. It collects also all of the literature that Hegel used and all literature concerning Hegel. At the present time the Archive has in its Hegel library over three thousand books and over fifteen thousand photocopies. By the end of 1971 we are to have acquired the basic collection of necessary books and photocopies. Then the Archive is to be made available to a wider public, offering in a unique way the possibility of studying a classical German philosopher from the sources. Eighty years ago Dilthey demanded an *Archiv der Literatur* to preserve the literary remains of philosophers; under different conditions and with the restriction to Hegel, the Hegel Archive seeks to meet Dilthey's demand. Dilthey knew that the literary remains of even the great philosophers had been scattered; that, for example, Kant's papers had been used to wrap coffee and herring. Today, to be sure, such papers are not used as wrapping paper; yet they have become collectors' items, a means of building prestige and capital. In this way, too, the papers are too often lost to scholarship. For the most part the possession of the papers is set; high prices make purchase of the larger collections impossible. Still, with photography, the manuscripts can be reproduced for scholarship.

Further, the Hegel Archive seeks to contribute to the promotion and coordination of Hegel research; it does this above all through the journal *Hegel Studien*. Since in recent years Hegel research has become more and more extensive, a survey of it is indispensible for those who want to work on definite questions, taking the research of others into account. Such a survey is possible through bibliographical reviews and abstracts of the individual contributions from the various countries and linguistic regions. It is important that the editing work remain in close contact with Hegel research. The best Kant scholars worked on the Kant edition; today such an arrangement is impossible because of the overload which burdens the university teacher. This makes it all the more important that the younger men who take over the job of editing remain in constant contact with the Hegel scholarship of our time. Constant reciprocity alone can be fruitful. For example, a new chronology of the Jena manuscripts forces interpreters of Hegel to ask new questions; on the other hand only a statisfactory interpretation of Hegel, one which gives the history of his development, can certify this chronology. The one implies the other; they will arise simultaneously or not at all.

III

In 1893 Wilhelm Dilthey suggested to the Prussian Ministry of Education and the Berlin Academy of Sciences that there be issued an edition of Kant's works. He stressed that all of the prerequisites for editing Kant's entire intellectual legacy existed then in a way that could never be duplicated. In the preface to the Kant edition Dilthey formulated these prerequisites in this way: "a strong interest, extending to all branches (of Kant's legacy), men who have dedicated their lives to these studies, and a wealth of works which have been devoted to this legacy." Although Dilthey certainly did not foresee that the coming decades would bring at least two world wars, he did see clearly that, given the usual dispersion of philosophical remains, the possibility of collecting together the papers Kant left behind would not soon return. Now appears to be the time to take for Hegel the step which was taken for Kant. There has been a widespread interest in Hegel for more than fifty years; his papers are for the most part gathered together (even if the last war, once again, brought great losses; for example, lost forever are the transcripts of Hegel's lectures which were in the Königsberg municipal library).

The complete edition should make easier the study of Hegel and should make possible a new understanding of Hegel. In order to do this it must completely encompass the existing Hegelian texts – even the preliminary studies and sketches, the various drafts or editions, and the variant readings of single formulations. In general, all of the documents which give us Hegel's thought are significant and informative. Thus, the Hegel edition does not face the danger which confronted the Nietzsche edition of the Nietzsche Archive at Weimar: there philological receptiveness acquiesced to the piety of Nietzsche's sister, who had preserved her brother's every scrap of paper, and so, did not advance beyond the insignificant early texts to Nietzsche's real works; overlooked was Nietzsche's genius for snatching up everything preliminary into that will concentrated upon the single task it had finally grasped. Hegel's texts are in all essential respects chronologically ordered, that is, they are grouped together according to the stages of his life and work. Within the individual phases which thus emerge (for example, the group of Jena texts) there can be doctrinal divisions. As opposed to the Academy editions of Kant's and Fichte's works, the Hegel edition will not separate from Hegel's publications the unpublished texts of the literary remains. Every volume will carry an editorial statement about the texts, supplying their dates of composition, chronological order, and tradition. This, of course, is not intended as an interpretation of Hegel's historical development. The *Anmerkungen* will identify quotations, elaborate on historical facts, etc., without becoming a commentary on the Hegelian text.

Dilthey proposed the Kant edition in 1893; he wrote his preface to the first volume in 1902. But even today we do not have that part of the Kant edition entitled *Vorlesungen*. It is to be hoped that the Hegel edition will be completed in a shorter time, that the *ca* 40 volumes can be published in about 40 years. Since it is clear that the framework of the historical development must still be worked out even for the early Hegelian texts, the editorial activity has concentrated on the volumes up to the *Phänomenologie* and the Nürnberg *Wissenschaft der Logik*. These volumes should be published in the next ten years. Already published is Volume 4 (*Jenaer Kritische Schriften*). At the printers are volume 1 (*Jugendschriften I*), volume 3 (*Exzerpte 1785-1800*), volume 7 (*Jenaer Systementwürfe II*) and volume 6 (*Jenaer Systementwürfe I*). A French translation of this edition is being prepared. Further, there are to be published student editions in German as well as French, which should make the Hegelian text available to a wider public (for example, in the German student edition by adapting the Hegelian text to contemporary spelling).

IV

It is estimated by those who are involved that, were the work of editing to be pursued continuously at its present rate, the Hegel edition could be finished in about 2007. One wonders what the world will be like when a complete edition of Hegel stands on the library shelves. It would be interesting above all to know whether this world will still be able to do anything with Hegel; more, what this world will in fact do with Hegel. But broad, rambling speculations are idle. Nevertheless, it is important to ask how Hegel philology can fit into Hegel research and how Hegel research can fit into philosophy.

With regard to the Kant edition he planned, Dilthey said that only by its means would there be possible a history of the development of Kant's thought. Dilthey stressed the history of Kant's development even though he knew that it would have been utterly foreign to Kant himself to see his work from this perspective (indeed, Kant did not want any of his pre-critical writings included in a Kant edition). In his preface to the Kant edition Dilthey links his interest in Kant's historical development to an "ultimate goal," "the historical understanding of the life's work of Kant," a goal to be achieved "by the ever-repeated confrontation between the historical situation in which Kant's thought occurred and the entire fruit of his intellectual activity as it has come down to us." The new complete Hegel edition should make possible such a historical understanding of Hegel's work as well. To be sure, Hegel philology will take a path other than that of Kant philology. Neo-Kantianism and Kant philology took Kant's critical work as the firm foundation from which to approach the pre-critical work; only gradually did Kant philology learn to relativize this starting point and examine in its own right the early thought which Kant later sought critically to surpass. Likewise, the editors of Hegel sought a firm foundation in the Hegelian system; but even Hegel's first followers and opponents looked upon the *Phänomenologie des Geistes* as the system's "crisis." Since Dilthey, the moving force of the interpretation of Hegel's development has been the antagonism between system and history (to which the young Hegel was devoted). Nevertheless, although Hegel always took his earlier drafts with him whenever he changed his residence, there can be no doubt that he too never wanted to see his thought from the perspective of its development. Friedrich Schlegel, indeed, planned an "autonoography," and Schlegel and Schleiermacher investigated Plato's development; but Hegel never recognized Schlegel and Schleiermacher as thinkers. While he applied the genetic point of view to the whole history of philosophy, the genetic view of a single philosopher was foreign to him. In general he was concerned to relate history to its taxonomy. So historical understanding (upon which there falls a special accent in the work of editing) can be only one of our possible approaches to Hegel. Other ways of approaching the subject-matter Hegel dealt with must have a place beside this one, while not combining with it in the same way in which Hegel sought to make system and history coincide.

Above all Dilthey also expected from research devoted to Hegel's development the scientific objectification of the approach to Hegel. "The age of the struggle with Hegel is over; the age of his historical recognition has arrived," Dilthey wrote in 1888 in that same review of *Briefe von und*

0149040

an Hegel, in which he first pointed to the significance of the Hegelian literary remains. We may here leave undecided whether what Dilthey's expectation implies, namely the ideal of a final historical explanation, is not altogether unrealistic; the fact is that in the eighty years since Dilthey's prognosis there has not occurred by means of historical research the expected objectification of the approach to Hegel. In the first place, the historical scholarship was shattered along with its most important results – the presumptuous ascription of the *Systemprogram* to Schelling, the chronology of Hegel's Jena manuscripts, and the description of the genesis of the *Phänomenologie*. But above all, the historical scholarship increased rather than decreased the controversies which arise from the confrontation with Hegel.

This is shown very clearly, for example, in the case of the so-called *Altesten Systemprogramm des deutschen Idealismus.* Rosenzweig edited this Hegelian text in 1917 and sought to establish that it derived from Schelling, that is, that Hegel's notes were a mere copy. Then for a while Hölderlin was regarded as the author. Now it is asked whether indeed Hegel is not the author. Until now Hegel scholars have supposed that the thinking displayed in this *Programm* was not Hegel's. Thus to establish Hegel as the author, it would have to be shown that the young Hegel thought in the manner of the *Systemprogramm* but not in the manner attributed to him by Hegel scholars. The *Systemprogramm* proves to be an attempt to institute the idealistic philosophy in order that a revolution of German thought or spirit might yet achieve that revolutionizing of the traditional structures which had failed politically in France. The young Hegel wrote to Schelling, "on the basis of the Kantian system and its utmost completion, I expect in Germany a revolution from principles now at hand and needing only to be universalized in order to be applied to all accumulated knowledge." Manifestly from the point of view of historical philology the controversy about the *Systemprogramm* is not so simply resolved. Yet this controversy does bring to light new themes of Hegel's early thought. Indeed, this controversy forces us to correct decisively the usual schemata drawn from the presentation of the history of German idealism. If Hegel himself wrote the *Systemprogramm,* or even thought in the manner of this *Programm,* then it was he who understood Hölderlin's criticism of idealism and Hölderlin's mythic poetry (while the young Schelling, to whom alone this understanding is attributed, quarreled more with Hölderlin, as the tradition also reports). In Jena Hegel opposed Schelling from a thoroughly independent position; he did not need to be led by Schelling to a new philosophical starting point; rather, Schelling's starting point could have

Otto Pöggeler

been grasped by Hegel from within that criticism of Fichte which he shared with Hölderlin.[6]

The same is true of the *Phänomenologie des Geistes*. The solution to the controversy proposed by Haering was philologically indisputable but philosophically frivolous. Today the new chronology of Hegel's Jena manuscripts makes it possible to write a history of the development of Hegelian logic and metaphysics and, on the basis of the latter, of the *Phänomenologie*. Such attempts, however, introduce new motifs into Hegel interpretation. In Kierkegaard's doctrine of the stages, in the young Marx's history of nature and of society, in Dilthey's critique of historical reason, and in the French philosophy inspired by Kojève, Hegel's *Phänomenologie* was taken primarily as "history," his logic as the useless shell which still clung to this philosophical egg of Columbus. But attention to Hegel's historical development reveals how much the *Phänomenologie* owes to the logico-metaphysical problematic and remains embedded in it.[7] In this way philology becomes the advocate of Hegel himself; it lets Hegel's own voice be heard in the dialogue in which we seek with him and against him the correct point of departure for philosophy.

In a sketch of Kierkegaard's Hegel arrives in the underworld and Socrates immediately takes an interest in him. Socrates hears with astonishment that for Hegel the truth is the whole and that, if one would philosophize at all, he must study Hegel's system – indeed, must study this system as developed in the edition of Hegel's students. In the Socratic spirit we still pursue truth; but our lives are so short – should we really permit Hegel to speak for twenty volumes? And in the future should we permit him to speak for forty volumes to be produced only after forty years of historical-philological labor? But manifestly there is in scholarship a point of no return: once a science has taken up a subject, be it the eyes of insects or the works of Hegel, it must pursue its work to the end. Curtailment is failure – at least in our society, which still has such little self-understanding with regard to the place of its scientific and technical possibilities. Besides, Hegel research has in fact only the choice between many dispersed attempts at editing, which bring no final result, and the adequate organ-

[6] Cf. my article: "Hegel, der Verfasser des *ältesten Systemprograms des deutschen Idealismus*," *Hegel Studien*, Supplement 4 (Hegel Tage, Urbino, 1965), Bonn, 1969, 17-32.
[7] For a discussion of the *Phänomenologie* cf. my essay "Die Komposition der Phänomenologie des Geistes," *Hegel Studien*, Supplement 3 (Hegel Tage, Royaumont, 1964), Bonn, 1966, 27-74. With regard to the chronology of Hegel's Jena writings cf. Heinz Kimmerle, "Zur Chronologie von Hegels Jenaer Schriften," *Hegel Studien*, Vol. 4, Bonn, 1967, 125-176.

ization of that editorial activity which has been under way for the past seventy years.

If we succeed in synchronizing and pursuing systematically the historical-philological-editorial work on Hegel's writings, then the achievement of Hegel research can certainly be increased greatly. Of course there is in this a danger as well as an opportunity. The danger is that Hegel's philosophy might no longer survive as philosophy, but only as the object of scientific, i.e. philological interest. The opportunity is that the utilization of Hegel's work in philosophy could strengthen a thinking that is not only aware of being called to the methodological control of given scientific behavior, but asks also about the sense in the totality of our lives of the powers which determine our lives (e.g. science, technology, art, politics). Whether we exploit this opportunity depends essentially upon the strength of our philosophizing, the strength of our philosophical confrontation with Hegel, and, in general, the strength of our tradition.

A CRITICAL SURVEY OF HEGEL SCHOLARSHIP IN ENGLISH: 1962–1969[1]

Frederick G. Weiss

Since the publication of J. N. Findlay's *Hegel: A Re-examination* in 1958 (paperback edition, 1962), there has been a remarkable outpouring of Hegel scholarship in English. Undoubtedly there are a number of factors responsible for this resurgence of interest, but Professor Findlay's efforts here and on a number of other fronts, before and especially after the appearance of his re-examination, surely must be placed near the top of any list of such factors. It is noteworthy, for example, that for nearly a decade preceding his exposition, only two books on Hegel appeared in English,[2] while the ten years since have witnessed the publication of some thirty volumes, including several new translations, four comprehensive reinterpretations, and a number of monographs and studies of Hegel's influence. While it has since become the fashion among writers on Hegel to begin by shattering negative Hegel legends, Findlay was the first to do so effectively, and I think few of us are fully aware of how instrumental his work

---

[1] This is an expanded version of the paper given at the Marquette Hegel Symposium; in its present form, the paper earlier appeared in the *American Philosophical Quarterly* 8, no. 3 (July 1971).

[2] Friedrich's *The Philosophy of Hegel*, an anthology of Hegel's writings, and Hartman's *Reason in History*, a translation of Hegel's Introduction to the *Vorlesungen über die Philosophie der Geschichte*, both published in 1953. Some of Findlay's other efforts: "Some Merits of Hegelianism," read before the Aristotelian Society in 1955; "The Contemporary Relevance of Hegel," given at a London Colloquium on Contemporary British Philosophy in 1959, and reprinted in his *Language, Mind and Value*, and in Alasdair MacIntyre's *Hegel*; "Hegel's Use of Teleology," first published in *The Monist*, 1964, and reprinted in Steinkraus' *New Studies in Hegel's Philosophy* and in Findlay's *Ascent to the Absolute*. Findlay has been instrumental in the publication of A. V. Miller's new translation of *Hegel's Science of Logic* (1969), and has also worked with Miller in providing the first English translation ever of Hegel's *Philosophy of Nature* (1970), together with new and emended editions (with *Zusätze*) of the existing Wallace translations of the first and third parts of the *Encyclopaedia*. Findlay has also contributed papers and commentary at three major Hegel symposia held in this country since 1968. He has been a Counselor for the *International Hegel-Vereinigung*, and is a member of the Advisory Board for *The Owl of Minerva*, the quarterly publication of the Hegel Society of America.

has been in bringing the objective study of Hegel's thought once more to the fore in English-speaking countries.

The argument that the current Hegel renaissance in America is a carry-over of the work of the European Marxists and existentialists is not borne out to any significant extent by the books here under consideration, for these are largely free of social and political axe-grinding, and left- and right-wing in-fighting. The tendency, on the contrary, has been to separate Hegel from the "Hegelians," and to assess his importance and relevance on the basis of his texts, and not those of some partisan interpreter who had long since taken leave of the original. Furthermore, the vigor of scholarly events surrounding the celebration of the second centenary of Hegel's birth this year is less a cause than an effect of the revival which we have been experiencing, and which is showing no signs of subsiding. Fichte's birthday, by comparison, passed nearly unnoticed in 1962.

Despite Findlay's clearing of the air, the habit of attacking the Hegelian bogeyman has been hard for some to break. A number of writers on Hegel have felt it necessary to begin (or end) by excusing themselves for having anything to do with what Popper once called "the Hegelian farce." Kaminsky's *Hegel on Art*,[3] for example, opens by approvingly reiterating the charges that Hegel's views "illustrate the hazards of uncontrolled speculation," that they entail "notorious totalitarian conclusions," and that they are couched in "linguistic and conceptual obscurity." What remains is but to "determine whether some portions of the Hegelian philosophy might be salvaged." [4] What Kaminsky seems unaware of is that it is just such "salvaging" of certain portions of the Hegelian system and a disregard for its integrity which has led to many of the intellectual and political grotesqueries since fathered on Hegel. At any rate, the *Aesthetik* is presumably a candidate, and in between a half-baked account of Hegel's metaphysic and a Humean critique of it, we find a fairly harmless and (aesthetically) erudite exposition of Hegel's *Philosophy of Fine Art*. But Kaminsky asserts that while "Hegel's observations about the arts can be appreciated without entailing a commitment to his ontology," it is still "necessary to understand Hegel's metaphysics in order to attain a clear comprehension of his aesthetic theory." [5] This seems to suggest that Hegel's aesthetic is best appreciated when it is not understood, and makes his added claim that "while Hegel's metaphysics can be sharply criticized, his

---

[3] Jack Kaminsky, *Hegel on Art: An Interpretation of Hegel's Aesthetics* (New York: State University of New York, 1962). 207 pp.
[4] *Ibid.*, p. vii.
[5] *Ibid.*, pp. viii, 3 respectively.
[6] *Ibid.*, p. 178.

aesthetics cannot be dismissed lightly" [6] even more puzzling. As with most of those who repeat the old Schopenhauerian charges of obscurantism and charlatanism, and then go on to find much that is lucid and true in Hegel, Kaminsky makes us wonder how Hegel's vision of the arts can be so clear and incisive, when his "metaphysical" point of view is so clouded and erroneous.[7]

The integrity of Hegel's *Aesthetik* with the rest of his system is masterfully manifest in Anne and Henry Paolucci's edition of *Hegel on Tragedy*,[8] where we find selections from Hegel's *Philosophy of Right, Philosophy of Religion, History of Philosophy, Phenomenology,* and *Philosophy of History* as well as the *Philosophy of Fine Art,* woven into a penetrating panorama that would have been impossible if it had not issued from a mind in which form and content, theory and practice, result and process, were one and inseparable. As the editors note in their introduction,

> Hegel's study of tragedy is penetrating and original precisely because he comes to it, as Aristotle came, not with a merely literary interest, but with profound philosophic regard for the problems of personality and for the ethical, political, and religious implications of the actions presented by the great tragedians.[9]

On the difficulty of the Hegelian language:

> ... a literary generation addicted as ours has been to deciphering the verbal puzzles of modern poetry and exploring the mazes of existentialist frustration should not be seriously troubled by that. It is, after all, merely the difficulty of permanent and universal intelligibility. Often a work that one generation, or one group of specialists, finds transparently easy proves to be, for every other, either impossibly obscure or unworthy of being read at all.[10]

Hegel's political thought has been subject to more mis-interpretation and abuse than perhaps any other facet of his system. G. R. G. Mure remarks that he hopes such "shamelessly ill-informed criticism" had reached "its expiring splutter" in the chapter on Hegel in Popper's *Open Society and its Enemies*." [11] Toward this end, *Hegel's Political Writings* provides us

---

[7] See Friedrich's Preface to *The Philosophy of Hegel*: "Someone who knows my other work may well be surprised to find me dealing with Hegel. For the philosophy of Hegel has always seemed to me fundamentally wrong. Perhaps this very prejudice is responsible for my undertaking this re-evaluation." p. ix.

[8] *Hegel on Tragedy*, edited, with an Introduction, by Anne and Henry Paolucci (Garden City, N. Y.: Anchor Books, 1962). 404 pp.

[9] *Ibid.,* p. xxix.

[10] *Ibid.,* p. xiii.

[11] G. R. G. Mure, *The Philosophy of Hegel* (London: Oxford University Press, 1965), p. viii.

for the first time with a complete translation by T. M. Knox of Hegel's minor political essays, and a lengthy, sympathetic exposition and analysis of them, and of Hegel *qua* political pamphleteer and journalist, by Z. A. Pelczynski.[12] The translations and notes are what we have come to expect from Knox, excellent, although he was apparently unaware in remarking that "none of these essays has been translated before into any language" that Friedrich's *The Philosophy of Hegel* included partial translations (by Friedrich) of three of the essays.[13]

Pelczynski's commentary and the translations reveal Hegel's lifelong interest in politics, his deep concern for and knowledge of contemporary political events, and perhaps most important, they demonstrate the growth and direction of Hegel's thinking during periods otherwise obscure for us, and in a way that his major works cannot. "Perhaps the greatest virtue of Hegel's political writing," Pelczynski notes, "consists in their non-technical language and common-sense argumentation." He adds elsewhere that "when he chose, Hegel was capable of writing fresh, vigorous, and readable prose . . . yet, paradoxically, it is precisely here that he plumbs depths of mysticism rare among political thinkers, and in a few bold sentences anticipates his future speculative philosophy of history." [14] In these pages, the myths of Hegel's reactionary conservatism and statism are not exploded, but rather quietly embarrased into silence. In his conclusion on "Hegel the Political Philosopher," Pelczynski remarks that "One can dispute the merits of Hegel's theory, point out its weaknesses or contradictions, question assumptions, and so on, but such treatment would not be different from that normally meted out to other thinkers."[15] This volume, together with Knox's translation of the *Philosophy of Right* (a comparable edition of the *Philosophy of History* is a desideratum), provide a clear, comprehensive and authoritative picture of Hegel *qua* political theorist which is unlikely to be superceded.

Between 1965 and 1968, four broad commentaries on Hegel's philosophy appeared, together with the first book-length study of the *Phenomenology* in English. With respect to Kaufmann's *Hegel: Reinterpretation, Texts and Commentary*,[16] with foresight we can see that in a review of Findlay's *Hegel* in 1961, he is already comparing it with this yet-to-be-

[12] *Hegel's Political Writings*, translated by T. M. Knox, with an Introductory Essay by Z. A. Pelczynski (Oxford: Clarendon Press, 1964). 335 pp.

[13] *Ibid.*, p. 141. Friedrich, pp. 523 ff.

[14] *Hegel's Political Writings*, pp. 24, 69.

[15] *Ibid.*, p. 135.

[16] Walter Kaufmann, *Hegel: Reinterpretation, Texts and Commentary* (Garden City, N. Y.: Doubleday & Co., 1965). 498 pp.

[17] The review is in *Mind*, LXX n.s., 1961, pp. 264-269.

published volume, and Findlay is portrayed here as a lisping Walter Kaufmann.[17] Kaufmann seems to regard his own book on Hegel as embodying the ideal balance between the consideration of Hegel's development and his mature thought, and between sympathy and criticism. But sympathy does not run very deep in Professor Kaufmann. He says that what is needed is not for somebody to score on Hegel by tripping him up on details, yet he often does precisely this both in his book and in his reviews of those he apparently regards as his competitors in the exposition of Hegel. In his review of the late Professor Loewenberg's *Hegel's Phenomenology*, for example, he suggests nastily at the close that the best thing about the book is the superb photograph of the author on the jacket, and the quality of the paper on which it is printed![18] Kaufmann had criticized Loewenberg and Findlay for ignoring previous work on Hegel, and thus he does not fall into that error himself. He tells us that Rosenzweig stuck only to Hegel's political writings, while Haering expired after only reaching Hegel's first book and Glockner added little to this. Of Wallace's *Prolegomena*, "the less said the better." Mure's *Introduction to Hegel*, "if not as perverse as it appears to be . . . is at least far-fetched," and "too little space remains for Hegel himself." Kuno Fischer's approach leads to the absurd. Stace's *The Philosophy of Hegel* is "misnamed," is based upon Wallace's "inadequate" translations, and "ignores all primary and secondary non-English sources." Findlay's *Hegel* ignores these sources *and* Hegel's development, etc.[19]

Kaufmann often criticizes what he calls "play-by-play" accounts of Hegel's writings, typical, he thinks of most treatments. He repeats in his book what he has said in his reviews, that the ideal book on Hegel should include "a detailed discussion of a very few sample sections," rather than "a thumbnail digest of almost all." "The reader of the *Phenomenology* or the *Logic*," he says, "does not so much need to be told what happens, section by section, as he wants to know how these books are to be taken: what Hegel attempted to do – and what he did in fact." [20] If this is true anywhere in Hegel, it is surely not so with regard to the dark progress of the dialectic in the *Phenomenology* and *Science of Logic*, where a chief problem for the reader is precisely, if only initially, to be able to follow the movement of Hegel's thought, to know what is happening. The kind of "comprehensive reinterpretation of Hegel – not just of one facet of his

---

[18] *Philosophical Review*, LXXVI, 1967. pp. 389-392.
[19] Most of these comments are found in the Preface to Kaufman's *Hegel*; others like them occur throughout the text.
[20] *Ibid.*, Preface, p. 13.

thought but of the whole phenomenon of Hegel" (which Kaufmann says he is giving us) is not in fact provided in this book at all. Kaufmann largely substitutes for a play-by-play account of Hegel's *philosophy* a day-by-day, season-by-season, year-by-year, letter-by-letter, edition-by-edition account of Hegel's life, and the historical background of his writings. In his discussion of the *Phenomenology*, for example, he is never really able to leave the book's immediate historical context, and treat at any length the substantive philosophical issues which it embodies. There is even a serious suggestion that the growth of the *Phenomenology* under Hegel's hand in 1806 was significantly related to the growth of Hegel's bastard son, Ludwig, in the womb of his Jena landlady![21]

Kaufmann speaks of going beyond Hegel, but he seldom even reaches him. The best thing in Hegel, we are told, is the famous Preface to the *Phenomenology*, and it seems the only part of Hegel that Kaufmann is up to dealing with directly, and even here, his commentary on his own translation of it is not philosophical but philological and historical, a welter of *Zusätze* markedly superficial in comparison to the additions to Hegel's own writings and lectures which Kaufmann disparages. "Royce," he says somewhere, "has no time for philological correctness," but Kaufmann has plenty. At those few places in his book where he rises from intellectual biography to philosophical criticism, he passes the gauntlet to Nietzsche whose aphorisms, he suggests, throw more light on "the secret of Hegel" than the massive work by Stirling of the same name. Hegel is not Kaufmann's favorite philosopher. I surmise that Nietzsche is, however, and an extensive comparative study of the two might have been a more philosophically rewarding labor for both Kaufmann and his readers.

Still, Professor Kaufmann has written a good book in spite of himself. It has already been pointed out in lengthy reviews by Hook, Crites and Findlay that the work contains a wealth of valuable information, much of it otherwise inaccessible, especially to the average American student. In the words of one reviewer: "Gossipy and talkative, a little disorganized, in love with itself [Kaufmann's own motto for the book: *wer ihn kennt, soll ihn hier erkennen*; may those who have long known of Hegel here come to know him], forgetful and repetitious, prejudiced and not exactly guileless, the book has the charm of all these little vices." [22] But if we take Kaufmann at his own word, that this book constitutes a complete reinterpretation of "the whole of Hegel," we must judge that he has failed, or

[21] *Ibid.*, p. 113.
[22] Walter Cerf, in *Philosophy and Phenomenological Research*, 28, pp. 601-603. Kaufmann's motto is found on page 293 of his *Hegel*.

that he has seriously mistaken the significance of "Hegel." If, rather, a supplement to existing works on Hegel and to an understanding of Hegel which, due to the nature of philosophy itself will likely never be complete, it stands thus as a significant contribution to this understanding.

Also published in 1965 is G. R. G. Mure's *The Philosophy of Hegel,* which must be reckoned the best small volume to have appeared on Hegel in the English language since that of Edward Caird.[23] Professor Findlay has referred to Mure as "a deep student of Hegel." That this is the case is manifest from the fact that, in the nearly three decades between the publication of the original English translation of the *Science of Logic* and Findlay's *Re-examination,* the most substantial and significant Hegel scholarship in English was carried on by Mure and his colleague in Scotland, Sir Malcolm Knox, and this at a time when Hegel's "popularity" was at its lowest ebb, and in a part of the world where the name itself often invited laughter and/or scorn. We get some idea of the bleak character of this period from Mure's somewhat despondent but brilliantly critical and deeply axiological book *Retreat From Truth,* where he says in the Preface:

This book grew, slowly and intermittently, from a mood of deep depression. In the years between the wars I had watched without enthusiasm the return of British philosophy to its native empiricist tradition. After the last war it appeared to be reducing itself from naïveté to absurdity with such speed and such conviction that I began to think it might soon be time to cry stinking fish.[24]

The book closes with the remark that "at present if I had an intelligent son coming up to Oxford, I should not regret it if he turned his face away from all the three Honour Schools that include philosophy, even from Greats." [25]

In his *Introduction to Hegel,* criticized as a book not about Hegel at all, Mure tried to tell us that the best commentary on Hegel is the history of philosophy itself, not only before, but after Hegel also.[26] It manifests his belief that the proper (though of course not the only) way to study the history of philosophy is to study at least two important thinkers together in some detail, and "the greater they are, the less it matters how many

---

[23] Caird's book was originally published in 1883, and has recently been reprinted by Archon Books.

[24] G. R. G. Mure, *Retreat from Truth* (Oxford: Basil Blackwell, 1958), p. vii.

[25] *Ibid.,* p. 250.

[26] Findlay, for example, points out in "Some Merits of Hegelianism" (see note 2 above) that "the whole development of our British thought over the past half-century is a museum-specimen of Hegelian dialectic."

centuries divide them." Mure holds, in the spirit of Hegel's *History of Philosophy*, that "philosophy in each age of civilization is at once a product, a criticism, and a reconstruction of the values and insights of its own past," and that "it therefore contains its history as a constituent element of its own nature." [27] He characterizes Hegel's own conception of philosophy as

in a broad sense of the term, historical; one might call it "developmental." Significant truth, he believed, is always and everywhere a result which contains and consummates its own process, and the only way of expressing it philosophically is to exhibit process and result together. There is no other way, because philosophy itself is thought as process culminating in result.[28]

Thus Mure regards Hegel's lectures on the history of philosophy as "perhaps his most brilliant work.[29] Some commentators devalue materials such as the Lectures and editorial Zusätze because they are not "from Hegel's own hand," but I should think it a misguided effort of philosophically sterile, nit-picking scholarship to point out that the *Lectures* are not from Hegel's own hand, and are thus unworthy of serious consideration. (As if philosophy has ever come from anyone's hand!) If we found the lecture notes in a clump in the street, without any indication of their source or authorship, they would still be deserving of our carefullest attention, because of their vision and wealth of insight. And if we reconstructed from their content the world this vision discloses, it would be and is none other than that revealed in Hegel's own four major published writings. In fact, as Professor Findlay notes in his Foreword to Miller's translation of the *Philosophy of Nature*, without these lectures and *Zusätze*, that latter world would be sparsely populated indeed, and a good deal less interesting and intelligible.[30]

I think there is little question that the anti-Hegelian (or a-Hegelian) aspect of the recently dominant empiricist-positivist philosophies in Britain and America has gone hand-in-hand with its anti-historical character. In those philosophies for which history is a fundamental category, such as Marxism, Hegel's thought has always been an object of concern. Mure, of course, does not emphasize Hegel's examination of philosophy's history to the exclusion of all else, as some have emphasized the *Phenomeno-*

[27] From his Foreword to my Hegel's *Critique of Aristotle's Philosophy of Mind* (The Hague: Martinus Nijhoff, 1969), p. xi.
[28] Mure, *The Philosophy of Hegel*, p. vii.
[29] *Ibid.*
[30] *Hegel's Philosophy of Nature*, Being Part Two of the Encyclopaedia of the Philosophical Sciences (1830), translated from Nicolin and Pöggeler's edition (1959) and from the *Zusätze* in Michelet's text (1847), by A. V. Miller, with Foreword by J. N. Findlay (Oxford: Clarendon Press, 1970), p. vii.

logy. His lengthy *Study of Hegel's Logic,* as well as other works we have noted, surely indicate otherwise. He regards the study of these lectures, however, as "a quite indispensable introduction" to the system, especially for the professional student.

The method of exposition Mure employs in his *Philosophy of Hegel* approximates that of Findlay.[31] They both (as does Kaufmann) follow Hegel's own order of exposition of the system, but in contrast to Kaufmann, neither of them pays much attention to biography, and of the two, only Mure has much to say about Hegel's early writings. Findlay's attitude toward the juvenilia is manifest in his Foreword to the *Philosophy of Nature,*[32] while Mure's position regarding Hegel's life is best illustrated in this passage from his *Introduction to Hegel:*

> The biography of a philosopher gains importance only so far as he fails to express himself fully in his writings, and it then serves to explain his failure rather than his philosophy. The half-philosopher, the empiricist in whom the philosophic interest is never, or for a period only, dominant, can to some extent be legitimately interpreted through the facts of his life; but the great thinker, so far as a man may, goes whole into his thoughts. In him the order of connexion is reversed – I might say restored – and his philosophy explains the rest of his life.[33]

The most attractive feature of Mure's little book is the 40 page introductory essay on "The Principles of the System." Here, Mure deals briefly but lucidly with those issues in Hegel which are basic and perennial in philosophy, and which the student in particular must come to see, and see clearly, if he is to understand either. They are the relation of God and man, of subject and object, the "unity" of thought and being; the no-

---

[31] Also, compare their respective notions of philosophy and dialectic: ". . . philosophy in the full sense of the word is a criticism of this or that mode of experience from a level above it, a criticism which displays the lower level as a privation and not a mere absence of the higher . . .," Mure, *Retreat From Truth,* p. 56; "I should say that the basic characteristic of the dialectical method is that it always involves *higher-order comment* on a thought position previously achieved . . . to operate at a given level of thought, to accept its basic assumptions . . . go to the limit in its terms, and then to stand outside of it . . . become conscious of it . . . as to what it really has achieved, and how far these achievements do or do not square with its actual professions." Findlay, "The Contemporary Relevance of Hegel," in *Language, Mind and Value,* pp. 219-220.

[32] "It may, further, be wondered whether the concern for Hegel's 'development' displayed by many writers, is not excessive, especially in a situation where there are no reliable, detailed commentaries on his major works. The Juvenilia of Berne and Frankfurt have been studied exhaustively for very many decades, and have thrown very little light on any major notion or position in Hegel's mature work: they remain writings, interesting as reflections of their time and place, which give absolutely no indication that their writer was ever destined to be a great philosopher, let alone one of the greatest of all philosophers." Foreword to *Hegel's Philosophy of Nature,* pp. vii-viii.

[33] G. R. G. Mure, *An Introduction to Hegel* (Oxford: Clarendon Press, 1940), p. xvii.

tions of negation and otherness, of the finite and infinite, of consciousness and self-consciousness, truth and error, and the inherent dialectic of all these relations. "The reader who tackles a work of Hegel for the first time," he says

should, as a preliminary exercise, take any process of development, the growth of an organism, an historical movement, or the course of what strikes him as a well constructed novel or play, and try to reflect on it at a level beyond pictorial thinking. He should try not to dwell in the stream of imagery which will at once arise in his mind, and not to stop at the abstract level of quantitative measurement, but to think what really is that movement which he already calls development. Then, as he reads Hegel, he should treat the triadic notation as an indispensable but rough sign-posting of the route, and watch to see whether there may not be triads (on any scale) which not only reveal sublation in the very heart of things but suggest that it cannot be something merely sporadic and accidental.[34]

The problem of at once employing and transcending *Vorstellung* and *Verstand*, however, pre-occupies Mure in much of his writing on Hegel, and is the chief basis of his critical stance toward Hegel and, indeed, philosophy itself.[35] At the close of *The Philosophy of Hegel*, he writes:

Because the Hegelian philosopher is himself at once and contradictorily the whole and a part of it, "infinite in faculty" but "owing God a death," he can think the Logic as a circle but he cannot articulate its every phase as a timelessly necessary transition, and in the philosophies of Nature and Spirit he cannot so comprehend the eternal as to dispense entirely with the *Vorstellung* of a limited temporal process which presents itself as a section of a spurious infinite. He is doomed to accept in his philosophic thinking the aid of what he knows to be a lower form of thought.[36]

And elsewhere:

Before we become entangled in such problems as the validity of the categories or the transition from pure thought to Nature, there are simpler questions to be asked. If pictorial thought begets only endless repetitive regress when it strives to make a finite image commensurate with the universe, what of speech, which has its roots in imagery and perpetually constrains the philosopher to precarious metaphor which his colleagues seldom interpret precisely as he does. Can pure thought be expressed in words? Again, if human self-consciousness both constitutes and is constituted by absolute spirit, how can it tell a plain tale of its own nature and destiny? [37]

The dialectic, he concludes, involves as much restless dissatisfaction as

---

[34] *The Philosophy of Hegel*, pp. 38-39.
[35] See also Mure's essay "How, and How Far, is Philosophy Possible?" forthcoming in my *Hegel: The Question of Knowledge*.
[36] *The Philosophy of Hegel*, p. 204.
[37] Weiss, *Hegel's Critique of Aristotle's Philosophy of Mind*, p. xxiv.

happy harmonizing, and in Hegel's own concept of history can "be no
more than a phase in a development inherently beset by the dilemma of a
docta ignorantia." [38]

For many years during the period when Hegel was in eclipse in this
country, a few "bold spirits" continued to lecture on his philosophy, particularly on the *Phenomenology*.[39] One of these was Jacob Loewenberg,
whose edition of *Hegel Selections* (Scribners, 1929) was the only one available in English for a quarter of a century. His *Hegel's Phenomenology* is
apparently the fruit of these many years of guiding his students at Haver-
ford, Columbia, Harvard and California along the route of Hegel's "voyage of discovery." [40]

The book departs markedly from most treatments of Hegel in that it
is cast in dialogue form, and has little concern for the paraphernalia of
scholarship. Other Hegel commentators are barely mentioned, and of
these the only one whose influence is apparent is Royce, with whom Loewenberg studied at Harvard. Thus he views the *Phenomenology* as the
"biography" of consciousness, a "tremendous debate, the subject debated
upon being the claim to exclusive truth on the part of every human persuasion." [41] Hegel's "phenomenological method" is that of "histrionic impersonation," and the dialogue between Hardith and Meredy, two emi-
grants from Loewenberg's *Dialogues from Delphi*, is calculated to sharpen
and deepen the "inner tensions and incongruities," the tragi-comic paradox of consciousness:

The *Phenomenology* is a sort of comedy of errors ingeniously devised to serve
as "deduction" of organic truth. And in Hegel's comedy, too, the incongruities exposed are visible, not to those who enact them, but only to those watch-
ing them as spectators. Comic figures, not perceiving what goes on "behind
their backs," to use Hegel's expression, are unaware of their own folly. The
absurdity of their ways, so transparent to us, is not apparent to them. Successive impersonation of types of persuasion as comic, comic because they betray
to us the contradictions hidden from their adherents, this is the task Hegel
assigns to the dialectical method.[42]

Professor Loewenberg carries this thesis throughout the book, and where

[38] *Ibid.*
[39] Professor Werner Marx of Freiburg recently remarked in a letter to me that
"When I taught Hegel's *Phenomenology* 20 years ago in my courses at the Graduate
Faculty of the New School, this was considered a very strange and unnecessary undertaking, and they were at that time considered to be the only ones offered in the States."
[40] Jacob Loewenberg, *Hegel's Phenomenology: Dialogues on the Life of Mind* (La
Salle, Illinois: The Open Court Publishing Co., 1965), 377 pp.
[41] *Ibid.*, p. xxi.
[42] *Ibid.*, p. 20. *Cf.* Kenley Dove's interesting article on "Hegel's Phenomenological
Method" in *The Review of Metaphysics* (XXIII, June 1970, pp. 615-641), where he
argues that Hegel's method in the *Phenomenology* is not dialectical, but descriptive.

it not for the fact that this "comedy" is in some sense a *"divine* comedy," i.e., revealing an "irrepressible nisus toward the Absolute," the entire course of man's "spiritual odyssey" as portrayed by Hegel would become a "Demonodicy." In his introduction to his Hegel anthology, the tenor of which differs little from the present volume, he writes:

> The world, indeed, is a comedy, since all its parts are awry and absurd, but these very parts are "the great world's altar-stairs, that slope through darkness up to God." The *whole* is spiritual . . . Only the "happy ending," so to speak, in a preternatural sense and on a cosmic scale, saves Hegel's picture of the world . . . from assuming the character of an unmitigated tragedy.[43]

But the ending of the *Phenomenology*, the chapter entitled "Absolute Knowledge" by Hegel, is not a particularly happy one for Hardith and Meredy who become involved in a tragedy of their own making because they are unwilling (or unable) to come to grips with a chief problem of the *Phenomenology*, i.e., its place and function in Hegel's system and the related question of the place and function of human knowing with respect to "absolute" knowledge. Loewenberg chooses to retitle the chapter "The Philosophical Consciousness' and make it just another "posture" of human mind (albeit one which somehow "absorbs and transmutes all the others") because of the "anomalies of absoluteness."

What is the chapter's essential purpose? Does it or does it not belong to phenomenology? Does it contain the conclusion *drawn from* the series of the antecedently exhibited forms of consciousness or is its aim rather to serve as *transition to* an investigation by the same method of the objective ways of being instead of the subjective ways of knowing? Should the chapter be read as epilogue or as prologue? [44]

All of these questions and the many more raised in this dialogue revolve around Loewenberg's initial construal of Hegel's *Phenomenology* as some sort of biography. "If all knowledge presupposes a subject in pursuit or possession of it, what subject is capable not only of seeking but of attaining the totality of knowledge in which alone its truth resides?" [45] If the *Phenomenology* is a biography, whose is it, and who is the author? Prior to the advent of religious phenomenology, the human psyche alone has been the subject; but "the center of the stage now comes to be occupied by the Absolute," whose consciousness "must now be found to lie hidden in man's." [46] Either the apparent biography of the human psyche must be

---

[43] *Hegel Selections*, ed. by Jacob Loewenberg (New York: Scribner's, 1929), p. xli.
[44] *Hegel's Phenomenology*, p. 357.
[45] *Ibid.*, p. 359.
[46] *Ibid.*, p. 365.

construed rather as God's *auto*biography, or the dialectical development of the various postures of mind is "completely at loggerheads" with this non-phenomenological result. The first alternative is "preposterous," and thus Loewenberg's interpretation leaves us with another *docta ignorantia*. Like Book Lambda of Aristotle's *Metaphysics* and the doctrine of active *nous* at the close of the *De Anima*, the last chapter of the *Phenomenology* is to be regarded as another Platonic wild oat come home to roost, somehow out of joint with the rest of Hegel's teaching. But as Bosanquet once remarked, "the hardest of all lessons in interpretation is to believe that great men mean what they say. We are below their level, and what they actually say seems impossible to us, till we have adulterated it to suit our own imbecility." [47]

While the publishers may have gone too far in hailing this book as the "definitive work on *The Phenomenology* for which the Hegel scholars of the world have long been waiting," inasmuch as it is the only full-length treatment in English, such a claim will have a measure of truth until such time as it is properly challenged by an equally comprehensive exposition. With so many presently teaching Hegel from the *Phenomenology*, and with a new translation in the works, perhaps it is not too much to expect that someone else soon will have the courage of his classroom convictions and put his interpretation in print.

Emil Fackenheim's *The Religious Dimension in Hegel's Thought*,[48] in contrast to Loewenberg's "quasi-lay conversations" on Hegel's first book, is an impressive work of erudition and argumentation, a complex tapestry of interpretation and reinterpretation, not just of Hegel's philosophy of religion, but of the entire Hegelian system. But Fackenheim does not come to praise or even merely to expound Hegel, but to bury him. He calls up many of the negative Hegel legends, some of which he appears to refute; but some, on the other hand, persist and even evolve in Fackenheim's hands, and if a few early signs are missed or disregarded, there is the continued expectation that the author will eventually arrive at a resolution of the questions which gather like threatening clouds in their wake, "questions on which, by its own confession and insistence, the fate of Hegel's philosophy as a whole depends." [49] But as it turns out, the book is in fact a long, many-faceted *rhetorical* question, the ultimate message of which

---

[47] *The Introduction to Hegel's Philosophy of Fine Art*, translated by Bernard Bosanquet (London: Kegan Paul, Trench & Co., 1905), p. xix.
[48] Emil Fackenheim, *The Religious Dimension in Hegel's Thought* (Bloomington: Indiana University Press, 1967). 274 pp.
[49] *Ibid.*, p. 9.

is that the entire Hegelian enterprise, judged by what Fackenheim takes to be Hegel's intentions, is a failure.

This question is first raised as "the impenetrable mystery of Hegel's thought": how can he "put forward an absolute philosophy, that is, an all-comprehensive and therefore final system of an all-comprehensive and therefore infinite Reason . . . and yet take existence seriously?" [50] How can Hegel's thought rise to absoluteness or divinity, yet not "flee from but stay with" the world? This question becomes transformed into the problem of "the relation between all of human life and an all-comprehensive philosophical thought," found decisively, Fackenheim argues, in religious life, and specifically in modern Protestant Christianity. The author's interpretation of the *Phenomenology* throws considerable doubt on its ability to provide a ladder to the absolute standpoint: "The phenomenological road to science can be a road only if it is *already* scientific. Phenomenological thought must already *be* at the absolute standpoint if it is to 'hand the individual the ladder' to it." [51] His treatment of the *Encyclopaedia* (the Hegelian "middle") similarly fails to reveal the "overreaching power" which the mature system of science must have to prevent it from falling into fragmentation:

Hegel's "appearing science" and his "science proper" must both fail to *demonstrate* their crucial assumption unless the final dualism can be disposed of: between the totality of non-philosophic life and the philosophic thought which is to comprehend it.[52]

The last half of the book examines the dependence of philosophy upon religion, and the former's ability, or lack of it, to at once "transfigure" and preserve non-philosophic religious content: "Can it make peace with the faith it comprehends? Or only be hostile to it?" [53] In a brief passage, a ray of "Divine Love" seems to penetrate the clouds and provide the elixer needed for this peace, but again, another condition must be met: philosophic comprehension must preserve not only the content but the *form* of faith as well; human receptivity must not be preempted by divine *self-othering*. Such, argues Fackenheim,

would surely end the life of faith. And it would end, as well, a thought which, rather than simply dwell with the Divine, is perpetually to reenact its rise *to*

[50] *Ibid.*, p. 4.
[51] *Ibid.*, pp. 34-35.
[52] *Ibid.*, p. 112.
[53] *Ibid.*, p. 204.

it. It seems that Hegel's peace between the final philosophy and Christian faith must become – for *both* religion and philosophy – a peace of death.[54]

This repugnant conclusion is again postponed, but not denied, by noting that such was certainly not Hegel's intention. "Its crucial condition," argues Fackenheim, "is that a conflict which in one sense is yet to be resolved by thought is in another already resolved in life." [55] Only if Reason is already actual in the world can a peace be won between it and the final philosophic thought. It thus emerges that Hegel's belief in the "actual – and, in principle, final – secular-Protestant synthesis in modern life" is the ultimate condition for the possibility of the Hegelian *philosophic* synthesis. But the heart of the argument, if this labyrinth of "crucial" questions, "decisive" dilemmas, and unacceptable alternatives may be said to have a heart, is found in this passage in the introduction, where Fackenheim writes:

No wisdom is required today for the insight that the Hegelian synthesis, if ever a genuine possibility, has broken down beyond all possible recovery. Shortsighted academic critics may focus their criticism even now on the Hegelian system, taken in isolation from the world which it seeks to comprehend. Prophetic non-academic critics such as Marx and Kierkegaard focused their criticism, even in the nineteenth century, on that modern world which Hegel could still view with so colossal an optimism. Today, no prophetic insight is needed for the perception of universal fragmentation. The sins of colonialism have come to visit Hegel's modern Europe. America – Hegel's "land of the future" – has lost its innocence at Hiroshima and Nagasaki. Hegel's own countrymen – in his view permanently raised above their original barbarism by a Christian culture originally alien to them – have shown at Auschwitz a depravity unequalled in all history. Modern secular self-confidence, if surviving at all, has lost its titanic quality, and the God who speaks to present-day faith speaks ambiguously if He is not wholly silent. This writer – a Jew committed to Judaism – would in any case be at odds with the Hegelian synthesis, which, after all, is Christian or post-Christian. In the world of today, no one can accept this synthesis – Christian, post-Christian, or non-Christian ... and it is entirely safe to say that Hegel, were he alive today, would not be a Hegelian.[56]

It is indeed a pity that Fackenheim did not approach this work as a philosopher committed to philosophy, rather than as a Jew committed to

[54] *Ibid.*, p. 206.
[55] *Ibid.*, p. 207.
[56] *Ibid.*, p. 12. Fackenheim assumes the position of a latter-day Krug, requiring Hegel not only to deduce but to justify the unjustifiable horror of Auschwitz. Typical of much of Fackenheim's current writing on Hegel is this passage which concludes his article "On the Actuality of the Rational and the Rationality of the Actual" in *The Review of Metaphysics* (XXIII, June 1970, p. 698): "This modest essay has inquired only into the meaning of Hegel's philosophy. Any inquiry into its truth must confront its claims with the gas chambers of Auschwitz."

Judaism. What his study reveals is how the same elements in Hegel may (unfortunately) serve to show that Hegel is essentially dead or essentially alive for our time, depending on whether one is concerned to grind one's own or Hegel's axe. In Hegel's world, and particularly in Hegel's state, a Jew is secure in his Judaism; but in Fackenheim's world, Hegel must cease to be a Christian, must cease to be an Hegelian, to survive.

On the so-called sins of colonialism, what we are witnessing today is but a hurried realization of Hegel's prophecy that the exploited servant who serves well is being equipped in the process to become his own master, and that the ideal relationship is one in which the exploiting master comes to recognize and to intend the inevitable result. Suggestive, and in its final clause precisely to the point, is Hegel's observation in the *Philosophy of Right* that "Colonial independence proves to be of the greatest advantage to the mother country, just as the emancipation of slaves turns out to the greatest advantage of the owners." [57] On America's "lost innocence": it surely misrepresents Hegel to suggest that he thought America was ever innocent or that it could avoid passing through the stages of development that would force it beyond its own territorial limits when all its critizens aspired to full equality in political freedom. And as for the significance of the atomic bomb, Hegel would likely have welcomed its development as proof that, in the modern world, not one, not some, but all are free and equal in the sovereign rights and responsibilities (risks) of political freedom. Again in the *Philosophy of Right*, speaking of the advance of equality in freedom marked by the transition from feudalism to the first phase of the modern state, Hegel writes: "It is for this reason that thought has invented the gun, and the invention of this weapon, which has changed the purely personal form of bravery [the aristocratic form] into a more abstract one [democratic form], is no accident." [58] And on the character of the Germanic people, on modern secular self-confidence, and on God's voice in the world, it is likely that what Hegel has had to say will remain fresh and true long after Fackenheim and his peers have mounted other hobby-horses.

But most important of all, Fackenheim mistakenly ascribes to Hegel a practical intent. His criticism is thus beside the point, except on the assumption that Hegel is advocating a political-social program, so that, to be an Hegelian would mean that one wanted to see realized or preserved what Hegel *advocated*. From that point of view, Hegel ceases to be what

[57] *Hegel's Philosophy of Right*, translated with Notes by T. M. Knox (Oxford: Clarendon Press, 1958), p. 278.
[58] *Ibid.*, p. 212.

he is in fact. Twice in the Preface to the *Philosophy of Right,* a book
which, given the nature of Fackenheim's critique he is unjustifiably completely silent on, Hegel reminds us that "as a work of philosophy," his
politics "must be poles apart from an attempt to construct a state as it
ought to be." The other passage at the close of the Preface concerns "the
owl of Minerva," and although Fackenheim refers to it more than once, its
famous significance seems to have been missed.

Finally, it might be pointed out that while Fackenheim attacks on a
number of levels Hegel's attempt to construe the world rationally, he
nowhere in this volume adequately examines the Hegelian texts on which
the ability or inability of the dialectical *Begriff* to bring this about depends. The *Logic,* for example, is barely mentioned. Instead, his text
abounds with metaphorical language at crucial points in the development
of the argument, and comment on wider but equally crucial issues is
relegated to extremely condensed and sometimes question-begging appendices and footnotes.[59] This needed examination, or re-examination
has only just begun, and we shall surely be best advised to wait until it
has borne its fruit before we put Hegel in his grave.

Until quite recently, there has been very little available for English
readers on Hegel's life and the background of his writings. Prior to the
appearance of Kaufmann's *Hegel* in 1965, the only books in English that
devoted much space to Hegel's biography were Caird's *Hegel* and Luqueer's *Hegel as Educator.*[60] The standard German accounts are those of
Karl Rosenkranz, a devoted disciple of Hegel, and Rudolph Haym, whom
Caird aptly describes as "a critic whose opposition to Hegel's philosophical
principles has passed into a kind of personal bitterness." [61] Both of these
remain untranslated. In 1959, Gustav Emil Mueller published his *Hegel:*

---

[59] "Science," for example, continually appears in inverted commas, and its meaning
for Hegel never receives the close, detailed scrutiny which alone would reveal whether
or not Hegel's understanding of it could prevent the "fragmentation" which throughout
his book Fackenheim rhetorically assumes as a *fait accompli.* Fackenheim's writing is
also needlessly ambiguous, allowing him to pass from half-statement to half-statement
without obviously committing himself to the patent absurdities implied. His style exemplifies "the peculiar technique of writing between the lines" so deftly noted in Leo
Strauss' *Persecution and the Art of Writing* (Glencoe, Illinois: The Free Press, 1952),
and most of his negative conclusions, if they do not take the form of rhetorical questions, are put in the mouths of other Hegel detractors, such as Marx, Kierkegaard, and
Haym.

[60] On Caird, see note 23 above; Frederic Ludlow Luqueer, *Hegel as Educator* (New
York: Columbia University Press, 1896). 185 pp. Reprinted 1967, AMS Press.

[61] Caird, *Hegel,* p.v. Mueller (see next note) says "Rudolph Haym's brilliantly superficial and profoundly malicious book on Hegel is the start of most Hegel legends,
save the Marxistic one of 'thesis, antithesis, and synthesis,' " and "Again, we owe to
the prolific vituperations of Rudolph Haym the popular Hegel legend that he was
called to Berlin in order 'to be a servile tool of reaction.' " (pp. 317, 346 respectively.)

Denkgeschichte eines Lebendigen (Franke Verlag Bern), and an English version of this appeared in 1968 under the title *Hegel: The Man, His Vision and Work.*[62]

Mueller's treatment, in contrast to Kaufmann's, is thoroughly sympathetic, and manifests throughout Mure's remark above (p. 10) on the integrity of Hegel's philosophy and life. His Introduction ("Some Hegel Legends") emphasizes the theme of an earlier article, "The Hegel Legend of 'Thesis-Antithesis-Synthesis' ": "If you expect to find this nonsense in Hegel, then no text makes sense, because no text contains this." [63] The first third of the book follows Hegel's development through his *Lehrjahre* and *Wanderjahre* in Stuttgart and Tübingen, Bern and Frankfurt, drawing largely from Hoffmeister's edition of *Dokumente zu Hegels Entwicklung* and Nohl's *Hegels Theologische Jugendschriften* those excerpts and accounts which reveal the later system in germ form. "Hegel's philosophical development," he writes, "is a Hegelian development: He becomes for himself what he is in himself through hard and incessant labor and effort. The mature man is the explication of the boy, but it is almost uncanny to see how much is already implicit in his beginning!" [64] Typical of Mueller's approach is this appraisal of Hegel as a schoolboy in Stuttgart:

I doubt where we could find a second boy, whose years from 14-18 could match the same age in Hegel. This boy is a genius of learning, coupled with a critical spirit, which is not submerged by the substantial sum of appropriated materials; and what is even more amazing, this boy, in spite of his indefatigable diligence, is not an intellectualistic snob but a friendly and helpful comrade among others. His exceptional way of life seems natural to him; he swims in wisdom like a fish in water.[65]

At the *Stift* and as *Hauslehrer* at Bern and Frankfurt, Hegel's friendship with Schelling and Hölderlin, and his personal and "existential" encounters with theological and political "positivity" are thrown into a crucible from which will emerge his later philosophical principles:

Hegel discovered a dialectical reality in Christianity. Christianity thus, in turn, was bound to appear as one special symbolic expression of the universal truth that the whole of reality is a dialectical structure and process.[66]

---

[62] Gustav Emil Mueller, *Hegel: The Man, His Vision and Work* (New York: Pageant Press, 1968). 451 pp.

[63] *Ibid.*, p. 4; Mueller's article appears in *Journal of the History of Ideas*, 19, No. 3 (1958).

[64] Mueller, *Hegel*, pp. 15-16.

[65] *Ibid.*, p. 24.

[66] *Ibid.*, p. 59.

And again:

Hegel is already practicing a method of reflection, which later he calls phenomenological. This method consists in asking: What sort of object is evident
to what sort of subjective consciousness? What kind of certainty is aware of
what sort of truth?[67]

Mueller argues that this period culminates in Hegel's philosophical breakthrough: in Frankfurt he arrives at the realization that he is "condemned
by God to be a philosopher," and "begins to write his first purely systematic reflections on philosophy." Hegel's productivity henceforward is immense, and his reading voluminous. He continues to "live what he thinks
and think what he lives." In Jena, the *Phenomenology* ("the foaming
chalice of the spirit") "was hurled on paper in one flow," the culmination
of all his previous experience and writing into which it flowed. Rosenkranz
called it "the phenomenological crisis of the system":

How a system can experience a "crisis" is clear only to a "Hegelian"; "Hegelians" are more than ordinary mortals. What Rosenkranz probably means
is that Hegel in desperation gave up and was thrown into the convulsive act
of writing the *Phenomenology*. The first attempt at the "system" is such a
pitiful heap of unintelligible gibberish that it is rather amazing that out of it,
through incessant effort, finally emerged the clear structure of the *Encyclopaedia*.[68]

The last sentence of this passage displays the one criticism which Mueller
allows to creep into his adoration of Hegel. In his "rendition" (one can
hardly call it a translation) of Hegel's *Encyclopaedia,* he says "To translate
the world's worst stylist literally . . . is perfectly pointless; the translation,
then, is every bit as unintelligible as the original. But the world's worst
stylist," he continues, "is, alas, also one of the world's greatest thinkers,"
and "in the whole history of philosophy there is no other single work which
could hold a candle to his *Logic*; a work incomparable in its range, depth,
clarity of thought, and beauty of composition . . ." [69] Again, how such
profundity can "hide under" such a "dead heap of abstactions" must
present itself as a real puzzle to mortal, non-Hegelian students, and how
such a devotee can curse the darkness in the admitted presence of such
light is even more puzzling. One would think that Mueller might rather

[67] *Ibid.*, p. 106.
[68] *Ibid.*, p. 207.
[69] *Hegel: Encyclopedia of Philosophy,* translated and annotated by Gutsav Emil
Mueller (New York: Philosophical Library, 1959), p. 1.

have reconsidered the meaning of "clarity" with respect to Hegel's philosophical thought.[70]

The rest of Mueller's book traces the systematic embodiment in Hegel's mature writings and lectures of the kaleidoscopic vision of *Geist* presented in the *Phenomenology*. His account is both insightful and inspiring, and in the space of 200 pages, manages to shed considerable light not only on the historical circumstances of Hegel's teaching and writing, but also upon many of the significant philosophical issues with which they are concerned. Mueller's interpretation focuses upon Hegel's claim that "the truth is the whole," a whole which presents itself as an infinite, encyclopedic "circle of circles," each of which reflects the whole in its own medium:

This whole is too rich to be expressed in any one-sided "system." The various "isms" (rationalism as well as irrationalism, subjectivism as well as objectivism, idealism as well as realism) must be educated to realize their limitations and their value within their limitation.[71]

This dialectical *paideia* emerges from the *Phenomenology* and moves through the system as it had moved through Hegel's life.

Critics and scholars of Hegel's development will undoubtedly find much in this book to which they will object. The cutting and rewriting of the German version was apparently done somewhat impressionistically, and we have already noted with what self-willed devotion Mueller applies himself to the task of presenting to us this "famous stranger of strange fame." He has also taken many liberties with the Hegelian texts, and it is often difficult to tell whether we are reading Hegel or Mueller. At several places, quotations begin, but there is no way of telling where they end, and there are many uncorrected misprints. But the charm, vigor, and intimacy of Mueller's style more than compensate for these shortcomings, and his knowledge and sincere appreciation of Hegel – the man, his vision and work – are unmistakable: even Professor Kaufmann would have to admit that the book is aptly titled. Finally, it presents throughout the religious dimension of Hegel's thought almost totally missing from Fackenheim's volume which bears that title.

Worth mentioning briefly in this context is another, smaller and less devoted treatment of Hegel's life by Franz Wiedmann titled *Hegel: An*

---

[70] *Cf.* Bosanquet's remark in a letter to Hoernlé: "To me [Hegel] has not, and never had from the first, that foreignness or essential difficulty. Not that I can 'explain' him any more than others can, but that when I do seem to understand he speaks to me as the only writer I can understand . . . every one else seems distant and artificial beside [him]." *Bernard Bosanquet and His Friends*, ed. by J. H. Muirhead (London: George Allen & Unwin, 1935), p. 116.

[71] Mueller, *Hegel*, p. 239.

Illustrated Biography.[72] This monograph adds little, if anything, to Mueller's account, and does not attempt a philosophical appraisal, but rather sticks largely to dry reports and extensive quotations from the writings and letters of Hegel and his contemporaries. Wiedmann simply remarks, for example, that Hegel's philosophy of nature "is the weakest part of the system," and seems to regard the "historical power of Hegel's ideas," i.e. their influence on Marx, etc., as their chief importance. "Even today," he says, in something of a naïve concession, "Hegel's philosophy is taught at universities." [73] The book does contain a variety of interesting photographs: the house in which Hegel was born, the *Tübinger Stift*, examples of Hegel's handwriting, and even one of Hegel's grave in the *Dorotheenstadter Friedhof* next to Fichte and near his friend Solger.

In 1969, the most productive year thus far with respect to books in English on Hegel, no less than seven volumes appeared, including a new translation of the *Wissenschaft der Logik*, translations of the work of two influential French Hegel commentators, a study of the intellectual, moral and political background of Hegel's thought in Rousseau, Kant and Fichte, and three monographs, two of which approach Hegel through Kant, the third through Aristotle.[74] Since, at this writing, most of these have been available for a very short time, and since my consideration of Hegel scholarship in English must in any case be a limited one, I wish to comment briefly on only the three monographs.

Soll's *Hegel's Metaphysics* is a welcome study for several reasons. First, it approaches the subject in terms of the Kantian problematic, and more specifically, through Hegel's critique of Kant. While Hegel's metaphysic is much more than just a response to the Critical Philosophy, the influence of Kant's *Critiques* is especially important in understanding and assessing Hegel's position. Every teacher of philosophy is aware that Hegel "rebell-

---

[72] Franz Wiedmann, *Hegel: An Illustrated Biography*, translated from the German [Wiedmann's *Georg Wilhelm Friedrich Hegel in Selbstzeugnissen und Bilddokumenten* (Reinbek b. Hamburg) Rowohlt, 1965] by Joachim Neugroschel (New York: Pegasus, 1968). 140 pp.

[73] *Ibid.*, pp. 120, 129, 121 respectively.

[74] In order, they are: *Hegel's Science of Logic*, translated by A. V. Miller, Foreword by J. N. Findlay (London: George Allen & Unwin, 1969). 844 pp.; Alexandre Kojève, *Introduction to the Reading of Hegel*, edited by Allan Bloom, translated by James H. Nichols, Jr. (New York: Basic Books, 1969). 287 pp.; Jean Hyppolite, *Studies on Marx and Hegel*, edited and translated by John O'Neil (New York: Basic Books, 1969). 202 pp.; George Armstrong Kelly, *Idealism, Politics and History: Sources of Hegelian Thought* (Cambridge: Cambridge University Press, 1969). 387 pp.; Ivan Soll, *An Introduction to Hegel's Metaphysics* (Chicago: The University of Chicago Press, 1969). 160 pp.; W. H. Walsh, *Hegelian Ethics* (New York: St. Martin's Press, 1969). 84 pp., and Frederick Gustav Weiss, *Hegel's Critique of Aristotle's Philosophy of Mind*, (The Hague: Martinus Nijhoff, 1969). XXVIII + 56 pp.

ed" against the limitation Kant placed on knowledge (although he was neither the first nor the only one to do so), and that he rejected the doctrine of the *Ding-an-sich*, but few are more than superficially aware of the grounds and detailed nature of this criticism. This is not surprising, since there does not exist in English a systematic and thorough examination of Hegel's critique of Kant.[75] The chief sources for such an examination are the *Lectures on the History of Philosophy*, and the larger and especially the lesser *Logic*. Soll completely ignores the former,[76] and concentrates on the latter, drawing also upon the *Phenomenology* where, although Kant's name is barely mentioned, the stance of the Critical Philosophy is often clearly before Hegel's mind.

Secondly, Soll's commentary on the historical *Vorbegriff* or exposition which precedes Hegel's treatment of Logic proper in part one of the *Encyclopaedia* helps to fill another gap in the existing English Hegel literature, as well as show how deeply rooted Hegel's metaphysic is in the thought of his predecessors.[77] The importance for Soll's book of these opening chapters on the various "attitudes of thought to objectivity" is emphasized by the fact that they were intended by Hegel to serve his own students as an introduction to the system outlined in the *Encyclopaedia*.

Thirdly, Soll's brief and clearly written treatment of several of the key issues in Hegel's epistemology and metaphysic makes it ideally suited for its purpose, which is to provide a means of access to Hegel's thought for budding undergraduate philosophers, and in an area that still suffers from a marked deficiency of such texts. The future of the present Hegel revival is going to depend largely upon re-instating Hegel in the mainstream of western philosophy and clearly establishing at the "grass-roots" level his relevance and importance for a host of problems that beset the inquiring minds of students and scholars alike.[78]

Whatever shortcomings this study has attach mainly to the fact that due

[75] There are, of course, a number of studies of the *development from* Kant to Hegel, notably those of Seth and Royce, and there is even a small book by Josef Maier titled *On Hegel's Critique of Kant*. This latter, however, is actually a Marxist critique of both Hegel and Kant.

[76] Quite justifiably of course, since he is not primarily concerned with Hegel's critique of Kant, but with a more general exposition of Hegel's metaphysic.

[77] There is no commentary in English on these chapters, which not only show Hegel at work in the history of philosophy (modern philosophy in particular), but clearly demonstrate the difference between his own metaphysic and the "metaphysics of the understanding."

[78] See Mueller's *Hegel*, p. 11: "Once the Hegel legend was established, writers of textbooks in the history of philosophy copied it from their predecessors. It was a convenient method of embalming Hegel and keeping the mummy on display for curious visitors of antiquities."

to its size, it cannot do all these things well. In an attempt to illustrate
the relation between "Philosophy, Truth and Human Activity," the author devotes the first third of the book to a commentary on Hegel's chapter
on "Self-Consciousness" in the *Phenomenology*. In these pages, there is
no discussion of Kant at all, and given the orientation of the rest of the
book, an exposition of §§1-18 of the lesser *Logic* would have been much
more suitable in answering the question Soll raises on his first page, i.e.,
"What . . . does Hegel take to be the goal of philosophy?" This initial
excursion into the *Phenomenology* seems influenced by Walter Kaufmann, whose inimitable style is also manifest in his Foreword for the
book.[79] Soll also invokes a relatively superficial debate between Kaufmann
and Royce on the interpretation of the *Phenomenology* (and at the close,
between himself and Kaufmann), which adds little to his project.

Walsh's *Hegelian Ethics*, an even smaller volume than Soll's, sets itself
the task of introducing Hegelian ethics "by means of a comparison with
the parallel doctrines in Kant, doctrines which I can perhaps assume to
be generally familiar to the reader." [80] In this Professor Walsh does a
very good job, considering the space that he has. Indeed, he even manages
within a scant 80 pages to significantly introduce material from Hegel's
early writings, and to include chapters on Hegel's life and the British Hegelians. But Hegel's ethical theory, like Plato's, is much richer and more
extensive than such a restricted comparison can reveal, and although
Walsh seems to be aware of this, he nonetheless often leaves us with a
negative impression, not only with respect to the wider context of Hegel's
ethics in the state, but also in the narrower realm of personal morality. The
author's treatment of "concrete ethics" and particularly Hegel's theory of
the state is just too brief (about a dozen pages) to do it justice, and the
result more often than not leaves the subject in an ambiguous and com-
promised position. With respect to personal ethics, Walsh says at one
point that "Where Hegel is unsatisfying is that he apparently leaves no
room for personal morality of any kind," and "It must be confessed that
Hegel is insensitive to this [necessity of being a good man, of cultivating
one's soul] whole dimension of the moral life."[81] Later however, he writes:

The argument that Hegel neglected the more personal aspects of morality
has already been considered above (Section III). The probabilities are that
he always meant to leave room for what might be called cultivation of the

---

[79] "This book is my intellectual grandchild. It has others ancestors, and I have
other offspring, but I am proud of it without always agreeing with it. And, of course,
it does not always agree with me." Walter Kaufmann, from the Foreword, p. ix.
[80] Walsh, *Hegelian Ethics*, p. 6.
[81] *Ibid.*, pp. 18-19.

individual soul, but saw the primary concern of ethics as being with men's interpersonal transactions. An impatience with mere conscientiousness, the pursuit of the good will as an end in itself ... doubtless reinforced this attitude of his. *In my opinion he was entirely right to take such a view.*[82]

And, as Professor Paolucci remarks in his review of this book:

Professor Walsh makes no effort to examine the *articulation* of Hegel's ethical thought as presented under the headings of Abstract Right and Morality in the *Philosophy of Right*. To pursue that articulation from the first claim of personality on what it deems, abstractly, to be its own, through the forms of "taking possession" by grasping, reshaping, marking, and using, to the "full possession" that permits one to "contract" with another personality for the alienation of what is possessed; to trace the emergence of the possibility of *wrong* – of tort, fraud, crime – out of the mutual recognition of wills in contract; to follow the logic of *righting* wrongs through personal *revenge* and *punishment* by a third party, to the emergence of the subjective, inner conviction that one can still claim to be *right* morally while being judged wrong objectively; that, surely, is the way Hegel would have us approach the profundity of his ethical doctrine.[83]

For an understanding of Hegel's ethics that may suitably serve as a basis for criticism, Reyburn's *The Ethical Theory of Hegel* is a far better text.[84]

Finally, of my own book on *Hegel's Critique of Aristotle's Philosophy of Mind*, I shall say very little. Like Soll's *Hegel's Metaphysics*, it was not orignially written for publication, but rather constituted part of my own "voyage of discovery" into the rich background of Hegel's thought. If there is reason to examine the influence of Kant on Hegel, there is even more to locate the authority for Hegel of Aristotle, and of all things Greek. "The development of philosophic science as science," teaches Hegel, "and, further, the progress from the Socratic point of view to the scientific, begins with Plato and is completed by Aristotle. They of all others deserve to be called teachers of the human race." [85] We have also to remember that Professor Findlay ends his *Hegel: A Re-examination* with the remark that Hegel is "without doubt, the Aristotle of our post-Renaissance world, our synoptic thinker without peer." The purpose of my own study was really to explore a small part of the truth of this remark, to call attention to Hegel's neglected and disparaged *Lectures*, and to follow up Mure's pio-

[82] *Ibid.*, pp. 57-58, emphasis mine.
[83] Henry Paolucci, from his review of Walsh's *Hegelian Ethics* in *The Owl of Minerva*, I, 2, 1969, p. 6.
[84] Hugh A. Reyburn, *The Ethical Theory of Hegel: A Study of the Philosophy of Right* (Oxford: Clarendon Press, 1921). 271 pp. Reprinted 1967.
[85] *Hegel's Lectures on the History of Philosophy*, edited and translated by E. S. Haldane and Frances H. Simson (London: Routledge and Kegan Paul, 1963), vol. II, p. 1.

neer work on the subject.[86] For many years it was thought that Hegel's philosophy grew solely out of Kant, and constituted an even more preposterous reaction to him than those of Fichte and Schelling. But Hegel's mind was not one to be influenced only by his more or less immediate surroundings, his intimate knowledge of them notwithstanding, and only a close study of his philosophy as a whole, and his *Lectures on the History of Philosophy* in particular, can reveal this. For Hegel, "the study of the history of Philosophy is the study of Philosophy itself, for, indeed, it can be nothing else." [87] Whoever forgets this remark is apt to miss a good deal of Hegel's meaning throughout his work.

In conclusion, and given the tenor of this paper thus far, it might be appropriate to give the last word on Hegel studies to a philosopher who was among the first to assess "what is living and what is dead of the philosophy of Hegel:"

Now, if any one were to ask me if he should or should not be an "Hegelian," and if I am an Hegelian, I might, after all I have said, dispense with a reply. Yet I wish as a corollary, to answer here this question in a way which is perhaps derived from that very philosophy. I am, and believe is necessary to be, an Hegelian; but in the same sense in which any one who has a philosophical spirit and philosophical culture in our time, is and feels himself to be at once: *Eleatic, Heraclitean, Socratic, Platonic, Aristotelian, Stoic, Sceptic, Neoplatonic, Christian, Buddhist, Cartesian, Spinozist, Leibnizian, Vichian, Kantian;* and so on. That is to say, in the sense that no thinker and no historical movement of thought come to pass without bearing fruit, without depositing an element of truth, which forms part, consciously or no, of living modern thought. Neither I nor any sensible person would wish to be an Hegelian, in the sense of a servile and obsequious follower, who professes to accept every word of the master, or in the sense of a religious sectarian, who considers disagreement a sin. In short, Hegel too has discovered a moment of the truth; to this moment we must accord recognition and value. That is all . . . .

But the first condition for resolving whether to accept or to reject the doctrines which Hegel propounds (I am constrained to make explicit what I should have preferred to leave to be understood) is to *read his books*: and to put an end to the spectacle, half comical and half disgusting, of the accusation and the abuse of a philosopher by critics who do not know him, and who wage a foolish war with a ridiculous puppet created by their own imaginations, under the ignoble sway of traditional prejudice and intellectual laziness.[88]

---

[86] See above, pp. 8-9.
[87] *Hegel's Lectures,* vol. I, p. 30.
[88] Benedetto Croce, *What is Living and What is Dead of the Philosophy of Hegel,* translated by Douglas Ainslie (London: Macmillan & Co., 1915). Reprinted (New York: Russell & Russell, 1969) pp. 216-217.

THE HEGELIAN DIALECTIC*

Eric Weil

In his last text intended for publication, signed just a week before his death, Hegel was led to speak of a difficulty inherent in every philosophic exposition intended to be comprehensible to the public of its own day. By right, the simple presentation of the thought should suffice. Indeed, it alone would be adequate. At the very most, there might be added "negative reflections aimed at repressing and removing what otherwise might be introduced by the representation or a poorly ordered thought."

But the problem is hardly soluble. For one thing, such additions are by their very nature fortuitous and give this defence the same character; not to mention the fact that, because errors are fortuitous and hence inexhaustible, no precautions will ever suffice. Moreover, "the peculiar unrest and distraction of our modern consciousness force us to take into account reflections and fancies that lie more or less near at hand"; inevitably, there will be a compromise. (*Preface* to the 2nd ed. of *Logic* I, ed. Lassen, 1932, p. 29).

Still more will there be compromise for the interpreter of philosophic thought. The text is there at the disposal of everyone, and those wishing to know the work need only be sent to it. After all, the commentator who believes himself better able than the author to express what the latter intended puts himself above the one whose work he explains. He would do better to express this superiority without lingering at an undertaking for which he'll have the gratitude only of those who wish to avoid the work of understanding by themselves.

But here again, Hegel's reflection is well founded and apropos. The reader is not contemporary with the text. And in breathing the atmosphere of his own time, he has heard and accepted opinions on the subject of that *-ism* into which a philosophy that claimed to be comprehensible

* Transl. L. Rice.

in and of itself on the sole condition that we let it speak and listen attentively to it, has been transformed under the influence of adversaries and, perhaps especially, of disciples and disciples of disciples. Reductions to what is *essential*, condemnations without appeal sustained by the dogmatic convictions of judges, the effusions of manuals that must treat everything and in fact only summarize that whose entire value consists in its elaboration – all of these contribute to the fact that the entry into the great edifices of philosophy is blocked and forever in need of being freed of obstacles which time incessantly piles up. Thus, the interpreter's work is at once useful and impossible: useful because it can eliminate certain misunderstandings, impossible because their number is legion; for if truth is one there is no limit to errors.

In full consciousness of this difficulty I will attempt to speak about the Hegelian dialectic. Moreover, if I may be permitted to employ a paradoxical formulation, I intend to show that one cannot *speak about* the Hegelian dialectic; that one may follow it, or refuse to follow it, but that one cannot summarize it without denaturing it.

I

Everyone knows what dialectic is. Hegel himself, in a conversation with Goethe, formulated it perfectly. Asked by the poet what the dialectic is, the philosopher responded that it "is nothing other than that spirit of contradiction, well regulated and methodically formed, which dwells in every man – a gift that shows its greatness in the distinction between the true and the false." And to Goethe's remark, "If only such arts and skills of the mind were not so often used to make the true false and the false true," Hegel, obviously desiring not to continue on this track, answers that, indeed, "this happens, but only with persons of sick mind" (Eckermann, *Gespräche*, 18 October 1827). It is evident that here Hegel is not speaking as a philosopher, that he is aware of dealing with one who has always distrusted philosophy. And yet, the terms he uses, if they do not perhaps characterize his own conception of the dialectic, do characterize the one current in his day; even as these terms will probably appear both natural and sufficient to the great majority of our contemporaries. *Contradiction* and *method*: these are the two concepts by which the dialectic is to be defined, unless one wished also to emphasize that the spirit of this contradiction is *natural* to every man.

Now, even an imperfect acquaintance with the Hegelian texts shows clearly that none of the traits listed fits what, in Hegel's own view, the dialectic is and should be. It is, on the contrary, so little natural to man that the individual has to traverse anew the entire history of the spirit in order to arrive at a point where philosophy, and more particularly the dialectic, become accessible and comprehensible to him. The enormous work accomplished in the *Phenomenology of Spirit* has as its sole aim to answer the need of man situated in the finitude of ordinary life, and to offer him the ladder he needs and has the right to demand of the philosopher, who, for his part, would not accomplish his task if he required of ordinary consciousness that it make a standing jump into the Absolute. What the non-philosopher thinks to be is not what he is, and what he truly is he discovers only at the end of the long work of historical reason. To retranslate Hegelian terminology into that of Aristotle, what is first in itself, the foundation and the essential, is last for us in the order of discovery. No doubt, the spirit progresses by contradiction, by the spirit of contradiction, which is indeed strong in the distinction of true and false. But the false was true in its own moment; it does not vanish, because what succeeds presupposes what preceded it, is not the latter's absolute negation, annihilation, or disappearance pure and simple, but rather the comprehension of its insufficiency which preserves in itself what is comprehended, assigning its place and its limits; which shows that, being of finite nature, this particular and partial comprehension was wrong in taking itself for the Whole, for the In-finite. That the attitude be thought is enough for it to be recognized as *one* attitude among others, and for Spirit and history – i.e. man in history – to go beyond it; because they discover that it is able to be transcended, i.e. is already transcended, though this transcendence is not yet thought, but shows itself only to the philosopher who has arrived at a totality which is thought and is thought in him. It is the spirit of contradiction that leads history, and particularly the history of consciousness, and it must indeed characterize man. But a long process of investigation is not needed to establish that what is at issue is a very special spirit of contradiction, a spirit that is *regulated* and proceeds *methodically*. The Hegelian formulas that indicate this are, so to speak, omnipresent in the work.

Indeed, anyone can object to anything. Who does not see that every thesis can be opposed by another, that every point of view can be refuted, rejected, declared insufficient from another point of view? There is no shortage of arguments either for or against. But for Hegel, this is a poor kind of contradiction; it is that of the understanding, which separates and holds things and concepts in separation and in opposition and, what is most serious, in an opposition that understanding will never overcome.

Caught in its own nets, it attributes the contradiction either to its own nature or to that of the world in its totality, to declare that it is unable to attain true reality, truth as it is in itself and, in the end, for itself, truth of the world, truth of reason itself. But if philosophy is to be something other than the affirmation of its own failure, of its own impossibility, if it is to become knowledge, absolute knowledge, it must transcend the contradiction of static understanding, and above all that between subjectivity and objectivity, that of the finite and the infinite, that between reality and thought.

In other words, it is a matter of comprehension and self-comprehension, of the decision to philosophize in view of arriving at the truth, at the reasonable being of reality, more exactly, at the revelation of this reasonable being, at the conscious grasp of what, in all his acts, in all of his language, man knows without comprehending. We would not be oriented within the world, even at the level of the most current experience, we would not seek to grasp the true nature of things behind what presents itself to animal experience as fluid and without consistency, if we were not profoundly sure that thought grasps the truth, i.e. the true nature of things and – since each thing is only understood in its place in a world that is *one* – of this world. So Hegel, when he keeps his language under control, does not recognize the plural of the term "concept"; empirical notions are innumerable, but they have meaning only within the unity of the concept, which is unique, as are both reason and the world. It is not, therefore, a question of presenting the absolute as that which is *wholly other* vis-à-vis the relative and the finite, or of throwing oneself into it to be freed from contradiction: an infinite opposed to the finite would itself be finite by this opposition which would limit it. Nor is it any more permitted to bypass, negate or rule out the contradiction: one must think it, and think it – and this follows immediately from what was said above – in view of and within the unity of the concept. The unity of the concept must be reconciled with contradiction and with contradictions in order that man achieve peace, achieve satisfaction of his deepest desire – at least if he thinks and wishes to think his own thinking, the desire, namely, of consciously recovering what he has never in his life doubted, the unity of thought with reality, of reality with thought, of that comprehension which recognizes itself as total comprehension of the truth of what is real and *one*.

This means that contradiction and dissatisfaction are at the origin of reflection, and that appeasement, satisfaction – or as Hegel very early put it: holy joy (*seliger Genuss*), the highest idea as well as the highest felicity, beatitude, the blessed sight of the eternal vision (*Anschauung*)

(*Glauben und Wissen, Intro.*, Erste Druckschriften, ed. Lasson, 1928, pp. 226 f.) – are found only at the end. This expression is to be taken literally; they *are found* by the consciousness which overcomes the fundamental contradiction between thought and that object that had appeared to be external, the contradiction between the thing itself, the essence that is pure thought (and has always been, though without our having understood this) and the pure thought that is equally the thing in itself (*Logic* I, p. 30). We, finite beings, live within the finite, within the accidental. Only by seizing our liberty, the possibility of not resting content with what, being accidental, continually perishes and is never real in the strong sense of the term,[1] a possibility possessed by, even *identical with*, dissatisfaction, only by letting this thirst for felicity and total harmony work in us and in the world, on the world of experience, will we transcend the finite, the accidental, the contradictory, that whose being is to not be itself, that which claims, and which we claim to be other than thought.

II

All the work that Spirit has accomplished in the long history of philosophy and before that in the history of human thoughts and actions, that work which *is* history, consisted only of raising to consciousness, of making *for-itself*, what until that moment had pushed history *a tergo* and within the world of the *in-itself*. Now thought knows what it desires in starting again, always anew, within and from the finite; it knows also what it is, and it grasps itself in its own essence, which is its effective, efficacious reality (*Wirklichkeit*), and in its reality, which is its essence present to itself. The *Phenomenology of Spirit* leads to this unique presupposition of absolute Philosophy, of Knowledge (*Logic* I, p. 30), just as the same presupposition is set up by that other Phenomenology, freed of every external and purely historical element, which is the Introduction to the Logic of the *Encyclopedia*, under the highly significant title, "Positions of thought before reality" (*Enc.*, 3rd ed., ## 26-78). The basis of departure is thus assured; we now know what we desire if we desire to comprehend; we even know what it is to comprehend: unification (for us), the unity (in itself) of reality which is being thought and of the thought of reality. But this is a base for departure, and not a point of arrival except for finite

---

[1] *Zufälliges=Fallendes*: a philosophical word play (cf. *Encyclopedia*, 3rd. ed., ed. Nicolin and Pöggeler, 1959, p. 75) to which corresponds the thesis, everywhere repeated, that the finite is *nichtig*, is as such without consistency or substantiality, and falls on the side of non-being.

consciousness which, traversing the retraced road which is its own, becomes capable of elaborating science, science that does not consist in the simple affirmation of the Absolute and of the Infinite. Within the Absolute and the Infinite, consciousness must think the finite and the accidental inasmuch as these two contain something of absoluteness and infinity. What the concept grasps, or better that in which it grasps itself, is not the dark night of an empty Absolute; it is the World-as-Thought.

It is of utmost importance to retain, at one and the same time, the non-essentiality of the Finite as such, and the fact, philosophically fundamental, thit this Finite exists in its own way but only insofar as it is founded on the Infinite, the eternal, the non-accidental, and contains it so as to both conceal and reveal it. Reality, that which is commonly – or vulgarly, from the philosophical point of view – so-called, this *being-there*, this *existence* of what is accidental, of what is always perishing, this *Nichtiges,* is not nothing; the accidental has its existence within it, precisely the existence of that which is in process of disappearing. In other words, it can be thought in its specific essentiality, thought through the concept, comprehended by the concept as what it is: the actuality of that which is only in potency insofar as it is in potency – to cite an Aristotelian definition which constitutes a strict analogy with Hegel's conception of the finite (and indeed appears to be its source). Thought grasps the eternal within the transient; it is within the transient that it sees, within the twofold transiency of finite objects and of subjective and empiricist thought, which conceives its objects as opposed and outside of itself, as an externality it must dominate without being able to imagine the means and manner of doing this.

Now, if this approach is the fruit of work done by thought unconscious of its infinity and its liberty, if it is not a matter of a leap into an Absolute which, opposed to the finite, would be at once finite because opposed to the finite and empty because emptied of all content (which would remain on the side of the finite), if – to express it differently – the concept, the true concept, the concept of the world as thought and of thought as real world, is a result and not a revelation, then the concept itself *becomes*: it does not exist, it is not there before our eyes, wholly constituted like something which it would suffice to take to oneself. As we have seen, it is attained through dissatisfaction, through the desire to comprehend, beginning with a comprehension that is insufficient, partial, incomplete. If it reveals itself, it does so starting from its diffraction within the finite.

Thence arise what Hegel calls the *categories*, those concepts which are situated, to speak with Plato, between the sensible and the Idea. These are not the pseudo-concepts, these *notions*, these fluid classifications without precise limits, which are familiar to, and the life-blood of, the empirical sciences, and which everyday living handles without reflection. Neither are they *the concept*. But they constitute the concept, or more exactly, they are the aspects, the *moments* of the concept as it unfolds itself, developing itself within the intellectual, philosophical experience of human thought. No one among them is *the* concept; but if the concept is not to be identified with the finite and empty Absolute, these notions are the concept itself in its organization and in its structure, which is not revealed but which reveals itself. It is understanding, *the admirable force of understanding*, which is at the beginning of the long work of reflection; it is the will to distinguish and to fix the oppositions among the philosophical concepts that gives birth to the movement within these oppositions, within the negation of its own substantiality which the finite is. We distinguish Being from Nothing, cause from effect, force from its expression, subject from object. We utilize the categories, but we do not think their nature and we thus fall into contradictions that are insoluble and irreconcilable as long as we persist in handling them naively; and we are surprised and shocked to note that these concepts lead back from one to the others, *reflect* themselves reciprocally, and in this way limit themselves by contradicting one another. In a word, it is their finitude that creates, that *is* the dialectic; and it is the particular and fragmented concepts, these categories in which every thought thinks (even the thought which wishes to be, and believes that it is, the most positive and empirical), which put in movement, which indeed are the movement of the thought of reality and of reality as thought, of reasonable reality and of a reason that is real, active and efficaciously present. All else exists; the sensible is not denied; but it is only the hale, the bark, the domain of that which – at once irreducible and always to be reduced to its reasonable essence – remains inessential, accidental, and arbitrary. What is neither accidental nor arbitrary is the dialectical play of the particular philosophical concepts, a play which produces itself with necessity the moment that thought, conscious of itself and what it desires as liberty, grasps them in their purity. Being, when it is maintained in its nature and without exterior addition, becomes and reveals itself to be Nothing; the cause would not be cause without its effect and is thus founded on what it produces; and so on, not *ad infinitum* nor indefinitely however, but until the circle reveals itself as a circle, closed and infinite inasmuch as it knows no limit that separates it from something else. Only the reflection of the understanding is finite because it persists in holding separate what can only be separated as a multiplicity of aspects of the same thing, of the reality-reason that is *one*. Even what the understanding believes it cannot know, the thing-in-itself, is thought and known; it is the finite thought of fixed oppositions that sees there only an empty spectre, an object forever indeterminate. In truth, philosophical truth, nothing is better known nor more knowable: it is the totality of its manifestations – logical, natural, and historical.

The dialectic is, consequently, a dialectic of the concept, which excludes, any dialectic of propositions, of mutually opposed theses, excludes, that is, that dialectic of the understanding, a subjective dialectic (in contrast to the objective dialectic of the concept, which could also be called a dialectic of objectivity, on the condition that this objectivity mean precisely the concept-world, the world as thought and as thinking itself), a subjective dialectic which was that of Plato, according to Hegel, and which, moreover, constitutes the Aristotelian logic and the logic of the schools up to Wolff. The proposition (*Satz*) is, without knowing or saying it, dialectic in the bad sense, because it contains the contradiction of concepts, but camouflages it at the same time: "In the judgment, what is first possesses, as subject, the appearance of an autonomous consistency (*Bestehen*); while it is, on the contrary, suppressed, conserved, and elevated (*aufgehoben*) in its predicate, which is its other. This negation is doubtless present in the content of these propositions (*Sätze*), but the positive form of these contradicts this content. Consequently, what is contained therein is not proposed (*gesetzt*)." (*Logic* II, p. 495; cf. *Enc.*, pp. 62 f.; and also *Phenom.*, pp. 52 ff. – a text from the *Preface*, a fact which has an importance of its own.) At the risk of shocking those who hold to a tradition too much accredited, the Hegelian dialectic does not proceed by thesis, antithesis, and synthesis; it derives nothing from the Fichtean dialectic, to which it is violently opposed. It grasps the particular concept, purely and in its purity, sees it pass into its contrary, and testifies that this contrary is not $= 0$, but is the contrary of the first, which is thus preserved within it, mediated with itself and, thus mediated, is itself preserved in being elevated and liberated from its particular finitude into a higher logico-ontological concept that is a result and at the same time the point of departure and uncovery of a new contradiction-harmony. The substance-accident pair moves into that of cause and effect, which passes into the category of interaction (*Wechselwirkung*), a still-not-established presence of *the* concept, the point of departure of a new chapter of the *Logic*. No particular concept is *the* concept; but the concept is only its own becoming within the movement of the particular concepts throughout the categories.

III

It would be superfluous to insist upon the identity, always affirmed by Hegel, of this dialectic with ontology. If reason *is*; if the world is reasonable; if the totality of what is real and active is comprehensible; and if comprehension seizes what gives to each particular its consistency, its essence, and its true substance – then discourse is necessary in itself (it could not be otherwise without ceasing to be coherent) and reveals the necessary in reality. True logic, in contrast to the subjective logic of the understanding, is inherently theory, that is, the *view* of that which is, insofar as it is real and is the foundation of what the vulgar call reality, i.e. of this domain of the fleeting, the accidental, the inconsistent, of unmediated contradiction produced by the fixity of the understanding's thought. It is this thought which, wishing to be subjective, conceives itself as other than the world then considered as inaccessible in its substance.

What is of greater importance than this identity of dialectical logic with ontology is that it is born of no theses whatever. Hegel always acted with extreme (and unjust) severity towards Fichte, in whom he recognized (and then only in passing) merely the merit of having demanded a philosophy authentically systematic. Here, as at other points, Hegel returns past the Kantians to Kant himself, to the one who first discerned the objective character of dialectic and who was, again, first to show (though he himself did not entirely understand it) that finite philosophical concepts, once they are taken to be valid without limitation, forestall access to the infinite thought of the infinite, access to reason. For despite the appearances they assume within the Kantian presentation, finite concepts overturn, so to speak, when applied to the infinite, and manifest to the thought which wishes to think them and not simply use them, at once their necessity and their insufficiency, i.e. their dialectical character, which is not the character of any propositions whatever, or of theses, but rather that of the movement of *the* concept within *the plurality* of particular concepts, of the onto-logical. All in quest of its own comprehension, in the two senses of (1) comprehension of its own nature and (2) comprehension through itself.

Everything thus begins with the immediate. But this immediate contains its contrary, its *other* (to remain faithful to the Hegelian terminology), an other that negates it, but that also, because it is *its* other, preserves and contains it. Being, to return to that, passes into Nothing; but this Nothing is and remains the Nothing of Being; and it reveals itself as Becoming, which is a unity, not an extrinsic reunion of the two. The first *moment,* this first negation, is now posed, enunciated, understood in its nature and its function, but not completely, in all its truth; and it will not be so understood until the contradiction itself is grasped not only as pure contradiction, but also (and especially) as a unity of the contraries, as a second negation which negates the first by preserving it within its unity. This is the central point of the entire dialectic. It is here that the concept exists for itself, that it refers to itself through the double mediation of double negation. It is here that the concept becomes subjectivity, which is nothing other than the fact (or rather, the activity) of existing for itself.

IV

To speak of "triplicity" is thus at the same time both justifiable and open to criticism. The same text just summarized in the preceding paragraph, and which is found at the end of the *Logic*, speaks to this point with all the clarity desirable: "Inasmuch as the first negative is already the second term, one can just as well count as the fourth what has been counted as the third (moment or term), and thus take quadruplicity in place of triplicity as the abstract form." (*Logic* II, p. 497 f.) It is true that Kant had *the infinite merit* of having distinguished the triplicity of dialectical movement; but "this is only the superficial and external side of this mode of knowing, and is no more than that"; and the greatness of Kant is found in his "more determinate application" (*ibid.*), precisely within the dialectic of the categories. But what Kant is credited with remains incomplete; in a manner of speaking, movement is revealed within it, but it is not comprehended as movement. The concept, inasmuch as it exists in itself immediately, contains the contradiction that is its own negation, which must be *posited*, affirmed, and allowed to affirm itself. Once posited, the contradiction leads to affirmation, to the positing of a unity of opposites (the *difference*) that formerly was only contained in the opposition and so remained pure and simple separation. The negation of the bare opposition posits the unity within the difference; and this second negation, a negation of the first, establishes a new positive. Triplicity exists, but it is somewhat peculiar: the new positive is, in effect, the third moment if one begins counting with the first moment; but it is at the same time positive with respect to the second negation (i.e. the negation of the first negation), and thus is fourth with respect to the first moment; and "what has been counted as third may also be counted as fourth" (*loc. cit.*).

We shall retain here only a single aspect of this considerably complicated development. If the celebrated triplicity retains a meaning for Hegel, it is certainly not sufficient to characterize the dialectic "even if one insists on counting" (*loc. cit.*), which does not for Hegel seem to be an ideal procedure. What, on the other hand, is essential is that, beginning with the immediate, via the negation of this immediate and the negation of that negation (the affirmation of the unity of opposites), one arrives at a new immediate destined in its turn for the same fate; and this continues until the circle is closed and every being-for-itself is recognized as in-itself, until every immediate, every being-in-itself is thought and thinks itself, and until the in-itself and the for-itself coincide – until thought knows itself as all reality and all reality is revealed to thought in its truth and its substantiality, within the presence of the concept, a comprehension real and objective, a concept objective and subjective, objective-subjective, indissolubly *one* in its development.

V

To summarize: Hegel is not interested in that extrinsic dialectic of the understanding, that sophistry that Kant had already distinguished from what, in his view, was apparent but inevitable contradiction, consequently, objective dialectic. Nor, further, is he interested in a dialectic of theses and antitheses and syntheses. He is not even interested, in the strict sense, in a simple triplicity. In a word, he is not interested, in positive affirmations. What is at issue then, one will say, is a mere method, a reflection on method, a methodology.

In fact, Hegel himself used such expressions. It is also a fact that especially but not exclusively within the tradition of Marx and Engels, the methodological character of the dialectic has been emphasized to the point of often obliterating every other aspect. Hegel, an idealist as a philosopher and consequently to be cast into the outer darkness, remains the great methodologist of the sciences of nature, history and society. Yet, to begin on this note, it is remarkable that from his earliest writings Hegel thinks dialectically, in the sense that he seeks to grasp unity in difference, that he rejects unmediated opposition, that he thinks in terms of concepts not theses, that the individual and the particular must pass from themselves into a Universal which is not their *other* but their result (in the matter of coming to consciousness) and their foundation (in the matter of their ontological status), and that this same Hegel, the young Hegel, does not use the term "dialectic." He is a dialectician, but he does not proclaim himself such. Even in the *Phenomenology of Spirit* the word is found very rarely. It appears twice in the chapter on "Sense certainty" (p. 83 and p. 86 of the

Lasson ed., 1928), and three times in the chapter on "Scepticism" (pp. 155 ff.), where it denotes the experience produced by sense certainty; in the chapter on "Religion" (pp. 518 ff.), where the allusion to Socrates and Aristophanes is evident; in the "Introduction" (p. 73), which likewise speaks of the experience of consciousness; finally, in the *Preface*, where the word occurs (pp. 53 ff.) seven times, but only there in what will be its proper sense thereafter: movement of the concept, in contrast to the "empty form" of the proposition which "does not grasp the speculative predicate as concept and essence," while "the presentation . . . must preserve the dialectical form and admit nothing except insofar as it is comprehended (*begriffen*) and insofar as it is the concept (*Begriff*)." Here in the *Preface* we are not, to be sure, face to face with a developed onto-logic; but the principle for one is *established*. It is only at this moment, after the completion of the *Phenomenology*, at the moment Hegel wants to introduce the reader to his system, that the dialectic is considered according to its true and essential nature; it is only here that it is reflected (in itself, Hegel would have added).

This simple review of the literary facts will already suffice to make suspect the claim that Hegel had at his disposal a method worked out at the beginning and subsequently applied. When he speaks of method, especially in the last part of his *Logic*, this could not be the kind of method encountered in Descartes, Kant and Fichte (to cite but a few names), i.e. a procedure established prior to entering into the subject matter. To be certain of this it suffices to turn to the texts that speak of dialectic as a method. To begin with, the categories of *form* and *content* are in themselves dialectical, that is to say, inseparable. Every content is the content of a form, and every form the form of a content. The refusal to concede their dialectical unity is precisely what characterizes the procedure of the understanding and makes comprehension impossible by emptying the one and the other. More profoundly, a reflection on the possibility of knowing and of thinking quickly reveals its own impossibility: there can be no thought prior to thought (something, nevertheless, demanded in demanding that the tool be submitted to an examination before being used). This is like wishing to have completed the study of physiology before beginning to eat or digest (*Enc.* #2, p. 35), or to learn to swim before entering the water (*ibid.*, #10, p. 43). The method is only the final result of the elaborated Logic, the final conscious grasp of what in the course of the development has shown itself in action, of the dialectic at work, which cannot know itself as dialectic until it has traversed the road of living thought, the living reality which is thought and which thinks itself.

So it is not a question of trying to know an object which (no one can say how) would be *given* in advance, and in relation to which the method would be only a form, an external and therefore arbitrary determination: "The method is born (*sc.* as a result, *hervorgegangen*) as the concept which itself knows itself and which has for its object itself as the absolute, subjective as well as objective, consequently as the pure adequation (*Entsprechen*) between the concept and its reality, as an existence which it itself is" (*Logic* II, p. 486). Or, in terms perhaps still more clear: "Method is the pure concept which refers and is related only to itself; it is thus simple self-reference, which is Being [i.e. at the end of its course, the onto-logical return to its beginning, which at first had the appearance of the immediate]. But this Being is now equally Being filled with content (*erfüllt*), the concept which comprehends itself, Being as the totality which is concrete and at the same time absolutely intensive" (*ibid.*, p. 504).

To these texts, which date from 1813, one could add others of later date. Thus the *Encyclopedia* of Berlin declares (#243): "Method is thus not an external form, but the soul and the concept of the content, from which it is distinguished only insofar as the moments of the concepts in themselves come into appearance in their *determinateness (Bestimmtheit)* as the totality of the concept." Or in the "Introduction" to the first volume of the *Logic* (1812, but revised and thus maintained in 1831): "The exposition of what alone can be the true method of philosophical science is part of the treatment of logic itself; for method is consciousness directed at the form of the internal *self-movement* of its content." And, not to multiply the citations beyond what is necessary, a final quotation from the *Philosophy of Right* (#31): "Dialectic is not an external *doing* by a subjective thought, but the very soul of the content, a soul that organically produces its branches and its fruits. To think it subjectively is only to assist as a spectator, adding nothing, to the development of the Idea as a proper and internal activity of its reason."

The dialectic does not proceed from the empirical, psychological, historical individual (except historically, *phenomenologically*); he has not to invent a procedure, he has only to assist as a pure spectator at what takes place within the concept, to receive what presents itself if he renounces every desire other than that of receiving, in other words, the desire to comprehend. He does not get to this point through his thinking activity, he arrives there through objective thought (*Logic* I, Intro., I, p. 31), from the content of what I think, from what is thought, not from my thinking which, itself subjective, must be comprehended in its truth and in its limits. But it will be so comprehended only through the logico-ontology, through onto-logic.

Method? Certainly, but on the condition that one not see there a pre-existent or pre-developed procedure, a way of doing that would stem from the needs, the preferences, the decisions of an empirical subjectivity. The method exists, but it is the consciousness of a path which has been trod, a result, not one of those methods which are applied to objects taken to be given and immediate. Even where a superficial view would distinguish such an employment of the dialectic in the fields of exteriority (nature) and of the return to self (in the philosophy of Spirit), the dialectic is the pure development of the concept in the different forms of its exteriorization. To cite the admirable formulation of Johann Eduard Erdmann, Hegel's disciple and probably the greatest historian of philosophy: "The logic that we see, for example, in the world consists in the dialectic of the Idea," that is, the realized concept, reality as reasonable; "the science of logic does no more than accompany step by step (*Mitgehen*), whence the name 'method' = *methodos*" (*Grundriss der Geschichte der Philosophie*, 3rd ed., 1878, II, p. 584).

VI

What, positively speaking, is the Hegelian dialectic? To one who asks this question the sole response one can give conscientiously will be: read Hegel. Accordingly, we have not undertaken the construction of the royal road to philosophy which is so often sought, and which does not exist because it cannot exist. As we said at the beginning, it can be useful to indicate how one must not proceed, what the extrinsic opinions are which it is best to do without, what the summaries are that would distill and *reduce to essentials* that of which the essential is precisely not an abstract principle but a living development which alone and at its conclusion reveals not the principle but the meaning of that which is the beginning for a reflection that while seeking itself knows also that it seeks to go beyond itself.

Nothing, however, prohibits our asking questions of this dialectic, questions that are pertinent so long as they touch on what this thought itself considers to be its own conditions. Philosophy seeks to be absolute knowledge. What price must it pay to achieve this goal? Hegel tells us clearly: one must be rid of the accidental, of the fortuitous, of *that which perishes*. It is logical that Hegel reproaches Kant for his *tenderness for finite things*; they are indeed what cannot be grasped without remainder, without an external bark that is impenetrable to the concept. The sacrifice seems considerable, for after all we live, finite, within the finite. Hegel himself sees what this reproach of tenderness for the finite implies, and he does not hesitate to juxtapose the two aspects: "It will be recalled that in his fundamental thought and attitude (*Gesinnung*) man must raise himself to that abstract universality (sc. of Being, as opposed to particular and finite being) in which it is indeed indifferent to him whether the hundred thalers (sc. of Kant) exist or do not exist, just as it is indifferent to him whether he himself be or not be, that is to say, within finite life (for it is a matter of a determinate state (*Zustand*) of a determinate being" (*Logic* I, p. 74)). One can refuse to accede to knowledge at this price, as the course of history has shown. Whether there still can be a philosophy that is something other than an edifying (in a positive or negative sense) sermon is another question . . .

It should next be noted that the path leading to absolute knowledge begins within immediate certitude and with the declaration of the contradictions at which this certitude terminates when one seeks *to speak* of this experience. In other words, philosophy begins in language. Now Hegel, who celebrates the grandeur of language in magnificent texts, especially in the *Phenomenology* (and, in a narrower context, in the *Encyclopedia*, #459), does not treat of it explicitly, does not *thematise* it. One could answer that the whole of the *Phenomenology* is a history of discourse. But defensible as such a thesis might appear to us to be, it seems to lead to another, no less disturbing difficulty: it would then be necessary that the system, in order to preserve the circularity that alone proves it, lead back to that departure within the finite which is the *Phenomenology*, which, as Hegel originally affirmed, would thus necessarily be the first part of the system; while the *Encyclopedia*, which has the greatest difficulty in situating the *Phenomenology*, returns to the beginning of the *Logic*, to Being, and ends with a text of Aristotle that affirms the *Nous* as substance-subject and as life, as object-subject of vision, of *theoria*, in which language disappears at the same time as the individual.

Finally, one can consider the relation between experience which is historical (and concretely, scientifically empirical) and dialectic, which is the "thought of God before the creation of the world." Is it not then the created which forms the point of departure as well as the point of arrival of philosophy, which would remain the activity of finite being, even though it would terminate at the Absolute and the (Aristotelian) union with *Nous*? In other words, and to put it in current language, is it not the structured that interests us, whereas the structure interests us only insofar as it sheds light upon the structured? Or finally, to formulate the problem in still another way, ought not the System proceed by way of regressive reflection (transcendental-analytic), instead of being presented as deductive?

Let us stop at this point. The response that Hegel would have given is, if not furnished, at least clearly indicated by the System. Your questions, he would probably have said, can be justified as meaningful, i.e. non-arbitrary, universally valid, necessary, only within the dialectic. They cannot be so justified if they are presented as preliminary, drawn from who-knows-where, from your prejudices, from your judgments made in advance of any comprehension of comprehension. We would be saying the same thing, but in another way, if we affirmed the necessity of choosing between, on the one hand, a discourse that is absolutely coherent, a discourse of the Absolute (as subject and as object) and, on the other hand, the arbitrary, an arbitrary that exists only under the form of violence, the sole means of deciding when no philosophical criterion exists.

COMMENT ON

ERIC WEIL
'THE HEGELIAN DIALECTIC'

John N. Findlay

I am going to press certain criticisms of Prof. Weil's paper. But I want to say first how very much I admire it, because not only is it a very profound paper, but it is also very useful. It shows, I think, the imprint of Hegel's *Phänomenologie*. It cares for and promotes a working understanding of Hegel rather than a precisely directed rearward looking glance. Now, since I admire Hegel's system much more than I do the *Phenomenology*, I shall differ from Prof. Weil on certain points, though not actually many, and really none of them at all fundamental; and my differing with him does not mean that I haven't been greatly charmed and stimulated by what he has said.

Now, in his opening paragraphs and also in the paragraphs at the end of his paper, Prof. Weil articulates a view of Hegel that is certainly Hegelian, that is to say in keeping with what Hegel said of himself. But it is a view which I believe to be only partially true and helpful. It is a view of his own procedures and of their foundation and outcome; but it is also the kind of thing that Plato and Wittgenstein and a great number of other philosophers held about their own opinions. What is this view? It amounts to saying, my thought has absolutely no presuppositions; I take nothing for granted, as others do; my thought has no foundational principles, no dogmas; everything in it is radically in question and only assumes definition as the argument proceeds; in fact, I'm starting in a void, the whole thing is a sort of ectoplasmic seance; I have no advance program, I haven't even an advance goal; and what I'm moving toward is going to come as a surprise even if when it does come as a surprise it will be surprisingly familiar. And the path I'm following I can't tell you about in advance. My method is not characterizable in advance; or if I say anything about it, this is mis-leading. Winding in and out according to the exigencies of the terrain, it adopts different techniques on different occasions. As Plato says, the Logos is like a wind, and moves in whichever direction the wind blows. And similarly, it's generally said that the outcome cannot be understood until you've taken the whole journey.

Now, if all these contentions are in part true and sincere, wholly true and sincere, they are also in part false but deeply sincere, and in part false and insincere. And while they in some respects help the student a great deal, in other respects they confuse and mislead him. And I think we ought to clear them up. Now, they are true and sincere insofar as the working out of the detailed kind of thought-structure like Hegel's necessarily involves problems and solutions and various methods which he adopts and which cannot be foreseen in advance: the treatment of electricity or the treatment of the French Revolution, for example, can only be worked out in a concrete struggle with particular notions or material. This is clear and obvious. But these statements are sincere and false, I think, insofar as it is impossible for a thinker really to be aware of his full motivation, his full cognitive motivation, of exactly what leads him to say something, or to say what he says, and when he says it, and so on. Many thinkers come to mind here. Husserl, for example, comes to mind particularly. He very seldom says what he's doing, because he doesn't really know. He's inspired about something that rather differs from what he actually manages to put down. And the same is, of course, true of Hegel. But this doesn't mean that the person who studies the product of such a philosopher cannot discover the actual techniques he adopted, the actual ruses he employed, and cannot classify them.

I think that the ruses of Hegel are definitely classifiable, and fall into a definite number of classes. It's not easy to do so exhaustively, and there are many cross-classifications and so on, but they certainly do fall into recognizable types. Finally, I think such statements are insincere in all the cases where the philosopher does start with certain preconceptions which he pretends he is going to evolve out of the material. Now, I think there is no doubt whatever that Hegel has certain basic preconceptions which not everybody would accept; they are Hegel's dogmas, which he doesn't set forth immediately and frankly because for one thing he would expose himself to very serious criticism if he did. Rather, he lets them spring upon you bit by bit, and they become clear only as one goes on. But he knows them all along, knows what he is taking you to, and sees how he is to manage it, what strategy he is to employ at a given moment to get to his result in the particular predicament in which he is. Now, these Hegelian dogmas are such things as the falsity of the independently finite, mentioned by Prof. Weil, the primacy of the whole, the primacy of conscious spirit, and so forth. And he pretends to elicit these from the thought material as it comes out, as a surprise. Now, the motive for this is the desire for invulnerability, the desire that made Wittgenstein state all his most contentious dogmas in the form of rhetorical questions; that which made Socrates never start with saying that virtue is knowledge, but rather move through an entirely impersonal, impartial discussion which somehow always came to it, while people who were subject to this sophistry didn't know that they were gradually being forced to the position that virtue is knowledge.

Now, all these contentions that establish invulnerability are very helpful to the student because they force him to read the philosopher and read him very closely. He musn't imagine that Hegel can be characterized according to general forms. They also make him scorn secondary literature. I mean the really great philosopher reads only the very best secondary literature, the most helpful kind; and unless you are a rather superficial person, avoid reading the less profound kind. But these contentions are also very misleading in that very often they let the student flounder about in minutiae without really mastering the thing at all. And this is true of Hegel above all: there are dozens of students who get nowhere with Hegel because he is too difficult. They wander about like people in a forest without a guide; and Hegel does not provide them with a guide. He says something mysterious, and they are supposed to be equally satisfied with this mysterious something, and the whole thing appears not very suitable for ordinary folk. The point is, with Hegel it is very important to have people who, as it were, give really good guidelines and enable you to understand the way the whole thing works and the goal of the whole system. Hegel approaches Nature, purvading its essentials and endless contingencies in detail. He says that one has got to seize the sea-god, Proteus, covered with barnacles, and you have to make him declare himself in true conceptual form. Now, I'm afraid that Hegel himself is in part just such a sea-god. In the case of the *Phenomenology* the barnacles almost completely veil the conceptual form.

Now, proceeding to matters of detail, there is a point mentioned by Prof. Weil which is, of course, very important to stress, namely that Hegel's contradiction is not the contradiction between two theses: I say it's so, and you say it's not so, and we say these things in the same sense, and I just cancel out what you are saying, and so on. I mean, the kind of contradiction Hegel is dwelling on is a distinction between the moments in a single concept which have a tendency to make the notion fall apart and become two incompatible notions. But you cannot really pull them apart without destroying the notion altogether. And so you have to become conscious of the deep unity of these two striving aspects or moments of the notion. Now, this is not contradiction in the ordinary sense at all, because the very fact that reconciliation is possible means that it isn't contradiction in the formal logical sense. You can't reconcile formal logical contradictions because the whole meaning of them is that they are irreconcilable; they are not on speaking terms. In other words, you cannot bring them together. But then that you can bring certain things together means that they are another sort of contradiction. And I agree with Prof. Weil that in Hegel's system you don't have separate concepts, but you have *der Begriff*, the one *Begriff*, the active Universal, the force of thought, as it were, collecting various aspects together and holding them in unity, and you are going from a certain measure to more adequate measures of unity. But, as I have said, in this whole thing there are these deeper preconceptions which I've mentioned; and I think it's very important to realize that the Hegelian preconceptions are such that many people who would not want to follow the dialectic as Hegel wanted them to could always refuse to do it. You know for instance that whenever Wittgenstein asks a rhetorical question and says, "Is it not perhaps the case that . . .?" you can simply say, "No, it's not the case that . . ." And to Socrates, you can simply say, "Oh, power and wealth have value in themselves; and they're not the only good things, Socrates, but they're damned good in their own way." Now, I am not a man of the Understanding, and I repudiate the thought of the Understanding; but one has to recognize that a really determined person of the Understanding just refuses to make the Hegelian move: he refuses, for instance, to say that mechanism is inherently teleological, that it's a sort of imperfect teleology; or that teleology expresses itself in life; that life is an imperfect form of a kind of higher unity that we get in cognition; and that volition is even more expressive of what we are trying to do in cognition than cognition is, and so on. A determined man of the Understanding will say, no, cognition is cognition and volition is volition, and so forth, and mechanism is mechanism, there is no necessary life coming out of it; it just goes on being mechanical, and so on. Many people are content with this; they like a world in which there are a lot of loose episodes like a bad tragedy; and if you like a world such as this, then nobody can force you out of it. Wittgenstein once said to me personally that he could take me to the water, but couldn't make me drink. And this is true of Hegel. Though I drink the Hegelian water, there is an act of will in it, a belief that unity is somehow more important than mere diversity or difference.

I agree with Prof. Weil that Hegel's dialectic is a dialectic of concepts, not of propositions or positions. And I also agree profoundly that this was an ontology rather than an idealistic, idealized history of thought postures. In the *Phenomenology* you restore the logic of thought postures; but this is all over at the end of the *Phenomenology*. And then what we have is a series of self-displays by being, by that which is – I could probably use the word "reality," which is probably the word we would use –, displays which are at first one-sided, then become more and more rich, until we get the whole diamond with all its facets and gleaming with its own mystery, all shown together. Now, I do not myself believe that the display is neatly ordered and arranged in the way Hegel arranged it. But I applaud the final result; and I do not think there is anything in all philosophy or all religion that is more magnificent. I say "religion" advisedly because I think Hegel's writings are scripture. That is, I do not think they are solely a philosophical treatise. And many obviously find that passages in Hegel are scriptural.

I also agree with Prof. Weil and am interested in his doctrine that Hegel's triplicity should be made into a quadruplicity. I've never understood this before, that is, that you have a notion and then you have a negation of the notion, then you negate the negation, and then there is a fourth step and you get a new positive notion emerging from it. I mean, it's tetradic rather than triadic. This is an interesting and valuable concept, and of course there are passages where Hegel says things of this sort. I actually use only a one step dialectic. I think that each step of the dialectic criticizes the one that went before. I don't myself like this circular spectrum; I think that this is a kind of *penchant* of Hegel. I think it is an important fact about Hegel that there is a tremendous amount of arbitrariness in the course that he takes; because I do not think that dialectic, which is sort of criticism that passes on to a more comprehensive concept from a less comprehensive one, necessarily involves a single route; that is, you can supplement a deceptively one-sided concept in various ways, and you can get the ultimate result which will be a completely comprehensive truth. But you can arrive at it by different routes, just as you can protect your character by removing different thoughts. There is not necessarily a single way in which you can become the perfect character, such as cutting down on drinking or limiting your swearing or something like that. I mean there are many ways toward becoming a desirable person. Similarly with the Idea. Hegel is always perfectly clear about what he's getting to, and I think Prof. Weil admits this. Some of the time I really think that Hegel ought to be improved considerably. For instance, I think that the long discursis in the doctrine on essence needs improvement; i.e. where we end up with absolute necessity, and then we are told that the truth of necessity is freedom. What then do we get into? We get into formal logic: the *Begriff*, the *Urteil* and the syllogism. But really what we should have gone on to there is to teleology, the mechanism leading on to teleology, and we ought now to take a straight leap up to life. I think that the whole of formal logic there is a discursis which should be fitted in somewhere else. Well, this is just one example; and I think that the whole of the system is riddled with things that should be differently placed. I don't think that a sound Hegelian criticism would deny this.

Now, I'm coming to the end of this criticism. Prof. Weil at the end of his paper went into some interesting questions regarding the position of the *Phenomenology* in Hegel's system. And he asked whether, since it is the beginning of the system, since it is the start of the whole Hegelian thought, shouldn't you insist on a return to a phenomenology; that is, when Hegel has got an absolute Idea known in itself in the form of philosophy and so on, ought he not then start with *das sinnliche Bewusstsein* instead of going to *Sein*, i.e. going back to the beginning of the *Logic*. Now I personally think that if this is Prof. Weil's view, if he thinks we should do this, then he is wrong; and I think that all people are wrong who make the *Phenomenology* an integral part of the Hegelian thought-structure. The *Phenomenology* describes what you have to have been through in order to pursue *Wissenschaft*, but it doesn't tell you what you ought to have studied in order to do *Wissenschaft*. You needn't ever have read the *Phenomenology*, you needn't read it now, provided you've got the point of view which in the end it expresses. The *Phenomenology* starts by giving the position of a person who still thinks in subjective terms, subjective approaches, doubts whether he can get things as they really are, and so forth. But at the end of the *Phenomenology* this has vanished, and a person now has that which is declaring itself in ever more complicated form; in short, we've gotten into ontology. The whole thing is framed in objective terms. Subsequently, of course, spirit comes into the picture, but spirit and the phenomenology get repeated in a rather cut-down, reduced form. But this repeated phenomenology is merely a stage in the system, and, I think, rightly occurs where it does; this is the only place the phenomenology should really have in the complete system. The whole system is a quest for the logically stable, and it starts with extremely abstract things and it gets on with more and more logically stable things until we get into spirit, where we get things that have this complete self-sufficiency, this *Selbstständigkeit*, and this complete explanation of everything in and for and through themselves. And this is where the thing belongs, that is within Absolute Spirit. I think, therefore, that the *Phenomenology* has a certain meaning, but that it's not immensely illuminating or important because it describes the human passage to the capacity for scientific knowledge; but it isn't itself a part of scientific knowledge itself; rather, it is taken up in scientific knowledge in a strangely different form when it occurs in the *Philosophie des Geistes*.

Now I want to conclude by saying that Hegel was a very great philosopher. He started as a subjective German thinker, the progeny of Kant and Fichte, and more remotely of Kant, and he had the idea of the ego underlying everything, and no doubt believed in the transcendental machinery by which the ego constructs the world and sees categories in the world because it's really put them there rather in the Kantian sense. Now the *Phenomenology* contains the last dying notes of this position, suggested rather than stated. But still many people see it in the *Phenomenology*. Now I take the view that in his later developments Hegel is the progeny of Plato rather than of Kant and Fichte; that is, that the Idea, a timeless logical ideal takes the place of the ego, and the displaced ego appears as a goal of the system, it appears as Spirit, what you get when the Idea is worked out in concrete reality. It's the highest perfection of the working out of the Idea; it's not anything that constructs the world. It's that for the sake of which the world exists rather than the other way around. And, of course, at the same time the idea of Plato, which in him is rather an inert thing, becomes dynamic, becomes something which specifies and instantiates itself and comes to itself in the course of time.

One concluding remark. Prof. Weil says that dialectical philosophy involves an arbitrary element. I agree. But he goes on to say, "an arbitrary that exists only under the form of violence, the sole means of deciding when no philosophical criterion exists." Now, I'm not happy with this violence. Is it merely the intellectual violence of making a philosophical decision as to how to interpret things, or is it the sort of thing that was practiced by the students at Nanterre? I have no sympathy with the latter: it is not necessary, it is not rational, it is not Hegelian; but I think that no doubt Prof. Weil agrees.

HEGEL AND THE PHILOSOPHY OF PHYSICS

John N. Findlay

My aim in this paper is to make a fairly close study of the conceptual structure of Hegel's *Physik*, the second, most difficult section of his *Naturphilosophie*.[1] I do so for two reasons. The first is part of the general effort to
plumb the nature of the Dialectic, as Hegel conceived it, the method of
steady advance from one thought-determination to another, the latter being regarded as a more adequate vehicle of interpretation and understanding than the former, since it incorporates the thought-content of the former
yet adds to this comments and criticisms which make it part of a more
completely understood and self-consistent whole than it would be formerly. For Hegel, the Truth is the Whole, and we only achieve it by a process
in which the one-sided partiality of our notions is overcome by seeing them
in a context which includes other, perhaps even superficially incompatible,
notions. This unique thought-method has been extensively studied in the
case of the *Phenomenology of Spirit* and the two versions of the *Logic*:
it has also been studied in the Philosophy of History, the History of Philosophy, the Philosophy of Religion and other concrete forms of the Philosophy of Spirit. But no careful study of the Dialectic in the Philosophy of
Nature has been recently attempted, possibly owing to fear aroused by
the wealth of scientific difficulty in that work. The difficulty of the material has been much over-estimated; much of it falls within the bounds
of ordinary school-science, and it is interesting material dialectically since
it studies the Idea in its utmost remoteness or alienation from self, in its
breakdown into items which, superficially regarded, seem mere matters of
contingent experience and which moreover often seem as near mutual
independence and irrelevance as it is possible for thought-material to be.
Such material, by its stark alienness, shows the working of Hegel's thought-
mechanisms with more perspicuity than *geisteswissenschaftliche* material

---

[1] The quotations from Hegel's *Naturphilosophie* in this paper are from A. V. Miller's
recent translation (Clarendon Press, Oxford, 1970).

such as Stoicism, the French Revolution or Cartesian Philosophy, and *if* Hegel's methods can be shown to have purchase and illumination in this unpromising region their philosophical merit will be well attested.

I am also studying this part of Hegel's work for its intrinsic interest. There are two basic ways of regarding Nature, one Cartesian, which sees the superstructures of purpose, life, consciousness as more or less irrelevantly imposed on an order of things which has nothing teleological, organic or conscious about it: the other Platonic and Aristotelian, which sees the substructures of bodily mechanism and inorganic existence as in some way serving the organic structures which emerge out of them, and as teleologically geared to produce the latter. The former epiphenomenalistic view has been tried long without achieving conspicuous success: it has never shown that the classical approach is not after all the more explanatory. Hegel's Philosophy of Nature is in my view the best Nature-philosophy of the classical type. If unacceptable or outmoded in detail, it may yet be a type of thought that quite well permits of successful modernization.

There are certain basic misunderstandings regarding Hegel's Nature-philosophy which must be removed at the outset. Hegel's Nature-philosophy, despite much concrete detail, does not purport to deduce, in the strict formal sense of "deduce," the empirical facts of Nature, nor is it even concerned with them in all their detail. It accepts the existence of a vast amount of natural detail of which no philosophical treatment is either possible or desirable, the number of species of tropical parrots, the shape of the ear-lobes, etc. There is in Nature and Mental Life a purely contingent element that gives these spheres their final concreteness: things could in such respects have been otherwise and it is philosophically inept to try to show that they could not have been so. It is in the welter of such details that what Hegel calls an "instinct of reason" directs the man of science to find a law, a specific pattern, a *Begriff* or notion, and it is on the conceptually transformed material of the man of science that the philosopher must go to work, using his own instinct of reason, and discovering in scientific concepts the more general, and also more deeply unitive concepts that are properly philosophical. For the philosopher, e.g., Light and Gravitation are both cases of the same *actio in distans*, the same collusive unity of the remote, which is philosophically interesting. There is no case in Hegel where a philosophical interpretation of Nature is not scientifically documented: Hegel sometimes sides with one scientific view rather than another, but he is never without scientific backing. And if he backs the wrong horse, as when he said there could only be seven planets in his Jena

Habilitationsschrift, he changes his mind when better data are available. The most austere empiricist could not object to the sort of philosophical interpretation Hegel performs, or, if he does, he is merely opposing *his* Philosophy of Nature or his methodological assumptions to Hegel's.

Hegel's interpretation of Nature is, further, realistic rather than idealistic, and perhaps too much so for modern taste. He is not concerned with subjective "models" and the other structures with which modern philosophers of science concerns themselves, but believes, in Greek fashion, that there are Forms, Concepts, Laws actually at work and immanent in Nature. There is an objectivized quasi-thought, consisting of "petrified" thought-categories rather than subjectively live thoughts, which is at work in the world, and which only achieves *subjective* status in the mind of the scientist and the philosopher. It exists in an unconscious form in the world long before the scientist or the philosopher pries it out. For Hegel Nature is the *real* realm par excellence even if its final destiny is to be thoroughly absorbed and set aside in the spiritual medium of conscious thought and action.

Hegel's general view of Natural Philosophy is set forth clearly in the introductory paragraphs §§ 245-252 of his Nature-philosophy, and in the transitional § 244 which leads us from the logic to the Nature-philosophy. The Logic, though increasingly "concrete" in the sense of increasingly rich in conceptual content, has none the less abstracted from the spatio-temporality, the self-externality of the natural world, and from the intuitive-sensuous specificity which that spatio-temporality makes possible. It is that spatio-temporal externality and that intuitive-sensuous specificity that must now be explicitly brought into our philosophical purview: they stand, of course, in a timeless relation of "requirement" to the abstractions of the Logic, though this relation is only clear to the Hegelian philosopher when he reaches 244 of the Logic. It is important when considering the celebrated and not really obscure *Entäusserung* of the Hegelian Idea to realize that it takes place on two planes at once, as it were. It "takes place," on the one hand, as the eternal relation of a series of categorial thought-patterns to the actual realm of concretely specified being in Space and Time, but it also takes place in philosophical thought, in the passage from the abstract thinking of the Logic to the more richly specific, but still abstract thinking of the Nature-philosophy. What we have in the Nature-philosophy is not real spatio-temporality and its diversifying content but this spatio-temporality and its content transformed in the medium of *das absolute Wissen*, of philosophical thought.

As to the reason why spatio-temporality here enters the philosophical picture, it is plainly that Logical Ideality presupposes a contrast, an element of "otherness" or of application, and that this is precisely what spatio-temporality provides. Spatio-temporality not only contrasts with the unextended unity of logical patterns, but it also involves an inner repetitiousness which makes instantiation and individuation possible: one part of Space is alongside another, one part of Time comes after another etc., and logical patterns can be multiply exemplified and so really enjoy the universality which, on Hegel's view, is always inseparable from specification and individuation. The possibility of a specifying and individuating medium *other* than the spatio-temporal is a modern conceptual excess that Hegel would rightly have regarded as empty. The task of a Nature-philosophy is then clearly set forth; it is the discovery in Nature of a series of stages leading from the sheer side-by-sideness and one-after-anotherness of pure spatio-temporality to a stage in which unity, totality, the presence of all in each and each in all, becomes fully explicit. Nature, on Hegel's view gives separate existence to all these stages: there is a discoverable natural phenomenon corresponding to each dialectical stage which the natural philosopher is able to distinguish. But Nature being externalized and spatio-temporal never fully expresses the thread of logical necessity which binds all its stages together: this only exists for the philosopher who can distinguish and arrange Nature's stages because he has, in a sense, gone right behind Nature and released its meaning. It does not, in particular, exist as an actual evolutionary history of the Natural World: histories only enter the picture where Spirit has given a living, progressive sense to the barren successiveness of mere Time. Hegel further plots the division of his Nature-philosophy according to distinctions previously worked out in his Logic: there will be a Mechanics which does not probe beneath the descriptive surface, the qualitative-quantitative accoutrement of bodily being, and so may be fitly compared with the logical Doctrine of Being, there will be a Physics whose dodging to and fro from surface manifestations to underlying, unmanifest patterns will connect it with the logical Doctrine of Essence, and there will finally be an Organics or treatment of Life which will parallel the unitive, teleological treatment of the logical Doctrine of the Begriff or Notion. Hegel also connects his three divisions of Nature-philosophy with the Universality, Specificity and Individuality which are the three aspects of his logical Notion, and makes use of these distinctions within each of these divisions.

A brief sketch of the main dialectical points in the Mechanics will now be attempted in order to lead up to the Psysics, which we mean to study more intensively. Hegel proves the mutual requirement of Space and Time in that, while both illustrate Quantity, and so the conjoined moments of Discreteness and Continuity, Space is more emphatically continuous and less emphatically discrete than Time, since Time essentially gives separate being to the present moment, and so to all contents associated one by one with that moment. Time as it were primarily dirempts while Space primarily unifies, and each as it were borrows its other aspect from the other. Both are further inseparable from material masses which diversify them and from the motions of these material masses. All this Dialectic is wholly acceptable: it merely points to the necessary supplements without which an abstraction makes no sense. In Matter Hegel sees the necessary unity of a repulsive force, a diremption into separated parts against which an attractive, unifying force necessarily fights: only in the balance of these two forces is material being possible. But this view is not merely scientific but philosophical: the Notion, the Philosophical Universal, requires precisely the separateness of far-flung instances in order that it should be a Universal, present in all of them, but it also requires some holding together of its instances if its instantiation is not to be lost in the inane. From this conception of Matter (which Hegel of course inherited from Kant) it is natural to see Inertia and Gravitation as notionally combined. There is a merely dispersive tendency manifest in pure Inertia, and an attractive tendency manifest in Gravitation, and we must envisage these tendencies as but two sides of the life of Matter, distinguishable yet not separable. It is therefore of the essence of Matter, as exemplifying the partless unity of the Idea, to organize itself around centres which themselves are organized around centres so that complex patterns like the solar system arise, in which there will be a central sun, orbiting planets, captive satellites and loosely attached, wandering comets. And the elliptical movement of the planets round the solar centre is no odd amalgam of mutually irrelevant centrifugal and centripetal forces, as Newton wantonly imagined: it is an organic performance expressive of the two constitutive tendencies in material being. All this was clear (Hegel conceives) to Johannes Kepler who analysed the dynamic nature of Matter which Newton then tore apart into abstract shreds of the centrifugal and centripetal. Hegel's reverence for Kepler, expressed in his first Jena writings, never left him, nor did his contempt for the unphilosophical empiric Newton. We are now at the point where we can begin our consideration of Hegel's Physics.

Hegel begins with a Physics of General Individuality which sets forth the most general differences of Matter. He deals with a materiality whose Thrust or Impact is no longer external to itself, but represents, as he says, its own internal, immanent Thrust: we have different forms of *self*-moving materiality. The kind of mutual influence which spread through the system of the Sun, planets etc., is now seen as concentrated in various types of body in that system. Matter's unity now comes to be in its parts rather than hovering among them. A new manifestation of material unity now comes to the fore, a manifestation most evident in the sun and the stars, but in other things also, the manifestation known as Light. Hegel's characterization of Light is typical of the sort of concept he develops in the *Naturphilosophie* and in the Dialectic generally. In Light Hegel tells us (§ 275) we have the pure self-identity of Matter raised to a sort of independence, a *Selbständigkeit*, from the other determinations of natural being. Nature throughout offers us non-independent moments *as if* they were independent existences, but the special oddity of Light is that it raises the universal *non*-independence of everything from everything (for such is for Hegel the meaning of identity) into an as-it-were independent existence. Light has several peculiarities: it is emphatically community, connection, continuity without any clearly contrasting note of enmity, opposition, exclusion etc. The unavoidable opposition to Light is therefore projected outside it, and appears in the dark substances that it illuminates and not in itself. Physical Light therefore both resembles and differs from the spiritual "Light" of consciousness, which has its objects, its elements of darkness, within itself. Light also has a detachment from reality which renders it somewhat incorporeal: it shows up other things rather than itself, and when it does show itself in the form of a sun or a star, there is nothing in this revelation *but* a revelation. A star or a sun is essentially a featureless, abstract case of shining: it derives full reality from the system that it illuminates and of which it is, in fact, the connective expression. When realistic picture-thought denies that ideality is present in Nature one has but to refer it to Light, the pure making manifest which is nothing but a making manifest (§ 276). From such an insubstantial conception of Light it follows at once that Light cannot be divided into the spatially distinct rays in which Newton believed and that its travelling, even if it takes time, is rather a deferred arrival, strictly proportioned to distance, than the stage-by-stage traversing of a route. It will be noted how gracefully empty, how free from substance or mechanisms, is Hegel's conception of Light. It obeys a new form of Ockham's Razor: *Entia non sunt characterizanda praeter necessitatem.* And *because* it is so abstract it can lead on to grosser forms of community such as those of Sound, Electrical Transmission and Chemical Interaction. By avoiding the treatment of Light as a substantial thing, it avoids the innumerable pseudoquestions which such a treatment suggests: What is Light like apart from its con-

nective function, after what fashion is it present in Space as it travels, why
do bodies radiate or absorb Light, why does Light travel rectilinearly, etc.
All the questions are as meaningless as the question "Where is Fancy
bred?" Possibly the difficulties attendant on the modern physics of Light,
its loyalty to a dead ether instead of to the bodies it departs from or arrives
at, its inability to decide whether it is a particle or a wave etc., all spring
from a love or superfluous quasi-sensuous characterization and from an
unwillingness to rise to the austere emptiness of Hegel's physical concepts.

Light as the being-of-everything-for-everything necessarily posits or requires opposed bodily forms dark in themselves but capable of being illu-
minated, and here Hegel simply reverts to the solar, planetary, lunar and
cometary types of dark body which all stand in a differing relation to Light.
But these variants of body must be represented in each type of body and
particularly in the planetary, though "in the planet the bodies of the solar
system are no longer self-subsistent but are predicates of a single subject"
(§281 *Zus.*). The four types of Matter in the solar system therefore show
themselves as identical in principle with the four states of Matter found on
this earth: the Airy or gaseous state which corresponds to the Sun and
Light, the Fiery or inflamed state which corresponds, oddly enough, to the
moon, the Watery or liquid state which corresponds to the comets, while
the solid, Earthy state corresponds, very properly, to our planetary earth.
There are a large number of points which here deserve comment. First we
may point to the fluid operation of the Hegelian concept of identity. Since
identity is not for him a matter of vanishing individual embodiment, but
of notional content, he can very well trace an identity moving and developing itself as we pass from the luminous sun, whose very being is illumination, to the transparent Air, which though not actively luminous is
intrinsically set to transmit it and is in fact a lineal successor of the διαφανές,
the Transparent of Aristotle. We can trace a similar identity, somewhat
more creakingly, as we move from the spikey intransingence of lunar geo-
graphy to the all-devouring negativity of Fire. The equation of watery
liquidity with the state of comets is a little less tenuous; perhaps Hegel believed that comets shone by reflected light. In the identification of solid
earthiness with the planet Earth, there is almost a Mooreish use of the
notion of identity. The Dialectic certainly takes great leaps, but its leaps
always season arbitrariness with genuine affinity. We may next comment
on Hegel's characterization of the four elements or elementary states of
Matter that he has distinguished. Each manifests Universality in a peculiar
dynamic form: it negates, reduces to uniformity the specific differentia-
tions of Matter. Air subtly corrupts and decomposes whatever is exposed

to it: only the vacuum-sealed product evades this nemesis. Fire is even more actively reductive of differences: it reduces all to ashes and then extinguishes itself. Water explicitly embodies the neutrality towards which Fire tends, and acts as a universal solvent of all types of Matter. Earth, finally, harbours all differences in itself without actively levelling them in uniformity. What we have, then, is Nature in its naiveté giving us concrete phenomena which express a kind of Universality which is essentially destructive of the specific and concrete, a concrete which is inherently abstract and which struggles to remain such. I myself believe that there are and must be such phenomena in the world: abstraction and *Gleichschaltung* is not merely a thought-activity. What is further remarkable is Hegel's willingness to give a place in Natural Philosophy to the four classical elements, which were at the time of writing displaced by the new Pantheon of Nitrogen, Oxygen, Hydrogen, Carbon and so on. Hegel does not reject this new chemical Pantheon, but he believes it to be active and existent only in laboratory situations. The so-called chemical elements can be teased out of the natural ones by artificial techniques in artificial situations, and endure in these situations for a brief period, but they are not to be thought of as still present, though in latent or unmanifest form, in the good old phenomenological elements of our daily experience. There are not little particles of Oxygen, Nitrogen, etc. in the good air that we breathe: they can be coaxed out of this good air by abnormal torturing, but soon lose themselves in it again. The world-media, if we may so call them, are not made up of self-identical, diversified, enduring particles: to think that they are is to think with the English, with the analytic Understanding, that one cannot get something out of nothing or out of anything different. I shall not encourage you to go back to the Empedoclean elements, even on Hegel's recommendation, but I shall point to the fact that, in modern chemistry many elements have precisely this shortlived laboratory status which Hegel believes in, and that all are in principle such. And compounds in modern chemistry integrate their elements into a continuous pattern and do not contain them unchanged. Perhaps there is something yet to be said for the "shining Zeus, life-bringing Hera, Aidoneus and Nestis" of Empedocles.

From a pre-Socratic theory of the elements Hegel passes to a pre-Socratic meteorology: the elements evince their profound, underlying identity by a continuous passage into one another, which must at all costs not be interpreted, in English fashion, as due to the latent presence of one material element in the vaster mass of another. Water when it evaporates really transmutes itself into Air, and does not hover about in merely suspended, latent form, waiting to precipitate itself in rain, dew etc. This is proved by the way in which, in Switzerland, rain suddenly falls from a wholly clear, dry sky. If Hegel is here wrong on a point of detail, I should hold him right on a point of principle, which is also accepted in modern chemical theory. Hegel's meteorology is particularly heavy with empirical documentation: in Chile there is always a thunderstorm at 3 p.m., in India the barometer always stands at the same level, no thunderstorms were found by Parry in the polar regions, meteoric stones fell on people's heads at Aigle in the last century, etc. etc. One wonders where the legend of the purely *a priori*, deductive Hegel was invented.

From the Physics of General Individuality, the theory of all-pervasive terrestrial differences, Hegel passes to the Physics of Specified Individuality. One can, on general notional principles, only exhibit the various forms of difference-overriding generality which are found in the elements, if one also exhibits these in various specific forms which differ from case to case, and which are essentially such as to be what they are in relation to all the others. This comparativeness or relativity of Matter reveals itself in Matter's essential role of space-filling: one type of Matter will be denser than another, will have a different Specific Gravity. One must not interpret such differences, in atomistic or English fashion, as a differing ration of fulness to void. One type of Matter will, in the same way, be more or less cohesive than another, it will differ in its implementation of a mandatory material "holding-together". And one type of Matter will, in the same way, be more susceptible than another to that general loss of specificity, that "existent dissolution" with which Hegel identifies Heat. It is in the strange context of this graded variation of different aspects of materiality that Hegel devises an extremely queer theory of Sound. Sound, he holds, is really Matter temporarily divesting itself of materiality and transmuting its spatio-temporal rhythms into a purely temporal "soul" which has nothing extended about it, but which none the less reproduces in subtle, qualitative fashion, the quantitative differences on which it is based. "The natural man," says Hegel, "marvels at Sound since in it an inner being is revealed; he does not presuppose a material basis for it but rather something psychic . . . This phenomenon of an inner being coming into existence cannot astonish *us*, for the basis of the Philosophy of Nature is that thought-determinations show themselves to be active principles" (§ 300 *Zus.*). Hegel's doctrine of Sound builds on his logical view that Quantity and Quality are interdependent: Quality becomes a surd unless given a place in an ordered march of Quantities, and Quantity equally becomes a surd unless given form and limitation by the Qualities which it measures.

If we accept all this, and refuse to tear the secondary qualities from Nature in the manner deplored by Whitehead, Hegel's theory of Sound as a sort of non-extensive, qualitative summing-up of motions and vibrations is highly acceptable, and it leads, as all good physical theories lead, to an extensive Pythagoreanization of sound-differences in terms of proportions and numbers. Material substances will of course differ in the quality and amount of the sonorous "soul" they give out when subjected to external impact. Hegel here shows astonishing knowledge of the Physics of Acoustics and Harmony.

Hegel now says that the ordered comparativeness involved in Density, Cohesion, Sonorousness and Heat must take wing and reappear in the form of an *internal* comparativeness and relativity, a static or dynamic total patterning of material being. This total patterning assumes a static Crystalline form and a dynamic Magnetic form, it appears in Colour-, Odour- and Taste-differences, the remaining types of secondary quality: it also appears in Electrical Charge and Shock, and, finally, in Chemical Process. We shall see that there is considerable artificiality and also considerable philosophical profundity in this dialectical arrangement.

As regards patterning in general, it appears in an abstractly punctiform guise in the fine grains of many types of solid matter and in the rounded drops of water: it assumes an abstractly linear form in the Magnet, and an abstractly superficial form in the Crystal. Great care must be taken in the case of each of these types of natural phenomena not to see in them more than they one-sidedly offer, and certainly not to erect them into cosmic forces of vast and vastly varied significance. "Magnetism," says Hegel, "is one of the determinations which inevitably became prominent when the presence of the Notion was suspected in specific natural phenomena and the idea of a Philosophy of Nature was grasped. For the magnet exhibits in simple naive fashion the nature of the Notion, and the Notion moreover in its developed form as Syllogism." (In the Syllogism Genus, Species and Individual each inferentially mediate the connection of the other two members, and Hegel sees similar mediation among the twin poles of the magnet and its neutral centre.) "The poles," he says, "are the sensibly existent ends of a real line ... but as poles, they have no sensible, mechanical reality but an ideal one, and are absolutely inseparable. The point of indifference where they have their substance is the unity where they exist as determinations of the Notion, so that they have meaning and existence solely in this unity; polarity is the relation of such moments. Apart from the determination here explicated, Magnetism has no further special property ... It would be unphilosophical to try

to show that a form of the Notion *exists universally* in Nature in the determination in which it is an abstraction" (§ 312). The specification of linear-
ity in the Magnet does not, however, differentiate the two directions or
ends explicitly: it can only differentiate them dynamically in terms of an
approach to or withdrawal from a third magnetized pole. Poles become
specified as *like* in virtue of their common attraction towards or repulsion
from a third pole, and the nature of the Notion, concerned to differentiate
the identical and identify the different, will then ensure that like poles
repel one another while unlike poles are mutually attractive. The core
of the Hegelian philosophy is thus perspicuously exhibited in the behaviour
of magnets, even if in a somewhat infantile, pictorial form. There is
moreover nothing more to Magnetism than this dialectical revelation. No
special stuff nestles in the interstices of magnets or issues from it as an
effluence: to believe otherwise is to be even more naive than Nature.

If we now turn from Magnetism to Crystallography we see Matter in-
formed by a superficial rather than a merely linear urge, an urge which,
apart from the growth of crystals, is static and not dynamic. The restrictions of one-dimensionality enforce on the Magnet and overflow into Time
which the Crystal does not need. In the crystalline state "the restless activity of Magnetism reaches complete rest. Here there is no longer approach and withdrawal, but everything is set in its place ... The individual Crystal, as Real Magnetism, is the totality in which the urge has died
down, and the oppositions have been neutralized into the form of indifference; Magnetism then expresses its difference as a determination of surface ... This is a silent activity of Nature which sets forth its dimensions
timelessly" (§ 312 *Zus.*). The shaping activity present in the Crystal perva-
des the whole: as a magnet breaks up into magnets, so a crystal breaks up
into smaller crystals having the same surfaces and angles. But in crystals as
in magnets, the analytic Understanding, the English principle, is still dominant: all is stiff and angular, and we do not have the freely flowing cur-
ves and ovals that we have in Life. Needless to say, Hegel does not conceive
of crystalline patterning as being due to a regular arrangement of mole-
cules: it is simply a specific form of superficiality, and of consequent solid-
ity, which is active in Matter.

Oppressed by difficulties of space and time, I shall now pass over a long
treatment where Hegel considers how patterned, total bodies necessarily
stand to the elementary existences evident as Light, Air and Water. He has
an interesting account of refraction where he has devoted particularly
deep thought to the phenomenon where objects seen through air and water
seem nearer than objects seen through air alone. He explains it on prin-

ciples which involve the reception by one form of matter of the deliverances of another so that the latter are modified to suit the former's limitations: the water's bottom is raised much as a hero's conduct is dwarfed when seen in the mirror of his valet's dwarfish soul (§ 318 *Zus.*). I suggest that such a theory is more interesting and arguably "truer," though incorrect in point of fact, than the theoretical accounts we learnt in our textbooks. Hegel also goes on to philosophize about Colour in a manner which contains much fine abuse of Newton and his use of the prism, but which is marred by an acceptance of the *Farbenlehre* of Goethe, the latter being, in my estimation, the regrettable incursion of a litterateur into the sphere of science. Goethe, Hegel tells us, "had a Bohemian wine glass, the inside edge of which he covered half with black and half with white paper; the glass then looked blue and yellow. This is what Goethe called the *Urphänomen*" (§ 320, *Zus.*). One could have wished that Hegel has contributed his own *Urphänomen* of Colour, illustrating some important dialectical principles rather than borrowed one from Goethe's unprincipled ruminations over Bohemian wine glasses. The *Farbenlehre* of Goethe and how Hegel might have bettered it are, however, matters too large to be considered here.

I shall pass over what Hegel has to say about bodily Odour and Savour: like Sound and Heat and Colour, these are true properties of Matter, and are in no sense conjured up by the senses which take cognizance of them. I shall pass on to Hegel's interesting treatment of Static Electricity which was practically all that was known of Electricity at the time. Hegel sees Electricity as restricted to phenomena involving an electric spark and shock, brought on by rubbing or stroking, and manifest also in certain quasi-magnetic effects. He has no patience with theories of Electricity which make it a universal agent, responsible for thunderstorms (of which he had quite a different account), chemical interaction and the activities of Life, nor can he stomach theories which make Electricity a matter of particular stuffs or currents. Electricity on Hegel's view is a kind of emphatic assertion, having some of the properties of anger, of the individuality of one body as against that of another, particularly when the bodies have been brought into irritating proximity and interference by stroking, rubbing and other such activities. The bodies then become oppositely charged, and they as it were acknowledge each other as opposed, and thereupon cancel this opposition in a shock or spark, accompanied by a characteristic odour or savour, but leaving the electrified bodies otherwise unchanged. "We, however," says Hegel, "see in electricity body's own selfhood which, as a physical totality, preserves itself when in contact with another body. It is body's own upsurge of anger which we see; no one else is there but body itself, least of all any foreign matter. Its youthful courage lashes out, it raises itself on its hind-legs, its physical nature rouses itself to struggle desperately against the connection with an other, and it does so as the abstract ideality of light. It is not only we who compare bodies, they themselves compare themselves ... the essential point is that what is here active is body's own immanent physical refractoriness" (§ 324, *Zus.*). This is all there is to Electricity, except that the two electricities which arise in such circumstances have many of the properties of magnetic poles: they approach or retreat from other charges of Electricity and are grouped into like sorts of Electricity by common attractions or repulsions, while the power of the Notion is again exhibited in making like charges unattractive to one another and unlike charges attractive. But the Electricities, unlike magnetic poles, inhabit sundered bodies, and Electricity is said, following Schelling, to be "ruptured Magnetism." The whole Hegelian philosophy is again illustrated in a physical phenomenon, but with greater stress on the differences that it bridges than in the case of Magnetism.

The path is now cleared for a transition to Chemical Process, with which Hegel is to end his treatment of Physics and pass on to Organics. The Chemical Process makes real what in the electrical response is only ideal, the non-independence of bodies, their deep identity with other bodies from which they lie sundered in Space. As Hegel puts it (§ 325): "The particularization of the individual body does not stop at the inert diversity of properties and their own, separate activities, from which in the (electrical) process the abstract pure selfhood of body, the light principle, first issues in the tension of opposed moments and then resolves the latter in their indifference. Since the particular properties are only the reality of the simple Notion, the body of their soul, of Light, and since the complex of the properties, the particular body is not truly independent, the *entire* corporeality therefore enters into tension, into a process which is at the same time the becoming of the individual body." The Chemical Process therefore carries out in sober reality, in the actual issuing of bodies out of other bodies, that denial of ultimate otherness and apartness which has been much more vaguely indicated in the phenomena of Electrical Tension, of Light and of Gravitation.

Hegel's account of Chemical Process involves a use of Contradiction obnoxious and unintelligible to what Hegel calls the Understanding: it supposes an actual state of things to be deeply self-contradictory, and it adds to this offence that of supposing that this self-contradiction is the source of an important natural process. The separateness and mutual in-difference of two chemical elements, Oxygen and Hydrogen, say, or Car-bon and Oxygen, is not for Hegel the plain, actual self-consistent, circum-stance that it gives itself out to be: it involves a deep rift of inner contra-diction, it being in a deep sense absurd and impossible that the elements in question, which are mutually *for* one another, should not be as insepa-rable in existence as they already are in intimate principle. It is this inner rift of contradiction that drives the seemingly independent substances to-gether to form a compound which is really built-in to their nature. "In in-dividuality developed into a totality," Hegel says, "the moments are determined as . . . whole particular bodies which, at the same time, are in relation only as different towards each other. This relation, as the identity of non-identical, independent bodies, is contradiction, and hence is essen-tially *process*, the function of which, in conformity with the Notion, is the positing of the differentiated as identical" (§ 326). Hegel is of course here not using "contradiction" in the sheerly self-cancelling sense con-demned by formal logicians: in making contradiction a real phenomenon, responsible for real change, he is automatically rejecting this interpre-tation. But he is using it in the way in which it is used in his own ever de-veloping, deepening discourse and, as so used, it may well have an ana-logue in the behaviour of the chemical elements.

The contradiction which leads to chemical union is, however, balanced by another contradiction: that of the elements united in the chemical combination. When separated, they are seized with a burning urge to combine, and, when combined, they experience the self-contradiction of their suppressed separateness, which leads, in suitable circumstances, to their disassociation. At the chemical level, accordingly, identity has not that overreaching power over difference which is required by the Notion: sundered bodies tend towards chemical union, but they come out of it sundered as they were before, unenriched by the "experience." What we therefore have is only a senseless oscillation from one unstable state to another, one of which, the combined state, only *ought* to be the truth of both. And because no decisive privilege or priority unifies the process, it is also not self-initiating: the combined substances do not seek to dissolve their union, but neither do the separated substances seek to consummate it. All depends on an *external* factor which brings them together in a suitable medium: Water is thus the medium of combination as Air is of disassociation. The process is not at all like Life in which the unity of the organism differentiates itself into sundered parts and functions only to negate their separateness in its use of each for all and of all for each. "If the Chemical Process could carry itself on *spontaneously*, it would be Life; this explains our tendency to see Life in terms of Chemistry" (§ 326 *Zus.*).

After a few complicated studies of particular chemical processes, we have the dialectical transition from Chemistry to Life. Hegel says (§ 335) that "the Chemical Process is, in fact, in general terms Life, for the individual body in its immediacy is not only *produced* by the process but also *destroyed* by it, so that the Notion no longer remains at the stage of inner necessity but is made *manifest*. But on account of the immediacy of the corporealities entering into the Chemical Process, the Notion is everywhere infected with division ... The *beginning* and *end* of the process are separate and distinct; this constitutes its finitude which keeps it from Life and distinguishes it therefrom." But (§ 336) "what is thus posited in general in the Chemical Process is the *relativity* of the immediate substances and properties. Body as an indifferent existent is thereby posited as a mere *moment* of the individuality and the Notion is posited as *the reality which corresponds to it* ... This concrete unity with self, ... a unity which is the activity of sundering and particularizing itself into the moments of the Notion and equally of bringing them back into that unity, is *the Organism*, the infinite process which spontaneously kindles and sustains itself." Chemical Process, in short, makes manifest a unity of sundered bodily substances which it fails to embody in a complete and satisfactory form. Life is precisely the complete and satisfactory embodiment of this unity. Life is therefore the "truth" of the Chemical Process, just as, at a later stage, *Geist* or Spirit will be held to be the "truth" of Life, realizing a unity in interior experience that is for ever barred to the merely self-external in Space. Our exposition of Hegel's Physics hereby comes to an end. We have only to raise a few final questions regarding the method and outcome of his treatment.

The argument of Hegel up to this point is most readily characterized as a progress guided by a conceptual ideal, which is also such that it cannot be reached or formulated except as the outcome of such a progress. The conceptual Ideal is one that is absolutely unitary in that it admits of no stark dualisms or pluralisms within itself, features which do not require one another, or which have nothing to do with each other, whose joint application is a mere fact, or a mere matter of experience rather than a necessary, conceptual fitting together. It is also one that must be intrinsically specified or differentiated if it is to make sense at all: no *blankly* unitary conception conforms to the ideal in question. It is also a conception that points to nothing outside of itself to which it merely applies externally:

it must outsoar, as it were, the normal limitations of concepts, and include all that it could be applied to, and, if there is an underivable contingency involved in such application, then it itself must in some manner explain and justify and in fact entail the presence of this underivable contingency. And while contrast is of its essence, the element with which it contrasts must also be required by, and in the last resort wholly a projection of itself. And if it emerges as the result of a process, that process too must be part of its final content. To many, the essential ideal which guides Hegel in the Nature-philosophy and elsewhere is self-contradictory and unintelligible, but Hegel would demonstrate its harmony and intelligibility by the fact that all concepts which fall short of it leave an unexplained residual element outside of them, which cannot be felt as anything but a surd and a defect by the enquiring mind, whereas it alone does not do so. And Hegel also contends that his concept is more than a logical ideal: it is present more concretely in the form of self-conscious Spirit, a unity which *requires* to face an Other in the form of an objective world-order, and to unfold itself in the otherness of a world of mutually recognizing Spirits, and to face and overcome endless contingencies, emergencies and untowardnesses whose endlessness is no more than what is required by its own endless vitality. The philosophers of old erred in making their logical ideal too flatly self-sufficient, too lacking in requirements, too unparasitic: Hegel by making his Absolute infinitely exigent, infinitely dependent, infinitely parasitic, paradoxically succeeds in giving its true self-sufficiency and total explanatoriness.

If we now turn to examine the ruses which enable Hegel to go from step to step in his dialectical progression, they are vastly various. Often they consist in reproducing the structure of a complex unity in each of its elements: to be enrolled in a solar system is to have the pattern of that system stamped on one's whole internal economy. A system which rejects the possibility of truly independent parts must necessarily find the structure of the whole present in each of the parts. At another time the ruse consists in calling up the forgotten contrast which shows up a Notion, the Darkness which is necessary to Light, the approach and withdrawal which is necessary to the distinction of magnetic poles or electric charges and so on. Particularly frequent in the Philosophy of Nature is the erection of some abstract connection or property into a separate existence: this is not an absurd proceeding, since all existences, however seemingly independent, are even less independent than the one-sided universals they exemplify. In a system where nothing is truly concrete but the Logical Ideal itself, there is not the sharp distinction between type and instance which obtains in other types of philosophy, and the Light that we see shining

upon us from all natural things may be nothing more than an intuitively
vested universal, a purely docetic expression of the necessary bearing of
all upon all. Another ruse, justified by the primacy of universals or notions that we have just mentioned, is the dialectical migration from one
quite different natural phenomenon to another, when the second is said to
express the "truth" of the first, to make explicit what the first only embodies "in principle." Electricity is ruptured Magnetism, Chemical Process is the full reality of the electrical spark and shock, Light is the full
meaning of Gravitational Attraction, etc. The only identity interesting
to philosophy is the identity of *Begriffe*, Notions, conceived, not as human
conceptions, but as the moving principles of things, and such notions may
be wholly the same even when the phenomena that instantiate them are
sundered and disparate. Magnetism is a different sort of phenomenon
from Electricity or Gravitation, and the individual instantiations of these
sorts are even more plainly different: all this does not prevent us from
seeing in them a sameness of principle which is most fully carried out in the
self-conscious unity of Spirit. I cannot in the few moments still at my disposal say anything more about Hegel's dialectical ruses, except to say that
they are all the infinitely varied tactics of a single strategy, and that, while
often prompted by the need to find a conceptual place for certain empirical data, they are never merely empirical. Hegel seldom or never moves
from one actual natural phenomenon to another without showing some
notional affiliation, relevant to his philosophy, in the whole transition. The
arrangement he imposes on his material may not be the only arrangement
he could have imposed on it – if it were his thought would be of the Understanding, not of Reason – but it is at least a genuine notional arrangement,
based on a single fixed principle, and it genuinely does fit his empirical
data with a greater or lesser degree of illuminating "truth."

Is Hegel's treatment valid? The question is too large to be answered. If
complete intelligibility is an intelligible ideal and a necessary feature of
what exists, then it is likely that Hegel's conceptualization of Nature and
of everything else involves less surds than any other system. But if surds
are to be accepted and swallowed in devout deference to empirical reality
and the limitations of explanatory reasoning, then there are ways of looking at Nature that would seem to fit its observed details better than Hegel's.
I myself believe that the steady collapse of the piecemeal, pictorial naturalism of the sort Hegel excoriates will lead to a climate in which Hegelian
interpretations will enjoy greater currency in natural science. The *Naturphilosophie* may then become an inspirational background for methodo-
logists in the place of, or together with Bacon, Mill, Carnap and the like.

I believe this because I think that the analytic Understanding, though mighty and important, has in the end no function but to serve as a handmaiden to the superior insights of Reason.

COMMENT ON

J. N. FINDLAY
'HEGEL AND THE PHILOSOPHY OF PHYSICS'

Frank Collingwood

One of the problems a reader has in pursuing Hegel is that of knowing when he has arrived at the truth of the matter, for any grasp of the real by the mind is necessarily incomplete and one sided and easily falsely taken for the complete and correct account. To the Greeks of Aristotle's era the hot the cold the dry and the moist combined in various ways to produce the four elements – air, earth, water and fire. If such an account of physical nature were in any sense true, it should still be found in some form in the present day works written by chemists and physicists. It is to be found only in poems or in prose which makes no pretense of accounting for the physical world in statements testable by anyone. I do not see any grounds upon which Hegel's adoption of this thesis about the four elements is defensible as being science or philosophy.

I understand the notion of intelligibility to be that of a rational grasp of a matter that is possessed by the mind in such a manner that there is no irresolvable conflict between it and the whole area of understanding already achieved upon previous occasions. That is, to be intelligible is to be in agreement in some aspects with the knowledge already possessed even though there may also be many novel aspects in the newly achieved consciousness. The human mind, according to Hegel, singly and corporately, goes from one truth to another on the way to the Truth. In doing this, it achieves ever greater intelligibilities as each succeeding intelligibility surpasses those which preceded it thus enlarging simultaneously the rational grasp of the real and also the real itself which is identified with consciousness of it.

At any moment in the Hegelian development of his thesis one will expect to find consciousness doing something and to find partial truths rising into view as consciousness progresses toward its goal, the Truth. There are many aspects to consciousness: idea, concept, notion, reason, understanding. These are terms used by Hegel to express precise viewpoints on consciousness as it is at work both within itself reflecting and also external to itself objectifying itself. This working of consciousness is also termed by some Hegelians a dialectic for they wish to stress the tension within consciousness as its realization of the incompleteness and one-sidedness of a notion forces it to consider an opposing claimant for consideration and then eventually to surpass the limitations of such partial intelligibilities by achieving a more global one which saves the truth of the former as it adds to them.

There are many individual consciousnesses at work simultaneously, Hegel's is that of the outstanding ones which we are being asked by Professor Findlay to take seriously; yet consciousness may be considered as in some sense one. Consider this illustration. The notion of twoness will be grasped in much the same way by every mind and thus there is really only one idea of twoness which is thought in the same way in various times at various places. In other words, there is one consciousness of twoness. Let your own mind now surpass this illustration and entertain the notion of a unitary consciousness going by the name of Idea. It differs from the concept of twoness by its immense comprehension – it is all intelligibility. Just as we talk of our own conscious life, imputing many activities to the mind, so Hegel talks of the duration and activities of the Idea. When we possess a perfectly clear notion, we enjoy its full intelligibility. But when we seek to recognize such an idea in the realm of singular existents, we often are hard put to find it for the multitude of details is a problem to the probing mind. When we are forced to seek in the shifting flux of sensory details to find an intelligibility where one has not yet been discovered, then the task is formidable indeed and many a human mind has striven zealously in the endeavour called physical science, only to arrive at a mistaken notion which, although it was clearly intelligible, as is the four element theory, was nevertheless abandoned at a later time as being to some degree false.

Hegel sees our minds as engaged in a contest in which we strive to arrive at the Truth which is found in a grasping of the Idea, but our progress toward this goal is impeded by the diffusity and unlawlike behavior of the singular existents in which the notions about material being are shrouded. It appears to me that Hegel in his own lugubrious way is including in his philosophical system that item which Plato posited in the *Timaeus* as a locater of sensible qualities and mathematical forms – the matrix of becoming – space, and which Aristotle reasoned to as the ultimate substrate of becoming, matter. All three philosophers find the irregular and endlessly detailed appearances of things an obstacle to seizing the intelligibility which they believe is there. Plato and Aristotle discuss it in terms of an errant cause and a real indeterminacy to indicate their opinion that there is an anti-intelligible factor to be reckoned with in man's attempt to relate material being to intelligible principles. Hegel speaks of a diremption which diversifies into innumerable details the perfectly clear notions which the Idea objectifies. Each of these men felt it necessary to find an excuse in the nature of things for the human mind's failure to render Nature clearly intelligible.

For these three philosophers, the goal of human knowing is the comprehension of all of the intelligibility there is. Their instructions for achieving this differ. Plato talks of a dialectic progress within the mind which would start from sensible reality and pass to the realm of mathematicals and thence to the realm of the Forms and ultimately to the Good which could be identified with the model for the Maker in the *Timaeus* and with the Divine Mind as locus of the divine models of reality in the works of St. Augustine and St. Thomas. Aristotle stressed more the steady progress to be expected from man's endeavor to carefully observe nature and to skillfully phrase the orderly and lawlike behavior therein so as not to overleap the limits of experience nor to understate the richness of intelligibility to be found there. For both Plato and Aristotle it is an effort to be carried out by human consciousness in the face of great difficulties caused both by the opacity of sensible reality and by the weakness of the human mind as a gainer of knowledge. For Hegel man makes steady progress in sounding out the physical world through new experiences and by elaborating ever better notions which capture increasingly greater intelligibilities as they approximate the consciousness of the Absolute.

By taking a position outside of the parameters that all three men were constrained by I see the problem as one of attempting to find out by human means what the Idea (Absolute, The Good, God) is doing as it objectifies itself in sensory being. Dialectic is a name for the process of passing to a better understanding of what there is. Idea is a name for the supposed source of sensory being and its intelligibility. Nature is a term for sensory being considered as existing in its own right. Alienation is the name for a feeling that all is not right and that something radical must be done to overcome the alienation and return to a state of full identification between what is known and what there is. The aim of the game is to make sense out of what the various forces and trends in nature are up to and thus to understand and thereby proceed along the various paths which lead eventually to the Truth. Assuming that this brief overview is sufficient to locate Hegel's Philosophy of Physics I will now attempt to analyse what Professor Findlay has done and to proffer some evaluation.

Professor Findlay has admiration for Hegel's way of achieving intelligibility in the sensory realm. The aim of his paper is to plumb the nature of the Dialectic as it is at work in a realm where the Idea is most alienated from itself. The consequence of this alienation is an appearance of great independence and unrelatedness of physical beings with respect to one another. Thus the challenge to the Dialectic is great, providing a severe test of Hegel's methods in bringing clarity into apparent disorder. Findlay holds that if Hegel's methods provide illumination here we will have a further confirmation of the fruitfulness of this approach to achieving the tautology, the real is the rational.

The Dialectic may be expressed in a variety of ways and is concerned with the forms of things of consciousness. For example, there are expressions conveying the notion of a progression within consciousness from a thought form which is onesided and therefore insufficient as a presentation of the fullness of the object to a fuller and more complete determination of consciousness which includes all of the content of the earlier thought plus another side of the object plus a realization that this is a more comprehensive awareness even though it may still be insufficient in presenting all that there is to be known. For example, gravitation and inertia are notions which are based on experience and are formulated by minds occupied in the elaboration of Physics. Each *Begriff* taken by itself presents a single form of physical being with no relation to any other. A more comprehensive *Begriff* sees them as physical forces whose complementary influences are indispensable to grasping the dynamic and the static characteristics of bodies in our solar system. In arriving at this more comprehensive notion reason posits identity occurring when only difference was realized in the first apprehension. In a manner such as this the mind is to wend its way to the total viewpoint, the Truth. The moments in this dialectic may also be expressed in terms of the self and the non-self. This is a passing from conscious self to the other and back to the self. Thus Idea passes from itself into Nature. Such an activity is termed alienation because of the non-self aspect. Nature is the alienation of the Idea. It also in its turn is alienated from itself. Further it is even alienated from its alienation from itself. This only means that it returns into itself but with a greater intensity of self realization.

The locus of Findlay's analysis is consequent to the passing of the Idea into Nature, which is characterized as the relating of thought patterns to the actual concrete types of things. The alienation of Nature from itself is manifested in the multifarious intermeshings of the qualitatively and quantitatively characterized material things of sensory experience. The analysis of this process is to be scrutinized so that we with Hegel may discern the Dialectic at work. We are to discover the abiding physical intelligibilities which tie the material universe into a conceptual whole. As a way of manifesting Hegel's success in this endeavor Findlay singles out for the reader's attention some of the integrating physical concepts which enable one to assimilate an area of experience which if taken only by itself apart from such integration, would be a sheer multiplicity of material beings. By the use of such concepts the mind gathers into a unified rational comprehension the endless diversity of sensibilia by grasping a logical unity in the diversity of the spatio-temporal things around us.

The alienation of Nature is found in its depiction of material being as endlessly diverse and separate, as in the great variety of colors and smells, etc. This appearance is its naive presentation which is overcome by abandoning its preoccupation with these appearances to realize the conceptual links (the variety of forms) which logically interrelate its manifestations.

The focus of attention then is the spatio-temporal world of sheer multiplicity and qualitative diversity. In it the men of science find notions which they express as conceptualizations or as laws. Thus the concept of light and the laws manifested by its behavior or the concept of gravitation and its law-like behavior are notions formulated by scientists as a result of their analysis of physical phonemena. These in turn are transformed by the philosopher into properly philosophical notions such as "action at a distance" which in this instance states a common element in light and in gravitational attraction while respecting their phenomenal differences. Here we have an example in which the apparent unconnectedness of the sensible types around us which screened their real relationships gives way to the philosophic penetration which attains to a view that shows them as inexorably linked together. This exemplifies the work of philosophical notions throughout the Nature Philosophy in forging a logical chain whose links are forms which vary from the most externally based interconnectedness considered in the section on Mechanics to the forms most immanently possessed by the living things considered in the section on Organics. The task of reason is to discern the forms.

Nature Philosophy sets out to discover in Nature a series of conceptualizations progressing from sheer extensionality and the minimal interdependence of spatial and temporal relationships to the explicit totality where all material beings are seen as contained in and as containing one another. This is penetrating to the meaning of Nature. Of the several parts which constitute this endeavor Professor Findlay has singled out the second one, the physical realm, for our attention. It is his opinion that Hegel's Nature Philosophy is the best Nature Philosophy of the classical type. He understands the classical type of Nature Philosophy, set forth by Plato and Aristotle, as one which sees the whole of Nature as teleologically opened to conscious purpose. In contrast a mechanistic Nature Philosophy views consciousness as rather arbitrarily imposed on an order of non-conscious things which partake mulishly if at all in conscious enterprises. The superior type, the organismic Nature Philosophy, both Greek and Hegelian, survives the inaccuracies of incompletely apprehended details (the number of planets observable at any given time, for example) and permits itself to accomodate its unifying principles to new empirical evidences. Its openness to discoveries and its wide-ranging explanatory notions are the ingredients which make for its superiority.

A critic of this claim might well ask whether an explanation of the activities of Nature which accomodates itself to all inaccuracies and to all accuracies equally well is not so general and vague as to relinquish its claim to be a reasonable account of anything. An analogy comes to mind with the principles of potency and act in Aristotelian Physics which remain intact after all of the inaccuracies have been selectively deleted because they can make no pronouncement regarding either the accuracies or the inaccuracies of the detailed physical explanations of the material universe.

It is in the physical domain where both general principles such as all-encompassing telism operate and where more limited principles, such as gravitational attraction are also discernible that Professor Findlay invites us to find far-ranging intelligibilities. We are warned that the details involved will have to be declared false but that "the principle and the method are true." Let us reconsider two instances mentioned by Professor Findlay which he claims substantiate his position regarding the correct or true method and the false details plaguing it. I.) Hegel sees both time and space as illustrating quantity. Space is a unifying factor and time is a diremptive factor although neither one is such exclusively. The dialectic is found in their mutual interaction. Diremption into separate parts as in time separating each successive instant is complemented by an attractive unifying force of space unifying all the material things at any moment. Only in the balance of these two is material being possible. Philosophically expressed this becomes: "the Notion, the Philosophical Universal requires the separateness of far-flung instances in order that it should be a Universal, present in all of them and it also requires the holding together of its instances if its instantiation is not to be lost in the inane."

Is there, in this latter reference, any implied intractable and unintelligible element or principle at work in Hegel's world such as there is in the Platonic physical world formed in the matrix of becoming? For if there is one must remember that such a cosmogony saw the physical universe as a chaos with a rather arbitrarily imposed set of forms forcing nonconscious things to partake mulishly and fleetingly in conscious enterprises. [*Timaeus*]

II.) Professor Findlay presents Light as a manifestation of material unity which typifies the conceptualization of the Nature Philosophy and of the Dialectic generally. Light, for Hegel, presents the pure self-identity of matter as a kind of independence from the other determinations of natural being, thus giving to each thing an as-it-were independent existence. Here I became confused as to exactly what the philosophical conceptualization of light expressed. What is the self-identity of matter – this nonindependence of everything from everything? Is light in giving an as-itwere independent existence doing nature a service or a disservice? A further clarification is desirable here regarding the consequence following from Hegel's insubstantial concept of *Light as a revelation*, the consequence namely that light cannot be divided into the spatially distinct rays that Newton differentiated with his prism. Is this one of the false details? And further, *what* is it that causes Professor Findlay to champion the "austere emptiness of Hegel's physical concepts," in this case his concept of light, in a universe characterized by Hegel as abundantly rich in material diversity – is it that the greater the diversity of specification and instantiation in material reality, the more encompassing is the unitive principle by its stark simplicity?

If the principle and method of procedure are true as is claimed – they are not obvious – *is* there a paradigm of the method that Hegel used in the Physics? If there is much would be gained presenting it as a direction for the Dialectic in the progress of Reason. If there is not, in what sense is there a method of procedure? The discussion of the philosophic view of magnetism reveals it as similar to that of space and time and of inertia and gravitation: all three views involving the antagonism between diremptive and unitive tendencies. The concepts involved have that stark simplicity which Hegel approves of but in so doing they prescind from the actual details of the material phenomena stressing identity but omitting differences. Is *this* desirable or undesirable in science's world view? Would the conceptualizing of most material activities in terms of transformations of energy be in line with the thrust of Hegel's thought?

The opposition that Hegel voices to the analytic method of understanding seems capricious and destined to hold to archaic supposedly wholistic unitive aspects in the face of much more complete accounts of material reality achieved by an analytic method.

Had the world followed Hegel's method there would be none of the fantastic advances produced by reductionist mechanistic methods – nor any further progress along teleological lines, for our understanding of parts as ordered to wholes depends upon the mechanistic reduction of wholes into their component parts. Purpose as man discerns it is directly experienced only in his self-conscious actions and in the ineluctible consequences of activites of nature whose end results are well known. As a factor in discerning the intelligibility of the material universe it has yielded no fruit for it is uncompromisingly inscrutable.

HEGEL AND MARX

Jean-Yves Calvez, S.J.

I should probably have entitled this "Marx and Hegel," since I do not
wish to attempt a study of the influence of Hegel through Marx, but rather
of the position taken by Marx with regard to Hegel. What follows, then,
is first of all a study of something *in* Marx himself. True, one says a good
deal about Hegel also in asserting that there is no Marx without Hegel,
without the problematic of Hegel. And I should recall in passing that this
assertion – no Marx without or outside of Hegel – is completely denied by
those who insist on a radical break in the course of Marx's intellectual
career. According to this school of thought, there was a time when Marx
was effectively dominated by Hegelian problematics; and then there was
in Marx's mature years, beginning more or less with *The German
Ideology*, a time at which he escaped definitively from those problematics,
from the "siren" who, he told us, earlier haunted him, and whose charms
he could not rid himself of.

I am not in a position to effect a full and erudite demonstration of a
thesis on this problem. I can, however, present the manner in which I
viewed these matters in studying for itself the *Thought of Karl Marx* in
1956, and propose certain positions at which I then arrived to the critical
scrutiny of our friends and colleagues of the Marquette Hegel Symposium.

I

I think the first impression gained by one approaching the relationship of
Marx to Hegel is that Marx, while criticizing what he calls the idealism
of the Hegelian dialectic, nonetheless retains much of Hegel, specifically
the dialectic itself, "the dialectic of negativity as the moving and creating
principle." [1] "Hegel grasps the self-creation of man as a process, objectifi-

---

[1] *Economic and Philosophical Manuscripts* (in the part of Ms. III entitled "Critique
of Hegel's Dialectic and General Philosophy," in *Karl Marx: Early Writings*, tr. and ed.
by T. B. Bottomore (N.Y.: McGraw-Hill, 1964), p. 202.

cation as loss of the object, as alienation and transcendence of this alienation, . . . he, therefore, grasps the nature of labor, and conceives objective
man (true, because real man) as the result of his own labor." Marx develops the notion further: "The real, active orientation of man to himself as
a species-being, or the affirmation of himself as a real species-being (i.e.
as a human-being) is only possible so far as he really brings forth all his
species-powers . . . and treats these powers as objects, which can only be
done at first in the form of alienation." [2] The greatness of Hegel lies in
his having grasped the fact that man is thus process, labor, and that a negativity is at the heart of the process.

Thus the first impression – and it is one confirmed by the long developments in the chapter on Hegelian dialectic at the end of the Third Manuscript – is that, while Marx takes exception to Hegel's transposition of the
movement of man into a movement of the self-consciousness of spirit, he
recognizes at least that Hegel perceived the *law* of this movement, the
dialectic.

II

Yet if we look more closely, and in the very vicinity of the texts just cited,
a second impression can easily follow the first: contrary to what first
appeared to be the case, Hegel, as Marx represents him, *did not truly
understand negativity*. Marx has just told us that Hegel grasps the "nature
of labor"; and he continues: "labor as the essence, the self-confirming essence of man." But he quickly and somewhat bluntly adds: "he observes
only the positive side of labor, not its negative side." [3]

Put somewhat differently, this seems to mean that Hegel recognizes
exteriorization or externalization – yet a quite limited exteriorization, because the object is not really placed in opposition –; while, on the contrary,
he does not really understand alienation, negativity in the strong and strict
sense. Hegel sets up an objectivity which is so little objective, so little
"other," that he has no difficulty in reabsorbing it through a speculative
process that is little more than a facile play.

Correlatively, this also means that there is no real suppression of the
alienation, no real transformation, but rather conservation, and thus no
real negation of the negation. But here, too, it is a question of a deficiency
in negativity. For example: "after superseding religion, when he has recognized religion as a product of self-alienation, he then finds confirma-

[2] *Ibid.*, pp. 202-3.
[3] *Ibid.*, p. 203.

tion of himself in religion as religion." [4] Marx denounces this as "*false positivism.*" Hegel's criticism is "merely *apparent* criticism." Or again: "Man, who has recognized that he leads an alienated life in law, politics, etc. leads his true human life in this alienated life as such. Self-affirmation, in contradiction with itself, with the knowledge and the nature of the object, is thus the true *knowledge* and *life.*" [5] To read this rightly, an exclamation point must be added.

Marx pursues the point: "In Hegel, therefore, the negation of the negation is not the confirmation of true being by the negation of illusory being. It is the confirmation of illusory being, or of self-alienating being in its denial (negation); or the denial (negation) of this illusory being as an objective being existing outside man and independently of him, and its transformation into a subject." [6] After the objection of positivism, we thus have that of total subjectivism."

Hence we are led to say that, in Marx's view, we find in Hegel a rather poor understanding of the dialectic and of negativity. True, this does not completely contradict the first impression mentioned earlier, namely that Marx grants Hegel the merit of having clarified dialecticity, negativity. It is simply the case that, with the movement being perceived only in the realm of selfconsciousness or spirit, as it is with Hegel, dialecticity and negativity themselves change in character; they are impoverished, rendered pale. But to say that, for Marx, the dialectic has only this profoundly mystified sense in Hegel is to begin thinking that, all things considered, there is rather little of Hegel in Marx. Apparently then, Marx separates himself much more from Hegel than he recognizes a resemblance.

To be sure, Marx will continue to say that idealism, in opposition to "all materialism up to the present, including that of Feuerbach," has the merit of having recognized the "active aspect" of reality ("Theses on Feuerbach," No. 1). But is there great merit in this recognition when, as it appears to Marx, everything is so profoundly perverted in the view of reality and of history maintained by every philosophy except materialism, and when, again as it appears to Marx, "activity" was so recognized only in the domain of thought, of consciousness, of spirit – all having precisely secondary status in the view of things had by Marx himself.

Must we not say that what counts with Marx, *vis-à-vis* Hegel, are the radical adoptions of position such as these. In Hegel, Marx comments, " 'thinghood' (*Gegenständlichkeit*) is totally lacking in independence, in

[4] *Ibid.*, p. 210.
[5] *Ibid.*
[6] *Ibid.*, p. 211.

being, *vis-à-vis* self-consciousness; it is a mere *construct* established by self-consciousness. And what is established is not self-confirmation; it is the confirmation of the act of establishing, which for an instant, but only for an instant, fixes its energy as a product and *apparently* confers upon it the role of an independent, real being." [7] Marx responds categorically: "When real, corporeal man, with his feet firmly planted on the solid ground, inhaling and exhaling all the powers of nature, posits his real objective faculties, as a result of his alienation, as alien objects, the *positing* is not the subject of this act but the subjectivity of *objective* faculties whose action must also, therefore, be *objective*. An objective being acts objectively, and it would not act objectively if objectivity were not part of its essential being. It creates and establishes *only objects, because* it is established by objects, because it is fundamentally natural." And again: "Man is directly a *natural being*." [8] More precisely, he is at once both active and passive.

These themes of 1844 are shortly after taken up again by Marx in *The German Ideology* which, on this score, does not represent a real rupture in the development of Marx's thought; and they continue to underlie the later works. In other words, these themes are truly Marx's own thought. They are in singular opposition to Hegelian thought as Marx understands it.

III

It would be useless to go further, one might add, if all philosophical problems are decided in a certain choice between materialism and idealism. Indeed this is what Marxism has, in general, thought; and Marx encouraged the posing of all philosophic questions in this way by his insistence on the theme of historical materialism. Nevertheless, it seems possible to take a further step: it may be that, removed as we are from the period in which Hegel and Marx both lived, we can discover all the same that the two, despite their differences, are common in many respects, and particularly in one problematic which reunites the one and the other and opposes them in common to other philosophers, more recent ones especially, who tend to challenge that problematic.

First, in their search for a *philosophy of history*, Hegel and Marx are, in effect, brothers. Marx judges that Hegel presents history only in a deformed mirror – that of self-consciousness, spirit, ideas, knowledge; but he well knows that Hegel aimed to produce a comprehension of historical movement. Marx, too, meant to provide an expression of the same move-

[7] *Ibid.*, p. 206.
[8] *Ibid.*

ment of history, though no longer "abstract, logical, speculative," but rather concrete, non-alienated; he tried to reach the level of its real presuppositions, its true reality, its concrete texture.

Further, Marx and Hegel are together in one and the same attempt to reabsorb in a certain way the whole of what stands as exteriorization, finitude, limit or alienation. From a sufficiently broad point of view, and despite a fair number of nuances, we can throw all of these terms together. For Marx as much as for Hegel, this second ambition specifies the expression, "philosophy of history," that I just attributed to each of their works; for philosophy of history can have other meanings. Both Marx and Hegel understand it in ways not too dissimilar: both the one and the other attribute the greatest importance to the overcoming of exteriorization or alienation (the use of these two terms maintaining sufficiently the reality of the divergence which at the same time remains between them). As an example, we need only recall the famous text of Marx: "Communism as a fully developed naturalism is humanism and as a fully developed humanism is naturalism. It is the definitive resolution (*Auflösung*) of the antagonism between man and nature, and between man and man. It is the true solution of the conflict between existence and essence, between objectification and self-affirmation, between freedom and necessity, between individual and species." [9]

Within this same effort, there is with the one and the other a kind of quest for historical "totalization," whatever ambiguity has to be recognized in such a project. Absolute knowledge with Hegel; birth or liberation of man with Marx (or again, a kind of universal reconciliation among men as well as between man and nature).

Marx and Hegel share as well a certain humanism, precisely one attacked today as characteristic of an epoch that has run its course. No doubt, with Hegel it is, overall, a question of the man of self-consciousness; with Marx, on the other hand, man the natural being, as spoken of a moment ago. But we should note that Marx wished at the same time to underscore the specificity of man: "But man is not merely a natural being; he is a *human* natural being. He is a being for himself, and, therefore, a *species-being* (*Gattungswesen*); and as such he has to express and authenticate himself in being as well as in thought." [10] And, it must be added, neither is this denied in the later works of Marx; as when, for example, in the beginning of *Capital* he speaks of the irreducible traits of human labor as opposed to the instinctive activity of the animal.

[9] *Ibid.*, p. 155.
[10] *Ibid.*, p. 208.

IV

Yet, for all this underlining of similarities in the problematics of Hegel and Marx, I do not return to the first impression called to mind in my exposition. According to that impression the principle thing the two have in common would be the dialectic. It is other aspects that I have emphasized more.

But if we must, nevertheless, return to this question of the dialectic, we should emphasize again that, if Marx could reproach the Hegelian dialectic for being essentially too little dialectical, in the sense that it does not take hold of the real but rather dissolves the real in thought, and that the *Aufheben* is not a true negation of the negation but rather conservation and confirmation, then doubtless an analogous reproach can be leveled at Marx himself: that of giving in the end greater weight to a kind of monistic naturalism than to the dialectic or to negativity. Everything appears to be rather precontained in a nature that opens out, to be sure, through successive determinations, in particular through the fact of man – who is a "natural being" but a "human natural being" –, but which nonetheless has in itself the force to restore everything precisely back to itself. What is called for is an end to the struggle between man and nature, and this is subtended by a conviction that in fact, and in the very course of the process, nature carries this out. For the forces of man that set the movement to work were, after all, only "natural forces"; and if they encountered "objects," these objects were intimately tied to the natural forces; they are "objects of (man's) needs." [11]

In closing the works of Marx, and after all the discussions on the role of determinism and that of revolution, one can never wholly refrain from thinking that for him there is an irresistible, natural-historical force that clears the way. *Capital* itself has something of the character of a positive demonstration of this necessity (tendential law of the decline in rate of profits, etc. . . . .).

Thus, despite the place given to an "active" aspect (retained from idealism, as Marx wished us to do in his "Theses on Feuerbach") we have, for all that, the sense of a materialism opposed from end to end to idealism.

But it must be added finally – and this is the final remark I wish to make in summary concerning the relationship of Marx and Hegel –, between this materialism and idealism (which Marx denounced in Hegel), there re-

[11] *Ibid.*, p. 211.

mains, with reference to the form of the thought, profound resemblances. Whatever concern Marx manifests about the concrete nature of the alienations to be suppressed, he first of all resolves them in thought, in a theory (called "scientific"); and it has happened that several of his successors have, as a result, given primary importance to a "scientific" dogmatism with a contemplative cast. It was with this conviction that I wrote at the end of *La Pensée de Karl Marx* (1956): "The total act, the completeness of the proletarians' essential action, is an *idealist* postulate when compared with the dialectical conditions of History." [12] And I tend more and more to think that, despite some denials by Marx (who wanted to avoid making recipes for the cook-shops of the future), he could not refuse to give first importance to the task of an intellectual construction and totalization of history: in that he was Hegelian, in any case if we refer to what Marx himself understood by this adjective. In that, too, he belonged to a well defined philosophical world, from which an appreciable number today wish to separate themselves without any intention to return.

[12] *La Pensée de Karl Marx*, 7th edition (Paris: Editions du Seuil, 1961), p. 620.

COMMENT ON

JEAN-YVES CALVEZ 'HEGEL AND MARX'

David McLellan

I will address myself, in turn, to the structure, content and scope of Professor Calvez' paper. First, with reference to its structure, I see in his paper a triadic element: it contains a very determinate thesis, then an antithesis, and finally a synthesis. The thesis I take to be that Marx first takes a very positive view of Hegel's dialectic. He thinks Hegel has got quite correctly negativity, man as self-creator, etc. However, there is an antithesis, namely that the sense of negativity and dialectic in Hegel is nevertheless deficient, because there really is no object, for Hegel, outside of man's consciousness; the object is simply a thought-object; and thus the dialectic is deficient. Yet – and here comes the synthesis –, to some extent Hegel and Marx are brothers in that (1) they share an essentially similar philosophy of history, with history being a process capable of being totalized in that all man's alienations can be reabsorbed in the end; and (2) they are both essentially humanists in that they commonly hold that man cannot be reduced to elements outside of him.

Now, I am in general agreement with this admirably dialectical approach to the problem of the influence of Hegel on Marx. And while I think that the first part of the paper accurately describes Marx's critique of Hegel – and thus what Marx took over and what he rejected –, the further question could be asked as to how accurately Marx interpreted Hegel. It could well be argued that Marx to some extent misinterpreted Hegel and that his criticisms, particularly in the *Paris Manuscripts* of 1844, are misdirected.[1] From this it would follow that the relationship between Hegel and Marx cannot be fully revealed by Marx's own account of their relationship.

[1] Cf. L. Dupré, *The Philosophical Foundations of Marxism.* New York: Harcourt, Brace and World, 1966; J. Maguire, *Marx's 1844 Manuscripts: An Analysis.* Dublin: Gill Macmillan, 1972.

As to the content of Professor Calvez' paper, there is one point I wonder about, and another to which I object. The first has to do with the quote from his book, *La Pensée de Karl Marx*: "The total act, the completeness of the proletarians' essential action, is an *idealist* postulate when compared with the dialectical conditions of History." The meaning of this quotation is not particularly plain to me. Furthermore, I do not understand in what sense Marx could be said to have resolved alienations in his own thought, in his own theory, such that this could be a basic objection against him. On this point I am not so much objecting as wondering precisely what Professor Calvez is saying. The second point, and this is the one to which I do object, is Professor Calvez' treatment of an opposition in Marx's writings between materialism and idealism. I believe there is misplaced emphasis here: I believe it is incorrect to think that Marx opposed materialism and idealism as two opposite poles and then came down himself on the side of materialism. Marx himself in the *Paris Manuscripts* – which is the writing on which Professor Calvez bases his interpretation – comments on his own approach: "We can see here how consistent naturalism or humanism is distinguished from both idealism and materialism and constitutes at the same time their unifying truth." [2]Professor Calvez' treatment of the materialism-idealism opposition seems to me to be too much on an ontological, or metaphysical plane; whereas in Marx it would seem to be rather a methodological question, with Marx using expressions like "the materialist conception of history," which means the way in which you start into a problem, the end from which you approach it.

Finally, as to the scope of Professor Calvez paper, I question the adequacy of relying, as he does, solely on the *Paris Manuscripts* in treating the relationship of Hegel and Marx. I think that questioning the relationship of the two is automatically to raise the question about the continuity of Marx's thought, and thereby, according to the answer you give, to assert one or another view as to whether or not there was one Marx or two; and if there was one, in what did the continuity of Marx's thought consist. Now, as we know, there have been many views on this subject, all of which seem to me to be to some extent mistaken. The older view, that which obtained before the publication of Marx's early writings, was that there really was only one Marx, the Marx of *Das Kapital*, primarily a "scientific" economist. This view is still held, in most cases by orthodox communists, and has been recusitated most recently by the French philosopher

---

[2] Karl Marx, *Early Texts*. Ed. D. McLellan. New York: Barnes and Noble, 1971, p. 167.

Louis Althusser. It is a view of Marx which seems to me totally mistaken. Then there is the opposite view, which seems to me to some extent contained in Professor Calvez' book, *La Pensée de Karl Marx*, and in English typically in Fromm's book, *Marx's Concept of Man*, and which is quite prevalent in books written in German and inspired by the Landshut-Mayer Introduction to their edition of Marx's *Frühschriften*.[3] Then there are certain writers who attempt to hold something of a middle course by saying that, of course, there is continuity in Marx's writings, and we don't want to emphasize either *Capital* on one hand or the *Paris Manuscripts* on the other. This position is probably best exemplified by Maximilien Rubel.[4] Now, what seems to me to be lacking in all these accounts, and to bear directly on the question of the relationship of Hegel to Marx, is full attention to the massive manuscript of Marx written in 1857-58 preparatory to the actual drafting of *Capital* and other works, and which is known as the *Grundrisse*. Marx himself characterized this as a *resumé* of the work that occupied him during fifteen of the best years of his life; and it is in many ways a synthesis of his leading ideas – the only place where he brought together at any length the philosophical and economic elements of his thought.[5] In this unique writing Marx's debt to Hegel and his method, with emphasis on the *Logic* rather than on the *Phenomenology*, comes through quite as strikingly as in the *Paris Manuscripts*. There are an enormous number of Hegelian elements in it. Not only is the concept of alienation central to the work, but the whole range of concepts of alienation, objectification, appropriation, man's dialectical relationship to nature, and man's generic, or social nature are again taken up and filled with more specific content than in the *Manuscripts*; the treatment of capital, labor, labor-time etc. seem to me clearly and totally Hegelian. So in conclusion, I would like to make the point that insofar as the *Grundrisse* expresses Marx's mature and full thought large space should be afforded to the discussion of this work, rather than the early writings and *Capital* in any discussion of the continuity of Marx's thought, which in turn goes back to the question of the influence of Hegel on Marx.

---

[3] *Karl Marx/Der historische Materialismus*. Ed. S. Landshut and J. P. Mayer. Leipzig: Kröner, 1932.
[4] Esp. M. Rubel, *Karl Marx: Essai de biographie intellectuelle*. Paris: Marcel Rivière & Cie, 1957.
[5] Karl Marx, *Grundrisse der Kritik der politischen Oekonomie (Rohentwurf), 1857-1858*. Berlin: Dietz Verlag, 1953; first published in two volumes by the Marx-Engels-Lenin-Institute, Moscow, 1939-41. For excerpts in English see Karl Marx, *The Grundrisse*. Ed. D. McLellan. New York: Harper and Row, 1971.

THE CONCEPTUALIZATION OF RELIGIOUS
MYSTERY

AN ESSAY IN HEGEL'S PHILOSOPHY OF RELIGION

Kenneth L. Schmitz

I. The Problematic

We will soon pass the one hundred and fiftieth year since Hegel began his
Berlin lectures on the philosophy of religion.[1] Since that time he has appeared as mystagogue to some, arch-rationalist to others, and more recently as a host for fragmentary existential insights. During these one hundred
and fifty years it has not been uncommon to hold two assumptions concerning religious mystery and Hegel's philosophy. First, much writing
about Hegel seems to assume that he has touched upon all forms of what
might be called religious mystery. It is dangerous to assume that he has
not, but, as with all great minds, equally dangerous to assume that he
has. Second, a widely spread opinion holds that, at the very least, Hegel's
philosophy is uncompromisingly hostile to any attempt to have knowledge
pass ultimately over into mystery.

It is not easy to get the truth or falsity of these two assumptions right.
Concerning the first, it seems a straightforward matter to line up Hegel's
own considerations of religious mystery, and to check them off with those
described in the history of religions. That, of course, might prove onerous
enough, but a qualitatively different difficulty immediately appears when
it is attempted. For Hegel forces a would-be critic to reformulate more
than once what the critic takes religious mystery to be, so that at points of
crisis in his reflection the critic finds himself driven to ask whether there
is anything which Hegel has not considered in the matter of religious mys-

---

[1] The edition used throughout the essay is that of Georg Lasson, 1925, 1927: G. W.
F. Hegel, *Vorlesungen über die Philosophie der Religion*, 2 Bde., Hamburg (F. Meiner)
1966. Hereafter VPR. For a discussion of the considerable textual problems see the
Appendices. In recognition of them (g) will represent Hegel's own autograph text, (k)
the students' notebooks and materials from earlier editions. The English translation
from Bruno Bauer's unsatisfactory edition is by E. B. Spiers and J. B. Sanderson, (1895),
Hegel's Lectures on the Philosophy of Religion, 3 vols. New York (Humanities) (1962)
1968. Hereafter LPR.

tery. The struggle to determine this question forms the essential theme of
the present essay.

Concerning the second assumption, we are familiar with Hegel's claim
to have laid bare the *telos* and dynamic of meaning itself, the inner necessity for completeness which is inherent in the pursuit of truth and the realization of existence. Would the elevation of religious mystery to a position
of honour, by giving it the last and highest word, jeopardize Hegel's paradigm of diremption and reconciliation, by robbing it of finality, ultimacy or
necessity? Let us suppose for the moment that some such elevation were
called for. What sort of change would that introduce into our estimation
of Hegel's philosophy? Could that philosophy remain essentially intact,
complete within itself, yet only partial in terms of dimensions which escape
it? Or would the introduction of a dimension so apparently alien to the
drive towards systematic rational completeness result in the destruction or
corruption of the Hegelian philosophical enterprise? To say it again, is
all discourse in the Hegelian sense snuffed out if God exceeds our grasp?
Does true and genuine discourse require exhaustive comprehension of
what is said?

Is there any sense of religious mystery that is compatible with the final
stages of Hegel's systematic reconciliation of meaning and existence?
James Collins insists that a certain sense of religious mystery remains to
the very end in Hegel's reconciliation, but he qualifies this admission very
seriously. It is found in the

conviction that a certain act of faith is still required at the very base of
philosophizing. The one holy mystery acknowledged by Hegel is found in the
act of mind whereby the philosopher accepts this ultimate concretion of the
infinite and finite, in an all-inclusive totality.[2]

Professor Collins hastens to add that

because the entire divine essence is involved in this self-realizing process, there
can be no residue of divinity left unmanifested . . . no hidden God.

We may agree that there is something holy at the centre of Hegel's
thought, and thereby lay aside the harsh and inaccurate charge that Hegel
is simply a bald and bare-faced rationalist insensitive to rich dimensions
of religious experience; but we may still wish to ask, whether there is anything mysterious left? Or, whether Hegel has displaced religious mystery
with an imageless faith in Reason? It is true, certainly, that a rational
faith underlies the Hegelian enterprise, but the difficulty remains: Is not

---

[2] *The Emergence of the Philosophy of Religion*, Yale 1967, pp. 403-05.

a rational faith a faith in rationality? And how is that equivalent to a faith in the positive religion of Christianity and in religious mystery? [3] Erik Schmidt asks, No matter how impeccable the logical characteristics of Hegel's final categories may be, are they not inadequate to prevent the religious beliefs of Christianity from being brought into grave danger, even into pantheism in the delicate relation between God and the world? [4]

On the other hand, if Hegel allows religious mystery to appear in the lower regions of the system, and if the lower is fully present in the higher,[5] we may well ask, whether the final stage does not contain religious mystery precisely as mysterious? M. Clark, while conceding that Hegel was in intent a rationalist, has concluded that he has actually (if inadvertently) transferred mystery to the very heart of his system.[6] Claude Bruaire, while conceding that Hegel ultimately fails to do justice to historical Christianity, brushes off the charge of a doctrinaire rationalism bent upon replacing Christianity, with something "higher." He argues instead that Hegel's philosophy is a serious attempt to fulfill Christianity's deepest aspirations.[7] Finally, Albert Chapelle, bolder than most commentators, speaks openly of

---

[3] VPR IV, 73 (k) speaks of "reverence" before God as absolute truth, but this is then interpreted in terms of the qualities of pure thought.

[4] *Hegels Lehre von Gott*, Gütersloh 1952, pp. 154-5 (fn. 38): "Logisch ist dieser Begriff unanfechtbar. Aber ist nicht seine Konsequenz in der speziellen Theologie der Pantheismus? Wenn Gott das Endliche als ein Moment in sich hat, besteht dann nicht wieder die Kontinuität zwischen Gott und Welt und ist dann nicht die Einheit ein gottweltliches Universum, in welchem die Transzendenz des überweltlichen Gottes nicht zur Geltung kommt? Wir sehen: Die Kategorien der Logik, so tief sie auch sein mögen, erweisen sich als Darstellung Gottes in seinem ewigen Sein nicht zureichend. Sie wollen die ungenügende religiöse Vorstellung von Gott begrifflich läutern. In Wirklichkeit bringen sie die Gottesvorstellung in die Gefahr, unaufgebbare Momente des Gottesgedankens preiszugeben oder zu verdunkeln."

For Dr. Schmidt's resolution see pp. 193-4 and fn. 45. The best Hegel can come out with is a "dialectical pantheism," even though he wishes to avoid Pantheism in all forms. This proves that "dies letzte Mysterium . . . ist nicht einer logischen Formel zu erfassen." Again, p. 239 (fn. 65): "Weiter kann man sich vom Evangelium nicht entfernen, als indem man an die Stelle des Geheimnisses des Kreuzes eine dialektisch-spekulative Formel setzt! Wir zweifeln auch hier nicht, dass Hegels persönliche Frömigkeit viel tiefer war, als seine Theorie des Kreuzes ahnen lässt. Aber auch hier ist Hegel ein Gefangener seiner Logik, die er für den Schlüssel zu allen Problemen hält." And finally, p. 257: "Hegels Gotteslehre ist eine säkularisierte christliche Eschatologie." Hereafter HLG.

[5] Cf. G. R. G. Mure, *A Study of Hegel's Logic*, Oxford 1950, especially cc. 1, 21-22. Also Malcolm Clark, *Logic and System*, Louvain (Univ. Werkgemeenschap), pp. 28-36. Hereafter LAS.

[6] LAS, p. 345: "In his doctrine of religion, Hegel has often been accused of "rationalism" in his rejection of "mysteries." The charge is probably justified. Yet its proof is no easy matter. For his system has – whether he wanted it or not – transferred mystery from a future "beyond" to the heart of his thought."

[7] *Logique et religion chrétienne dans la philosophie de Hegel*, Paris (du Seuil) 1964, p. 100. Hereafter LRC.

the presence of a certain mystery in Hegel's final synthesis.[8] Fresh winds of sympathetic consideration of Hegel's philosophy, coupled with changes in our understanding of religion and of religious mystery, may indicate the usefulness of another look at the question of Hegel's final reconciliation and the place which religious mystery may or may not have in it.

Is it absurd to rethink Hegel to see if his dynamic of reconciliation has room for holding and giving objective form to an encounter of God and man, an encounter, moreover, which transcends man in every respect? Perhaps it is not the most important thing to say about Hegel that his primary motive is to drive beyond religion to rational completeness? We know texts in which he exalts love to the highest motive, that longing for complete reconciliation between God and man in which self recognizes itself in the other and the other in itself and which yet preserves the integrity of each.[9] Of course, the character of the final reconciliation is for Hegel uncompromisingly conceptual, in his sense of the term, and it is therefore intended to be a reconciliation which is in accord with the demands of scientific reason as he understands them. Our question remains: Can religious mystery (however *it* is to be understood) have any reality in that reconciliation?

What, now, do we hope to accomplish? We hope to raise the possibility of an option open to one who retraces Hegel's path, – an option which Hegel may not have taken, – in order to see where it might lead. In the result, then, we hope to have an indicator with which to assess the Hegelian odyssey from a fresh perspective, one that is not an alien assault upon his path, and yet which is something of our own. In the following reflection several post-Hegelian influences will make their appearance. I am indebted to them, but I wish to take them only as suggestions and to develop them out of the present problematic and thereby to avoid saddling them with historical accoutrements which I may not wish them to wear.

We should not forget that it is an Hegelian principle that religion contains the fullness of truth, even the imperative to go beyond its form in order to realize its intentionality. Hegel interpreted that intentionality in such a way that he clearly gave certain forms of religious mystery a subordinate role. Suppose that we find in the Christian religion a mandate to interpret religious mystery in a different philosophical way? Are we then truer Hegelians than the master? But this is surely a thought which is too presumptious for scholars and too paradoxical for philosophers.

---

[8] *Hegel et la religion*, Paris (Universitaires), t. II (1966), pp. 60-62. Hereafter HR.
[9] VPR IV, 176 (g). Cf. Jan van der Meulen, *Die gebrochene Mitte*, Hamburg 1958, p. 299.

We turn rather to an attempt at extricating ourselves from the thicket we have been growing.

II. Revelation as Epistemic Manifestation

It is a famous principle of Hegel's philosophy that not only is the Christian revelation true but that it is the total manifestation of the deepest truth. Agreeing with many classical philosophers, he insists that God would not be God if he did not know himself.[10] Furthermore, since Hegel is sure that Christianity is actually *the* revealed religion, God must say something about himself in it;[11] it cannot be secretive or exclusive, but must be open and have a definite teaching.[12] To contemporaries who tried to use the imagery of the Bible in order to allege that man cannot know God, he replies that this is a mindless distortion, and that the Christian religion consists precisely in knowing what God is in his essence.[13] But he presses his principle further. God as he reveals himself in the Christian religion must be identical with God as he actually is.[14] In contrast to other religions, which stand under a sort of necessity, and in which God shows himself to be other than he really is, and in which his true nature remains hidden and unknown,[15] in the Christian religion God manifests himself so that nothing remains unrevealed.

In the *Phänomenologie* Hegel had already described the joy with which the religious consciousness greets the revelation and appearance of the ultimate reality in revealed religion:

The revealed which has come forth *entirely* to the surface is just therein the *deepest* reality. That the Supreme Being is seen, heard, etc. . . . God, then, is here revealed, as He is; He actually exists as He is in Himself; He is real as

---

[10] *Enzyklopädie der philosophischen Wissenschaften im Grundrisse (1830)*, (herausg. v.F. Nicolin und O. Pöggeler), Hamburg (F. Meiner) 1959, #564: "Gott is nur Gott, insofern er sich selber weiss."

[11] VPR IV, 34 (g): "[Die christliche Religion] erkennt Gott, wie er ist. Eine christliche Religion, die Gott nicht erkennen sollte, [in der] Gott nicht geoffenbart [wäre], wäre gar keine christliche Religion."

[12] VPR IV, 35 (k): "Diese Religion also ist die offenbare . . . Sie ist Religion des Geistes und nicht das Geheime, nicht verschlossen, sondern offenbar und bestimmt . . . Der Geist ist dies, sich selbst zu erscheinen." VPR I, 201 (k): "In der christlichen Religion ist kein Geheimnis mehr . . ."

[13] VPR IV, 25 (k): "Wer solche Vorurteile im Kopf hat, wie muss der die Bibel verdrehen! Das bringt man hinzu, obwohl die christlichen Religion gerade dies ist, Gott zu erkennen, und die Religion sogar, in der Gott sich geoffenbart, gesagt hat, was er ist."

[14] VPR IV, 32 (g): "Die christlichen Religion ist auf diese Weise die Religion der Offenbarung. In Ihr ist es offenbar, was Gott ist, dass er gewusst werde, wie er ist . . ."

[15] VPR IV, 33 (g): "Gott ist [aber da, d.h. in anderen Religionen] noch etwas anderes als das, [als] was er sich offenbart. Eine Notwendigkeit [steht] über den Göttern. Gott ist das Innere und Unbekannte . . ."

spirit . . . Ultimate reality is, then, and not till then, known as spirit when it is seen and beheld as immediate self-consciousness.[16]

In the Berlin lectures Hegel speaks in more public terms. By revealing himself God becomes the explicitly manifest, in whom nothing hidden remains any longer. God brings to appearance just what he is.[17] Indeed, the manner in which he appears in Christian revelation is not separate from what that revelation shows him to be:

The revealing manifestation is the characteristic and content itself, namely, revelation, manifestation, being for consciousness . . . .[18]

God, then, *is his revelation*,[19] for in revealing himself God is actually living his "interior" life. His appearing and his reality are one. According to Hegel, such an equivalence is implicit in the very notion of God as spirit:

Self-manifestation belongs to the very essence of spirit. Ein Geist der nicht offenbar ist, ist nicht Geist.[20]

As spirit, then, God is committed by his nature to the total manifestation of his inner being, for his act of revealing *is* his act of living and being. The Christian revelation is wholly adequate as epistemic manifestation. Nothing of God remains, in principle, unknown.

Hegel's understanding of the nature of Christian revelation is open to criticism and has received its share.[21] Moreover, it is not uninfluenced by his own search for systematic rational completeness which he is pleased to take up from the Greek philosophers. To insist upon the fullness of religious revelation is not, to be sure, to guarantee full comprehension in philosophy; but Hegel seems to have formulated his doctrine of the notion

[16] *Phänomenologie des Geistes* (herausg. v. J. Hoffmeister), Hamburg (F. Meiner) 1952. The translation above is by J. B. Baillie, *Hegel's Phenomenology of Mind*, (rev. 1931), New York (Macmillan) 1955. Hereafter PdG with reference to the German pagination, and B as key for the Baillie translation. Thus, here, PdG 529B760. Italics above are mine.
[17] VPR I, 205-06 (k): "Gott dadurch sich offenbarend, der Offenbare für sich selbst wird. Dann ist nichts verborgenes mehr in ihm; was Gott ist, hat er zur Erscheinung gebracht. Seine ganze Natur ist in die Erscheinung hinaus . . ."
[18] VPR IV, 32 (g): "Die offenbare Manifestation ist ihre Bestimmung und Inhalt selbst, nämlich Offenbarung, Manifestation, Sein für das Bewusstsein . . ."
[19] VPR. I. 200 (k): "Gott ist dies, sich zu offenbaren, offenbar zu sein. Diejenigen, die sagen, dass Gott nicht offenbar sei, sprechen ohnehin nicht aus der christlichen Religion heraus; denn die christliche Religion heisst die geoffenbarte. Ihr Inhalt ist, dass Gott den Menschen geoffenbart sei, dass sie wissen, was Gott ist. Vorher wussten sie es nicht; aber in der christlichen Religion ist kein Geheimnis mehr . . ."
[20] VPR IV, 35 (k). Bruaire, LRC, p. 27, speaks of "autology."
[21] See, for example, the stringent criticisms of Otto Kühler, *Sinn, Bedeutung und Auslegung der Heiligen Schrift in Hegels Philosophie*, Leipzig 1934.

(*Begriff*) at least as much in answer to a demand uttered by Christian revelation as by Greek science. For Hegel sees in the Christian revelation the mandate and even the demand to go beyond that revelation in its given form. The need to transform religion into philosophy arises from religion itself.[22] Indeed, the *Logik* and the *Realphilosophie*, taken as broad divisions of his philosophy, find their echoes in the religious imagery of God, on the one hand, in his eternal being (*Logik*) and, on the other, as creator of and reconciler in the world (*Realphilosophie*). In the introduction to the *Logik* he tells us that the realm of pure thought manifests the truth without any veil, adding that such a fully articulated content presents God so to speak as he is in his eternal essence.[23] Parallel to the religious error of thinking that God's essence remains unrevealed is the "usual" error which an abstract and superficial reflection commits, viz. that of taking as essential what is alleged to be merely inner.[24]

Nothing seems more certain than that in insisting upon the openness of revelation Hegel assumes the adequacy of language to express even the essential life to God. To be sure, Hegel complains often about the inadequacy of linguistic formulae,[25] but he thinks that this inadequacy can be overcome by a careful dialectical reflection. At an earlier time, and with less developed content, a certain adequacy of expression was already attained:

For the Greeks the highest could be spoken and was spoken in their art.[26]

Hegel also seems confident of attaining an adequacy of expression and content:

For Hegel, too, unlike the [modern] artist the highest could be spoken, but the language of this utterance was not art but philosophy.[26]

[22] *Hegel's Lectures on the History of Philosophy* (tr. Haldane and Simson), London 1896 (1968), III, p. 2: "Within Christianity the basis of philosophy is that in man has sprung up the consciousness of the truth, or of spirit in and for itself, and then that man requires to participate in this truth." Hereafter LHP. Cf. Chapelle, HR I, 107.

[23] *Wissenschaft der Logik* (herausg. v. G. Lasson 1934), Hamburg (F. Meiner) 1967, I, 31: "Die Logik ist sonach als das System der reinen Vernunft, als das Reich des reinen Gedankens zu fassen. Dieses Reich ist die Wahrheit, wie sie *ohne Hülle* an und für sich selbst ist. Man kann sich deswegen ausdrücken, dass dieser Inhalt die Darstellung Gottes ist, wie er in seinem ewigen Wesen vor der Erschaffung der Natur und eines endlichen Geistes ist." Hereafter WdL. English translations 1) by A. V. Miller, *Hegel's Science of Logic*, New York (Humanities) 1969, p. 50; 2) by W. H. Johnston and L. G. Struthers, *Hegel's Science of Logic*, New York (Macmillan) 2 vols. (1929) 1951, I, 60.

[24] *Enzyk.* # 140: "Es ist der gewöhnliche Irrtum der Reflexion, das *Wesen* als das bloss *Innere* zu nehmen. Wenn es bloss so genommen wird, so ist auch diese Betrachtung eine ganz *äusserliche* und jenes Wesen die leere äusserliche Abstraktion."

[25] For example, WdL I, 76 on the inadequacy of the propositional form to express speculative truths.

[26] J. Glenn Gray, *Hegel and Greek Thought* (1941), Harper 1968, p. 52. Hereafter HGT.

Indeed, one may suspect that his problem seemed somewhat easier to him to the degree to which he made no clear distinction between specific speech and speech about the totality; or rather, both seem to be treated by him as of pretty much the same order as far as the character of speech is concerned. Moreover, he exhibits a readiness to dispense with the sensuous element. Thus, in preferring the Aristotelian concept to the Platonic use of myth to express what escapes logical expression in his philosophy, Hegel remarks of Plato that

the myth belongs to the pedagogic stage (*Pädagogie*) of the human race ... When the concept has developed it no longer needs the myth.[27]

Nevertheless, we must be careful in interpreting such remarks. An abstract Aristotelian concept, for example, can do without much that his own concrete *Begriff* may need. Just how far Hegel can dispense with the sensuous in his reconciliation of meaning and existence is, perhaps, *the* central Hegelian problem.

Nothing grates more sharply or quaintly upon our ears today than a claim to linguistic and epistemic adequacy, whether it is made on behalf of a religious revelation or a philosophical reflection. Indeed, much of secular thought has reclaimed a sense of the non-lucidity of language, a sense which may break either towards despair over the crisis of meaning or towards a subtle sense of the mysterious. Both often urge a more radical role for the non-cognitive and non-rational than Hegel may have been willing to grant, even though he too recognized various pre-reflective strata of human life. Josef Simon has pointed to Hegel's awareness of the hiddenness (*Verborgenheit*) of the living body's structure in contrast to the pure objectivity proper to abstract understanding.[28] In settling the issue, however, it is necessary to isolate the precise question which is being asked. A determination of the transparency or opacity of speech in general may not help us much to arrive at a determination regarding the adequacy of God's own speech to us, or of our own reflective language about his speech. The *Verborgenheit* arising, for example, from the existential structure of the human body may be an obscurity due, according to Hegel, to sensuousness; and we must still ask what he thinks happens to speech as it makes its way from religious revelation through the pure understanding to the domain of speculative philosophy itself. If there is not a lucid transparency running through ordinary language and pre-philosophical revela-

[27] Gray, HGT, pp. 78-9, who quotes from LHP II, p. 20 with alterations.
[28] *Das Problem der Sprache bei Hegel*, Stuttgart 1966, pp. 51-5, especially 52-3. Clark, LAS, p. 162: "Language is an externality at the heart of thought." Also pp. 185, 202.

tion, does such a transparency at last break forth and recapture the substance of the lower orders once it reaches philosophical speculation? Professor Collins stresses Hegel's sense of adequacy:

Nothing is left mysterious or essentially unsayable about the divine nature.[29]

And Hegel agrees that if something unsayable were left, the revelation might be as complete as *possible*, but that it would not then be the *full* revelation of God's own life as he *actually* lives it. Hegel speaks clearly and forcefully on the issue: The revelation of God in the Christian religion holds back nothing. As the ultimate epistemic manifestation, Christian revelation is exhaustive, and only awaits transformation into the categories of the dialectic.

III. Revelation as Ontological Constitution

We have been examining the act of revelation from the point of view of its disclosure to consciousness. We turn now to look at revelation, not as a manifestation for knowledge, but as an activity of constitution *for being*. The being of spirit is revealed in its own activity of revealing, for it belongs to the nature of spirit to reveal itself to an other.[30] The spiritual need for truth is the need of objectification, according to Hegel, that is, of positing self as object for another consciousness.[31] This must not be looked upon as a deficiency, but as of the very nature of that generosity which characterizes being in its spiritual mode. Now such generosity finds its highest expression in the Christian conception of God revealing. To be sure, this insight into spiritual being is anticipated by some pre-Christian philosophers:

That God is devoid of envy undoubtedly is a great, beautiful, true and childlike thought. With the ancients, on the contrary, we find in Nemesis, Dike, Fate, Jealousy, the one determination of the gods; moved by this they cast down the great and bring it low, and suffer not what is excellent and elevated to exist. The later high-minded philosophers [i.e. Plato and Aristotle] controverted this doctrine [of divine envy].[32]

[29] Collins. *Emergence*, p. 337.

[30] VPR IV, 35 (k): "Aber Gott ist als Geist wesentlich dies, für ein anderes zu sein, sich zu offenbaren . . ."

[31] VPR I, 74 (g): "Die vollendete Religion ist diese, wo der Begriff der Religion zu sich zurückgekehrt ist, – wo die absolute Idee, Gott als Geist nach seiner Wahrheit und Offenbarkeit für das Bewusstsein der Gegenstand ist."

[32] LHP II, 73. See also the Zusatz to Wallace's translation of the *Encyclopedia* # 140: "Those who look upon the essence of nature as mere inwardness, and therefore inaccessible to us, take up the same line as that ancient creed which regarded God as envious and jealous; a creed which both Plato and Aristotle pronounced against long ago. All that God is, he imparts and reveals; and He does so, at first, in and through

What they glimpsed Christian revelation makes explicit.

The divine self-disclosure, nevertheless, has its moment of negativity. To recognize God as spirit is to set aside all attempts to represent him simply as a featureless substantial unity.[33] Beyond this impoverished natural sense of divinity we come at last to a disclosure which presupposes and includes within it the distinctions of subjective and objective consciousness. Within this disclosure religion moves towards its fulfillment in Christian revelation.[34] We cannot here follow the elaborations of the dialogue between divine and human consciousness in which the spiritual nature of both is finally revealed; but what we wish to recall is that in the dialogue a process of distancing and recovery is under way.[35] In it we overcome, on the one hand, the pure immediacy of a consciousness sunk in itself and therefore not yet aware of itself as a self, and, on the other, we overcome the pure immediacy of a divinity which is merely a natural force. The lesson we learn is that spirit is not immediacy, and that everything spiritual is touched by absence, distance, death and the power of the negative. Thus, for example, the first appearance of Christ on earth is a relatively immediate one, and before he can realize his spiritual presence, he must die, and having risen must still go to the father who is in heaven.[36]

This distancing is also a sort of doubling, in which spirit doubles itself so as to include the moments of the religious essence: singularity and universality, inwardness and outwardness, the subjective and objective, the finite and infinite. God and man meet one another in religion only as spiritual beings; for religion teaches that to the spirit only the spirit speaks:

nature." Total revelation, of course, only comes in the Christian religion, and total comprehension of it only in Hegel's philosophy.

[33] VPR I, 198 (k): "Gott ist das Eine, absolut bei sich selbst Bleibende; in der Substanz ist kein Unterschied." Bruaire, LRC, p. 20, remarks that to cling to such an indeterminate unity is not pantheism but atheism.

[34] VPR I, 199-200 (k): "Das Erste in dem Begriff der Religion ist diese göttliche Allgemeinheit, der Geist ganz in seiner unbestimmten Allgemeinheit für den durchaus kein Unterschied ist. Das Zweite nach dieser absoluten Grundlage ist der Unterschied überhaupt, und erst mit dem Unterschiede fängt Religion als solche an. Dieser Unterschied ist ein geistiger Unterschied, ist bewusstsein ... So haben wir den Standpunkt, hier erst haben wir zwei, Gott und das Bewusstsein, für das er ist."
dass Gott — Gott in dieser Unbestimmtheit überhaupt — Gegenstand des Bewusstseins ist,

[35] VPR IV, 62 (g): "Gott an sich nach seinem Begriff ist die unendlich sich dirimierende und in sich zurückkehrende Macht; so ist er dies nur als die sich unendlich auf sich selbst beziehende Negativität, d.i. die absolute Reflexion in sich, was schon die Bestimmung des *Geistes* ist."

[36] PdG 531B762: "He is the *immediately* present God; in consequence, His being passes over into His *having been*. Consciousness, for which God is thus sensuously present, ceases to see Him, to hear Him: it *has* seen Him, it *has* heard Him. And it is because it only *has* seen and heard Him, that it first becomes itself spiritual consciousness."

Only the relation of spirit to spirit is religion.[37]
Der Geist nur ist für den Geist.[38]

We are speaking here primarily and throughout of the fullest expression of the religious notion, that is, of absolute revealed religion, Christianity. In it spirit is just this mutuality of self-conscious being. The distancing and doubling, therefore, confirms the shared identity of the participants in the religious drama. It shows how the individual and universal in the spiritual world are inseparable, and how the primordial identity of man and God, finite and infinite, comprises the essence of religion. The distancing and doubling, therefore, is an explicit recovery of the character of spirit itself:

Spirit is the divine history, the process of self-distinction, diremption and the recovery of self.[39]

In the *Phänomenologie* Hegel had already described spirit as

the process of retaining identity with itself in its otherness.[40]

In the Berlin lectures the Biblical characterization of God as Love is taken to illustrate the way in which each consciousness, divine and human, may find itself in the being of the other even while it preserves the reality of each consciousness. The dogma of the Trinity, however, has unique revelatory power, for through it the essential process of spirit is demonstrated at the level of divinity. On the one hand, it raises the moment of difference and expresses it as the infinite singularity of each of the divine persons; and on the other, it reaffirms the unity of that Love which is the discourse between the substantive Father and the differentiated Son, an infinite Love which realizes itself in constituting the person of the Holy Spirit. In order to appreciate this religious image, we trace out with Hegel the sense of unity implicit within it:

---

[37] VPR IV, 14 (k): "Nur das Verhältnis des Geistes zum Geist ist Religion; so ist sich die Religion objecktiv geworden, indem der Gegenstand des endlichen Bewusstseins gewusst wird als der Geist, und so wird er nur gewusst, insofern das Allgemeine, – diese eine Substanz, die absolute Wesenheit, Wahrheit ist, – auch absolute Macht ist, in der alles als organisch gesetzt, ein Negiertes ist, die aber nicht nur als Substanz, sondern als Subjekt ist."

[38] VPR IV, 15 (k): "Es ist unzertrennlich der allgemeine und der einzelne Geist, der unendliche und der endliche; ihre absolute Identität ist die Religion." And earlier: "Der Geist ist identisch mit dem Geiste. Dies ist der Begriff der Religion."

[39] VPR IV, 65 (k): "Geist ist die göttliche Geschichte, der Prozess des sich Unterscheidens, Dirimierens und dies in sich Zurücknehmens."

[40]. PdG 528B758.

[1] God is one, at first [as] universal, [i.e. as an immediate and undifferentiated unity]. [2] God is love, [and while] he remains one, [he is] nevertheless more than [this simple] unity; [he is more] than immediate identity, not [however] as [a mere] negative reflection into himself [i.e. he is not simply the reflective withdrawal into a second immediate identity]. [3] God is spirit; [he is] one as infinite subjectivity, one in the infinite subjectivity of the distinction [which holds among the divine persons].[41]

The dogma of the Trinity, then, serves as paradigm for understanding the Hegelian spirit. Love is the recovery of what self is, a recovery achieved through losing oneself in the other, while at the same time maintaining and developing self-recognition and self-certainty. Trinitarian love is the process of objectification and subjectification at the apex of pure Being. It traffics in the exchange among infinite personalities. It is a process of divine othering and selving which is ontologically constitutive. Of course, it is God's very activity of self-knowing, but the usual senses of the term "knowing" may obscure Hegel's proper meaning. "Knowing" is the name we give to the way in which selving and othering goes on at a certain level of recovery, viz. that involving persons. Such a process of knowing and loving, however, is obscured if it is apprehended primarily as a psychological event, in which the involved consciousnesses undergo an experience. It is, rather, an *ontological* process through which being and non-being, positivity and negativity, unity and difference co-determine themselves in ways that bring both their singularity and difference, on the one hand, and their universality and identity, on the other, to the peak of pure constitutive reciprocity.[42]

IV. Negative Forms of Mystery, Representation and Abstract Thought

Christian revelation is both epistemic manifestation and ontological constitution; but the form or manner in which revelation manifests its constitutive spiritual content needs philosophical conceptualization. Without it, it will fall prey to distortions and inadequacies. These may arise from the original dogmatic representation given by the religion itself, or out of attempts of an abstract theological or philosophical sort to intellectualize that content. The major deficiency may be exhibitied in the following

[41] VPR IV, 57 (g). Insertions within the brackets are mine. The German text reads: "Gott ist Einer, das Allgemeine zunächst. Gott ist die Liebe, bleibt Einer, [ist] aber mehr als Einheit, als unmittelbare Identität, nicht als negative Reflexion in sich. Gott ist Geist, Einer als unendliche Subjektivität, Einer in der unendlichen Subjektivität des Unterschiedes."
[42] VPR IV, 11 (k): "... die absolute unendliche Subjektivität... Die unendliche Form ist der Kreislauf dieses Bestimmens; der Begriff ist Geist nur, indem er sich durch diesen Kreislauf hindurch bestimmt, ihn durchlaufen hat. So erst ist er das Konkrete." Cf. Clark, LAS, p. 19. Also VPR IV, 33ff. (g).

ways: 1) The content is merely given and the believer merely passive. 2)
Belief and believed-in, therefore, rest upon a merely contingent basis.
3) Moreover, only an external relational (i.e. relative) understanding of
God is reached. 4) No intrinsic unity is preserved. 5) An unknowable
Transcendent is introduced, which 6) dissolves into indeterminacy. And so,
finally 7), God and man are both reduced to finite and mutually exclusive
entities.

1) The content is merely given and the believer merely passive. The
teachings of Christianity are given in the form of a positive religion, i.e.
they come to us from outside.[43] *2) They appear, therefore, as extraneous
and contingent.* For example, the Incarnation is in truth a profound step
in the reconciliation of man with God, and yet it appears in the form of a
contingent event.[44] There is something inaccessible to reason in such an
irreducible existent, and what is irreducible remains untrue.[45] Comment-
ing upon the modern interest in subjectivity, not without appreciation and
even a certain irony, Hegel notices an instability in the structure of religious consciousness. On the one hand, it can pass over into a harmony of
devout and inward feeling, which, however, lacks intellectual content.
On the other, it can turn into a heightened sense of the separation of man
from God. This latter may happen when religious representations are
grasped abstractly by consciousness, so that the true spiritual content slips
away and at least appears to remain over against consciousness in objective form. Then, even the grace of God is thought to be an alien power
at work in the believer who for his part remains in a passive faith-posture.[46]
It is this posture which gives undue weight to miracles, church authority
and the works of man.[47]

[43] VPR IV, 19 (k): "Diese absolute Religion ist ... eine *positive* Religion in dem
Sinne, dass sie dem Menschen von aussen gekommen, ihm gegeben worden ist ... *Es
muss alles auf äusserliche Weise an uns kommen.*" It comes from God but appears
as from outside us, and so Hegel is led to distinguish between the merely positive and
that which contains a rational spiritual kernel in positive form (VPR IV, 20). Cf.
LPR II, 336ff.

[44] Cf. Chapelle, HR I, 162: "Si la foi proclame leur réconciliation, le Dieu justifiant
n'apparait, des lors, que dans la contingence finie de l'Incarnation, dans une revelation
mystérieuse, irreductible à la raison de l'homme qu'elle béatifie."

[45] Cf. WdL I, 138: "Das Unwahre ist das Unerreichbare." Also Bruaire LRC, p. 35.

[46] VPR IV, 16-17 (k): "Die Religion ist in der abstrakten Bestimmung des Bewusstseins so beschaffen, dass der Inhalt hinüberflieht und wenigstens scheinbar ein ferner
bleibt. Bewusstsein ist, dass mein Gegenstand ein Selbständiges ist, als ein anderes
gegenüber mir bestimmt ist, z.B. Berg, Sonne, Himmel. Die Religion mag einen Inhalt
haben, welchen sie will; festgehalten auf dem Standpunkte des Bewusstseins ist ihr
Inhalt ein solcher, der drüben steht, und wenn auch die Bestimmung von übernatürlicher
Offenbarung dazukommt, so ist der Inhalt doch schlechterdings wieder ein gegebener
und äusserlicher für uns ... Der Geist, die Gnade Gottes wohnt im Menschen, sagt
man, und denkt sich dabei, dass sie so ein Fremdes sei, dass er sich gefallen lassen muss,
ein Fremdes, das in ihm wirkt, zu dem er sich passiv verhält." Cf. LPR II, 330ff.

[47] On miracles, for example, see VPR IV, 21 (LPR II, 338). For his critique of

3) Only an external and relational understanding of God is reached.
An appeal to an immediate form of religious experience insists that we
can know only our relation to God within religious experience, and that
we cannot know his nature.[48] When abstract theology attempts to explain
the Biblical imagery, on the other hand, its interpretations rest upon presuppositions which are not themselves to be found in the words of the
Bible.[49] And even more removed from the given religious representation,
when metaphysical or natural theology describes God in terms of abstract
attributes, taken statically as predicates, each of them is distinguished from
the others in such a way that, although meant to become infinite, they
remain finite. Indeed, in their abstract form they express only relations
which we bear to God, and so they leave his nature unknown.[50] When
philosophy or theology proceed in this way, they frame a representation

church authority, for example, see his treatment of the Middle Ages in his *Philosophy
of History.*
   [48] VPR I, 50-51 (k): "Zugleich aber liegt in der Behauptung des unmittelbaren
Wissens, dass wir bei der Betrachtung der Religion als solcher, näher bei der Betrachtung dieser Beziehung auf Gott stehen bleiben sollen. Es soll nicht fortgegangen werden
zum Erkennen Gottes, zum göttlichen Inhalte, wie dieser Inhalt göttlich, in ihm selbst
wesentlich wäre. In diesem Sinne wird weiter gesagt, wir können nur unsere Beziehung
zu Gott wissen, nicht, was Gott selbst ist; nur unsere Beziehung falle in das, was
Religion überhaupt heisst. Damit geschieht es, dass wir heutigen Tages nur von Religion sprechen hören, aber keine Untersuchungen finden, was die Natur Gottes, was
Gott in ihm selbst sei, wie seine Natur bestimmt werden müsse."
   [49] VPR IV, 24-5 (k): "Sobald nun aber die Religion nicht bloss Lesen und Wieder-
holen der Sprüche ist, sobald das sogenannte Erklären anfängt, Schliessen, Exegesieren,
was die Worte der Bibel zu bedeuten haben, so tritt der Mensch ins Räsonnieren, Re-
flecktieren, ins Denken über, und da kommt es darauf an, wie er sich in seinem Denken
verhalte, ob sein Denken richtig ist oder nicht. Es hilft nichts, zu sagen, diese Gedanken
seien auf die Bibel gegründet. Sobald sie nicht mehr bloss die Worte der Bibel sind,
ist diesem Inhalt eine Form, bestimmter eine logische Form gegeben. Oder es werden
bei ihm gewisse Voraussetzungen gemacht, und mit diesen wird an die Erklärung
Vorstellungen mit, die das Erklären leiten. Die Erklärung der Bibel zeigt den Inhalt der
Bibel je in der Form einer jeden Zeit; das erste Erklären in den Anfangszeiten der
Kirche war ganz anders als der jetzige. Zu solchen Voraussetzungen, die man heut an
die Bibel heranbringt, gehören z.B. die Vorstellungen von der Natur des Menschen, dass
er von Natur gut sei, oder von Gott, dass man Gott nicht erkennen könne."
   [50] VPR IV, 54-55 (g): "Indem es Bestimmungen sind, [sind sie] verschieden von-
einander, obgleich unendliches Sein *sensu eminentiori, excellenti,* aber [sie] sind
bestimmt, somit endlich, und dies wird so gesagt, dass sie nur Beziehungen von uns auf
Gott ausdrücken, nicht aber seine Natur, die somit, da keine Weise sonst, sie zu ex-
plizieren, vorhanden sei als durch jene Prädikate, uns unbekannt, unerklärt sei." Again,
VPR IV, 75-76 (k): "Wenn von Gott gesprochen wird, was Gott ist, so werden zunächst die Eigenschaften angegeben: Gott ist das und das; er wird durch *Prädikate*
bestimmt. Dies ist die Weise der Vorstellung, des Verstandes. Prädikate sind Bestimmt-
heiten, Besonderungen: Gerechtigkeit, Güte, Allmacht, usf... Das eigentlich Mangel-
hafte dieser Weise, durch Prädikate zu bestimmen, besteht darin, wodurch eben jene
unendliche Menge von Prädikaten kommt, dass sie nur besondere Bestimmungen und
dass es viele solcher Bestimmungen sind, deren aller Träger das Subjekt ist. Indem es
besondere Bestimmungen sind und man diese Besonderheiten nach ihrer Bestimmtheit
betrachtet, sie denkt, geraten sie in Entgegensetzung, Widerspruch, und diese Wider-
sprüche bleiben dann unaufgelöst." Only in the speculative idea will they be resolved.

of God and his relation to the world which is ultimately incomprehensible, a result that is satisfying to those who want to know nothing of the nature of God.[51]

4) No intrinsic unity is preserved in the conception of God. Such a manner of representation, in which we speak of God's properties as indeterminately determinate, as when we say that God is all-just, all-wise, all-merciful, – such a way of speaking illustrates an imperfect form of reflective thought which leaves unresolved the conflict among the distinct and even incompatible predicates. Now the Living God cannot be reached in this way, for

he is absolute activity, actuality, and his activity is to eternally reconcile the contradiction.[52]

Instead, in the form of representational thinking we lose the unity of God within himself and in his relation to the world. Thus, for example, God's creative act is seen as a single occurrence, when in truth it is eternally occurring.[53] It is impossible for representational thinking to reconcile the manifold of determinate perfections with the divine simplicity attributed to God.[54] Erik Schmidt rightly remarks that Hegel's objection to representational thinking is not that it is anthropomorphic but that it explodes God's unitary essence.[55]

5) An unknowable Transcendent is introduced. In the *Phänomenologie* Hegel had remarked that religious representation still encumbered spiritual life with an unreconciled diremption into a "here" and a "beyond." [56] Such a representation is taken as pointing to that which lies beyond human

[51] *Enzykl.* # 573, especially p. 459.
[52] VPR. IV, 13 (k): "Wir sind gewöhnt, von Gott zu sagen: Gott ist der Schöpfer der Welt, er ist allgerecht, allwissen, allweise ... Dies aber ist nicht das wahrhafte Erkennen dessen, was die Wahrheit, was Gott ist; es ist die Weise des Vorstellens, des Verstandes ... ein reflecktierendes, unvollkommenes Denken, nicht Denken durch den Begriff ... Die Lebendigkeit Gottes oder des Geistes ist nichts weiter als sich zu bestimmen ... Das ist das Leben, das Tun, die Tätigkeit Gottes; er ist absolute Tätigkeit, Aktuosität, und seine Tätigkeit ist, den Widerspruch ewig zu versöhnen: das ist er selbst."
[53] VPR IV, 32-33 (g): "Gott hat die Welt erschaffen, sich geoffenbart usf. [Dieser] Anfang [gilt] als *getan*, d.i. als ein einziger Aktus, einmal, dann nicht wieder. [Gottes] ewiger Ratschluss [wird] als [einmaliges Tun] des Wollens, so als Willkür [vorgestellt, und also nicht wahrhaft], sondern dies ist seine ewige Natur."
[54] At another level, cf. Hegel's criticism of Spinoza's reflection in WdL II, 164ff. (Miller, p. 536ff.; Johnston and Struthers, II, 167ff.).
[55] HLG, pp. 142-4: "Nicht dagegen hat Hegel Bedenken, dass die Eigenschaften Gottes anthropomorph erscheinen, sondern dagegen, dass sie Gottes einheitliches Wesen sprengen." Only the true infinity can save this unity in a determinate form. See pp. 150-154, especially: "Hat Gott das Endliche nicht an ihm, so steht es ihm selbständig gegenüber, und dann ist die Unendlichkeit Gottes eine schlechte Unendlichkeit und Gott ist selbst endlich und beschränkt."
[56] PdG 532B763-4.

thought in a region of impenetrable darkness.[57] 6) *This hidden realm remains indeterminate.* It would be quite misleading, of course, not to recall the growing sense of inwardness to which Hegel attributes great importance and which culminates in the Protestant principle of the immanentizing of truth. Jacob Boehme, perhaps surprisingly when one remembers Hegel's tastes, receives a very sympathetic consideration because

what marks him out and makes him noteworthy is the Protestant principle already mentioned of placing the intellectual world within one's own mind and heart, and of experiencing and knowing and feeling in one's own self-consciousness all that formerly was conceived as Beyond . . . This solid, deep, German mind which has intercourse with what is most inward . . .[58]

Nevertheless, inwardness is not in itself satisfactory, for driven to its most inward it would lapse into indeterminacy.[59] The tendency towards indeterminacy of both a transcendent and an immanent sort is a counter-thrust within the religious enterprise that resists the specifically Christian demand for a fully determinate revelation of the Godhead. Indeed, the lapse into indeterminacy is properly pre-Christian. It is not the revelation of the Living God, but a fantasy with merely subjective worth, a dead and empty God.[60] So the Christian as well as the philosopher is challenged by Hegel to give up this age-old prejudice [61] in order to take seriously the revelatory significance of the Christian religion. The prejudice consists, when all is said, in supposing that we save the transcendence of God by denying all language to him, so that he reveals nothing essential about himself, In addition, an efficacious language is thereby denied to us when we wish to speak to him or about him, so that in that event we have nothing to say.

---

[57] VPR IV, 83 (k): Speaking of the gradual development of the Idea, and having discussed the wild yet explicable speculations of the Gnostics, Hegel concludes: "Diese Idee nämlich ist eigentlich jenseits des Menschen, des Gedankens, der Vernunft gestellt worden und zwar so gegenübergestellt, dass diese Bestimmung, die alle Wahrheit und allein die Wahrheit ist, als etwas nur Gott Eigenttümliches, jenseits stehen Bleibendes betrachtet worden ist . . ."

[58] LHP III, 191, 193. Of course, Hegel considers Boehme's method "barbarous."

[59] Nor is symbolism an adequate outer expression, for religious symbols are flawed, according to Hegel, by a certain disproportion between an inner content and its outer expression. Cf. WdL II, 59. There remains always an indefinable ambiguity inherent in the "degeneration" of the genuinely speculative truth contained in religion into sensuous representations, for men must not have to wait until philosophy to acquire a spiritual life! Cf. *Enzykl.* # 573.

[60] Hegel sees quite clearly that if indeterminateness is taken as exclusive of determinateness, and if what *we* call negative theology were to hold to such indeterminateness in the Absolute, then all determinations, all discourse, would have to fall back upon the subjective. Thus VPR I, 143 (k): "Fehlt nämlich dem Allgemeinen die Bestimmung, so fällt alle Bestimmtheit in das Ich, das nun das Setzende wird, alle Tätigkeit und Lebendigkeit erhält, während der Gott das leere, tote, das sogenannte höchste Wesen wird und eben durch diese Leerkeit eine nur subjektive Vorstellung bleibt."

[61] Cf. Bruaire, LRC, p. 14.

This reduces God to an indifferent and purely external non-entity. A dead God is surely not a transcendence worth keeping.[62]

7) *Finally, the divine and human are both reduced to finite and mutually exclusive beings.* Perhaps the most dramatic and fundamental denial of man's cognitive access to ultimate reality has been formulated in the philosophy of Kant, a philosopher who in Hegel's eyes glimpsed the character of philosophical conceptualization but remained fixed within the abstract categories of the understanding. Following upon him it would be tempting to lodge an unknowable God in the region of the unknowable thing-in-itself. It is clear to Hegel, however, that any appeal to an unknowable thing-in-itself would be a relapse into the finite, so that religious man would then find himself closed within a finite order, phenomenal and ultimately subjective, an order of abstract categories of the understanding, on the one hand, or of vague religious sentiment on the other.[63] Pressed to its furthest, such an isolating reflection would pursue the logic of exclusion so that in the end the infinite would be reduced to one finite extreme set over against the finite itself. The unknowable God, then, would become wholly alien to man, wholly negative and entirely indeterminate. The religious understanding could find no names with which to name him.[64] We recognize such an indeterminate infinite in the pages of the *Logik*, where it is called the spurious infinite, spurious because it is simply the negative reciprocal of a finitude which is itself false and inadequate. Both belong within the same order, an order in which the true God cannot live. Even man cannot live there, for he too is constituted of infinite and finite,[65] just as God includes within his own essence the moment of finitude.[66]

We have explored the crevices in the lower levels of the Hegelian system to see whether we might legitimately lodge a negative sense of

---

[62] Cf. Clark, LAS, p. 19: "For Hegel there can be no ineffable, no 'beyond' to all words that try to express it."

[63] As, for example, rationalist theologians of the Enlightenment, on the one hand, and Jacobi, on the other.

[64] Cf. Bruaire, LRC, p. 48ff.

[65] See K. L. Schmitz, "Hegel's Philosophy of Religion: Typology and Strategy," *Review of Metaphysics* (Hegel issue) June 1970.

[66] VPR IV, 7 (k): Fully conscious of being misunderstood as holding a phantheistic confusion of God and man, Hegel speaks of the relation of finite and infinite in the self-distinction that constitutes spirit: "[Der Geist] muss die Bestimmung der Endlichkeit an sich selbst haben, – das kann blasphemisch aussehen. Hat er es aber nicht an ihm, so hat er die Endlichkeit sich gegenüber auf der andern Seite, und dann ist seine Unendlichkeit eine schlechte Unendlichkeit. Wenn man die Bestimmung der Endlichkeit als etwas ansieht, das Gott widersprechend sei, so nimmt man das Endliche als etwas Fixes, Selbständiges, nicht als Vorübergehendes, sondern als ein solches, das wesentlich selbständig ist, eine Beschränkung, die schlechthin Beschränkung bleibt ... Wenn Gott das Endliche sich nur gegenüber hat, so ist er selbst endlich und beschränkt."

religious mystery there. If it were to gain a foothold, such a mystery would live on the negativity within the system as a sort of justified ignorance. As Hegel understands it, however, such a sense of mystery would be simply residual. We have indicated Hegel's moves to block up such crevices, or more accurately, to insist that there is no soil there for a consistent and valid rooting of mystery. Mystery as residue yields external relations within God and between God and the world; and in that gap between his nature and his relations, Hegel reads not genuine mystery but the failure to integrate multiple determinations with the divine unity. Any attempt to posit an interior hiddenness or a transcendent beyond ends in the loss of all determinateness and reduces religious revelation to a merely positive claim which sets man and God opposite one another as false finite to false infinite. If it is to survive in the final resolution as more than the element of arbitrariness and extreme particularity, mystery cannot mean the fallout of a too sensuous or too abstract apprehension of religious revelation.

V. Religious Mystery and Speculative Truth

Having seen what Hegel rejects, we turn now to trace the sense in which he accepts religious mystery. Basing his remarks principally upon ancient Greek, Neo-platonic and early Christian views, Hegel distinguishes the mystery of God (*Mysterium Gottes*) from the claim that God is unknowable. A mystery is a secret teaching known only to the devotees. If, as with the Eleusinian mysteries, a great many know them, they are still treated in a reverent manner and are not discussed in ordinary non-cultic situations. The important point is that the secret is not in itself incomprehensible; on the contrary, it is essentially something known.[67] Nevertheless, Hegel cautions us not to look to the Greek mystery cults for profound wisdom. Socrates knew better.[68] The Neo-platonists also used the word to designate the process of initiation into their own mystical speculative philosophy, and did not mean by it something unknowable.[69] So, too, the Christian mysteries are precisely the distinctive doctrines which

[67] VPR III, 177 (g): "Geheimnis ist wesentlich etwas Gewusstes, aber nicht von allen, hier aber ein Gewusstes von allen, aber als geheim Behandeltes . . . bekannt, aber wovon man nicht spricht." Cf. LPR II, 257-8: "In this religion [of humanity] there is nothing incomprehensible, nothing which cannot be understood; there is no kind of content in the god which is not known to man."
[68] *Philosophie der Geschichte*, Stuttgart (Reclam) 1961 (hrsg. v. F. Brunstäd), p. 350: "Die Mysterien waren vielmehr alte Gottesdienste, und es ist ebenso ungeschichtlich als töricht, tiefe Philosopheme darin finde zu wollen."
[69] VPR IV, 77 (k): "*Mysterion* nämlich ist das, was das Vernünftige ist; bei den Neuplatonikern heisst dieser Ausdruck auch schon nur spekulative Philosophie." LHP II, 448: "Thus Proclus for example says . . .: 'Let us once more obtain initiation into the mysteries (*mystagogian*) of the one.'" Mysticism is just this speculative consideration of Philosophy."

communicate knowledge of God. Quite the contrary to their being secretive, they are manifestive.[70]

As essentially something known, the mystery is something reasonable.
Now what is reasonable is the work of speculative thought and will remain a mystery to sense and understanding. Both of these build up their
representation of the meaning of revelation in terms of enclosed, self-
subsistent entities and their relation. In their representational field, um-
bridged difference is everywhere, and so everything is sculpted in an external manner which quite escapes the interpenetration of opposites that
characterizes speculative reason.[71] The understanding is governed by the
fixity of simple self-identity, an identity which excludes all difference and
opposition. For that reason the concrete process of selving and othering
which constitutes speculative thought must remain mysterious to it. Conceptualization as the reconciliation of opposites appears to the understanding as something inconceivable; and so the speculative and the reasonable
remain unthinkable to it. Moreover, if the speculative and reasonable
comprise what is spiritual, and if God is spirit, then the true nature of
God is indeed unknown and inconceivable to abstract thought.[72]

The true meaning of *religious* mystery, then, is to be found in the *speculative* capacity of religious revelation, and especially in the doctrine of the
trinitarian God. The Trinity is the "mystery of Reason:" [73]

God is spirit, i.e. that which we call the triune God, a pure speculative content,
i.e. the Mysterium of God. God is spirit, absolute activity, *actus purus*, i.e.
subjectivity, infinite personality, infinite distinction of itself from itself.[74]

---

[70] VPR IV, 77 (k): "Ein Geheimnis im gewöhnlichen Sinne ist die Natur Gottes
nicht, in der christlichen Religion am wenigsten." Cf. Chapelle, HR II, 66 (fn. 102):
"Comme chez les néoplatoniciens, le *mysterion* trinitaire est moins le secret interdit
à l'histoire que l'intelligibilité spéculative de sa tradition, de sa mémoire."

[71] VPR IV, 70: "Was für die Vernunft ist, ist für diese kein Geheimnis; in der
christlichen Religion weiss man es. Geheim ist es nur für den Verstand und die sinnliche
Denkungsweise. Da sind die Unterschiede unmittelbar, die sinnlichen Dinge gelten;
es ist die Weise der Äusserlichkeit. Sobald aber Gott als Geist bestimmt ist, so ist die
Äusserlichkeit aufgehoben. Doch ist es ein Mysterium für die Sinne . . ."

[72] VPR IV, 79 (k): "Man nennt es unbegreiflich, aber was unbegreiflich scheint,
ist eben der Begriff selbst, das Spekulative oder dies, dass das Vernünftige gedacht
wird." Cf. *Enzykl.* # 82, Zus. (Wallace trans.), p. 154.

[73] VPR IV, 69 (k): "Die Dreieinigkeit heisst das Mysterium Gottes; der Inhalt ist
mystisch, d.h. spekulativ." For the most extensive and serious consideration of the
Hegelian Trinity in English, see the perceptive study of E. Fackenheim, *The Religious
Dimension in Hegel's Thought*, Bloomington (Indiana University) 1968. See also J.
Splett, *Die Trinitätslehre G. W. F. Hegels*, Freiburg/Br. (K. Alber) 1965. For a criti-
cal view of the work of Chapelle, Bruaire, Splett, Wolf-Dieter Marsch and Traugott
Koch, see the review article of H. Kimmerle, "Zu Hegels Religionsphilosophie," *Phil.
Rundschau*, 15, Jan. 1968, pp. 111-135.

[74] VPR IV, 57 (g): "Gott ist Geist, d.i. das, was wir Dreieinigen Gott heissen, [ein]
rein spekulativer Inhalt, d.i. [das] *Mysterium* Gottes."

The discussion of the coming of spirit to explicit manifestation and constitution in the Trinity is in terms of the elements of speculative thought,[75] and these determine the nature of the opposition. It is not, therefore, the simple opposition of finite and infinite, but is rather the fixing and overcoming of differences which announce themselves at the level of sense and understanding as final and unbridgeable. In this sense, speculative thought is the very process of spirit by which contradictions are resolved; and this is the ultimate mystery.[76] Hegel's claim to the use of the term mystery is less artificial than it at first seems, for we are familiar with the religious use of the term as the *coincidentia oppositorum*, said of religious myths and dogmas. Hegel insists, too, that speculative thought seeks what religious mystery has always proclaimed: the union of all opposites, of man and God in the Incarnation, of mercy and sinner in religious forgiveness, and the like. For Hegel, the Trinity is the paradigm of such a union, for it is the "self-separating unity of absolute opposites," of infinite persons.[77] If speculative thought can run through such a process of opposition and union, it can indeed claim to have caught up with its own presuppositions.[78]

Albert Chapelle takes very seriously Hegel's attribution of mystery to the Trinity, and seeks to understand the speculative truth of such an attribution. His defence is cathartic against any glib characterization of Hegel as a hard-shelled rationalist. His chief concern seems to be with those who would charge Hegel with reducing God to man, the infinite to the finite, and the knowledge of God to the knowledge of man.[79] In the energy and subtlety with which he pursues his defence, Chapelle seems to include a full sense of mystery within the Hegelian Absolute, a sense which in some way is not to do violence to the more traditional meanings

---

[75] Cf. Chapelle, HR II, 62ff., who notes that Hegel displaces the traditional theological terms of generation and procession for the dialectical ones of differentiation and partition.

[76] Cf. LHP III, p. 152: "In Protestantism, on the contrary, the subjective religious principle has been separated from Philosophy, and it is only in Philosophy that it has arisen in its true form again. In this principle the religious content of the Christian Church is thus retained . . ." And p. 165: "Here [in modern as distinct from ancient philosophy] there is a consciousness of an opposition . . . [which] . . . is the main point of interest in the conception of the Christian religion. The bringing about in thought of the reconciliation which is accepted in belief, now constitutes the whole interest of knowledge."

[77] Said of Jacob Boehme's notion of God in LHP III, p. 198.

[78] VPR IV, 22 (k): "Das Zeugnis des Geistes in seiner höchsten Weise ist die Weise der Philosophie, dass der Begriff rein als solcher aus sich ohne Voraussetzungen die Wahrheit entwickelt und entwickelnd erkennt und in und durch diese Entwickelung die Notwendigkeit der Wahrheit einsieht."

[79] See his discussion in HR II, 75-6 and footnotes 141-3. The chief point is that God is the true infinite who is the Measure but who is not himself subject to measure.

of the term. He lodges the claim to mystery in the moment of negativity:

God is then for divine Reason the Mystery whose absolute presence does not exhaust the negativity of absence. God is not only Reason; he is negation of his knowledge and his revelation.[80]

There are two characteristics of this alleged Hegelian mystery of Reason which bear further comment. 1) It is a negative form of mystery, *a mystery of the absence of God* from himself. 2) It is a dialectical form of mystery, a mystery lodged in a moment of the final resolution, *a mystery of the moment.*

1) Since it is the speculative form of negativity, this mystery is unlike the other forms of negative mystery in two respects. First, it is a mystery of an absence which is sublated (*aufgehoben*) by the process of speculative recognition, whereas the previous forms of negative mystery were simple claims or confession of the unknowability of God. Second, it is a mystery of an absence which is absolute, since it is the moment of negativity within the Absolute. Now the moments of the Absolute must surely be themselves absolute, or the famous resolution is simply a patchwork job. Whereas the earlier forms of negative mystery were all relative and reducible to the finite, we are here confronted with the staggering thought of an absolute absence of an absolute presence from itself.[81] In the face of this infinite distance, the problem which seems to have been worrying Chapelle all along, the charge of confusing the divine and human, seems well taken care of!

The divine Logos is thus positively in theological Reason the Transparence of a total identity, at the same time as the Darkness proper to absolute Negativity verifies the divine non-identity of the Mystery of God and of human certitudes.[82]

2) As a dialectical mystery of the moment, it is not simply a moment "within" the final resolution in the sense that it is a part or principle or factor

---

[80] Chapelle HR II, 75: "Dieu est dès lors pour la Raison divine le Mystère dont la présence absolue n'épuise pas la négativité de l'absence. Dieu n'est pas que la Raison; il est négation de sa connaissance et de sa révélation."

[81] This must be one of the strongest interpretations of the "ungeheure, fürchterliche Vorstellung," of the death of Christ: "Gott ist gestorben, Gott *selbst* ist tot." VPR IV, 157-8 (g), italics mine.

[82] Chapelle HR II, 79: "Le Logos divin est ainsi positivement dans la Raison théologique la Transparence d'une identité totale, en même temps que la Ténèbre propre à la Negativité absolue vérifie la non-identité divine du Mystère de Dieu et des certitudes humaines." It is clear from fn. 146 that Chapelle takes this negative mystery to be harmonious with "the idealist conception of the absoluteness of the Absolute and of the negativity of mystical knowledge, [of] speculative knowledge, [which] reawakens the theological categories of Absence and of Distance from man, of the cloud of Unknowing."

in the resolution. That sort of thinking would make the resolution simply a totality of partial moments. We are far beyond the overcoming of the distinction of part and whole, for each moment is now the whole.[83] Nevertheless, unless speech is to lapse into an indeterminacy of nonsense or into silence, there must be interpretive meanings with which to differentiate the role of one moment from the other. In this sense, then, we can say that the whole Absolute is being "mystified" through the moment of its self-absence. Mystery arises in the capacity of the Absolute to be absent from itself. But now we must ask what it might mean for the Absolute to absent itself? And here we see two possible meanings. First, it might mean that it becomes finite, as in the Incarnation, so that when Jesus the Christ died, the Absolute died. This lodges mystery in the distance between finite and infinite, between God and man. However, it can also mean the absence of the Absolute from itself, that eternal process whereby the Absolute recognizes itself in each of its moments. To speak again of the Trinity, mystery would then mean that eternal process whereby each of the divine persons recognizes himself in the others, and recognizes his own otherness in them. It is even more, perhaps; it is that constitutive process whereby the divine persons in their own being pass over into the being of the others in the spiritual identity of their shared being.

This mystery of the negative moment is the mystery of identity-in-difference, of non-being in being, of untruth in truth. It is the farthest reaches of Reason, not because there is more which is inaccessible to it, but because Reason here exhausts all that can possibly be. It is in this sense, then, that the mystery of the negative moment is a dialectical work of speculative reason, *das Vernünftige*. It is the final statement of the Reasonable, and the first. For, I suggest, here in this absolute distance between God and himself, between the persons of the Trinity, the entire movement of the Logic can be cradled. So far can we go with Hegel, it seems to me. But to you, it may seem that we have gone by far too far.

VI. Religious Mystery: Absence and Presence

Throughout most of the essay, and with our own emphasis, we have tried to reconstruct the sense of religious mystery according to Hegel. Towards the end, taking an insight from Albert Chapelle, we have developed a mystery of absolute absence. This is a turn which Hegel does not seem to have taken explicitly. His tone is usually confident and affirmative,[84]

---

[83] WdL II, 138ff. (Miller, p. 513ff.; Johnston and Struthers, II, p. 143ff.).

[84] Although see the closing pages of the Berlin lectures on the philosophy of religion. Each commentator on the *Logik* as well as on the Berlin lectures has to comment upon the threat of a resurgent dualism at the apex of the system. See a discussion of the

whereas the turn taken might appear to imperil the success of the Hegelian enterprise by raising the negative to so great a power that it threatens a new and absolute dualism. Such a threat is implicit in the conception of the Trinity itself. After all, a distinction of absolute persons is an absolute distinction, which must be neither wiped away into an indeterminate ground, nor advanced by the abstract understanding to three distinct gods.[85] Hegel thinks that he has met the threat by sublating the differences as moments of the concept. Where might we begin to probe the efficacy of Hegel's resolution?

The other as negative moment. If criticism is to be entered into, it might best begin by looking at the Hegelian "other," which is construed throughout his philosophy as a "moment" within a process of self-resolving moments. The characteristic movement of Hegel's thought is from the otherness implicit in a multiplicity to its explication in difference. With that explication, difference becomes opposition, that is, the difference of one with respect to an other. The final moment in the hardening of conflict and the beginning of its resolution arrives with the self-contradiction inherent in explicit opposition. The original entity finds itself constituted through its opposition, and therefore through its other. With this realization, the conflict moves from an external rebuff of a separate other to an internal conflict within the original entity itself. The dialectic takes the form of exploring every possibility of resolution through the co-constitution of opposed entities until this develops the process of explicit spirituality described earlier. Here the self recognizes its essential being and destiny in its mutuality with the other. Self and other, then, become "moments" in a self-differentiating and self-resolving process.

A question of presence. Hegel called the speculative comprehension of this process of moments the *Mysterium* of God; and we have suggested that an absolute mystery of the negative moment is consonant with his philosophy. It remains to ask: Is there a mystery of presence?

Before we reply, it is necessary to establish the scope of the mystery to which the following remarks are taken to apply. A claim that Being is mysterious is distinct from the claim that God is mysterious. The mystery of Being is an intelligible and philosophical claim; the mystery of God is a metaphysical, theological or religious claim to a mysterious being. Fur-

literature on this in Clark, LAS, especially touching Litt, Iljin, Coreth, Gregoire. See also van der Meulen, *op. cit.* and the comments of E. Fackenheim, *op. cit.* concerning the closing pages of VPR.

[85] VPR IV, 71 (k): "Da *scheint* der Widerspruch so weit getrieben, dass keine Auflösung, keine Verwischung der Person möglich ist." Italics mine. The *reality* is, of course, the resolution of this contradiction in the process of spirit, in the *Begriff*.

thermore, the mystery of God may allege that God is mysterious only to man, or that he is also mysterious to himself. Throughout the essay we have directed our attention to the Trinitarian God as revealed in Christianity, and so in order to sketch out a possible mystery of divine presence, we wish to present a strong claim, the claim that God is mysterious not only to man but also in and to himself. To present a claim is not to prove it, of course, but is merely to suggest a line of reflection that might test the efficacy of Hegel's resolution.

A trans-Hegelian power of the negative? As negating the whole process, the moment of absolute negativity poses a threefold option. First, if absolute negativity is understood to be a detailed reversal of all that absolute presence affirms, it can be safely tucked within the final resolution as a moment correlative to affirmation. Second, if absolute negativity is understood to be a collapse of the developed synthesis which spirit has laboured to achieve, such a relapse into absolute indeterminacy will put us at the beginning of the Logic or the Phenomenology, so that we may begin the long climb again. Third, if, however, we understand by absolute negativity a stance of critical reflection which withdraws from the entire process of self-developing moments, then there arises out of the Hegelian dialectic the possibility of a non-dialectical presence. Like the Phoenix from the ashes, so too from absolute negation a new presence may arise which may appropriate for itself other presuppositions than those which sustain the dialectical movement. This presence may bear traces of the dialectic, even as it stands free from it. The third option may seem like a *tour de force* turned against the Hegelian dialectic, but it is, after all, not unlike what has actually happened since Hegel. It is characteristic of the history of philosophy that it breaks free of its prior presuppositions and that it breaks the exclusive claim which a philosophy like Hegel's makes and thereby de-absolutizes it.

The question of indeterminacy. The Hegelian objection to such a "free" spirit, of course, is that it would be indifferent to man unless it were "run through" by him,[86] and that at best it would be externally related to him. For such a charge to be effective, however, we must accept the Hegelian interpretation of what it means to be related to something. The first step in acceptance is to permit Hegel to attribute to the negative a constituting power. Such an attribution already determines the character and possibilities of the other in a definite fashion, so that intelligible being is con-

---

[86] The phrase is meant to capture the methodical ratiocination required to follow the path of the dialectic from moment to moment, stage to stage, and to hold it together.

stituted of internally correlative moments. It follows, then, that there
can be no "other" which does not also fall under the necessity of constitutive correlation. The Trinity comes to be the paradigm of such correlation. The nature of conceptuality (*Begriff*) and the being of spirit (*Prozess*)
is fixed. It is a version of the demand for reciprocity which defines the
ultimate resolution as one of self-recovery and mutual constitution.

If for purposes of critical reflection we can put aside the Hegelian presuppositions, we might then recognize negation but not consider it as that
which needs to be overcome in the form of self-recovery or self-identifica-
tion. Suppose that spirit does not need to recover itself in the other? Or
that it does not need to identify with *its* other? What, after all, is the
force of the "its?" It seems that it is the bond of equals, or more exactly,
of those which equally need each other. A more radical other, "free" from
the burden of correlative constitution, would not be so related. It would
be an Other so radical that its being would not be defined by its "otherness." Such an Other would be radically free and would not need to
occupy its correlative in order to reconstitute and recover itself and its
other.

The question of necessity. Nevertheless, the correlation of moments in
the Hegelian system and their being "run through" *seriatim* was meant to
secure necessity. Even the final negative mystery which appears in the
Hegelian philosophy is a necessity of thought-thinking-being. Certainly,
some sort of necessity seems to be the condition for any philosophical re-
statement of mystery, whether on Hegelian or non-Hegelian grounds.
Mystery as contingent or arbitrary cannot be the foundation of being and
knowledge. On the other hand, if mystery arises through the necessity
of thought-thinking-being, it will have both epistemic and ontological
authenticy. Now, if the Other is freed from the logic of moments, its
necessity too will be of another order than dialectical necessity; and it
remains to suggest what the character of that order might be.

Mystery as determinate actuality of another order. A pre-Hegelian
model may serve to indicate a kind of absolute presence which might be
recovered through the moment of absolute negation. To make the argument cogent, the third option would have to be reduced from a "maybe"
to a "must." That is, the determinated character of mystery here suggested would have to be developed *out of* the absolute negation. One way
would be to recapitulate the whole system in terms of a latent presence in
it.

The history of some religions, to which Hegel also appealed, tells of
the manifestation of the sacred as announcing itself in a way that bespeaks

its compelling existence, a unique sort of necessity which is not incompatible with a certain appearance of arbitrariness that confirms the absolute status of its presence. Reflecting upon such experience, metaphysical theology among Jews, Christians and Moslems came to attribute to the holy God a *mystery of excellence*. He was figured as a too bright light for clear sight, a too precious good to be measured or weighed. This central conviction characteristic of a certain classical understanding of these theistic faiths offers us a distinction between what I might call mystification and mystery. A state of mystification rises out of the darkness of ignorance due to the weakness of our faculties, the poverty of the object or the obscurity of the medium. Mystery, on the other hand, arises out of the light of knowledge in the presence of that which excels and outstrips every effort to "run it through," to define it in concepts or to embody it in words. The Hegelian dialectic may purge the presuppositions underlying the metaphysical theology associated with this sort of mystery, but that in itself does not invalidate its testimony to an extraordinary presence. Such a mode of mystery would point to a peak of actuality, seen not as the assertion of contingent particular existence from below, but as a transparency, a luminosity, a necessary existence from on high. Such a presence would not be apprehended as indeterminate in the Hegelian sense, but its determinacy would be of an order of actuality that stands free from all conceptual moments. Concepts would not comprehend it, but merely open out towards it.[87] God would exceed all predicates and outstrip all moments. Mystery, inseparable from his presence, would manifest itself as power, abundance, openness, apprehended either through a religious faith or through an intellectual reflection. As with the Hegelian spirit, so too with this mysterious God, his mystery would be both his act of revealing and his act of being, so that God would not be mysterious simply for us. "Mystery" would be the name of God and his way of being present to himself.

Mystery as trans-verbal, trans-conceptual presence-in-absence. When those who assent to the mysterious character of God say that he "exceeds" all dogmatic formulas, that he is "more" than Father, "more" than Love, this mysterious excess does not have an ordinary meaning. It is not a "more" that can be filled in by speech that is being held back from crossing an alleged limit. This "more" does not mean that speech about God is "less" than it might be or will sometime be. Just as colour does not restrict flavour, so mystery does not restrict speech. Hegel, of course, might ask whether a spirit can settle for a speech that reaches "less" than total comprehension of all. Those who might uphold a mystery of excellence

---

[87] Obviously, an appropriate theory of meaning is required here.

and defend it on the grounds of religious faith or of thought-thinking-being might reply as follows. Spirit (both in its divine and human forms) has access to the full mystery which is at least implicit in the apprehension of reality and of the sacred. The "more than speech" does not designate a simple lack, but rather a trans-verbal, trans-conceptual mode of presence. Speech is not thereby limited; everything that is sayable of God remains sayable. No propositional truths are withheld. It is, rather, to use Spinoza's term, that speech is infinite in its own order. It is not limited by anything else, and yet it is a determinate mode with its own possibilities. Trans-verbal presence is another determinate mode of being, the mode of silence. Now this silence is not merely a correlative absence of the speech of the dialectic, for it manifests a meaning of its own.[88] Such a silence is not perspectival, but it is determinate and actual. The "more" is not simply negative as though lying out of reach of speech. It is, for example, the unsayable in the religious myth. Now the unsayable is not a simple negative. The "beyond" which remains unsaid and unsayable in the saying of the myth is carefully determinate and carries its own meaning. That determination is not of the same order as the representational or conceptual elements but is even more actual. Indeed, it is the actualizing power of the myth. Whereas for Hegel the Logic is the thoroughly conceptual and comprehensible discourse of God, the negative in the unsayable announces itself as a transforming power and presence of the sacred.[89] Mystery is God's way of being present and a manifestation of a meaning that is trans-propositional. The proponents of the mystery of excellence might reply that, like Hegel's spiritual process, the divine mystery is both the ontological foundation and the epistemic presupposition for all being, knowing and speaking.

The negativity of the third option, through which we first suggested a mystery of excelling presence, is strikingly manifest in the religious myth. For what is there revealed is also hidden from conceptual thought and propositional speech. In revealing himself, God also "hides," – not because he withholds part of himself out of envy or fear, but because his revelation exceeds the capacity to be comprehended. The final word of his manifestation is that he is mysterious. Religious mystery is incomprehensible, because if it were comprehensible it could be "run through." To comprehend something is to "run through" it, to occupy it, to gather it up into a totality. This is what Hegel's discourse does, moving ultima-

---

[88] A theory of religious language is needed here.
[89] For this view of religious myth, see Kenneth L. Schmitz, "The Philosophy of Religion and the Redefinition of Philosophy," *Man and World* (forthcoming).

tely to the absolute. Indeed, a moment is the "other" in the form of being able to be run through. Even Hegel's mystery is *in this sense* comprehensible; and it is just *in this sense* that the mystery of excellence, presence and silence is not. According to the mystery of presence which we are sketching we cannot run through the divine nature to gather it up. This is not because it lies "beyond" a barrier in a unknowable darkness, but because it lies infinitely open. Now it is not only that *we* can't run through God's nature in order to gather it up, but that "gathering up" is always short of the "free" infinite. God cannot gather himself up. God is ultimately incomprehensible to God, not by a failure of knowing but by an excess of a kind of presence that is not a running through.

A selective affinity between thought and images. A philosophical reflection is an interplay between leading ideas and suggestive images, and so a philosophy draws towards itself those images towards which it is drawn. The mystery of presence sketched out above draws its own images towards it. Perhaps its most preferred images are those associated with a properly religious joy. This is not an ordinary happiness or pleasure. It is sometimes lived as sublime peace, but at others in the most trying anguish. It includes the joy of consolation which a community of believers suffer in the death of a person. It is, above all, in the feast – solemn and funereal, or alight with joy – that the mystery of presence is caught in flight. When Hegel speaks of the feast he speaks of the fruits of earth rising to a new possibility, that of being eaten in enjoyment by a self-conscious being; and the mystery resides in the revelation of the unity of earth and self in this act.[90] But, in truth, who surrenders to the feast is carried along, poured out into a festal freedom that has no goal, – into a domain that is the play of the divine. The image of the feast seems to underly the Greek Father's understanding of the Trinity, and a sense of divine play.

Hegel's consideration of the Trinity differs considerably from previous traditional understandings, especially from those of the Greek Fathers.[91] The most significant difference, perhaps, is that Hegel describes the Trinity as a movement from the Father to its culmination in the Holy Spirit, a process which allows for the appropriate Hegelian function of the negative, and which allows a portrayal of the Trinity as a rational process of

[90] PdG 503B726.
[91] For a good discussion of the differences, see Chapelle, HR II, 55-109, including the discussions in the footnotes. See especially, p. 106: "La spéculation trinitaire de Hegel ne s'organise donc pas comme la théologie grecque selon un principe de génerosité communicative ... Le principe de la génerosité paternelle fait place à la négativité ..." And footnote 321: "Le pôle extatique de la contemplation patristique grecque est le Père, Source abyssale de toute la divinité. Dans la spéculation hégelienne, les moments du Concept s'organisent en référence à leur finale en l'Esprit."

development and fulfillment. The Greek Fathers see it rather differently. Their stress is rather on the Father and his superabundance of ontological generosity, of which the other persons are the response.[92] Hegel's Trinity is sombre and hard-working, a striving towards the goal which it appoints for itself. It is a marvellous goal, to be sure, but one which is arrived at by careful steps, and whose exact stages we can recount with precise, methodical conceptual clarity. There is everything here that some philosophers might want, and almost nothing that some religious persons might recognize. In the Greek Trinity, the Father, so to speak, finds himself with a family; in the Hegelian Trinity, he plans it. The Greek theologians celebrate the Father as generous source; Hegel ushers in the Holy Spirit as a primordial *telos* achieved. Nevertheless, he has taught us the power of the negative and made us realize that one-sided affirmative images and conceptions of presence have no exclusive role in teaching us of God, and that without the qualifying power of the negative they distort and corrupt. He has justified the images of absence and the thinking of "not" at the highest reaches of reflection. It is not accurate, I think, to say that Hegel has rationalized or secularized his Trinitarian paradigm. It is more accurate, perhaps, to say that he catches the more sombre shadows of religion, and, above all, its relentless energy. – But not its dalliance and pleasure. There is no ambrosia in the Hegelian synthesis, even as it foams forth its own eternal moments.

---

[92] Cf. Hegel's comments on the *kenosis* in PdG 534B767.

RELIGION AS REPRESENTATION

Louis Dupré

Hegel's theory of representation is original. Yet it was not conceived in a vacuum. Three major insights of his predecessors contributed to its conception. They all refer to qualities of the imagination: its detemporalizing function (Kant), its creative force (Fichte), its religious impact (Schelling).

For Kant the imagination construes representations without subjecting them to critical analysis. It synthesizes appearances; it is not concerned with the conditions which insert this synthesis into an objective world. A representation develops into a full-fledged image when the imaginative function lingers over it rather than delivering it outright to the objectifying process of the understanding. If this happens the representation is detached from the stream of sensation and synthesized into an independent unit without being inserted into the continuous totality of the *real world*. It is precisely this self-sufficient independence which predestines the image for aesthetic expression. Here we are interested only in the way in which the detachment both from sense perception and from objective reality is achieved. Kant describes the product of the imagination as a synthesis *in accordance with time*. Of course, temporality is not restricted to the production of images, since succession is the very form of sense perception. Yet it is only by means of new temporal syntheses that percepts can be detached from the continuous stream of perception and made into independent images. Only by withdrawing from the successive "presents" of the past is the inwardness acquired which characterizes the image. Mikel Dufrenne merely interprets Kant's position when he describes the independence of the aesthetic image in purely temporal terms. "To withdraw is to take refuge in the past."[1] Hegel will develop this aspect of the representation in his theory of recollection.

The creative power of the imagination is commonly associated with Fichte's name, but it was already introduced by Kant. To reproduce a

---

[1] *Phénomenologie de l'expérience esthétique*, Paris, 195, p. 434.

percept, as the imagination does, is to take it out of its original mode of giveness and to place it in a temporal setting which essentially transforms it. What results is not merely a reproduction, but as Kant knew, a novel production. Liberated from the actuality of perception the future is no longer tied to the past in rectilinear determination. By escaping from the *merely* present the imagination makes the future into a genuine possibility. This explains why the mind's awareness of freedom grows with the trust in its powers of imagination. Kant's theory of the *productive* synthesis inspired Fichte (and to some extent also Schelling) to conceive the imagination as the moving power of the mind. For Fichte the productive imagination precedes all conscious activity and thus allows the mind to be totally autonomous, that is, at once determining (through the imagination) and determined (as actual consciousness).[2] The imagination alone provides all the determinations of the real, even the complex articulations of the object-appearance which Kant ascribed to the categories of the understanding.[3] Nor is there any fundamental distinction, as Kant assumed, between the sensuous intuition and the non-intuitive understanding, for the phenomenal intuition is the first stage of a process which eventually will be liberated from its spatio-temporal setting and converted into a reflective cognition, valid for all time, that substitutes for the direct apprehension of the object the permanent symbol of a concept. The productive imagination is spontaneous yet not random, for it constitutes the very laws which structure the real. Thus it produces the controlled concepts of the scientist and the philosopher as well as the phantasies of the artist and the myths of the primitive. Nor is its productivity limited to the cognitive order. The very ideals of freedom by which the mind attempts to overcome its finite determinations are as much constituted by the productive imagination as the determinations themselves.

Schelling developed Fichte's insight in showing how the myth, and therefore also the roots of the religious conceptualization, are to be found in the productive imagination. Indeed, for him the imagination is essentially religious. The perfect unity of the real and the ideal in God, which became lost in the finitude of nature, is reconstituted by the creative imagination, the *Einbildungskraft*, that is, the power of "uniformation." The imagination reunites what is one in God. Its divine character becomes manifest in its exclusive power to create the representations of the divine –

---

[2] *Grundlage der gesamten Wissenschaftslehre*, in *Sämtliche Werke*, Vol. I, ed. by J. H. Fichte, Berlin, 1845, p. 227.
[3] *Grundriss des Eigentümlichen der Wissenschaftslehre*, in *Sämtliche Werke*, Vol. I, pp. 376-87.

the gods.[4] In the gods the imagination combines the reality of nature with the ideality of spirit. Hegel will follow Schelling's insight. Yet Schelling failed to distinguish adequately the mythic-religious representation from the aesthetic image. For him the prime object of art is mythology. Hegel will be more cautious in his interpretation of the relation between the aesthetic and the mythic-religious imagination. Let us now consider his own theory of religious representation.

For Hegel also the roots of religious concepts must be found in the imagination. Religion is representation which differs from pure thought even though it has the same content. Representation appears in the section on psychology, the final stage of the subjective spirit in the *Encyclopädie*. Once the mind has overcome the opposition between itself and the object-out-there in the early stages of consciousness, it gradually synthesizes the two essential functions of knowledge: on the one hand to regard the object of consciousness as its own (*das Seinige*) and, on the other hand, to project it into an ontic reality where it has more than a purely mental existence (*das Seiende*). In the representation the mind becomes aware that its content is not bound by the space and time restrictions of the sensuous intuition. What I intuit in space and time is *eo ipso* singularized to a *here* and *now*. The representation preserves the intuitive content, yet re-presents it in a way which is no longer tied to the *here* and *now*. The content is still represented temporally – rather than in the universal form of thought – but the temporality of the representation is no longer that of the sense intuition: it is, so to speak, a free temporality of the subject.

How the mind is able to interiorize by means of a new temporality appears clearly in the first form of representation, the *recollection* (*Erinnerung*). Etymologically the term *recollection* implies interiorization as well as temporality.

As first recollecting the intuition the intellect posits the content of feeling in its inwardness, in its own space and its own time. Thus it is an *image* freed from its first immediacy and its abstract isolation from others, assumed in the universality of the ego as such. The image is no longer completely determined as the intuition and it is, deliberately or accidentally, isolated from the external place, time and immediate connection in which the intuition occurred. The image taken for itself is transitional and the intellect is, in the form of attention, its time and space, its when and where.[5]

Time remembered differs from the time of perception even though it relates to it. In recollection I select only those intuitions to which I decide

[4] *Sämtliche Werke*, ed. by Manfred Schröter, München, 1958, p. 410.
[5] *Encyclopädie* (1830), # 452.

to pay attention. By being detemporalized the recollected representation becomes detached from its original setting. This enables it to stand for a number of similar experiences and to achieve a certain measure of universality. Yet this representation does not attain the logical coherence of thought. Its coherence remains one of succession and juxtaposition.

The coherence of the determinations appears to the representation as successive, not necessary (as only in the notion). The necessary interconnection of the determinations of the absolute content can be grasped only by the timeless, non-sensible notion. The representation retains these determinations as a succession in time. In religion we narrate. The abstract content comes first, its concrete fulfillment appears as a natural event, that is, as a happening in time.[6]

In the recollection the singular intuition is assumed into a representation with a universal content.[7] The form remains singular. Yet by omitting a number of particularities the recollection attains a meaning-potential which far surpasses that of any single intuition. The universality of the representation, then, consists in the transcendence of the content with respect to the singular form.

The interiorization of the *Vorstellung* with respect to the intuition appears even clearer in the productive imagination or *phantasy* which totally abandons the order of succession of the original intuitions in favor of a succession in the subject's inner life. The images of phantasy are no longer experienced as *re*produced, but rather as produced by the mind. At the same time they bring the mind closer to the awareness of an ontic, that is, a not-purely mental reality. The process of interiorization is also one of objectivation. While the mind progressively interiorizes its images it simultaneously rids itself of the subjectivism of the senses by opening up a new sort of exteriority *within* the interiority of the mind.[8] In the phantasy image the mind associates a number of intuition images moulding them into one universalized totality. The process of association is directed by an overriding representation which itself is not an image. The guiding representation may play an even more universalizing role by endowing images with a symbolizing power which allows them to transcend their concrete determinations. Thus we obtain concrete universal representations which Hegel calls *symbols*, and abstract ones, called *signs* and *allegories*. Strangely enough, Hegel rates signs higher than symbols. For him the symbol retains too much of its original image autonomy to

    [6] *Vorlesungen über die Philosophie der Religion*, ed. Georg Lasson, Hamburg, 1966, Vol. I, p. 297.
    [7] *Encyclopädie*, # 454.
    [8] André Léonard, *La foi chez Hegel*, Dissertation, University of Louvain, 1968, pp. 259-60.

be entirely clear in its meaning.[9] The sign enjoys no such autonomy. To posit a sign is to refer directly to the signified, since the sign has no other meaning. "The sign differs from the symbol, an intuition whose own determination according to essence and notion is more or less the content which it expresses as symbol. In the sign, on the contrary, the content of the intuition and the content of what is signified remain unrelated." [10] What matters in the sign is that there is an intuitive form; *which one* is unimportant. "The sign retains nothing of itself; it sacrifices itself to its sense." [11]

The representations of symbols, allegories and poetic images prepare the objectivity of thought by raising the question of their own objectivity status. In *representing* something I am critically aware that a question about its objective reality may be raised, even though I choose not to raise it. This indicates that the representation already points beyond the merely accepted intuition toward the object *in itself*.[12] The representation knows itself to be only a representation. One commentator describes Hegel's representational consciousness as "picture thinking in which the pictures are recognized as such." [13] But to know a representation to be *only* a representation is to relate it to objective, not purely representational being and thus to initiate the problem of objectivity. *What* constitutes objectivity is not revealed in the representation which remains too much caught in subjectivity to distinguish the real from the non-real. It merely posits its content as objectively *problematic*. To do more would require that the mind be conscious of its own power to constitute the real as real. The representational consciousness merely raises a question and invites a deeper reflection which will eventually result in full objectivity. To *know* will consist in realizing that the representation represents *something*. The representation *re*-presents objective reality by letting a particular intuition take its place. Thought will *present* reality itself and thereby reveal the full meaning of the representation.

In his *Lectures on the Philosophy of Religion* Hegel strongly emphasizes the objective character of the representation. It is precisely the representation which prevents the subjectivity of religious feeling to degenerate into

---

[9] This explains why the "symbolic" art of Egypt and the Orient ranks lowest in the *Lectures on Aesthetics*.

[10] *Encyclopädie* # 458 Zusatz.

[11] Malcolm Clark, *Logic and System: A Study of the Transition from Vorstellung to Thought in the Philosophy of Hegel*, Dissertation, University of Louvain, 1960, p. 122.

[12] See J. Hessing and J. G. Wattjes, *Bewustzijn en Werkelijkheid*, Amsterdam, s.d., p. 339.

[13] Clark, *op. cit.*, p. 59.

self-deification, fanaticism and intolerance.[14] The religious representation first states the truth which philosophy will present in the form of thought. "Religion is the true content but in the form of representation. The substantial truth is not given first by philosophy." [15] The religious mind does not grasp its determinations in their intrinsic connectedness. It presents them in succession and juxtaposition, while thought shows the determinations in their development and, consequently, in their overarching unity. Thus in speaking of God religious man will mention a number of unrelated attributes: God is just, but he is *also* merciful. The representation strings together determinations which it is unable to *think* simultaneously.

Representations are not identical with "images." This is particularly important for understanding Hegel's philosophy of religion. In religion images are never used for their own sake, but always as *symbols* and *allegories* of a transcendent content. Moreover, the religious representation includes also mythical or historical developments.[16] The true content of religion can be *represented* by myth or historical narrative but it cannot be adequately expressed by them. A mere report of events can never convey the transcendent content of a religious faith. Finally, the religious representation includes even non-sensuous and, by all appearances, purely spiritual concepts. Creation is such a concept.

When we say: the world has been created, we refer to an activity which substantially differs from any empirical one. Even the expression "activity from which the world proceeded," although abstract is still representational and notional, insofar as the two sides are not connected in the form of necessity: the connection which in itself is entirely unique and incomprehensible is expressed and signified in an analogy with natural life and events.[17]

The image is always present in the religious representation, but usually in a subordinate function. The transcendent content overburdens it to the point where it loses its original meaning. This transcendent character makes the religious representation basically iconoclastic with respect to images.

Religion has a polemical aspect insofar as its content cannot be perceived immediately in the sensuous intuition or in the image, but only mediately by abstraction, this is, by elevating the imaginary and the sensible to a universal level. This elevation implies a rejection of the image. At first only the form would seem to be rejected, but in fact the content itself is affected insofar as the religious meaning is connected with the image and the image, the beautiful, precisely implies that the universal, the thought, the notion cannot be separated from the image . . .[18]

14 *Vorlesungen über die Philosophie der Religion*, I, p. 286.
15 *Vorlesungen*, I, p. 299.
16 In *Vorlesungen*, I, p. 284, Hegel includes the myth in the image.
17 *Vorlesungen*, I, p. 113.
18 *Vorlesungen*, I, p. 285.

Nevertheless the religious representation always requires images and the use of images is what distinguishes one religious faith from another. Thus Hegel describes Hinduism as a religion of fantasy, because the powers of the Hindu imagination are not subordinated to a higher instance: coherent images are all that is required for this sort of religious reality. The only criterion of the Hindu mythology is man's capacity to imagine it.[19] It is superfluous to point out the confident ignorance displayed in this simplistic interpretation of Hindu faith. The valuable point is that religious representation does not simply coincide with religious fantasy.

In Greek mythology the image is equally important, but it is controlled by an awareness of the divine as subjective and *free*. This freedom is still hidden in the many "powers" of nature. Nevertheless in their aesthetic representation the powers reveal a subjective spontaneity which both surpasses and unites nature as the human spirit directs and animates the human body.[20] The aesthetic mythology of the Greeks conveys a religious transcendence insofar as the images of the gods are conceived as much more beautiful than man's image of himself. Indeed, the Greek gods may be said to represent man's ideal of himself. Precisely because of its idealized form was Greek mythology able to accommodate so harmoniously the ideal content of religion.[21] Religion consists in lifting the natural and moral powers which rule human life above their ordinary context. Rather than being a negation of the human, Greek mythology was nothing more than idealized humanity. The cult beautified life rather than changing it.

In other forms of religion, sacrifice means to give up, to bring forward, to deprive oneself. But here . . . sacrifice consists in drinking the wine and eating the meat . . . . Thus higher meaning and enjoyment is given to all activities of life. Here one finds no self-denial, no apology for eating and drinking. But every occupation and pleasure of daily existence is made into a sacrifice.[22]

Yet the limitation of this ideal is that it is caught in its own aesthetic *image* character. The Greek gods, at least as we know them through Homer and Hesiod, became exclusively ideals of beauty. The more aesthetically perfect they grew, the more they lost their meaning as religious symbols, that is, as finite appearances which reveal an infinite *transcendence*. Their perfect containment within finite forms made them aesthetic before poets and sculptors made them into works of art. It was their own aesthetic potential which killed the Greek gods: their very conception demanded an artistic treatment which they could not religiously survive.

[19] *Vorlesungen* II, p. 144.
[20] *Vorlesungen* III, pp. 119-25.
[21] *Vorlesungen* III, p. 144.
[22] *Vorlesungen* III, p. 170.

HEGEL AND THE SECULARIZATION HYPOTHESIS[1]

Kenley R. Dove

I. "Secularization" and the Modern World

"To seek for a point in history in which the middle ages 'end' and the modern world 'begins' is a sheer absurdity. But that does not do away with the necessity of looking for an *intellectual* line of demarcation between the two ages." [2] From Ernst Cassirer's monumental study, *Das Erkenntnisproblem in der Philosophie und Wissenschaft der Neueren Zeit* of 1906, to Hans Blumenberg's provocative and brilliant work, *Die Legitimität der Neuzeit* of 1966, the problematic of modernity has been the theme of countless books, essays and lectures. Since these quests for a concept of "the modern" may properly be thought of as "footnotes to Hegel," it is not surprising that Hegel's philosophy itself has been drawn into the controversy.

The following remarks are designed to throw some light on how this has happened by presenting a case study drawn from a selection of this vast literature. The general thesis to be examined is that an intellectual line of demarcation for the "beginning" of the modern world may be found under the general rubric "secularization." The term itself has been used to this end by a wide variety of scholars ranging from Max Weber,[3] John Neville Figgis [4] and Carl Schmitt [5] to Walter Benjamin,[6] Paul Til-

---

[1] For many discussions of this and other topics over the past five years, I am deeply indebted to my colleague, Rulon Wells.

[2] Ernst Cassirer, *The Myth of the State*, New Haven; Yale U.P., 1946, p. 130.

[3] Max Weber, *Gesammelte Aufsätze zur Religionssoziologie*, Tübingen: J. C. B. Mohr, 1920, Vol. I, pp. 24, 87n, 196, 199, 212, *et passim; Wirtschaft und Gesellschaft*, Tübingen: J. C. B. Mohr, 1922, pp. 405, 408, 417, *et passim*.

[4] J. N. Figgis, *Political Thought from Gerson to Grotius: 1414 - 1625*, Cambridge: The University Press, 1916 (1st. ed. 1907), pp. 22, 27, 249-50.

[5] Carl Schmitt, *Politische Theologie: Vier Kapitel zur Lehre von der Souveränität*, Munich and Leipzig: Dunker & Humbolt, 1922, p. 37.

[6] Walter Benjamin, *Illuminationen*, Frankfurt am Main: Suhrkamp, 1961, p. 274.

(no heading)

lich,[7] Friedrich Gogarten [8] and Harvey Cox.[9] Figgis, for example, concludes his seventh and final lecture on *Political Thought* by stressing "the general secularization of life which followed the destruction of religious unity and the *Aufklärung* of the eighteenth century. What is to be noted is that only through this revolution did ideas no less than facts take the shape in which they influenced the modern world." [10] And, to the extent that he has one, Weber's philosophy of history is guided by his concern for "the steady progress of the characteristic process of 'secularization' to which in modern times all phenomena that originated in religious conceptions succumb." [11] The thesis has also been exploited to account for specific dimensions of modernity, as, for example, in M. B. Foster's account of the rôle of Christian theology in the rise of modern natural science,[12] and in Carl Schmitt's argument that "all significant concepts of modern political theory are secularized theological concepts" [13] – both of which were formulated with reference to Weber – as well as in Hans Sedlmayr's theological critique of modern art.[14]

The notion that secularization, in one or another of its many senses, provides a key to modernity has, of course, been the object of criticism. In addition to the considerable literature evoked by Weber's famous 1905 essay on the Protestant Ethic, Hannah Arendt has attempted to show that the condition of man in the modern age is not to be understood in terms of increasing secularity (insofar as this is identified with worldliness) or any other religious phenomenon, but that "the hallmark of the modern age" has been the very opposite: "world alienation." [15] The tendency of secularization theorists to postulate the medieval or christian epoch as a

[7] Paul Tillich, *The Protestant Era* (Abridged Edition), Chicago: U. of Chicago Press, 1957, p. 24.
[8] Friedrich Gogarten, *Der Mensch zwischen Gott und Welt*, Heidelberg: Lambert Schneider, 1952, pp. 149 ff.; *Verhängnis und Hoffnung der Neuzeit: Die Säkularisierung als theologisches Problem*, Stuttgart: Friedrich Vorwerk, 1953, pp. 82ff, pp. 129ff.
[9] Harvey Cox, *The Secular City: Secularization and Urbanization in Theological Perspective*, New York: Macmillan, 1965, pp. 1 ff.
[10] Figgis, *op. cit.*, p. 250.
[11] Translated by Hans Gerth and C. Wright Mills, in *From Max Weber: Essays in Sociology*, New York: Oxford U.P., 1958, p. 307.
[12] M. B. Foster, "The Christian Doctrine of Creation and the Rise of Modern Natural Science," in *Mind* (October, 1934), pp. 446-68, and "Christian Theology and Modern Science of Nature," *Mind* (October, 1935), pp. 439-66 and (January, 1936) pp. 1-27. Also see: Pierre Duhem, *Le Système du Monde*, Paris: Hermann, 1913-59, 10 Vols, esp. Vol. I. p. 261, cited in Hartley G. Alexander, *Time as Dimension and History*, Albuquerque: U. of New Mexico Press, 194-, p. 70.
[13] Schmitt, *loc. cit.*
[14] H. Sedlmayr, *Verlust der Mitte*, Frankfurt am Main: Ullstein, 1955, pp. 156ff.
[15] Hannah Arendt, *The Human Condition*, Garden City: Doubleday, 1959, pp. 230-31. Also see: Arendt, *Between Past and Future*, Cleveland: Meridian, 1963, pp. 65-71; and *On Revolution*, New York: Viking, 1963, pp. 158-60.

"given" – itself requiring no interpretation – has also been subjected to severe criticism, at the level of onto-theological assumptions by Martin Heidegger,[16] and with respect to political theory by Eric Weil.[17] The most violent attack upon the secularization thesis may be found in the first part of Blumenberg's book.[18] But, helpful as these critiques are, each in its own way points to the necessity of coming to terms with Hegel in order to overcome the real intellectual difficulties indicated by the persistent attractiveness of the secularization hypothesis as an explanation of modernity. The present essay proposes to serve as a step in that direction.

II. *"Secularization" as a Critique of Hegel*

Of the many senses of the word "secularization," perhaps it would be helpful to isolate three recent usages in order to facilitate the development of our argument.

A. *Secularization as Liberation*

In the first, and least critical, of these, the word has been used to designate or, better, celebrate the liberation of modern man from his erstwhile religious and metaphysical tutelage. Thus Harvey Cox and other participants in the Bonhoeffer-inspired "Death of God" movement have revivified Auguste Comte's famous "three stages" argument, replacing the somewhat drab notion of "positivism" with the considerably more poignant – for theologians at least – idea of a "non-religious Christianity."[19] Despite the current waning of enthusiasm for this version of the secularization hypothesis, it will no doubt prove durable enough to undergo several future incarnations.

B. *Secularization Unmasked*

More pertinent to our topic is a second sense of the word – as an unmasking of false consciousness. This is the sense which has apparently prompted Blumenberg to defend the legitimacy of modernity against those who regard it as the unhappy offspring of the illicit marriage between Athens and Jerusalem, reason and faith. The sacramental formula employed by this school of secularization theorists turns upon the phrase "historization

---

[16] M. Heidegger, *Holzwege*, Frankfurt am Main: Klostermann, 1950, p. 187.
[17] E. Weil, "Die Säkularisierung der Politik und des politischen Denkens in der Neuzeit," in *Marxismusstudien*, Vol. IV, pp. 144-62.
[18] "Säkularisierung – Kritik einer Kategorie des geschichtlichen Unrechts," in H. Blumenberg, *op. cit.*, pp. 11-74.
[19] Ved Mehta's three "Profiles" of "The New Theologian" (*The New Yorker*, November 13, 20 and 27, 1965) present an appropriate sketch of this movement.

of eschatology." As their title indicates, this sense of secularization was very much at the center of Rudolf Bultmann's 1955 Gifford Lectures, *History and Eschatology*.[20]

A study of the text, however, indicates that Bultmann's Hegel critique and other formulations of the secularization thesis are heavily indebted to Karl Löwith, whose *Meaning in History* (which bears the more revealing title, *Weltgeschichte und Heilsgeschehen*, in the German version) [21] constitutes the *locus classicus* for this sense of the word "secularization." [22] Löwith's argument in this book, which may be put very succinctly, is that the philosophy of history developed in the occident depends for its essential character upon the presupposition that the Christian religion is the absolute truth. This assumption, says Löwith, was shared without question by historically oriented philosophers from Augustine to Hegel.

What distinguishes Hegel from Augustine in principle is that Hegel interprets the Christian religion in terms of speculative reason, and providence as "cunning of reason" .... As the realization of the spirit of Christianity, the history of the world is the true theodicy, the justification of God in History.

With this secularization of the Christian faith, or, as Hegel would say, with this realization of the Spirit, Hegel believed himself loyal to the genius of Christianity by realizing the Kingdom of God on earth. And, since he transposed the Christian expectation of a final consummation into the historical process as such, he saw the world's history as consummating itself. "The history of the world is the world's court of justice" (*Die Weltgeschichte ist das Weltgericht*) is a sentence which is as religious in its original motivation, where it means that the world's history is proceeding toward its judgment at the end of all history, as it is irreligious in its secular application, where it means that the judgment is contained in the historical process as such.[23]

The most fateful aspect of the Hegelian philosophy, as Löwith sees it, is that Hegel himself failed to grasp "the profound ambiguity" at the heart of his own thinking. The subsequent history of philosophy – or at least Germanic philosophy until Nietzsche – may therefore be read as a modern dress version of the Oedipus tragedy, in which the rôle of protagonist is played in turn by Hegel, Marx, Kierkegaard (together with other lesser

[20] R. Bultmann, *History and Eschatology: The Presence of Eternity*, New York: Harper & Brothers, 1957. For specific discussions of secularization and Hegel, see: pp. 56, 62-70, 73, 82, 89, 120. In addition, see: Mircea Eliade, *The Sacred and the Profane*, New York: Harper & Row, 1961, pp. 117: "Hegel takes over the Judaeo-Christian ideology and applies it to history in its totality ...."

[21] K. Löwith, *Meaning in History: The Theological Implications of the Philosophy of History*, Chicago: U. Of Chicago Press, 1949; German version: *Weltgeschichte und Heilsgeschehen. Die theologischen Voraussetzungen der Geschichtsphilosophie*, Stuttgart: Kohlhammer, 1953.

[22] See Löwith, *Meaning*, pp. 2, 19, 49, 57, 58, 193, 200, 201, 202.

[23] Löwith, *Meaning*, pp. 57-58.

"left" Hegelians) and, finally, Nietzsche, who comes closest to a full realization that the philosopher of history has murdered his holy father and desecrated his mother faith in producing that bastard quest for a "meaning" of history "determined absolutely from within history itself. . . ."[24] This, of course, is the basic plot outline of Löwith's most famous study, *From Hegel to Nietzsche*, which remains, so far as I have been able to determine, the *only* systematic interpretation of nineteenth century German philosophy.[25] That this should be so, despite the moot character of its central thesis, indicates the distance we will have to go before finally coming to terms with the tradition which has given birth to Marxism, Existentialism and various shapes of linguistic and analytic philosophy. For although the word "secularization" plays no significant rôle in Löwith's *From Hegel to Nietzsche*, the version of the secularization hypothesis now under consideration is clearly present:

> Whoever has really experienced a slice of world history, rather than merely knowing it through hearsay, speeches, books, and newspapers, will have to come to the conclusion that Hegel's philosophy of history is a pseudo-theological schematization of history arranged according to the idea of progress toward an eschatological fulfillment at the end of time; it does not correspond at all to visible reality.[26]

That Hegel, the "master" of irony,[27] and the only philosopher since Aristotle to deal with tragedy "in a manner both original and searching," [28] should be open to such an interpretation is indeed one of the more astonishing and ironical aspects of contemporary Hegel scholarship. For however valid the unmasking theory of tragic recognition may be, and despite the fact that Löwith himself does not explicitly make use of the Oedipal analogy, his interpretation of Hegel and the nineteenth century depends fundamentally upon the characterization of Hegelian philosophy as a horrendous, albeit unconscious, ἁμαρτια, the speculative secularization of the Judeo-Christian eschatology.

But assuming that Hegel does make this mistake, what precisely does

[24] K. Löwith, *From Hegel to Nietzsche: The Revolution in Nineteenth Century Thought*, trans. D. E. Green, New York: Holt, Rinehart and Winston, 1964, p. vi. (Original German text completed in 1939).
[25] There have, to be sure, been many compendia and chronicles of philosophy in this period, but, with the possible exception of G. Lukács' *Die Zerstörung der Vernunft* (Berlin: Aufbau, 1955) – a highly illuminating study, despite its polemical veneer – no other book even bears comparison with Löwith's masterful presentation.
[26] Löwith, *From Hegel*, p. 219. German edition: *Von Hegel zu Nietzsche*, Stuttgart: Kohlhammer, 1964, p. 239.
[27] Søren Kierkegaard, *The Concept of Irony*, trans. by L. M. Capel, New York: Harper & Row, 1965, p. 260.
[28] A. C. Bradley, *Oxford Lectures on Poetry*, London: 1950, p. 69.

the mistake itself consist in? What does it mean to schematize history pseudo-theologically? to secularize an eschatology? Hegel himself calls attention to the resemblance between two forms of "die allgemeine Ueberzeugung, dass Vernunft in der Welt und damit ebenso in der Welt-geschichte geherrscht habe und herrsche" [29]: (a) the affirmation of Anaxagoras "dass der Nus, der Verstand überhaupt oder die Vernunft, die Welt regiere" [30] and (b) the Christian belief "dass . . . eine Vorsehung die Welt regiere." [31] But does this *eo ipso* constitute a *reduction* of the presupposition [32] of a lecture course on world history to the specific structure of a Christian's belief in divine providence? The reader of Löwith's *From Hegel to Nietzsche* or *Meaning in History* will discover no answer to these questions. Löwith simply states his thesis again and again, that Hegel unconsciously identified the orientation of philosophy with that of the Christian faith.[33]

There is, nevertheless, an argument, or at least the makings of one. Just as the concept of "secularization," first articulated in *Meaning in History* (1949), epitomizes in a word the thesis of *From Hegel to Nietzsche* (1939), where the term does not appear, so too Löwith's response (1968) to Blumenberg's attack on the secularization thesis provides a retrospective clue to the unstated assumptions of the earlier studies.[34] But to take up this argument will require us to consider a sense of "secularization" which goes beyond the "vulgar Marxist" technique of unmasking a false form of consciousness.

C. *Hermeneutic and Historicity: The Shadow of Heidegger*

It should be noted at the outset that Blumenberg's book is neither an interpretation nor a defense of Hegel. But his own philosophical thesis – that historical epochs, modernity included, arise through a process of discontinuity – need not concern us here. The secularization thesis is simply that variant of the continuity thesis which Blumenberg finds most pre-

---

[29] Hegel, *Die Vernunft in der Geschichte*, ed. Hoffmeister, Hamburg: Felix Meiner, 1955, pp. 36-7.

[30] *Ibid.*, p. 37.

[31] *Ibid.*, p. 38.

[32] It is odd that Hegel's explicit discussion of the "weltliches Reich" and "geistliches Reich" in *Die Vernunft in der Geschichte* (Löwith's major source) is not taken up in *Meaning in History*.

[33] Since 1949 the unmasking theory of secularization has become a household implement of literary scholars as a device for unlocking the secrets of Coleridge's *Ancient Mariner* or Milton's *Paradise Lost*. In one case at least, the process has even come full circle. See M. L. Abrams' paper "Hegel's *Phenomenology*: Philosophy or Literature?" (Presented at Yale University, April 18, 1969).

[34] I refer to Löwith's review of the first part, pp. 11-74, of Blumenberg's *Legitimität der Neuzeit*, in *Philosophische Rundschau*, Vol. XV, No. 3 (July, 1968), pp. 195-201. The rest of the book is reviewed in the same volume by Hans-Georg Gadamer, pp. 201-09.

valent today.[35] The model which he takes as his clue to the presumptive illegitimacy of "secularization" is the expropriation (*Enteignung*) of ecclesiastical property.[36] And this interpretation indeed has a good *prima facie* claim to appropriateness since the term was apparently coined on April 8, 1646 by the French delegates at the preliminary negotiations for the Treaty of Westphalia.[37] Here too we find a term which has come to designate retrospectively a phenomenon as old as the Christian church. But the aspect which Blumenberg focusses upon is the connotation of illegitimacy inextricably associated with the word from its first employment.[38] The "paradigm of expropriation" [39] is then subjected to a learned and subtle historical discussion ranging from Augustine on legitimate and illegitimate possession of the truth to the question whether the concept of infinity in modern physical theory was "taken over" from the attributes of the Christian god. The philosophical error which Blumenberg discovers "in the background" of the secularization (expropriation) thesis he designates as "a Platonism": "was wahr ist, ist dies kraft eines Herkunftsverhältnisses als Abbild zu einem Urbild von Wahrheit, das mit Gott identifiziert ist."[40]

Löwith rightly senses that he is the prime target of Blumenberg's attack (despite the fact that he is only mentioned on two pages), but he denies ever having questioned the legitimacy of modernity, much less regarding it as "a Christian heresy." "Denn auch unsere These besagt nicht mehr und nicht weniger, als dass alttestamentliche Prophetie und christliche Eschatologie einen Horizont von Fragestellungen und ein geistiges Klima *geschaffen haben* – im Hinblick auf die Geschichtsphilosophie einen Horizont der Zukunft und einer künftigen Erfüllung – das den modernen Geschichtsbegriff und den weltlichen Fortschrittsglauben *ermöglicht* hat." [41]

However accurate his disclaimers might be, Löwith has in this recent interpretation of this thesis introduced a new element: the doctrine of the *horizon* of questioning. He has thus explicitly associated the central thesis of his many writings with the theory of "the hermeneutical situation."

[35] Presumably Blumenberg would find a Hegelian philosophy of history equally incompatible with his discontinuity theory. But to specify this would require a discussion of the elements of continuity and discontinuity involved in the concept of "determinate negation." Blumenberg does not discuss this. But see: Blumenberg, *op. cit.*, pp. 21-3.

[36] Blumenberg, *op. cit.*, pp. 19ff, pp. 33ff.

[37] J. G. v. Meiern, *Acta Pacis Westphalicae publica*, II 15 § 14; cited in S. Reiche's contribution to *Die Religion in Geschichte und Gegenwart*, 3rd ed. (RGG³), ed., Campenhausen *et al*, 6 vols., Tübingen: J. C. B. Mohr, 1957ff., Vol. V, p. 1280.

[38] The Church has tended to regard these expropriations as illegitimate. For examples in English, see O. E. D.

[39] Blumenberg, *op. cit.*, p. 20.

[40] *Ibid.*, p. 47.

[41] Löwith, *Rundschau*, p. 198.

Hermeneutic, one of the most fashionable words in contemporary philosophy and theology, designates an activity which, like secularization (in the sense of expropriation), dates back to the earliest days of Christianity.[42] The distinction between *hermeneutica sacra* and *profana* (i.e., for the interpretation of classical literature) was first drawn in the 18th century and, through the work of Hegel's contemporary, Schleiermacher, as well as Dilthey, Heidegger and Gadamer, it has come increasingly into the focus of philosophical attention as a problem *an und für sich*.[43]

The word "hermeneutic" has been the object of a number of amusing etymologies, but it would be difficult to assign priority to any of its three generally accepted fields of reference: expression, explanation and translation-interpretation.[44] Of these, the last has been raised to a level of heightened philosophical (and ultimately theological) prominence through Heidegger's "ontological analytic of Dasein as laying bare the horizon for an Interpretation of the meaning of Being in General." [45]

Sein und Zeit is the best known of the many works – beginning perhaps with the writings of Emil Lask – in the neo-Kantian tradition which have sought to present an ontological interpretation of the concept of transcendental self-consciousness, or transcendental unity of apperception, which was first formulated in Kant's *Critique of Pure Reason*.[46] The desideratum of Heidegger's efforts is a rediscovery of the question of Being. And his method of going about this is to lay bare the structure of transcendental self-consciousness by reformulating Kant's theory of the apriori intuition of time. The critical move (as Cassirer has rightly pointed out [47]) is the

---

[42] According to Gerhard Ebeling, hermeneutic was born out of the problem of interpreting the Old Testament in light of the New Testament doctrine that the O.T. prophesy had been fulfilled. See RGG³, Vol. III, p. 246.

[43] Theologians such as Robert W. Funk, Gerhard Ebeling and Wolfhart Pannenberg have, on the other hand, tended to regard the "hermeneutical situation" as a "solution" to the problem of revelation. Pannenberg claims to derive some of his hermeneutical insights from Hegel, but, on the basis of my sampling from this literature, the shadow of Heidegger seems to delineate more precisely the thought patterns of these new wave theologians, "Hegelian" or not.

[44] See Ebeling in RGG³, III, 243.

[45] Heidegger, *Sein und Zeit* (1927), Tübingen: Max Niemeyer, 1960, pp. 15ff. Also see pp. 372ff. Since the English translation of Macquarrie and Robinson includes the pagination of the cited German text, double references would be superfluous.

[46] This is of course much more apparent in Heidegger's *Kant und das Problem der Metaphysik*, Bonn: F. Cohen, 1929 (English tr. by J. S. Churchill, *Kant and the Problem of Metaphysics*, Bloomington: Indiana U.P., 1962). Compare: *Sein und Zeit*, pp. 319-21. For an excellent, and to my knowledge unique, presentation of Heidegger's philosophy in its neo-Kantian historical context, see Manfred Brelage, *Studien zur transzendentalphilosophie*, Berlin: Walter de Gruyter, 1965. Especially helpful is the essay "Transcendentalphilosophie und konkrete Subjektivität," pp. 72-229, in which the ontological interpretations of the transcendental problem by Nicolai Hartmann, Martin Heidegger and Richard Hönigswald are presented in their interrelatedness.

[47] Ernst Cassirer, "Kant und das Problem der Metaphysik: Bemerkungen zu Martin

suspension of the epistemological question (and all talk about the validity
or foundations of knowledge) in favor of the ontological question. Indeed,
Heidegger tends to regard the quest for the foundations of knowledge, the
search for a *fundamentum inconcussum*,[48] as one of the major factors
contributing to modern man's *Seinsvergessenheit*.[49]

Transcendental self-consciousness, as an ontological structure, Heidegger calls *Dasein*. Thus interpreted, self-consciousness is not *in* time: it
"times itself." [50] Kant's transcendental unity of apperception is accordingly supplanted by the "Einheit der Zeitigung der Zeitlichkeit." [51] *Dasein*
is in-the-world *because* it "times itself," [52] because it is ecstatically
"thrown" out of time, is claimed by the world and responds to this claim
which it itself is.[53] The distinction between the "authentic" and "inauthentic" modes of Dasein's responses, which lends much of the pathos to the
argument of *Sein und Zeit*, need not concern us here.[54] What is important for an understanding of our third sense of the word "secularization" is the significance which Heidegger's analysis of *Dasein* has given
to the term "horizon." For if *Dasein* is not properly understood as being
"in" time (which Heidegger regards as the "vulgar" conception of time,
brought to its quintessential conceptual exposition by Hegel [55]), then the
primordial structure of *Dasein* must be comprehended in terms of its
various modes of "timing itself" into the world. "Die existential-zeitliche
Bedingung der Möglichkeit der Welt liegt darin, dass die Zeitlichkeit als
ekstatische Einheit so etwas wie einen Horizont hat." [56] *Dasein* is therefore
said to experience the directionality of its "timing ecstasies" in accordance
with the "horizonal schemata" of "Zukunft, Gewesenheit und Gegenwart." [57]

The critical point to notice here is that Heidegger, unlike Kant, does not

Heideggers Kant-Interpretation," in *Kant-Studien*, Vol. XXXVI (1931), pp. 1-26.
[48] Heidegger, *Sein und Zeit*, p. 24 *et passim*.
[49] Heidegger's rejection of the secularization hypothesis is based on this theory that
the process of decomposition culminating in modernity must be traced back as far as
Plato. Thus a recovery of the question of Being requires, according to Heidegger, a
destruction of the history of "metaphysics."
[50] "Sich zeitigen." See, e.g., *ibid.*, p. 304.
[51] *Ibid.*, pp. 365, 427, etc.
[52] "Wenn kein *Dasein* existiert, ist auch keine Welt 'da.' " *Ibid.*
[53] "Das Dasein ist der Rufer und der Angerufene zumal . . . ." *Ibid.*, p. 277.
[54] The basic principle of this distinction, "Entschlossenheit," disappears from Heidegger's writings after the "Rektoratsrede" (*Die Selbstbehauptung der deutschen
Universität*, Breslau: Korn, 1933). Its systematic function in Heidegger's later thought
comes to be played by the concept of "Gelassenheit" (see *Gelassenheit*, Pfullingen:
Neske, 1959).
[55] See: *Sein und Zeit*, pp. 428ff.
[56] *Ibid.*, p. 365.
[57] *Ibid.*

treat self-consciousness as a fundamental structure, *to which* the judgmental structure of all true propositions must be seen to conform; for Heidegger self-consciousness is the horizonal structure *from which* and *through which* Dasein projectively attains the definiteness and concreteness of Being-in-the-world.[58] It is through the "Zeitigung der Zeitlichkeit" that Dasein comes to have the character of "Geschichtlichkeit" (historicity).[59] And here, once again, Heidegger's inversion of the normal (vulgar?) mode of considering philosophical questions is evident: "Die Analyse der Geschichtlichkeit des Daseins versucht zu zeigen, dass dieses Seiende nicht "zeitlich" ist, weil es "in der Geschichte steht," sondern dass es umgekehrt geschichtlich nur existiert und existieren kann, weil es im Grunde seines Seins zeitlich ist." [60]

In *Sein und Zeit*, the question of the horizon for the "historizing" of *Dasein* leads to a discussion of the horizon defined by the "Zwischen" (between) of birth and death. And it is in terms of this latter especially that Heidegger affirms the "finitude" of *Dasein*. But once having been thematized, this horizonal problematic was easily adaptable as the touchstone for asking a critical question: What is the origin of the horizon necessary for the possibility of envisaging a unity in world history?

This is the question which Löwith finally comes explicitly to pose in his response to Blumenberg. That he was reluctant to do so we may extrapolate from his earlier criticism of the Hermeneutic School and its leading contemporary exponents, Gadamer and Heidegger.[61] For Gadamer had already formulated the hermeneutic version of the secularization thesis in the 1950's:

Dass "die Geschichte" zum Gegenstand der Erkenntnis wird, setzt aber auf alle Fälle voraus, dass sie als eine Einheit gedacht ist. Diese Einheit kann eine inhaltliche sein, und dann heisst das, dass sich die Geschichte der Menschheit zur Einheit eines verständlichen Zusammenhangs ordnen lassen. So ist in der jüdisch-christlichen Überlieferung das Wissen von der Geschichte Geschichts*theologie*. Erst als das Produkt eines Säkularisationsprozesses, der diese christliche Theologie der Geschichte auflöst, entsteht der moderne Begriff einer Philosophie der Geschichte. Von Voltaire bis Hegel und Comte

---

[58] Dieter Henrich has attempted to show that the revolutionary reorientation of regarding self-consciousness as an ontological *terminus a quo* rather than a *terminus ad quem* is properly to be attributed to Fichte. See: D. Henrich, *Fichtes Ursprüngliche Einsicht*, Frankfurt am Main: Klostermann, 1967. Henrich does not explicitly discuss Heidegger in this essay.

[59] See *Sein und Zeit*, pp. 372ff.

[60] *Ibid.*, p. 376.

[61] See, for example, Löwith, *Vorträge und Abhandlungen zur Kritik der christlichen Überlieferung*, Stuttgart: Kohlhammer, 1966, pp. 205ff. and Löwith, *Heidegger: Denker in dürftiger Zeit*, Göttingen: Vandenhoeck, 1960.

ist damit stets das gemeint, was wir heute eine materiale Geschichtsphilosophie nennen würden, und d.h. die Erkenntnis eines einheitlichen Sinnes in
aller menschlichen Geschichte.[62]

From Löwith's point of view, a hermeneutic formulation of the secularization thesis was no doubt entered upon with some reluctance. For, despite the fact that "unmasking" constitutes no real argument, Löwith had
previously argued very explicitly that the hermeneutic philosophy of historicity as developed by Gadamer, and, especially, Heidegger, was suspect
precisely because of its "Hegelian" character. "Im Prinzip sind jedoch
Hegels konstruktiver Fortschritt und Aufstieg und Heideggers destrukti-
ver Rückschritt und Abstieg nicht verschieden." [64] Contemporary Germany's most famous critic of Hegel and most prominent friend-enemy and
erstwhile disciple of Heidegger has now begun to make manifest the "dialectical" character of his relationship to both.

But perhaps there is a moral to this story of the secularization hypothesis
which ramifies beyond the limits of this most famous and (in its "unmasking" version) most facile contemporary interpretation of Hegel. Perhaps Löwith is not alone in his tendency to read an interpretation back
into Hegel from the mesmerizing cadences of Heidegger's thought. For
a survey of the non-trivial expositions of Hegel's philosophy since 1927
(studies which are more than mere philological exercises) reveals again
and again the heavy shadow of Heidegger. This is most obviously evident
in Marcuses's book, *Hegels Ontologie und die Grundlegung einer Theorie
der Geschichtlichkeit* [65] and in Kojève's lectures,[66] but it is also unmistakable in the writings of scholars such as Jan van der Meulen,[67] Manfred
Riedel [68] and even Jürgen Habermas.[69]

As profoundly searching analyses, these works, together with the valu-

[62] H.-G. Gadamer, "Geschichtsphilosophie," in RGG³, Vol. II, p. 1489. Also see:
Gadamer, *Wahrheit und Methode*, 2nd. ed., Tübingen: J. C. B. Mohr, 1965, pp.
195ff, 501.

[63] See the chapter on "Geschichte, Geschichtlichkeit und Seinsgeschick" in Löwith,
Heidegger, pp. 44-71, esp. 45-6, 53-4, 58, 67, 68. Hegel is also clearly alluded to in
Löwith's "... vor etwa hundertfünfzig Jahren..." on p. 70.

[64] *Ibid.*, pp. 45-6.

[65] H. Marcuse, *Hegels Ontologie*, Frankfurt am Main: Klostermann, 1932.

[66] A. Kojève, *Introduction à la Lecture de Hegel: Leçons sur la Phénoménologie de
l'Esprit, professées* de 1933 à 1939 à l'Ecole des Hautes Etudes, ed., R. Queneau, Paris:
Gallimard, 1947.

[67] J. van der Meulen, *Hegel: Die gebrochene Mitte*, Hamburg: Felix Meiner, 1958.
Van der Meulen's dissertation was on Heidegger and Hegel.

[68] M. Riedel, *Theorie und Praxis im Denken Hegels: Interpretationen zu den Grund-
stellungen der neuzeitlichen Subjektivität*, Stuttgart: Kohlhammer, 1965.

[69] J. Habermas, "Hegels Kantkritik: Radikalisierung oder Aufhebung der Erkennt-
nistheorie," in *Erkenntnis und Interesse*, Frankfurt am Main: Suhrkamp, 1968; and
"Arbeit und Interaktion: Bemerkungen zu Hegels Jenenser 'Philosophie des Geistes' "
in *Technik und Wissenschaft als Ideologie*, Frankfurt am Main: Suhrkamp, 1968.

able studies by Heidegger himself,[70] must be ranked among the best works on Hegel produced in our time. Perhaps we may hope that the period between this, Hegel's bicentennial, and the 200th anniversary of the *Phenomenology*, will witness the emergence of Hegel interpretations equally rich in profundity while adhering more closely to the Hegelian principle of "immanent critique." [71]

---

[70] In addition to *Sein und Zeit*, see "Hegels Begriff der Erfahrung" (now available as a separate volume in English, *Hegel's Concept of Experience, with a section from Hegel's Phenomenology of Spirit* translated by K. R. Dove, New York: Harper & Row, 1970) in *Holzwege*, Frankfurt am Main: Klostermann, 1950; *Identität und Differenz*, Pfullingen: Neske, 1957 (translated and with an Introduction by Joan Stambach, *Identity and Difference*, New York: Harper & Row, 1969); and "Hegel und die Griechen" in the *Gadamer Festschrift*.

[71] My own labors in the Hegelian vineyards suggest the following points about the problem of winning an immanent critique of Hegel. (1) It must consistently recognize that Hegel was, on his own account, the author of two, and only two, "works": *The Phenomenology of Spirit* and the System (i.e., the two editions of the *Science of Logic*, the three editions of the *Encyclopedia* and the *Philosophy of Right*). However stimulating and insightful they may be, all other parts of the Hegelian corpus are either anticipatory or derivative of the conceptual edifice articulated in these "works." Hegel interpretations which fail to stress this will be "systematically misleading." (2) We must take more seriously the conceptual (and not, following Theodor Haering, merely the genetico-philological) problem of an introduction to Hegel's System. This means that the question of Hegel's *Phenomenology* must be considered in the light of Hegel's own description of it as "the deduction of the concept of science" and not merely as a brilliant work in its own right (à la Kojève). The recent studies by H. F. Fulda, together with the critical responses of Otto Pöggeler, have rightfully recalled this question to a position of prominence. (3) As Otto Pöggeler has argued, Hegel's *Phenomenology* remains – despite the commentaries of Gabler, Hyppolite and Loewenberg – an unlocked mystery as a "through-composed" book. (The signal for this in Hyppolite and Loewenberg is the word "noumenology." Gabler's study was never completed; it breaks off after a treatment of *Phen.*, ch. V). The most searching study we have of the methodological problem of the *Phen.* is, alas, Heidegger's essay, *Hegel's Concept of Experience*. Perhaps a necessary first step in coming to an understanding of the *Phen.* will be to disentagle Heidegger's fateful identification of Hegel's *Geist* with his own concept of *Sein*. I have made a preliminary effort in this direction in "Hegel's Phenomenological Method," *The Review of Metaphysics*, XXIII, 4 (June, 1970).

COMMENT ON DOVE'S 'HEGEL AND THE SECULARIZATION HYPOTHESIS'

Howard P. Kainz

1 can hardly disagree with most of the remarks in Professor Dove's oral presentation. But as regards the Secularization Hypothesis – I think that this topic invites comparison with the theme of the paper which Professor Schmitz presented this morning. It seems to me that the thesis that Professor Schmitz proposed concerning the possibility of an Absolute Negativity beyond the Hegelian dialectic, is an attempt to find an autonomy or transcendence for religion after the fact of the Hegelian version of the "death of God" has been considered.

The obstacles that impede the acceptance of the Secularization Hypothesis and in particular Löwith's distress with Hegel's "secularization" of Christianity – seem to pose the same general problem confronted by Schmitz: How are we to maintain or preserve an autonomy for religion in view of what Hegel has done? In other words, what about the ancient controversy between reason and faith, the controversy that you read about in Augustine, Anselm, the Medievalists and Renaissance thinkers? Are reason and faith locked in a perpetual antinomy – or are they reconcilable?

Has Hegel, as he claims, solved this antinomy? In *Glauben und Wissen*, Hegel seems to think that he has solved this problem and that the ancient dichotomy between faith and reason has finally been superceded in his philosophy. So I think that the question of the validity of the secularization hypothesis has to be discussed in the context of this claim of Hegel's.

There are just a few points about Prof. Dove's paper that I'd like to touch on before I get to the substantive issues here. First of all, the last paragraph of his paper states that he deems it necessary to enter into a more "immanent" critique of Hegel than he has found in the various Secularization Hypotheses. This, as far as I can see, is the only place in the paper where Prof. Dove states explicitly that he disagrees with, or takes exception to, the Secularization Hypothesis. I think that the disagreement or the exception should be made stronger. Personally, I tend to agree with the Secularization Hypothesis as presented by Löwith and others, and I would like to hear a stronger argument to the contrary. But in Dove's paper there is no such argument; there is little more than a bare assertion.

Now perhaps the remarks that he just made about the Introduction to the *Phenomenology*, about the dialectic between the *an sich* and the *für sich,* are intended as "a more immament critique," insofar as this dialectic is a challenge to skepticism. I'm not sure. If that is the case, then the relevance should be made more explicit.

Secondly, on page 6* of his paper, he makes his only textual reference to Hegel, a reference to Hegel's *Vernunft in der Geschichte* in which there is a contrast of Anaxagoras' principle of an order-generating *Nous* with the Christian belief in Providence. Prof. Dove says the stated similarity between *Nous* and Providence would perhaps lead you to believe that Hegel does indeed adhere to something like the secularization theory. But the particular text that Dove focuses on, in so far as it shows a *similarity* between reason and the Christian idea of Providence, also (as any similarity) shows a contrast. And therefore, I think it is ambiguous. It doesn't really elucidate the problem as it stands, because one could just as easily maintain that Hegel emphasizes the *difference between* reason and Providence, on the basis of this text. So I think that a further explication of that text, or references to other texts in Hegel would be necessary, if we were to try to decide whether the Secularization Hypothesis is relevant to Hegel's philosophy or not.

Now, as far as regards the main issue of the paper (the viability of the Secularization Hypothesis) I would like to focus on just one comment of Prof. Dove, on page 4 and 5, † where he compares one aspect of the Secularization Hypothesis to the Oedipus tragedy. He says "the most fateful aspect of the Hegelian philosophy, as Löwith sees it, is that Hegel himself failed to grasp the profound ambiguity at the heart of his own thinking. The subsequent history of philosophy – or at least Germanic Philosophy until Nietzsche – may therefore be read as a modern dress version of the Oedipus tragedy, in which the role of the protagonist is played in turn by Hegel, Marx, Kierkegaard (together with the lesser left Hegelians) and, finally, Nietzsche, who comes closest to a full realization that the philosopher of history has murdered his holy father and desecrated his

* *Supra.*, p. 149.
† *Supra.*, p. 147.

mother faith in producing that bastard quest for a "meaning" of history "determined absolutely from within history itself." Let me restate the analogy: According to Professor Dove, a kind of philosophical Oedipus tragedy has been indicated and portrayed by Löwith's hypothesis: The "father" in this case, is Christianity; the "mother" is faith. Hegel, according to Löwith, has murdered, or done away with, Christianity *per se*. He has achieved an incestuous union with his characterized mother, faith; and the illicit product of this incestuous union is a teleological-eschatological concept of history – a history which is presupposed to contain an eternal teleology within itself.

Now, all I would want to do here is carry this analogy a little further – in a sort of Freudian way. As you know, the Oedipus complex does not usually end with the little boy murdering his father and marrying his mother. Ordinarily, this is not the resolution. Perhaps sometimes. But as Freud tells us, there is ordinarily a sublimation of sorts: the child, instead of murdering his father, "identifies" with his father. He overcomes his tendency to murder his father by incorporating him, internalizing him. He creates an internalized father, an ego-ideal or super-ego, and the father remains.

Neither does the child marry his mother. He internalizes her. And this results in a "motherly conscience," as one of the commentators on Freud calls it.

It is necessary to realize that there is not a real tragedy here, at least in the ordinary sense of tragedy.

Now, following the same line of thought, perhaps Hegel has gone a bit further, or the Secularization Hypothesis has gone further, than simply murdering Christianity and forming an incestuous union with faith. Has the process of secularization not perhaps incorporated Christianity through a kind of internalization, and thus brought about a reconciliation between reason and the Christian faith? I think this is a possibility we have to take into account. Perhaps this controversy about the relationship, and the distinction, between reason and faith has finally been solved by Hegel. If so, you can no longer dismiss this problem in such a way as to take for granted that we are still in the wake of the old dichotomy. You would have to take Hegel's "synthesis" as a starting point for all future discussion of the relationship between reason and faith. Perhaps the transcendent eschatological expectations of Christianity have been incorporated into the immanent teleology of the philosophy of history, as Hegel claims. If so, it would be as immature for Christianity to return to its primitive claims, as it would be for an adult to try to revert to the beginning of the Oedipal stage of development.

I would like to note that Hegel himself offers a formulation which bears a striking similarity to the Freudian metaphor: This formulation comes at the end of Hegel's chapter on "Revealed Religion" in the *Phenomenology*, after the advent of Christianity and the incarnation of Christ has solved the dichotomy between consciousness and self-consciousness. Around the last page in this chapter on "Revealed Religion" Hegel makes a comparison between Christ and the Christian. He says that, just as Christ had an explicit mother, a real mother, but only an implicit or implied father, the father being invisible and not directly accessible, so also the Christian has an explicit "father" (his own will and spontaneous action) and an implicit "mother" (the sentiment or feeling of love, which has not yet become predominant or explicated within Christianity).* The resolution of this dichotomy (which is found in different ways in Christ and Christianity, respectively) comes about by an *Aufhebung* which leads to "Absolute Knowledge" in the *Phenomenology* (Absolute Knowledge being a state in which the spirit of Christ's father becomes explicit and the (metaphorical) "mother" of Christians becomes explicit also.) What is the nature of this *Aufhebung*?

The explicitation of the Spirit of the Father of Christ takes place (according to Hegel) when the historical, imaginative presentation of Christ as a past figure is done away with. No longer is he an historical figure, but the historical emphasis is transcended. It is only when this takes place that the Spirit of the Father becomes explicit, so that the father is no longer an unreal "beyond." Correspondingly, the implicit love of Christians becomes explicit, according to Hegel, when the future expectation of salvation, of a Last Judgment (the eschatological expectations) is superceded, and is no longer an essential part of Christianity; so that the Christian lives completely in the present, no longer in and for the future. (Feuerbach's interpretation of the "essence of Christianity" dwells in depth on this latter aspect of the secularization of Christianity).

But the essential thing I'm trying to suggest here is that there are other ways of conceiving the Oedipal-type situation that Professor Dove refers

---

* Cf. *Phänomenologie des Geistes* (Hamburg: Meiner, 1952), S. 548: "Seine eigne Versöhnung tritt daher als ein *Fernes* in sein Bewusstsein ein, als ein Fernes der *Zukunft*, wie die Versöhnung, die das andere *Selbst* vollbrachte, als eine Ferne der Vergangenheit erscheint. So wie der *einzelne* göttliche Mensch einen *ansich*seienden Vater und nur eine *wirkliche* Mutter hat, so hat der allgemeine göttliche Mensch, die Gemeinde, ihr *eignes Tun* und *Wissen* zu ihrem Vater, zu ihrer Mutter aber die ewige Liebe, die sie nur *fuhlt*, nicht aber ... als wirklichen unmittelbaren *Gegenstand* anschaut."

to. Perhaps there has been a "sublimation" of the "Oedipal" problem. Hegel himself seems to portray this sublimation in the aforementioned passages in the chapter on "Revealed Religion."

Professor Dove takes exception to the secularization hypothesis. Does he reject the hypothesis in so far as Hegel was wrong in formulating it or does he do so in so far as Löwith was wrong in applying it to Hegel? If he is rejecting it because Hegel was wrong in formulating it, then I think passages such as the one I've mentioned have to be taken into consideration; for they suggest the contrary. If he is rejecting it because Löwith applied it wrongly, I think not only do such passages have to be taken into account; but also it is necessary to develop some type of critical argument as to whether or not this hypothesis can be usefully applied to the interpretation of Hegel (whether or not Hegel explicitly asserted such a hypothesis).

HEGEL AND JUDAISM:
A FLAW IN THE HEGELIAN MEDIATION[1]

Emil L. Fackenheim

1

In his *Hegels Leben* Karl Rosenkranz makes the following observation: Hegel's view of Jewish history varied greatly at different times. The phenomenon both repelled and fascinated him, and vexed him as a dark riddle throughout his life. At times, such as in the *Phenomenology*, he ignored it. At other times, such as in the *Philosophy of Right*, he placed it in close proximity to the Germanic Spirit. At other times again, such as in the *Philosophy of Religion*, he placed it on a par with Greek and Roman history, as together constituting the immediate forms of spiritual individuality. Finally – in the *Philosophy of History* – he made Jewish history part of the Persian Empire. All these are . . . justified aspects, . . . but only the whole can satisfy.[2]

This paper – an extensive commentary on Rosenkranz' observation – will seek to show (i) that if (like many Gentile philosophers before and after him) Hegel was "repelled" by Jewish history, it was, in his case perhaps alone, because of serious philosophical reasons rather than mere handed-down prejudice and traditional bias: Jewish religious existence is radically at odds with central commitments of his philosophy; (ii) that if Jewish history "fascinated" him, it was not because of titillation by the "exotic" but rather because of philosophical integrity: he was unable to ignore a millennial historical fact simply because it would not fit into his system; (iii) that the last sentence in Rosenkranz' observation reflects a mere pious sentiment on the part of a pious Hegelian: Jewish religious existence *remains* a "dark riddle" for Hegel's philosophy to which, much though it tries, it cannot "do justice." *Hegel's philosophy seeks to mediate*

---

[1] This article reflects the general Hegel-interpretation given and documented in my *The Religious Dimension In Hegel's Thought* (Bloomington: Indiana University Press, 1968), and therefore documents only its own specific contentions. These confine themselves to a critical exposition of Hegel's philosophical mediation of Jewish history. A much more extensive account, to be published by Basic Books in my forthcoming *Encounters Between Judaism and Modern Philosophy*, will confront Hegel's mediation *of* Jewish history with Jewish self-mediation *in* history.

[2] Karl Rosenkranz, *Hegels Leben, Supplement zu Hegels Werken* (Berlin: Duncker & Humblot, 1844), p. 49.

all things, divine as well as human, transforming all absolute into relative distinctions. Jewish religious existence, in contrast, remains stubbornly committed to at least two absolute *distinctions – between the Divine and the human, and between the One true God and all the false. Indeed, these distinctions are reimposing themselves in the present age on Jewish existence – obsurely but unmistakeably – despite its thorough exposure to modern secularism.*

2

To the superficial reader Hegel's account of Judaism reflects simple re-pulsion. It seems to differ from, say, that of Kant only in its greater respect for historical phenomena and to be no less a caricature. Both thinkers ap-pear to view Judaism as a barren legalism, the one taking it as illustrating the vices of "theological morality," the other, as illustrating those of re-ligious "positivity"; and there seems little to choose between Kant's re-commendation of "euthanasia" for Judaism and Hegel's demonstration that Jewish religious existence is an anachronism. The best, it appears, that can be said is that, influenced as they were in this matter largely by Spinoza and Moses Mendelssohn, these two non-Jewish thinkers cannot be blamed too much if they took Jewish thinkers as authoritative.

But closer inspection reveals that, whereas Kant fails to understand Ju-daism because he never tries, Hegel's failure, crucial though it is, results from serious and even desperate attempts to do Judaism – like all profound spiritual phenomena – genuine "justice." Kant simply judges Judaism to be an anachronism by standards which are not questioned. Hegel's cor-responding judgment is self-exposed to the fact of Jewish survival through-out the ages; and such is the integrity shown in this self-exposure that Jewish existence, supposedly rendered anachronistic by the Christian world if indeed not by classical antiquity, keeps reappearing in his thought. The God of Israel alone survives the death of all the ancient deities in the Roman pantheon. Jewish history is somehow connected with modern Germanic history, thus emerging as in some sense dialectically superior to the entire Christian Middle Ages. Assuming in Spinozism the form of modern philosophical thought, Judaism is the indispensable beginning of all philosophical modernity. Finally, there is a cryptic footnote in the *Philosophy of Right* which, if understood in Hegelian terms, can mean nothing else than that there is a future for the Jewish people in the modern world, the dialectical dissipation of their religious past notwithstanding – a view lending more than poetic truth to the fact that the first Western

Zionist philosophy – that of Moses Hess – was largely Hegelian.[3] Kant (and many other philosophers one could cite) judge Judaism *ab extra* and never take it seriously. Hegel's philosophy immerses itself in the Jewish religious self-understanding before venturing criticism; and such is the profundity of its self-immersion and its criticism that both, even though failing in the end, remain significant to this day.

This would never have come to pass had Hegel's mature thought not turned sharply from the standpoint of his so-called *Early Theological Writings*. These early fragments, never intended for publication, remain with a dualism wholly alien to Hegel's mature philosophy. A religion of true inwardness is contrasted with one of mere "positivity" or external observance, and of this latter Judaism serves as the prime example. To be sure, Hegel surpasses Kant even then in his historical realism, and his brief recourse to an unhistorical mystic-romantic divine-human "union" is accompanied by a tragic awareness of divine-human "nonunion" in actual history. Even so, however, a dualism remains between sheer virtue or spirit and sheer vice or letter, and, as has happened with such depressing regularity in the history of Christendom, Judaism is the prime villain. However the realm of religious truth is to be circumscribed – and on this subject Hegel's views shift quickly in this early period – Judaism falls outside it.

In Hegel's mature thought Judaism is drawn into *the sphere of religious truth.* This monumental change is part and parcel of a no less monumental overall change in Hegel's mature philosophy of religion. First, every trace of (Kantian or romantic) subjectivist reductionism, if ever genuinely present at all, has disappeared: the religious fact for philosophical thought is not subjective or human, but rather (as all serious religious self-understanding takes it to be) subjective-objective, or a divine-human relationship. Second, this latter relationship is characterized by divine-human "nonunion" *as well as* divine-human "union": the tragic realism which in the *Early Theological Writings* falls *outside* the realm of religious truth now lies *within* it. Of these two doctrines the first is already present in Hegel's transitional romantic phase. But not until both doctrines are fully developed has his philosophy of religion reached maturity.

Hegel's mature doctrine is as follows. Without divine-human "union" there is no genuine religion but only mutual divine-human indifference and irrelevance. (Deism, ancient and modern, is no genuine religion but only a disguise for a lack of religion.) Without divine-human "nonunion" religion is idolatrous or frivolous: the first if the divine Infinity is

---

[3] See his *Rome and Jerusalem*, tr. M. Waxman (New York: Bloch, 1945).

reduced to *sheer* finitude; the second if the human self has fled from its real finitude into the shapeless "fog" of an infinite but unreal pious emotion. Hegel holds that no *genuine* religion is *simply* idolatrous, for the divine Infinity is at work *in* every such religion even if it does not, or only inadequately, become conscious *for* it. He also contrasts romantic frivolousness with Christian seriousness. The one flees from the actual divine-human discord into the sheer "union" of mere feeling. The other finds its climax in the Easter – a "union of union *and nonunion*" [4] which *both* preserves *and* conquers the Good Friday, the whole pain of absolute discord.

Within this overall conception, Judaism appears as the stern, stubborn, incorruptible witness to divine-human nonunion. The Jewish God is One, Infinite, universal, wholly incommensurate with multiplicity, finitude, particularity. On his part, His human worshiper exists in stark human finitude and particularity, a "family" even when "expanded into a nation." [5] Hegel sees a "strange, infinitely harsh, the harshest contrast" [6] in this divine-human relationship, and everything will in the end depend on why he sees a harsh contrast here and how he copes with it. For the present, however, all attention must be focused on his view that the Jewish divine-human relationship is a dimension of religious truth despite and indeed because of this contrast. *In spite* of it: Judaism is by no means (like Deism) a mutual divine-human irrelevance and indifference; within the divine-Jewish "nonunion" there lives a real "union" when man recognizes God as Lord and himself as His servant, and when God assumes lordship over him. *Because* of the contrast: the Jewish testimony to the divine-human nonunion has an absolute right over against all efforts to deny or dissipate either the finitude of the human or the infinity of the Divine. More: it has a role within the total realm of religious truth which is unique and indispensable. The Jewish fear of the Lord is not one religious wisdom beside others. It is the beginning of *all* religious wisdom.

The philosopher can elicit from Judaism (as from every genuine religion) a "metaphysical notion." The Divine is "infinite Power." A Power is *infinite* only if it is not beside, or indifferent to, the finite, but rather

---

[4] *Early Theological Writings*, tr. Knox-Kroner (University of Chicago Press, 1948), p. 312. Richard Kroner rightly calls this formula Hegel's "future philosophic system in a nutshell" (p. 14). He fails to add that it also expresses Hegel's mature view of Christianity, considered by him the "true content" necessarily preceding his own philosophy which gives that content its "true form." The present article makes ample use of the formula just cited.

[5] *Vorlesungen über die Philosophie der Religion*, ed. Lasson (Hamburg: Meiner, 1966), vol. II, p. 82 (Subsequently cited as *PhR*).

[6] *PhR*, II, p. 81.

Power *over* it. It is *divine* only if it is not *sheer* Power (no object of possible *worship*) but rather "Power of Wisdom." The world of finitude is „absolutely posited" by this Power, the "purpose" being divine lordship over the "world." Such in utmost brevity, is the metaphysical notion of Judaism.[7]

It would be a mere philosopher's abstraction except for its "realization." This occurs *in and for the religious consciousness* – in Judaism, in a human acceptance of both world and human self as products of a divine *creatio ex nihilo*. In this acceptance divine Power reveals itself as Goodness and Justice. *Divine* Goodness is absolute, manifesting itself primordially not in *what* finite things are but rather in *that* they are at all – granted independent existence, despite their finitude, side by side the divine Infinity. (For idolatrous or atheistic consciousness the existence of the world is an unquestioned fact. For Jewish religious consciousness it is *the* primordial miracle since the world is finite, and God, infinite.) No less absolute is divine Justice, its primordial manifestation being the revelation that, over against the divine Infinity, the finite owns no claims. By virtue of divine Goodness the world is forever already created and forever being maintained. By virtue of divine Justice it is forever destined to perish. He who in the beginning alone was will be alone in the end.[8]

This "realization" of the "metaphysical notion" of Judaism brings about the "demythologization" (*Entgöttlichung*) of the world. In nature religions the natural is itself divine, and even for Greek religion (no nature religion) the world is "full of gods." (Thales) Because in Judaism nature is posited *by* the Divine it is itself *un*divine, and this is true as well of man or "finite spirit": *all* finite things are divinely posited. Only on this "prosaic" presupposition can there be *miracles*. When as in Indian religion the Divine and the worldly freely intermingle "everything is intrinsically topsy-turvy." [9] Only when the world is in principle *distinct from* the Divine can it have a finite order of its own, and only then can there be miracles, or "sporadic manifestations of God in something particular." [10] Such manifestations must here be possible and indeed necessary, for the distinction between God and a divinely posited world takes place in a religious consciousness existing *in the world*. To the "prose" of the world corresponds "holiness" in Divinity, and *the religious consciousness is the*

[7] *PhR*, II, pp. 55-59.
[8] *PhR*, II, pp. 59-67. The traditional Jewish hymn *Adon Olam* contains the line "After all things shall have ended He, awe-inspiring, alone shall reign; He who was, is, and will be in glory."
[9] *PhR*, II, p. 70.
[10] *PhR*, II, p. 70.

place in which this "prose" and this "holiness" must meet even as they are held apart. But how could this be unless the Divine broke into the world's worldliness?

This "place," however, would be subjective only (i.e., divorced from both an objective God and the actual world) were it nothing but *mere* consciousness. There must be, and is, an *acting out* in which the actual world, the objective God and existing man in his psychosomatic totality are all involved. This occurs in Judaism when men "walk before God" so as to give Him "honor" in the "world." [11]

This honor is given by an affirmation of the divine Infinity which, made by the finite self, is at the same time a negation of the self by the self. Yet no less essential than this affirmation of the divine Infinity (and the self-negation of finite selfhood involved in it) is the self-affirmation of finite selfhood. Greeks submit to a blind divine Fate: Jews have "trust" in a divine Wisdom which will confirm the worshiping self not despite but precisely because of and *in* his human finitude. According to Hegel there is "fragmentation" in this togetherness of finite human self-negation and self-affirmation: even so there is truth in it. The Jewish "confidence" that "he who does right will fare well . . . is (not only) a basic trait of the Jewish people (but also) . . . one which is admirable.[12]

No less admirable (and ultimately for the same reason) is Jewish "steadfastness," a "fanaticism of stubbornness."[13] On the one hand, Jews worship the One, Infinite, universal God, rejecting all finite, particularistic deities. On the other hand, they remain a particular "family" even when "expanded into a nation," refusing to "absorb alien forms of religious worship." Hegel, as already mentioned, sees a "strange, infinitely harsh, the harshest contrast" in this relation, and he specifies it as between the "universal God . . . of Heaven and earth . . . (and) . . . His limited . . . purpose in but one family . . . in the historical world" – between "the demand that all nations give praise to His name (and His) real work (which consists) only . . . in the external, internal, political, ethical existence" of this one people.[14]

Hegel might have trivialized this "contrast" in the fashion of subsequent evolutionary liberalism, either by reducing the God of Israel to a mere tribal deity, or by dissipating the actual Jewish "family" into an abstract sect of "monotheists," or by contriving an "evolutionary process" from the one to the other in which the *terminus a quo* never meets the

[11] *PhR*, II, p. 78.
[12] *PhR*, II, pp. 78ff., 98.
[13] *PhR*, II, p. 97.
[14] *PhR*, II, pp. 81ff.

terminus ad quem. He resists that temptation. It is precisely *in* his finite, human, Jewish particularity that the Jew worships a God who *is* God for him only because he transcends all finitude and particularity. More: the Jew not only *does* hold fast to this "contrast"; he *must* hold fast to it and endure it. In Hegel's view this contrast could be overcome (rather than merely evaded) only by means of a divine-human mediation in which at once the Divine concretizes its own Infinity in finite human particularity while, as part of the same mediation, the particularity and finitude of the human were somehow raised and transfigured. Lacking a mediation of this sort, the Jew must hold fast to the contrast; to let go of it would be to lapse either into frivolousness (a flight from his actual Jewish particularity into some such abstraction as humanity-in-general) or idolatry (the reduction of the Lord of creation to a tribal deity.) To spurn both is to remain an uncorrupted witness to the incommensurateness of the Divine in its infinite Universality and the human in its undissolved particularity; and precisely this fidelity is "admirable."

For this reason the core of Jewish religious existence lies in a "renunciation of renunciation." [15] The worship of the infinite divine Power is the self-renunciation of human finitude. Such a self-renunciation, however, would be sheer self-dissipation were there not also a "renunciation of renunciation" – a "confidence" in a divine Wisdom which will confirm worshiping man in his very finitude. Thus "submission, renunciation, the recognition of the . . . purposive divine Power restores Job's former good fortune. Pure confidence, the intuition of the . . . purposive divine Power comes first; but it carries in train temporal good fortune." [16]

Thus, in brief, the Jew gives honor to God in the world. Yet this "realization" of the "metaphysical notion" of Judaism would remain unreal in an unreal world if it remained in heart and thought alone. It assumes actuality in the actual world only as it permeates and transforms the whole length and breath of real life – in the "labor" of cult. Jewish cult is obedience to a God-given law in the fear of the Lord.

Fear remains animal so long as it is dispersed into many fears geared to natural objects. Fear of the Lord, being one infinite fear, far from itself

---

[15] *PhR*, II, p. 99.
[16] *PhR*, II, p. 98. Hegel's Job has a remarkable resemblance to Kierkegaard's Abraham who in the very act of absolute resignation has faith that all well be restored to him. (See *Fear and Trembling*, New York: Anchor, 1954.) This resemblance is all the more remarkable because it is virtually impossible to assume that in this matter Kierkegaard should have been writing under Hegel's influence. That two Christian dialectical thinkers trying to understand Judaism should have arrived at similar conclusions is a fact worthy of close examination.

animal, on the contrary drives out all the many fears; and while the animal affirms its animality as it fears, the Jewish fear of the Lord dissipates human selfhood into nothingness. Yet – in the concrete labor of cultic life as in the abstract consciousness of heart and thought – the Jew "renounces renunciation." As the Jewish self recognizes God as Lord he finds himself recognized as servant, by both the Lord and himself. "The fear in which the servant regards himself as servant restores his being to him." [17]

This actual renunciation of renunciation comes alive in obedience to a God-given law. Solon and Lykurgos are the law-givers of the Greeks. God himself is the law-giver of the Jews, and Moses is only His instrument. Since God and man are incommensurable, "positivity" is not, in this context, a contingent and unspiritual trait to be done away with in the religious life and to be ignored by philosophic thought. The God-given law *must* be positive in both origin and content. "The most trifling ordinance" not only coexists with "the eternal laws of right and morality"; they also are "of the same rank." Nor are they alterable by human action, and human freedom is confined to accepting obedience. Hence "the details of the political constitution" are all determined – divinely, indiscriminately, and once and for all; they are neither left for the human will to determine nor in themselves determined with reference to a universal purpose. As for every kind of "political change," it is apostasy.

This acceptance (of the service of the Lord) is once and for all. It *takes the place of reconciliation and redemption.* In themselves reconciliation and redemption *have already taken place,* reflecting a choice by divine Grace *apart from all (human) freedom.*[18]

So much, for the present, in summary of Hegel's account of Jewish religious existence. To his account he adds the observation that the God of Moses is in strong contrast with the conception which "we" have of God.[19] It is not yet clear who this "we" is and how "our" conception of God is superior to that ascribed to Judaism. For reasons which have yet to emerge, Jewish religious existence, though an indispensable aspect of the totality of religious truth, is now as such an anachronism.

3

If the grounds of Hegel's criticism of Judaism have yet to emerge so do the grounds for his comprehension of it. Yet it is obvious that his compre-

[17] *PhR,* II, p. 94.
[18] *PhR,* II, pp. 96ff., 100. Italics added.
[19] *PhR,* II, p. 97.

hension, whatever its shortcomings, does not, at any rate, *wholly* fail to "do justice" to the Jewish religious self-understanding. To be sure, this latter takes itself as *standing in relation to* the Divine while the former seeks to grasp an inner logic in that relation from a standpoint external and somehow superior to it; yet the "logic" grasped reflects an uncanny empathy. Thus, e.g., it leaves far behind all liberalistic tribal deities, subjectivistic God-ideas, and evolutionary processes inserted between them. Instead it takes hold of and holds fast to the fact central to the Jewish religious self-understanding: a living relation *between* a radically universal God *and* one particular human "family."

Hence it is not surprising that much in Hegel's account passes critical scrutiny even by the most exacting and normative – i.e., rabbinic – standards of Jewish religious self-understanding, and this despite the fact that he shows no signs of acquaintance with the Talmudic and Midrashic sources. Thus (to give some examples) the rabbinic sources, while affirming an "oral Torah" which interprets and develops the "written" one, insist that the first is *in* the second, not a "free" human alteration of it; thus too, while searching for "reasons of the commandments" (*ta 'ame mitzvot*), they stress the validity of the commandments whether or not reasons are found. (Even modern non-orthodox Judaism pays liturgical if no other homage to the "positivity" of the Torah when it retains its reading in the weekly Sabbath service.) To be sure, this "positivity" does not render rabbinic Judaism incapable of "union" with the divine Giver of the Torah, for it insists that His law should and can be performed for *its* (and *His*) sake rather than merely extraneous motives. But then, Hegel himself surpasses Kant and all the other critics of Jewish "legalism" in just this – that he understands the law of Judaism not as a bar between divine Giver and human recipient but rather as a bridge. As antinomian a thinker as Martin Buber affirms an *immediate* (albeit, to be sure, not "harsh") relation between an infinite divine Thou and a finite, particular, human I; nor does that thinker fail to emphasize an immediate divine kingship exercized over an assembly of particular tribes in the pristine Biblical sources.[20] Clearly, the "contrast" between the Infinite One and one finite "family" is as central to the Jewish religious self-understanding as it is to Hegel's philosophical comprehension of it. Moreover, the crucial Hegelian concept of a dialectical "renunciation of renunciation" seems to do remarkable "justice" to it. How could a divine Thou – or King – possess infinity unless a finite "family" or "nation" renounced itself radi-

---

[20] See *I and Thou* (New York: Scribners, 1958); *Königtum Gottes* (Berlin: Schokken, 1936).

cally in His presence? And how could, nevertheless, an immediate relation exist between these two incommensurables unless there were also, and at the same time, "renunciation of renunciation?"

Yet just as Hegel *prima facie* succeeds so he *prima facie* fails as well. (We say "*prima facie*" in both cases as the *grounds* of Hegel's philosophical comprehension of Judaism have not yet emerged.) To begin with a by no means random example, (for to Hegel Job is the pious Jew *par excellence*), the Hegelian Job can receive the gift of an all-restoring divine Goodness only after an absolute renunciation before divine Power. In contrast, the Biblical Job (and any authentic Jewish comprehension of him) lodges an absolute protest – one remaining incommensurable with the divine Presence even when this latter manifests itself as absolute Power.[21]

This example once having been cited, others more central to our present purpose quickly force themselves upon us. Hegel *both* praises the Jew for his "firm" refusal to "assimilate alien forms of worship" *and* criticizes such lack of "universalism." The Maccabees were not stopped by their rejection of Hellenic gods from assimilating aspects of Hellenic culture.[22] Nor did rabbinic fidelity to the "particularistic" Sinaitic covenant prove incompatible with a belief on their part in a "universalistic" Noahidic one – a belief culminating in the doctrine that "righteous Gentiles" were equal to the high priest in the sight of God. Hegel's charge of "particularism" – "God is God of His people and not of all men" [23] – climaxes in *prima facie* absurdity with his statement that the Jewish doctrine of creation had effective reality, not in Judaism, but only in Christianity.[24] One Talmudic rabbi summed up the whole Torah with the verse "This is the book of the generations of man" (Gen. 5 : 1); [25] and orthodox Jews still thank God daily for renewing the creation.

No less *prima facie* absurd than the "particularism"-charge is the charge (as will be seen, related) that Judaism "lacks freedom." Hegel's Jewish

---

[21] See Buber, *At The Turning* (New York: Farrar, Straus & Young, 1952), p. 61: "Job ... charges that the 'cruel' (30 : 21) God has 'removed his right' from him (27 : 2) and thus that the judge of the earth acts against justice. And he receives an answer from God. But what God says to him does not answer the charge; *it does not even touch upon it*. The true answer that Job receives is God's appearance only . . . ." (Italics added).

[22] See Elias Bickerman's brief but great work *The Maccabees* (in: *From Esra to the Last of the Maccabees*, New York: Schocken, 1962), which demonstrates that the Maccabees *both* rejected Hellenistic gods *and* appropriated Hellenistic culture.

[23] *PhR*, II, p. 82.

[24] *PhR*, II, pp. 59, 62, 82. See my *Religious Dimension in Hegel's Thought*, pp. 129-33, 134, 189n.

[25] *Sifra*, 89b. Cited in Loewe-Montefiore, *A Rabbinic Anthology* (London: MacMillan, 1938), p. 172. Since rabbinic sources are not easily accessible to philosophical scholars I shall, wherever possible, give references to this excellent anthology. (Cited as *RA*).

God is Lord *only*, worshiped in *nothing but* fear. The God of the rabbis is Father as well as King, worshiped in love no less than in fear. Hegel's Mosaic law is *purely* positive, and Moses himself, a *sheer* instrument. The rabbinic Moses is no sheer instrument, and the rabbis are so "free" in their interpretation of his law that Moses himself, listening in heaven, cannot understand it.[26] The Hegelian Sinaitic legislation *"takes the place of reconciliation and redemption . . . and reflects a choice of divine Grace apart from all (human) freedom."* [27] In the rabbinic self-understanding, human freedom as well as divine choice are involved in the Sinaitic event; [28] and, far from taking the place of redemption, it on the contrary itself points to a Messianic future – one which is the joint work of God and man. Something, it seems, is seriously wrong.

What is wrong, however, is not merely Hegel's unfamiliarity with the rabbinic sources and our mere citing of these. For as we now turn from rabbinic to Biblical Judaism, the Jewish religious self-understanding still remains radically at odds with Hegel's philosophical comprehension of it. Presumably any philosophical account of an "essence" or "inner logic" of a form of religious life is problematic in being perforce selective in its use of source material. Hegel's selectivity *vis-à-vis* Biblical Judaism, however, is either totally scandalous in its arbitrariness – or else has a philosophical justification which has yet to emerge.

Consider the issues of "universalism" and "freedom" which will turn out to be crucial (as well as related). Hegel writes:

The Jewish God is the God of Abraham, Isaac and Jacob, the God who has led Israel out of Egypt; and there is not the slightest reflection that God has acted affirmatively among other nations as well.[29]

To cite no earlier sources, what of prophetic universalism – or of Amos' explicit connection between Israel's exodus from Egypt with that of Philistines from Caphtor and Aram from Kir (Amos 9 : 7)? Hegel disposes of prophetic universalism as follows:

The honor of God is to become manifest among all nations; especially among the later prophets this universality appears as a higher demand. Isaiah makes God say, "I will make priests and levites of those Gentiles who become wor-

---

[26] *Bab. Talmud, Tractate Menahot*, 29b (*RA*, p. 217).

[27] See above, note 18.

[28] The fact that the Torah was given in the desert is used by the rabbis to give Midrashic proof that it is "free to all the inhabitants of the world," that "everyone who desires to accept it may come and accept it," that no tribe may say to the others "I am better than you," and that "if a man does not make himself free to all as the desert, he is not worthy to receive the Torah." (A selection of the many relevant passages is assembled in *RA*, pp. 166ff.)

[29] *PhR*, II, p. 96.

shipers of Jehovah" (Isaiah 66 : 21). All this, however, is later; according to the dominant ground-idea (*Grundidee*) the Jews are the chosen people, and universality is thus reduced to particularity.[30]

But what if (as modern, sometimes Hegel-inspired Jewish thinkers were to argue) prophetic "universalism" is implicit in the original "particularism?" Or, more importantly (as is implied in the Biblical Jewish self-understanding since its origins), God chooses Israel for purposes transcending Israel from the start? What *Grundidee* (or characteristics of the *Grundidee* in question) deprives such universalism of truth or authenticity – when, in contrast, New Testament Christianity is permitted to explicate its universalistic implications throughout world history, despite and indeed because of its scandal of particularity?

According to Hegel, Biblical-Jewish "lack of freedom." The Biblical Jew can self-actively transform the world, and he can become "reconciled" with God, but he cannot unite these two aspects of being: any "free" Jewish self-activity *toward* God is inevitably a "falling away" from His law and an act of rebellion. Hence, so far as Hegel is concerned, Biblical Judaism implies, for man, a stance of frozen passive obedience; for God, a posture of frozen otherness; and for the law which spans the gulf between these two incommensurables an unalterable, uninterpretable, indiscriminately valid "positivity." And rabbinic Judaism, had Hegel been familiar with it, would have had to be disposed of in a manner similar to the disposal of prophetic universalism.

Yet this account is totally at odds with the Biblical sources. In his own self-understanding the Biblical Jew does not lack freedom *vis-à-vis* God, for he freely accepts the divine law; he does so, moreover, in love as well as in fear; and, having done so, he holds God Himself responsible for its terms. There is, in short, a *divine-Jewish covenant*, and such is the extent of its *mutuality* that God Himself may respond to an originally anti-divine human act by Himself accepting it. Thus "political change" – such as the demand for a human king, the kingship of God notwithstanding – while initially "called a falling away from God," is in the end accepted by God Himself; and such is the significance of this divine acceptance that *the descendent of David, the human king, is none other than the Messiah himself*. In Hegel's account of Judaism, however, two features startle above all others. One is that he mentions the concept of covenant but can make nothing of it. The other is that, incredible though it may seem, the Messianic belief is totally omitted – a fact all the more startling because

[30] *PhR*, II, pp. 95ff.

Hegel in his *Early Theological Writings* had himself described Messianism as essential to Judaism.[31]

Two explanations are possible for this state of affairs. Of these, one – that Hegel claims to *find* his *Grundidee* of Judaism *in* the Biblical sources – implies a degree of arbitrariness on his part which, in his case, defies all belief. We must therefore fall back on, and explore, the other explanation: Hegel (at least in part) *brings* this *Grundidee to* the Biblical sources – with a philosophical justification which has yet to emerge. If "we" have a concept of God superior to that of Moses – and can comprehend this latter in terms which render it anachronistic – this "we" must both identify itself and offer its credentials.

4

We shall presumably never find this "we" unless we somehow enter into Hegel's world of thought from the start. Yet, for the purpose at hand, the temptation to take a giant leap straightway into the complete and self-completing Hegelian system must be resisted. This latter, to be sure, being an infinite, self-explicating thought-activity which mediates all things, divine as well as human, may produce in this process a *Grundidee* in terms of which Jewish religious life is both comprehended and super-seded. We have, however, noted from the start a radical conflict between Hegel's commitment to universal mediation and the Jewish commitment to at least two absolute distinctions – between the Divine and the human, and between the One true God and all the false. If now in this conflict Hegel's commitment assumed the form of philosophical *thought only* it would provoke a protest from non-philosophical, religious, Jewish *life*; and since, by Hegel's own admission and insistence, a thought which is thought *only* could not mediate the conflict between itself and life, life would emerge victorious, disclosing the thought as having come "shot from the pistol." [32]

---

[31] *Early Theological Writings*, pp. 158ff., 203. Hegel states here that "the ordinary Jew," unwilling to let go of his God but faced with the "grim reality" of the loss of the Jewish state, "fled" from this reality by means of the Messianic hope. This view of Jewish Messianism as escapism may be an important clue (one which, after the Nazi holocaust and the rise of the first Jewish state in two thousand years, no Jewish thinker may take lightly) to Hegel's subsequent neglect of Jewish Messianism. But what might Hegel have to say about the state of Christian Messianism in the contemporary world? And, in view of the epoch-making events in contemporary Jewish history just referred to, could Hegel today still write: "The scattered remnants of the Jews have not abandoned the idea of the Jewish state, but they have reverted not to the banners of their own courage but only to the standards of an ineffective messianic hope" (p. 159)? See further below, section 10.

[32] This is argued at length in my *Religious Dimension in Hegel's Thought*, especially

By Hegel's own admission and insistence: his thought seeks to do far greater "justice" to Jewish religious life (as to all forms of life) than is held by his "panlogistic" interpreters. Hegel's philosophy does not *ab extra* impose a "law" of universal mediation *upon* historical life; it *observes* mediation as *already present in* historical life, although, to be sure, this observing cannot be done without certain qualifications. And whereas the *ultimate* mediation occurs *nowhere except* in Hegel's philosophical thought, this latter is itself possible only when the times are ripe for it. But the conditions making Hegel's own time ripe for the Hegelian feat include not only modern philosophical thought but also modern life.

The "we" we are in search of – the "we" whose concept of God renders the God of Moses anachronistic and enables philosophical thought to prove Him so – is therefore, at least in the first instance, not a society of philosophical minds inhabiting the Hegelian system. It consists of authentically modern inhabitants of the modern world.

                                    5

But an immediate recourse to the modern world would involve a leap hardly less great than that just rejected. Moving slowly and cautiously in our search for the Hegelian "we," we must begin with a crucial confrontation between Jewish "East" and Greek-Roman "West" as observed by Hegelian thought.

Jewish religion is human "service" of a transcendent "Lord." Greek religion is the "creation" of human "poets." The Jew's "holy" zeal smashes all man-made statues. The Greek creates just such statues – but they are "beautiful." The one will obey only a law of a God whose human messenger is nothing but an "instrument." The other will obey only a law given by men – but considered divine. As Hegel observes the oft-observed contrast between Athens and Jerusalem, it could hardly be more radical.

Hegel's philosophy *observes* this contrast. It adds, however, to *sheer* observation at least *one* commitment of its own. It will not suspend all judgment and simply look on. Still less will it simply side either with Athens or with Jerusalem. It rather perceives truth in *both*, in spite and indeed because of their contrast. In spite of it: there *is* truth in both. Because of it: the truth in each reveals a falsehood in the other. This commitment on Hegel's part is not a sheer or arbitrary commitment, for the truth and falsehood in both Athens and Jerusalem is not an insight unique

in chapter VI.

to Hegel's philosophy. As will be seen, it has long revealed itself in man's historical life.

In this conflict between Athens and Jerusalem Athens shows itself as endowed with a quality which gives us our first glimpse of Hegel's own ultimate judgment upon Judaism. It is true that the "holy," transcendent Lord of Judaism reveals Zeus and Apollo, despite their "beauty," to be mere finite God-projections. But, first, because of their beauty, these latter are not *simply* destroyed. Second – and this is crucial for our purpose – Athens does not depend on Jerusalem alone for the demythologization of its gods. The beauty of the gods manifests a Divinity immanent in the human spirit which has created them; and the Greek-Roman world explicates this Divinity as it shows a "freedom" and "universality" to rise above the gods of its own making. The Greek gods are demythologized in the sphere of thought by Greek philosophy as it "freely" rises to the universal, divine *Nous*. They are demythologized in the sphere of life by the Roman Empire as it shows its universal freedom by assembling all the gods in the pantheon, and by making them subservient to universal-political – but human – use. *Here appears first a "freedom" and "universality" which might conceivably produce a* Grundidee *in terms of which the scope and limitations of Jewish religious existence might be comprehended.* For the "freedom" displayed is a self-transcending human rise to oneness with Divinity, and the "universality" is achieved in this rise. Yet *such* a freedom and universality are beyond the scope of Judaism, not only as it appears in Hegel's philosophical comprehension, but also as it appears in the Jewish religious self-understanding. For the Jew remains a witness to the *otherness* of God – in his singled-out, Jewish *particularity*.

Might Hegel's *Grundidee* of Judaism have emerged, then, within the ancient Greek-Roman world? By no means. The Roman Empire assembles (and destroys) all the gods: the God of Israel alone remains without. Greek philosophy rises to true Divinity – but in a realm of thought which cannot touch or destroy the Jewish "confidence" in a God who is Lord of life. The ancient Greek-Roman world pays as price for its "freedom" the tragic choice between resort in thought to a worldless God and political existence in a godless world. The Jew, in contrast, serves *in* the world a God who is Lord *of* it. *Vis-à-vis* the Greek-Roman world he is a true, affirmative witness to a transcendent Divinity to which negative testimony is borne by the Roman Empire when, having "freely" rid itself of slavery to the gods, it becomes self-enslaved to Emperor-gods; and by Hellenistic philosophy, when, to preserve itself in its unsullied "freedom," it is forced to flee from the world.

6

No more could Hegel's *Grundidee* of Judaism have emerged in the Christian Middle Ages, and this despite the fact that this world-historical period is initiated and constituted by the most decisive "jolt" in all history – and one which makes actual *in historical life* a truth which we have thus far come upon only as observed by Hegel's thought: the higher truth that Jewish "East" and Greek-Roman "West" each contain both truth and falsehood. The "unheard of composition" of God and man in Christ contains the truth, and overcomes the falsehood, of both Greek-Roman "freedom" or divine-human "union" and Jewish "unfreedom" or divine-human "nonunion." The Hegelian philosophy does not, therefore, (as it did in the case of Athens) observe a confrontation between the old and the new Jerusalem. Since Christianity reconciles and supersedes Jewish "East" and Greek-Roman "West" the new Jerusalem renders the old anachronistic. Even so, however, the God of Moses, while *in Himself* an anachronism, does not become an anachronism *in and for* medieval Christian *life*; nor does He *prove* Himself so for medieval *philosophy*. Life becomes rent into a sacred heaven and a profane earth; hence philosophic thought loses its former "freedom" and Jewish existence survives, as a true (albeit negative) witness until the rise of the modern world.

Hegel's view of the achievement and limitation of medieval Christendom is as follows. In the Greek-Roman world "some" are "free," though a (religious, aesthetic, political, philosophical) human self-activity rising to "union" with Divinity. In the Christian world "all" are "free," made so not by a rise to Divinity possible for some, but by a divine descent into humanity made on behalf of all. In the Jewish "East" man serves the transcendent Lord in "nonunion." In the Christian "West" this "nonunion" is both preserved and overcome when the transcendent Lord, assuming radical immanence, Himself produces "union." Greek-Roman divine-human "union" is in flight from, or overwhelmed by, the reality of "nonunion." Jewish divine-human "nonunion" fails to achieve "union." Christianity is the divine-human "union of union and nonunion."

This world-historical achievement of Christianity remains, however, in principle limited throughout the entire Middle Ages. Salvation remains in heaven, leaving earth "unsanctified." "Free" in the sight of God, the medieval Christian remains "unfree" in the sight of feudal princes. In short, a split occurs between the sacred and the profane which has no precedent in either Jewish "East" or Greek-Roman "West." And the consequence is that whereas the Christian "content" supersedes both, its medieval "form" – the dualism of heaven and earth, the sacred and the profane – leaves both unvanquished. At one extreme Greek philosophy, become subservient to ecclesiastical authority in its medieval setting, longs, as it were, for the recovery of its former "freedom"; at the other, Jewish religious existence, albeit deaf to the Good News of the incarnate, dying and resurrected God, gives a true testimony with its stubborn search for salvation, not in Heaven, but on earth.

Hegel stresses this last-named point when in a brief, cryptic, but highly significant passage he states that the Jewish people was "held in readiness" by the "Spirit and its world" until the modern age, for a true (albeit negative) testimony to a divine-human "nonunion" persisting, and indeed accentuated absolutely, throughout the medieval period.

In the same passage he adds, however, that the truth of this testimony vanishes in the modern world. This latter is an "absolute turning point"; overcoming the medieval split between heaven and earth, Spirit turns "absolute negativity" into "infinite positivity." Only with this absolute turn is the "principle of the unity of the divine nature and the human," *in itself* actual since the rise of Christianity, *"grasped by"* a spiritual self-activity.[33] Only then a "we" appears on the historical scene whose concept of God has *wholly* passed beyond that of Moses. And only then can a philosophy manifest itself which will produce a *Grundidee* in terms of which Jewish religious existence is both comprehended and superseded.

7

Hegel's "absolute turning point" is produced by three distinct but inter-related modern revolutions: the Protestant reformation (in which the Christian God descends from a medieval heaven into a modern "heart" on earth); a secular revolution, assuming diverse forms in modern science, modern morality, and the modern state (in which man storms heaven); and a philosophical revolution which, recovering its ancient Greek freedom in the modern form of subjectivity, culminates in an absolutely self-active thought inclusive of all reality – the Hegelian system.

The three revolutions are distinct. Thus a veritable gulf may seem to yawn between a Protestant piety which, however emancipated in its "free" inwardness from all ecclesiastical authority, remains *receptive* of divine Grace, and, say, the French revolution which transforms and appropriates the external world in behalf of secularity as its supreme principle. Less obvious, but still unmistakeable, is the contrast between *both* these revolut-

[33] *Philosophy of Right*, # 358.

ions (which occur *in life*) and the third – that of philosophical *thought*.
"Freedom" or "self-activity" in the first two is limited by the fact that
they occur in and for men of flesh and blood. Self-activity in the third is
unlimited – but occurs in the realm of thought.

But if the three revolutions were distinct *only* no "absolute turning
point" would occur in world history; no "we" could emerge on the historical scene which could render the God of Moses anachronistic; and no
philosophical thought could appear productive of a *Grundidee* in terms
of which Jewish religious existence could be both comprehended and
surpassed. Hegel himself criticizes Protestant inwardness when it remains
inward only, hostile or indifferent to the external world, and, had he
considered the matter, might have found truth *vis-à-vis* such hostility or
indifference in a Jewish stubbornness which, however "unfree" in its
service of the transcendent Lord, at any rate serves Him *in the world*.
Likewise, he sees the nemesis of French revolutionary "freedom" (which,
in absolutizing secular self-activity, turns it into an idol) in French revolutionary "terror," and – again if he had considered the matter – he might
have seen truth in the Jewish God insofar as He testified against this
idolatry. The "law of Moses," to be sure, makes impossible revolutionary
"freedom" – but also revolutionary "terror."

Would the third revolution – that of philosophical thought – by itself
render Jewish religious existence anachronistic? We have already considered this question *in abstracto*, but find it no different as we now place
it into its historical setting. In Hegel's view modern philosophy begins
with "war" upon religion but ends with the Hegelian "peace." [34] But
whereas Christianity (as well as Judaism) would be forced to offer resistance in the war, Judaism (if not Christianity) would be forced to offer
resistance in the peace as well. And, on Hegel's own admission and insistence, in each case the resistance would be successful.

Initiating its absolute subjective self-activity in the realm of thought,
modern philosophy begins by "rising to the sun like a young eagle, a bird
of prey which strikes religion down"; [35] but such an attack on religion
would on Hegel's principles provoke a counter-attack by religion, and the
inconclusiveness of the contest would reveal onesidedness in both contes-
tants. This onesidedness is overcome, to be sure, when Hegel's own philosophy makes a "peace" with religion in which all truth is preserved and
united, and all things, divine as well as human, are mediated. This peace,

[34] See my *Religious Dimension in Hegel's Thought*, ch. VI.
[35] *Vorlesungen über die Geschichte der Philosophie. Einleitung: System und Geschichte der Philosophie*, ed. J. Hoffmeister (Leipzig: Meiner, 1944), pp. 190ff.

however, is resisted by Jewish (if not Christian) faith, committed as it is to the absoluteness of two distinctions – between God and man, and between the One true God and all the false. And, if the Hegelian peace were one of thought *only*, this resistance, far from failing, would disclose an *absolute* dichotomy between life and thought. On Hegel's own admission and insistence, his philosophic thought would reflect a onesidedness of its own; far from itself vaniquishing the testimony of life, it would reveal itself as having fled from it.

The three modern revolutions which produce and constitute the modern world are interrelated as well as distinct. Only thus is an "absolute turning point" produced in world history; only thus does a "we" come upon the scene of modern history whose "concept of God" does not merely differ from that of Moses but renders it anachronistic; only thus, finally, can there be a philosophy – Hegel's own – producing a Grundidee *which proves Judaism anachronistic by encompassing its limited truth without remainder in a higher, absolute truth of its own.*

The modern Protestant "heart" contains the "true content" of the unity of the Divine and the human: it overcomes its untrue "form" (receptive inwardness) only as it seeks self-active, secular expression in the external world. On its part, modern secular self-activity possesses the "true form" (*free* or *infinite* or *autonomous* self-activity): the "true content" eludes it as either a pure ideal or a fragmented reality until it passes beyond the dimension of secular – scientific, moral, political – action, to a religious dimension grasped by it as the source of all its acting. Only in this secular-religious union – which remains creative diversity – does "the principle of the unity of the divine nature and the human" come to life in modern spiritual self-activity; and only in this unity is this "principle" "*grasped*" as such *by* spiritual self-activity. Here, first, lies the turning from "absolute negativity" to "infinite positivity": secular-Protestant "freedom," taken as a self-differentiating whole, expresses a divine-human "union" in which all divine-human "nonunion" is forever *already* overcome in the Easter of the Protestant heart and forever *yet to be* overcome by self-active secular "self-confidence." Here, second, comes to life a "we" which *wholly* internalizes the God of Moses and liberates his Jewish servant from his Jewish servitude. Here, finally, arises an infinitely self-active, all-mediating, divine-human philosophical thought productive of a *Grundidee* in terms of which the scope and limitations of Jewish religious existence are both "done justice" and superseded. We have stressed that this feat remains impossible so long as it is one of thought *only*. It becomes possible and actual – so Hegel teaches – for a thought which merely completes and brings to absolute self-consciousness a divine-human mediation which, *except for that completion and self-consciousness*, is *already* complete in life. Only thus can Hegelian thought mediate the *ultimate* dichotomy – between itself and life – and "overreach" life itself.

Nor would it *demonstrate* its own overreaching power if the life-form comprehended were to vanish without remainder. To the application of this general Hegelian principle Jewish religious existence is no exception. Within the world of modern "infinite positivity" the Lord of Judaism, having lost His otherness, reappears in Spinozism in the form of modern philosophical thought. By itself, however, this dialectical preservation is onesided and inadequate. On the one hand, the One of Judaism pays for His loss of otherness by an "acosmic" loss of lordship *over the world* and a flight into *mere* thought. On the other hand – and this is a related loss – He also pays for this loss by a dissipation into an *abstract* universality divorced from concrete *particularity*. It is therefore not accidental that Hegel's dialectical transformation of Jewish religious existence shows signs – however cryptic and inconclusive – of wishing to preserve the Jewish people in their ancient particularity (as well as their ancient Lord) within the context of the modern world. In an enigmatic but highly important note [36] he strongly supports the emancipation of the Jewish people. Seemingly doing so on the liberal grounds that Jews are "above all, men," he immediately adds that humanity is no "abstract quality." Hegel states that modern Jews must be "free"; he also states that there is no such thing as humanity-in-general. But what "free" modern Jewish particularity is to be he does not – and perhaps cannot – say. Yet it is elements such as these in Hegel's thought which helped produce Moses Hess' Zionism.

8

In 1819 Eduard Gans, one of Hegel's most gifted, loyal and close disciples, wrote as follows:

Only a jarring independence which is reflected only on itself is to be destroyed (in Jewish existence), not an independence subordinate to the whole ... which is not to be required to lose its own substance. That wherein it merges (*aufgeht*) is to be enriched by what has become part of it; it is not merely to become poorer by having lost an opposition .... The specific character (of present Europe is) ... the fullness and richness of its particularities .... The comforting lesson of history, properly understood, is that everything passes away (*vorübergeht*) without vanishing (*vergehen*) and that everything

[36] *Philosophy of Right*, # 270.

persists which is long considered past. Hence neither can the Jews perish nor can Judaism dissolve; but in the great movement of the whole it shall seem to have perished and yet live on as the current lives on in the ocean.[37]

Barely six years after, the Jew Gans, once enthusiastically bent on a renewal of Jewish existence in the light of Hegel's philosophy, had become a Protestant; and the *Verein* he had helped found for the purpose of producing this renewal had collapsed a year before.

His case serves to dramatize the note of "riddle" on which Hegel's own thought on Jewish existence ends. Acquainted with such as Gans in the Berlin of his own time, Hegel cannot have been unaware of or indifferent to their dilemmas; nor is it compatible with his thought that the solution to these should be either wholesale conversion to Christianity or – in their case alone – a *simply* secular freedom without religious foundation. Least of all could Hegel's philosophy have advocated a Jewish identification with humanity-in-general which everywhere else he considered a lifeless abstraction.

The riddle of Jewish existence, once readmitted, reappears throughout Hegel's entire thought, all the careful and agonized mediations notwithstanding. Spinoza's "acosmic" God bears little (however dialectical) resemblance to the God of Israel who, whatever His shortcomings, is Lord *of the world*. The view of medieval Jewish martyrdom as a negative testimony to the power of Spirit becomes in Hegel's own terms dubious (as well as offensive in other terms) when Hegel himself holds that the crusades (a trauma for Jewish religious existence to this day) reflect not the power of the Spirit but rather its impotence. Hellenistic Judaism – insofar as it is *both* "universalistic" in partaking of Hellenic culture *and* "particularistic" in rejecting the Hellenic gods – is conspicuous by its absence from Hegel's writings. And even if the greatest *lacuna* – rabbinic Judaism – is accounted for, or even condoned, in terms of Hegel's unfamiliarity with it, the rock bottom difficulty still remains: Hegel's cavalier disposal of the two root Biblical concepts of covenant and Messianic hope. *By his own lights* the Jew persisted through Hegel's history by virtue of the Messianic hope: how can Hegel's philosophy, on *whatever* grounds, fail even to make mention of it? Again, while existing in this hope, the Jew had stood in a relation to his Lord which was *mutual*, and constituted by *love as well as* fear: how – once again, with *whatever* philosophical justification – can

[37] Rubaschoff, Salman, "Erstlinge der Entjudung: Drei Reden von Eduard Gans im Kulturverein," *Der Judische Wille*, I (1918), pp. 112ff. On this subject, see M. A. Meyer, *The Origins of the Modern Jew* (Detroit: Wayne State University Press, 1967), pp. 163ff.

Hegel's thought assert a "harsh contrast" in which there is no love and only sheer servitude?

It may be replied that Hegel's philosophical thought is in search of an "essence" or "inner logic" which has no room for inconsistencies or compromises, and that the facts of Jewish religious life cited by us *are* mere inconsistencies or compromises. In response, we must here confine ourselves to citing two Midrashim – and Midrash is the profoundest thought ever produced within Judaism.

Rabbi Azaryiah and Rabbi Aha in the name of Rabbi Yohanan said: When the Israelites heard at Sinai the word "I" (i.e., the first word of the ten commandments), their souls left them, as it says, "If we hear the voice . . . anymore, then we shall die" (Deut. 5 : 22) . . . . The Word then returned to the Holy One, blessed be He and said: "Sovereign of the Universe, Thou art full of life, and Thy law is full of life, and Thou hast sent me to the dead, for they are all dead." Thereupon the Holy One, blessed be He, sweetened (i.e., softened) the Word for them . . . .[38]

. . . When the iron yoke of the wicked kingdom will be broken . . ., then Moses will come from the desert, and the Messiah from Rome, each at the head of his flock, and the Word of God will mediate between them, causing both to walk with one accord in the same direction.[39]

Like Hegel's philosophical comprehension of Judaism, Jewish religious self-understanding, in the first Midrash cited, begins with a "renunciation" – as it were, death – and ends with a "renunciation of renunciation," "restoring being" and producing "confidence." Unlike for Hegel, however, this is no unilateral human dialectic, seeking to – but unable to – reach God in its self-negating-self-affirming stance. It is a bilateral dialectic in which divine Grace in its infinity accepts humanity in its finitude and Jewish particularity. This Grace acts, not subsequent to the law, but precisely *in* the law, rendering man free not despite but precisely *in* his humanity. Hence the law is received, to be sure, in absolute fear – and a love rendered radically astonished precisely because of the fear which precedes it. Thus there is not a master-slave relation but rather – astonishingly – a mutual divine-Jewish covenant.

In Hegel's view the law of Moses, despite its "positivity," "takes the place of reconciliation and redemption." For the Midrashic Jewish self-understanding, even the divine Jewish covenant cannot take that place. For whereas it rejects the Pauline (and Augustinian, and Hegelian) [40] view

---

[38] *Misdrash Rabba, Song of Songs*, V # 16 # 3. (*RA*, p. 60) I have expounded this Midrash more fully in my *God's Presence in History* (New York University Press, 1970), pp. 14ff.

[39] I quote this Midrash as retold in L. Ginzberg, *The Legends of the Jews* (Philadelphia: Jewish Publication Society, 1964), vol. II, p. 373.

[40] I have shown elsewhere (*Quest for Past and Future*, Bloomington: Indiana Uni-

that the law was given only to reveal sin, and hence rejoices in this gift of divine Grace rather than groaning under the burden of the law, it does not hold the view, supposedly "Pharisaic," that a *redemptive* performance of the Mosaic law is a human possibility, let alone ever an actuality. And since no *apriori* line can be drawn between what is, and what is not, within human power, a dialectic develops between the law of Moses which bids men work for Messianic redemption and the deed of the Messiah himself who will complete it – a tension so deep that the Word of God itself will be required in order to mediate, in the end, between them. But so long as this tension lasts the Jew is in his Jewish particularity a singled out witness for a universal redemption unto the nations of the world.

9

Might Hegel's philosophy have discovered a *Grundidee* doing genuine "justice" to a divine-human relation in which the Divine, remaining other-than-man, is the Infinite One; in which man, remaining other-than-God, is one particular "family"; and yet in which the relation between these extremes is not a "harsh" contrast foreordaining "unfreedom" and "particularism," but rather endowed with a free covenantal mutuality pointing to a Messianic future? If so, could a *Grundidee* of this kind have been fitted into the Hegelian system?

Surprisingly, our answer to the first question must be emphatically affirmative: Hegel not only *might* have developed an adequate *Grundidee* as his thought empathetically exposed itself to the Jewish religious self-understanding; his philosophy is, perhaps, of all philosophies the *only one* capable of doing so. In his account of Christianity Hegel sees himself required to put forward a concept of "double representation" which recognizes divine Grace, human free will, and a direct interrelation between them which is possible, actual and necessary despite and indeed because of the "antinomy" between Grace and freedom.[41] As one holds fast to Hegel's thinking on this matter, and calls to mind the world of Midrashic thought, one is surprised to discover that precisely the doubly-representational structure which Hegel detects and does justice to in Christianity is shown by the Midrashic religious self-understanding when, in the cove-

versity Press, 1968, pb. edition, Boston: Beacon Press, 1970, ch. 14) that Kant's concept of Jewish "theological morality" reflects an unconsciously Pauline view of Jewish revealed law. Hegel's view of Jewish "positivity" surpasses Kant's in understanding Jewish law as a bridge rather than a bar between the Divine and the human. It remains Pauline in its understanding of the *nature* of this bridge which, wholly lacking Grace, remains a divine-human master-slave relationship.

[41] See my *Religious Dimension in Hegel's Thought*, especially pp. 138-54 and 184-92.

nantal relation, it holds fast to the antinomy between the otherness of the
Divine and its involvement in a mutual relation with Israel; and when,
in the relation between covenantal present and Messianic future, it preserves the antinomy between human acting (which proceeds as though
all depended on man) and human hoping (which acts as though all depended on God.) Yet this resemblance is hardly accidental. Martin Buber,
inspired by Jewish tradition but, we suspect, unfamiliar with Hegel's concept of double representation, wrote:

I know that "I am giving over for disposal" and know at the same time that
"It depends on myself" .... I am compelled to take both to myself, to be
lived together, and in being lived together they are one.[42]

Any reflective thought which confronts, *and seeks to preserve*, the Infinity of the Jewish God, the finitude of Jewish man, and the *mutual* relation
that exists between them despite their incommensurability, is driven, it
would appear, to the kind of dialectic which Hegel terms doubly representational.

Why then did Hegel reserve the concept of double representation for
Christianity alone? Was it, in the end, after all nothing more than an
accidental factor – such as anti-Judaic prejudice or ignorance of rabbinic
Judaism – which caused him, all his labors notwithstanding, to ascribe a
Grundidee to Judaism implying depressingly familiar stereotypes?

We need not embrace this conclusion; indeed, perhaps we cannot. For
it would appear that Hegel *could* have recognized an adequate *Grundidee*
of Jewish religious existence only at the price of calling his *entire* philosophical system into question: here we find the *ultimate* significance of Rosenkranz' observation that Jewish history remained a "dark riddle" to
Hegel throughout his life. Hegel was able to recognize Christian religious
existence as doubly representational, for his philosophy was able to comprehend and rise above its antinomy to the absolute truth of "the principle
of the unity of the divine nature and the human." Had he recognized
Jewish religious existence as doubly representational, he would have been
forced to recognize it, like Christianity, as a witness *to* the togetherness of
divine Grace and human freedom – *but also as a witness* against *the unity
of the divine nature and the human*. To recognize and do justice to *this*
testimony would have meant nothing less than to accept that the Divine
is and remains other than the human, their relation notwithstanding; that
the human understanding of that relation is and remains confined to

---

[42] *I and Thou*, p. 96.

what Hegel calls the form of representation; [43] and that a philosophical thought which is at once human and divine – i.e., Hegel's own – is impossible.

<h1 style="text-align:center">10</h1>

Thus, had Hegel done justice to it, Jewish religious existence would have borne witness against him to one absolute distinction which it has affirmed through the ages – that between the human and the Divine. Two hundred years after Hegel's birth, even secular Jewish existence bears witness to the other – the *absolute* falseness of *some* gods. To be sure, the secular Jew of today does not affirm the Holy One of Israel: this is what makes him secular. His very existence and survival as a Jew, however, is a testimony against the devil. At Auschwitz was revealed an idolatry – total, yet wholly modern – which Hegel could not have anticipated and which, were he alive today, could not be mediated by his all-mediating philosophy. The Jew after Auschwitz, religious or secular, who raises Jewish children testifies absolutely against this absolute idolatry. Singled out by Auschwitz, he bears witness that there can be, must be, shall be no second Auschwitz anywhere; and he stakes on that testimony the lives of his children's children.[44]

Hegel states that no people appears on the world-historical scene more than once. Much has happened since his time to make one wonder whether Hegel, endowed as he was with a remarkable sense of history and a still more remarkable philosophical integrity, might not qualify or altogether withdraw this sweeping statement today. Not least among the epoch-making, radically astonishing, unanticipated events of the age which might shake his thought are Jewish death at Auschwitz and Jewish resurrection at Jerusalem.

---

[43] Midrashic thinking remains deliberately figurative or "representational," falling back, whenever necessary, on the expression *k'b'yahol* ("as it were"). See my *God's Presence in History*, ch. I, especially pp. 16ff.

[44] See my *God's Presence in History*, ch. III. For an interpretation of Nazism as an unmistakable, unsurpassable, yet wholly modern idolatry, see my "Idolatry as a Modern Possibility," *The Religious Situation 1968*, ed. D. R. Cutler (Boston: Beacon, 1968), pp. 254-87.

COMMENT ON FACKENHEIM'S
'HEGEL AND JUDAISM'

James Doull

"There are," says Goethe in an aphorism, "only two true religions: the one, that which recognizes and worships the holy that dwells in and around us without giving it any form whatever; the other, that which gives it the fairest form: whatever lies between is idolatry." [1] In antiquity these two religions existed independently of each other as the Jewish and the Greek. They had in common that they saw nature not as primary or independent but as that through which infinite purpose was realized. Human life had its meaning as participation in that purpose. The two religions differed in that, for the one, there was in truth only the actuality of the infinite purpose; in the other, artistic imagination presented the unity of nature and thought as a number of gods, inconsistently both absolute and special. The one detracted nothing from the divine; the other elevated the human as it limited the divine. Against both, another religion proved itself dominant in the world, which divinized the human and put finite purposes in place of the one infinite purpose. [2]

The olympian gods had already ceased largely to be the object of religious belief when the Greeks were subjected politically to the Roman principle. The Jewish people, though conquered and dispersed, were untouched in their religion: because divine and human were absolutely distinguished the thought which elsewhere dissolved all differences could obtain no hold. In the Jewish religion human remained human in relation to infinite divine freedom. The stability of the difference was their absolute unity in the infinite purpose. Abandoning all other ends before the one infinite good, the Jew knew his particular well-being as implied

---

[1] *Wilhelm Meister*, aus Makariens Archiv, 51 (*Werke*, Hamburger Ausgabe, 1967, Vol. 8, p. 468): "Es gibt nur zwei wahre Religionen, die eine, die das Heilige, das in und um uns wohnt, ganz formlos, die andere, die es in der schönsten Form anerkennt und anbetet. Alles, was dazwischen ist, ist Götzendienst."

[2] *Vorlesungen über die Philosophie der Religion*, ed. Lasson, Hamburg, 1966, Vol. 2, p. 48 foll.

in that obedience to the universal. Greek and Roman had sought universal freedom in the world and found the inadequacy of all natural content to self-conscious freedom. In the Jewish religion the infinite purpose had reality in the life of a particular people. To Greek, or to Jew lost to Hellenism, it must be unthinkable that this limited purpose be the primary revelation of divine will, and not rather the hidden unity of human and divine on which it rested. For the Greek and Roman religions had declared that the finite altogether was spirit, but did not know this truly as the meaning of the fate or necessity in which the finite perished.[3]

In the Christian religion, Roman subjectivity loses its destructive arrogance and is known as the infinite form which relates human and divine. Thereby the beautiful gods of Hellenic religion are freed of their multiplicity and finitude and known as the adequate revelation of the one God of Israel. The idolatry of the Greek and Roman religions is overcome; and the absolute difference of human and divine is revealed as also the negation of the negation, the moment which is also present in Judaism as the confidence in which man "walks before God." [4]

The new religion in one way reached its full development in the ancient world: doctrine and cult in general attained their adequate form. To that extent Hegel would undoubtedly say that Judaism and every religion had been superseded. But in another way the Christian religion was a mere belief without truth in human experience. The negation of classical culture, it had not shown the power to fashion a new world which would be the image and finite expression of its belief. To this extent neither Judaism nor the classical religions – so far as they had become philosophy – could be regarded as superseded.[5]

Judaism "vexed him (Hegel) as a dark riddle throughout his life." One may agree with Rosenkranz in so far as the realization of Christianity in the world was the whole problem of the Hegelian philosophy. The modern state was to Christianity what the polis had been to Hellas and the Jewish state to Judaism. In the states of Europe Christianity had that definite existence which Hegel admired and disliked in the exclusiveness of the Jewish people. The church no longer tried to rule the world as in the Middle Ages, nor did a fanaticism displace it which would destroy the finite to make room for an abstract truth. Rather the secular had in its finiteness the infinite Trinitarian structure of Christian belief. Religion was then no longer belief merely but the adequate knowledge of what existed and

---

[3] *Ph. Rel.*, 2, Die Religionen der geistigen Individualität, *passim*.
[4] *Ph. Rel.*, 2, p. 234 foll.
[5] *Vorlesungen über die Geschichte der Philosophie*, Berlin, 1844, pt. 3, p. 85 foll.: Die Idee des Christentums.

was done in daily life. At this point it would seem that the separate existence of the Jews as an excluded minority in Christian states had lost its meaning; that they should be emancipated and absorbed.[6]

But Hegel saw in his time no more the realization of Christianity than its disappearance. The ruin of ethical life was as much before his mind as its reality, and nothing was more lacking to religion and practical life than that substantiality and acceptance of law and truth which the Christians were thought to have learned from Judaism. In this view it would appear that Jews had a very different, and positive, role in the modern world than to disappear into Christian society; in a general desecration of everything holy, such as to recall the spiritual desolation of the Roman Empire, the Jews could not be thought to have less than a sacred duty to maintain the purity of their religion and their own existence as its guardian.[7]

II

It is insufficient to say with Rozenkranz that Judaism "vexed" Hegel and remained a "dark riddle" for him. Or, if it be true that he never solved the riddle, this is not a particular deficiency in the Hegelian philosophy but its ultimate and total failure. Certainly he did not ignore Judaism in the *Phenomenology*, where the opposition of the hiddenness of spirit in the Spinozistic substance to its appearances is altogether fundamental. In the *Philosophy of History* the Jewish people are seen not so much within the oriental principle of natural substantiality as having exceeded and completed it. "Therewith occurs the breach between East and West; spirit descends into itself and grasps the abstract underlying principle of nature as the spiritual." The Jews are, that is, divided from the Greeks and Romans in that they have the idea of spirit or the concrete unity of nature and thought. It is rather from the Egyptians and other oriental peoples that the Greeks receive the natural beginning of their culture, which they transmute to spiritual freedom under the form of the beautiful. But the Greeks and Romans may also be said to be at the same level with the Jews in that, however differently, free subjectivity is the common principle of their religions and cultures. In this they are alike distinguished from the oriental

---

[6] e.g., *Vorlesungen über die Philosophie der Geschichte*, Berlin, 1848, p. 514 foll.
[7] e.g. *Ph. Rel.*, 3, p. 230 foll.: "Wenn [man die religiöse Wahrheit] geschichtlich behandelt, so ist's mit ihr aus. Nicht die spekulative Wahrheit, wo den Armen wird das Evangelium gepredigt – si [sind es], die dem unendlichem Schmerz am Nächsten stehen, – wo die Lehre von Liebe in unendlichem Schmerz, [vom] substantiellen Bande der Welt verkündigt wird, ist noch zu hören;" etc.

world. From the Christian religion they are again separated in that all three set an absolute opposition between human and divine (if for Greeks and Romans fate and not the gods be taken as what is ultimately divine). Then, finally, the *Philosophy of Right* shows the elements of the Germanic or Christian realm as the intellectual spirituality into which classical antiquity dissolved and Jewish spirituality which held fast to the natural and particular. Having defined Judaism in its opposition to the Greek and Roman principles, as well as against the unfree Orient, Hegel's primary interest is its place in the modern world, where "the breach between East and West" is overcome.[8]

The Christian religion, and the culture which grew from it in the West, had its origin in the absolute scepticism and despair of the Greco-Roman world – "the absolute negativity which is also the absolute turning-point" where spirit "grasps the infinite positivity of this inner self, the principle of the unity of divine and human nature, of reconciliation as objective truth and freedom which has appeared within self-consciousness and subjectivity." To the oriental principle belonged as its infinite end objective truth, but freedom and subjective truth only implicitly. For the subjectivity and freedom of the Greek and the Roman principle an adequate objectivity and truth was beyond their finite realm of human freedom. But the loss of this freedom and its world disclosed that its hidden foundation had been the immediate unity of nature and thought of the oriental principle, as known in its truth by the Jewish people.[9]

The barbarous Germanic tribes which had overrun the Western Empire were capable of this new principle in that it was alike natural to them to recognize and submit themselves to the universal and, against it, to hold each to his particularity with the independence of infinite subjectivity. Only through the inward and concrete resolution of this extremest conflict of good and evil could Christianity either attain its adequate form as a religion or become the principle of a new secular order patterned after it. The way by which this most difficult task should be fulfilled was not direct but through the authority of other peoples who had already in some part attained rational freedom.[10]

Among the Greeks and the Romans themselves Christianity was not the source of a new secular order conformed to the inner order of belief. Rather, dividing the two realms, its tendency was to complete the corruption

---

[8] *Phänomenologie des Geistes*, ed. Hoffmeister, Hamburg, 1952, p. 557 foll.; *Ph. Gesch.*, p. 238 foll.; *Ph. Rel.*, 2, p. 48 foll.; *Philosophie des Rechts*, ed. Hoffmeister, Hamburg, 1955, pp. 296-7.

[9] *Ph. R.*, sect. 358.

[10] *Ph. R.*, sect. 359; *Ph. Gesch.*, p. 421 foll.; and elsewhere.

of the former ethical life. Through Christianity there was brought about among the cultivated people of the Empire the same contradiction between nature and reason as existed in the barbarous invaders. The difference between barbarism and classical culture was thus gradually obliterated. In a remote future the advantage lay with the barbarians that the older culture was alien – authoritative for them only while they were incapable of its abstract freedom. But at first the barbarians submitted to the church and the intellectual culture through which it mediated between the inner world of faith and the untamed violence of external life. They submitted as long as the difference of the two worlds, or of the universal and the particular, was the undetected presupposition of thought and practice. Through the corruption of the church and the suppression of feudalism the conclusion was imposed that the particular had no being independently of the universal, that the truth was rather the substance in which they were one.[11]

If this conclusion might be said to have been known already to Greek philosophy, and so to Medieval culture, it had not entered consciousness that therefore the distinction between the intelligible world and nature had no truth. To Jew or Moslem it was idolatrous to believe otherwise, though there too Hellenic culture might long persist along with that belief. It may thus be said that the oriental principle at this point is appropriated by the Germano-Christian world. It could thereby, as Judaism had done, establish for itself a realm of worldly activity which is other than but not unrelated to the ideal realm of faith. For the modern state, as against feudal society, begins with the surrender of all particular interest to the sovereign power of the king. But though substantial, this state also contains implicitly the Roman principle of infinite subjectivity. At the same point where Spinoza giving philosophical form to the Jewish principle, abandons the particularity of the Jewish people, Christian peoples assert their particularity against the universal church and make for themselves national churches. For the particularity is not immediate but founded on that subjectivity which Spinoza cannot find in separation from the One.[12]

The secular world which Protestant Christianity makes for itself begins as an ethical life in which it is well said that reconciliation through justification takes the place of the Jewish law. It is a freedom grounded in absolute obedience, which may be called rather servitude. But a servitude which liberates can as well be called freedom. Where in Antiquity the

---

[11] *Ph. Gesch.*, p. 408 foll.; *Gesch. Phil.*, 3, p. 129 foll.
[12] *Gesch. Phil.*, 3, p. 239 foll.; p. 356 foll.

freedom of a people to make laws for itself according to reason occurred in Greece independently of Jewish obedience to the divine law, here the same development is internal. The subjectivity present from the first asserts its claim against law and ethical life, and there arises in Protestantism an inner conflict from which there is no issue except in the self-destruction of subjective freedom at the point where it has seemingly destroyed its antagonist. It may be said that the Jewish and Hellenic elements of the Christian principle reach here their extremest antagonism. Here therefore the fanatical rage of Crusaders against the people who had once obstructed the visible presence of their Saviour is replaced by an inner and implacable hatred, which is nothing else than the disguised and hypocritical hatred of law and truth.[13]

It is only where this subjectivity has been raised, through the experience and education of civil society, to thought and the Idea – the unity of subjectivity and truth – that this opposition implicitly "loses its marrow and disappears." Then only "the present has divested itself of its barbarity and unrighteous wilfulness, and the truth of its distance and arbitrary force, so that the true reconciliation has become objective." [14]

This objective reconciliation Hegel knew could not take place within the Protestant principle as such. Indeed it was in overcoming its onesidedness that the extremest difficulty must occur. The "dark mystery" of which he said little, as though too much for his hearers to know, was the death and rebirth of Christianity itself. For the subjective reconciliation of Protestant faith can only become objective when religion again becomes speculative as in medieval Catholicism. But that speculation rather depended on the authority of an earlier experience than was the return to thought out of life and finite interests. To Protestant faith and to the secular rejection of it a renewed philosophy is intolerable, no less to the one than to the other. But only through philosophy can the bond be found between nature and the ideal world, and if the bond is not known speculatively – then buried in dead history – then the true knowledge of the state, as the image of the infinite truth, is only shown to the people through the external dialectic of war.[15]

The renewal of Christianity and of the practical realm in its likeness Hegel took to be the primary and moving interest of the new age he saw beginning in his time. Whatever else belonged to this renewal, it demanded certainly that the elements of the Christian religion – Jewish and Hel-

---

[13] e.g., *Ph.R.*, sect. 140.
[14] *Ph.R.*, sect. 360.
[15] *Ph. Rel.*, 3, p. 229 foll.; *Ph. R.*, sect. 324; sect. 360.

lenic – be known adequately and reconciled. In the one was the true
knowledge of God, in the other of the world. The realm of human action
had no direction save through the conjuncture of the two. As long as this
task was incomplete it must be thought to fall peculiarly to the Jewish
people and their principle to remind Christians of their idolatry of the
world or of themselves.[16]

III

"Hegel's philosophy seeks to mediate all things, divine as well as human,
transforming all absolute into relative distinctions. Jewish religious existence, in contrast, remains stubbornly committed to at least two absolute
distinctions – between the Divine and the human, and between the One
true God and all the false." [17] But to this Hegel would reply that the subjective logic, by which he had extended the Aristotelian philosophy in
the direction of its ultimate intention, respected both differences completely.[18] For in the Jewish as in every religion there is also relation between
human and divine. And in the Jewish religion this relation has the definite
form that finite spirit recognizes and is related to the one infinite purpose
in that it knows the nothingness of everything finite and turns freely therefrom to the infinite.[19] The philosophical expression of this relation is that
it is the immediate syllogism of absolute spirit.[20] In general the absolute
difference of human and divine and their relation in that absolute difference is the Idea:

Die absolute Idee als der vernünftige Begriff, der in seiner Realität nur mit
sich selbst zusammengeht, ist um dieser unmittelbarkeit seiner objektiven
Identität willen einerseits die Rückkehr zum Leben; aber sie hat diese Form
ihrer Unmittelbarkeit ebensosehr aufgehoben und den höchsten Gegensatz
in sich.[21]

What is avoided with the surest sense in the Jewish religion is that either
human freedom or anything natural should be mistaken for the divine.
This idolatry as it occurs in the pagan religions is obvious and no longer
a primary danger to those of a Christian, Jewish or Islamic tradition. What
is fearful is the idolatry that recurs in Christianity from the concreteness

---

[16] *Ph. R.*, sect. 360; and elsewhere.
[17] Fackenheim, *supra.*, pp. 161-162.
[18] *Wissenschaft der Logik*, ed. Lasson, Hamburg, 1963, vol. 2, pp. 211-13; 213
foll.; 235.
[19] *Ph. Rel.*, 2, p. 93 foll.
[20] *Enzyklopädie* (1830), ed. Nicolin u. Pöggeler, 1959, sect. 575.
[21] *W. L.*, 2, p. 484.

of its principle. The Jewish people know better than any other that the idea of the unity of divine and human nature can be productive of endless evil. This danger occurs because for the Christian the knowledge of "the absolute difference of human and divine" is not only immediate, but is mediated through the release of finite freedom. It is demanded of the Christian that evil – absolute evil – be negated in human self-consciousness. In this demand, if it be met, lies the strength of the Christian principle. For it must then indeed be true that not even the gates of Hell can prevail against it.[22]

The Christian religion in its objective Trinitarian form no more transgresses than Judaism the absolute distinction between God and man. The difference of the two religions is only that in Christianity the Jewish principle is explicated; in itself the logical form is unaltered.[23]

Had Hegel's logic of absolute spirit been available to Spinoza, he would not have found need to abandon Judaism. For it would have permitted him, first, to make philosophically the transition from his concept of substance to the *scientia intuitiva*; secondly, to know the particularity of the Jewish people as resulting from their concept of God as the first actuality of absolute spirit. But there is the difficulty that this last insight does not belong to a Jewish theology as such but to Judaism considered from a Christian standpoint. But then one might ask the question whether in the modern world Judaism exists independently of Christianity and not rather in relation to it – as Christianity again to Judaism.[24]

IV

Judaism is Christianity implicit: what is said of Jewish unfreedom in the *Philosophie der Religion* should be interpreted according to this concept. For then it is clear why Hegel finds in Judaism also unsurpassable freedom: man as turning from finite and selfish purpose is free or universal will. Not even the necessity before which the Hellenic gods resign their will exceeds human freedom in relation to God.[25]

The lack of freedom Hegel sees in Judaism, both in its essential religious attitude and in its ethical order, is that of an immediate or patriarchal relation to authority. It is the freedom of a family which has grown into a nation, but does not contain political freedom as a Greek would understand it. No doubt in one way the family is the freest society: children

22 *Ph. Rel.*, 3, p. 95 foll.
23 *Ph. Rel.*, 3, p. 6 foll.
24 *Gesch. Phil.*, 3, p. 356 foll.
25 *Ph. Rel.*, 2, pp. 78-9.

may remonstrate with parents, hold to how they would have it even as they freely yield theirs to a wiser will. What the family cannot suffer is that another law – that of individuals who legislate for themselves – be opposed to immediate trust and affection.[26]

Job certainly protests his sufferings, but he does not, as Achilles, follow his particular course to the limit, and only attend to the fate that is beyond the gods after he has destroyed all he loves. There is for the Greek a realm of finite freedom; subjection to fate is not so much the condition of human happiness as the recognition of its inevitable limit. In observing that it is subjection to God which restores Job to his former prosperity, Hegel has before him this fundamental difference.[27]

What Hegel says of the Messianic idea in Judaism is from the same standpoint: There is rather the formation of the concept than its explication as complete. Thus when Philo calls the Λόγος the image of God, Hegel objects that it could only properly be called this if God is known as concrete in Himself and not as the One simply to which everything finite returns as its end. In this he speaks of course as a Greek and a Christian. Obviously he knew the large place that Messianism in fact had in Judaism. But if his original concept of that religion be right, he is at any rate consequent in passing it over in his account. For God in relation to the Jewish people as his peculiar purpose is not the One but as well concrete spirit; and this concept Hegel sees as having its development in Greek and Roman religion, its adequate form in Christianity.[28]

To Hegel it is remarkable that Judaism did not lose this Messianic and particular side and become as Islam the universal religion of the One. There was very much the danger that with the growth of philosophical thought the whole religion would be conformed to the ideal of God as the One. The stubbornness with which the Jewish people held to the particular and concrete is also to him admirable. Thereby it became the substantial aspect of Christianity, and did this stubbornness not also mean that from the side of Judaism itself another outcome was possible than Spinoza's?[29]

That Hegel leaves the Covenant also untouched has no doubt the same

---

[26] *Ph. Rel.*, 2, p. 80 foll.
[27] *Ph. Rel.*, 2, pp. 75-6; *Vorlesungen über die Aesthetik*, Berlin, 1843, 3, p. 403.
[28] *Gesch. Phil.* 3, pp. 19-20; *Ph. Rel.* 3, p. 6 foll.
[29] In Judaism is also fully, but immediately, the subjective freedom of the Roman: the one side is the fear of the Lord and through it freedom from finite fear and concern; the other, resulting from it, is the "Seligkeit . . . sich zum Zwecke zu setzen, nicht Abhängigkeit, sondern die Bestimmung der Unabhängigkeit" (Ph. Rel. 2, p. 94). In Judaism the dependence of the one side on the other is immediately in view.

explanation: it has not the universality of the idea of God as the One, but is the Covenant of a particular people because it is founded on that abstract idea. But again this omission must be considered in relation to the refusal of the Jewish people to let go the concrete. The harsh contrast of both is his complete concept of Judaism. To equalise these aspects was the task of the Germano-Christian world, the faithfulness of the Jewish people the assurance that it would not be forgotten.[30]

<h1 style="text-align:center">V</h1>

The Jews, wrote Hegel against the anti-Semites of his time, ought to be given civil rights not only because they are men but also because they are Jews. In this he pointed to their essential role in the liberation of the Germano-Christian state. On the basis of human equality differences of thought and attitude would gradually be evened out. Hegel does not say that Jews would or should be absorbed into Christian society; that, for example, as Eduard Gans they become Lutherans. Rather he would lead them from the ghetto and make them part of the crucial and unsolved problem of Christian society: how is abstract equality – and subjective freedom generally – to become concrete? [31]

The sense of the problem cannot be stated more harshly and pertinently than if one consider that the final destruction of the Jewish people is permitted and encouraged by the two dominant Christian peoples, attached to rival forms of subjective freedom, neither seemingly capable of a rational und humane purpose.

---

[30] *Ph. Rel.*, 2, pp. 81-2. When Hegel sees in Judaism "der merkwürdige, unendlich harte, härteste Kontrast," this is not to be taken as a hostile comment but as the extreme opposite. In Christianity is the same contrast; but because its harshness, that is its immediacy, has been mitigated, that is mediated, the contrast itself which is the source of all truth and freedom can easily be lost from sight. The Christian feels not "Furcht" but "Ehrfurcht": "Im reinen Denken ist nichts zu fürchten; da ist schon alles Vergängliche, alle Abhängigkeit als negiert, als verschwindend aufgegeben, entfernt: Es ist ein einfach reines Verhältnis; man kann also Ehrfurcht sagen" (*Ph. Rel.* 3, p. 73). But how hardly can this simple relation avoid that it fall, if not into idolatry of the finite, into the emptiness of irony! V. *Enc.* 571: "Wird das Resultat, der für sich seiende Geist, in welchem alle Vermittlung sich aufgehoben hat, in nur formellem, inhaltslosem Sinne genommen, so dass der Geist nicht zugleich als an sich seiender und objektiv sich entfaltender gewusst wird, so ist jene unendliche Subjektivität das nur formelle, sich in sich als absolut wissende Selbstbewusstsein, die Ironie, welche allen objektiven Gehalt sich zunichte, zu einem eitlen zu machen weiss"; etc. When one has considered such a passage well, the meaning of the "infinitely hard contrast" becomes evident, and its infinite importance to Christianity. If the knowledge of it be lost, so is lost the knowledge of the Idea: "Alles übrige ist Irrtum. Trübheit, Meinung, Streben, Willkür und Vergänglichkeit; die absolute Idee allein ist Sein, unvergängliches Leben, sich wissende Wahrheit, und ist alle Wahrheit" (*W. L.* 2, p. 484).

[31] *Ph. R.*, 270, note: with its reference to 209.

LABOR, ALIENATION, AND SOCIAL CLASSES
IN HEGEL'S *REALPHILOSOPHIE*

Shlomo Avineri

The two sets of lectures given by Hegel during his period at Jena and generally known as *Realphilosophie* I and *Realphilosophie* II occupy a unique place in the development of Hegel's system.[1] *Realphilosophie* II, which is far more extensive in its section dealing with *Geistesphilosophie,* is the more important for any attempt to reconstruct the stages of Hegel's philosophy of society and state. Rosenzweig saw in it Hegel's first detailed attempt to describe the middle zone between the state and pre-political man, the zone Hegel will later call "civil society."[2] Marcuse sees here Hegel's first discussion of the historical realization of the free subject and the various spheres of integration through which consciousness has to pass.[3] And to Lukács the *Jenenser Realphilosophie* signifies Hegel's construction of man's own self-creation by himself, *die Menschenwerdung des Menschen.*[4]

It is indeed a remarkable set of texts. The theme first propounded a few years earlier in the *System der Sittlichkeit*, the self's struggle for recognition through the other, leading to the emergence of objective spirit in the form of social and political institutions, is here developed in detail. It has thus become accepted that the *Realphilosophie*, together with the preceding *Jenenser Logik und Metaphysik*, set the scene for the *Phenomenology.*

[1] For the problems of the status of the texts, see the editor's remarks to the re-edition of *Realphilosophie II*, in G. W. F. Hegel, *Jenaer Realphilosophie* (Hamburg, 1967), pp. v-vi. Though the editor denies that the text known as *Realphilosophie I* is an earlier version of an attempt at a comprehensive system, we shall, for convenience's sake, continue to refer to the two texts as *Realphilosophie I* and *II*. For the complex problem of dating Hegel's manuscripts of the Jena period, see H. Kimmerle, "Zur Chronologie von Hegels Jenaer Schriften," *Hegel-Studien* IV (Bonn, 1967), pp. 125-176. See also Kroner's Introduction to Hegel's *Early Theological Writings* (Chicago, 1948), esp. pp. 28-43.
[2] F. Rosenzweig, *Hegel und der Staat* (München/Berlin, 1920), I, p. 178.
[3] H. Marcuse, *Reason and Revolution*, new ed. (Boston, 1960), p. 73.
[4] G. Lukács, *Der junge Hegel* (Zürich/Wien, 1948), p. 415. See also J. Hyppolite, *Studies on Marx and Hegel*, trans. J. O'Neill (London, 1969), pp. 70-92.

But beyond this, there arises the question of the relationship between the *Realphilosophie* and Hegel's *Philosophy of Right*. In a way, Hegel tried all his life to write one book, and the *System der Sittlichkeit*, the *Realphilosophie*, the *Phenomenology* and the *Philosophy of Right* are different versions and drafts of the same opus. It is this aspect of the *Realphilosophie* which I would like to bring out in this paper. It will be my intention to show both the rare achievement of Hegel's understanding of modern society as well as some serious flaws in his claim to integrate the inherent tensions of this society into a comprehensive social philosophy.

Various writers, notably Lukács, juxtapose Hegel's radicalism in the *Realphilosophie* to the quietism of the *Philosophy of Right*, and thus oppose a young, radical and critical Hegel to the later author of the *Rechtsphilosophie* who limits himself to *Nach-denken* at the falling of dusk. It will be my argument that the *Realphilosophie* combines a radical analysis of modern society with a spirit of resignation and acquiesence, and that Hegel's political and social solutions in the *Realphilosophie* do not differ fundamentally from those proposed in the *Philosophy of Right*. The dialectical continuity of Hegel's thought seems to me to be vindicated by such a critical reading of the *Realphilosophie*: since his earliest writings Hegel has always been haunted by what he calls "positivity" in his Bern manuscripts and "destiny" in some of the Frankfurt fragments: the dialectical necessity of the combination between the process of man's creation of his own world and his alienation is the main theme of the *Realphilosophie*. Yet when Hegel has to face the extremities of alienation – poverty – he is at a loss: poverty in these texts is as much insoluble as it is in the *Philosophy of Right*, where Hegel bluntly admits that "the important question of how poverty is to be abolished is one of the most disturbing problems which agitate modern society" [5] – and leaves it at that. But despite the fact that Hegel is as reluctant in the *Realphilosophie* to give instruction as to what the world ought to be as he will later turn out to be in the Preface to the *Philosophy of Right*, the *Realphilosophie* manages to raise a number of crucial questions which continued to agitate 19th century thought: the text abounds in motifs anticipating Feuerbach's religious criticism and Marx's social critique – though neither Feuerbach nor Marx were ever acquainted with these texts. Yet it is the same motifs which later appear in the *Philosophy of Right* which thus serve as a link between the young Hegel and the young Marx.

The *Realphilosophie* deals with the philosophy of nature as well as

[5] G. W. F. Hegel, *Philosophy of Right*, trans. T. M. Knox (Oxford, 1958), Addition to Para. 244.

with the philosophy of man: but since the themes of social and political criticism figure so prominently in any contemporary discussion of Hegel's legacy, it seems to me appropriate to discuss at some length those texts of Hegel where these issues are treated by him most extensively. Hegel does come back to these problems in the *Philosophy of Right*, but in a much more cryptic way. He sometimes uses what looks like a code or a cipher to refer to issues settled by his earlier analysis of the subject. Without knowing what he is referring to one sometimes cannot fully grasp his intention.

For the purpose of this paper, a general acquaintance with the *Philosophy of Right* will be assumed, and I shall limit references to it to a minimum. It should, however, be understood that at the background of the argument the relationship to the *Philosophy of Right* will always be present, though the discussion will generally limit itself to the analysis of the *Realphilosophie*, and particularly to Part B (*Geistesphilosophie*) of *Realphilosophie* II. The parallel section in *Realphilosophie* I is much shorter and more condensed, and since its main argument is far better brought out in the later version, the references to this earlier version will be necessarily limited.

The struggle for recognition through the other, after finding its initial articulation in speech, comes up against the world of material objects. In his earlier *System der Sittlichkeit* Hegel has already shown how need is the feeling of being separated from the objective world and how through desire one achieves in satisfaction the transcendence of this separation on the immediate level.[6]

This need to assert oneself in the other is expressed very clearly at the outset of the section of the *Realphilosophie* dealing with the objective world. Through recognition by the other, the subject attains universality, his existence has a meaning for subjects outside himself: hence the transition to objective spirit, *"wirklicher Geist."* [7] Intersubjective relations attain this universality also through the device of contract, which elevates individual will to a universal object: "The universal is the substance of the contract." [8] In breaking a contract, one is injuring not only the immediate incidental subject who happens to be the other party to it, but a universal, objective and social arrangement. Society, not the individual,

[6] G. W. F. Hegel, *Schriften zur Politik und Rechtsphilosophie*, ed. G. Lasson (Leipzig, 1913), p. 422.
[7] *Realphilosophie II*, p. 210: "Everyone wants to count for the other; it is everyone's purpose to perceive himself in the other. Everyone is outside himself..."
[8] *Ibid.*, p. 219.

is hurt, and punishment thus expresses the general will and not merely the injured party.

The same universality appears in property. Hegel makes an initial distinction between possession and property; this distinction follows the traditional line, but then Hegel adds to it another aspect which brings out the centrality of the aspect of recognition in the constitution of property. While possession pertains to my relation to the *object*, property signifies my relation to other *subjects* who recognize my possession of that object:

> The right of possession relates immediately to things, not to a third party. Man has a right to take into possession as much as he can as an individual. He has this right, it is implied in the concept of being himself: through this he asserts himself over all things. But his taking into possession implies also that he excludes a third. What is it which from this aspect binds the other? What may I take into my possession without doing injury to a third party? [9]

It is from these considerations that Hegel derives the trans-subjective, non-individual nature of property: *property pertains to the person as recognized by others*, it can never be an instrinsic quality of the individual prior to his recognition by others. While possession related to the individual, property relates to society: since possession becomes property through the others' recognition of it as such, property is a social attribute. Thus not an individualistic but a social premise is at the roots of Hegel's concept of property, and property will never be able to achieve in his system an independent stature. This is significant because Hegel's description of the economic process is taken from classical political economy, yet on the basic nature of property he holds a totally different view. Property always remains premised on social consensus, on consciousness, not on the mere fact of possession.

Yet there still remains an element of accidentality in possession, even when turned into property, since the objects of possession relate to this or that individual in a wholly arbitrary way. It is only through labor that "the accidentality of coming into possession is being *aufgehoben*," maintains Hegel.[10] By thus appearing central to Hegel's views on property, labor becomes also a focus to Hegel's conception of the self.

It has already been pointed out by several writers that Hegel owes many of his views on labor to his early acquaintance with the writings of Adam

---

[9] *Ibid.*, p. 207. Cf. *Realphilosophie* I, p. 240, on the transition from possession to property: "The security of my possession (becomes) the security of the possessions of all; in my property, all have their property. My possession has achieved the form of consciousness."

[10] *Realphilosophie*, II, p. 217.

Smith and Steuart.[11] Lukács has however remarked that the way labor appears in Hegel's system integrates it most profoundly into speculative philosophy, for it is here "that the active principle (in German idealism, Thought, the Concept) must learn to respect actuality as it is." [12] It is through the instrumentality of labor that Hegel constructs his paradigm of a society differentiated according to types of labor, and it is on this stratification, based on a division of labor, that he later on builds his political edifice. It is in this discussion on labor that Hegel comes closest to motifs to be found later in Marx, and it is these motifs that appear again in the *Philosophy of Right* in those paragraphs (# 241-246) which seem to pose a question mark to the fundamental conservatism of the whole book.

Labor first appears in the *Realphilosophie* as an indication of man's growing awareness of his confrontation with and differentiation from nature. We have already seen how the establishment of property institutionalizes man's relations to other human beings through its integration and incorporation of the objective world into consciousness: nature becomes part of the natural history of man. In a parallel way labor is the transformation of the appetites from their initial annihilative to a constructive attitude towards the objective world; whereas primitive man, like the animals, consumes nature and destroys the object, labor holds up to man an object to be desired not through negation but through creation.[13]

Hegel's achievement in describing the movement of labor has a double edge: on one hand, Hegel shows how labor is necessarily connected with alienation. Alienation to Hegel is not a marginal aspect of labor which can be rectified or reformed: it is fundamental and immanent to the structure of society, it cannot be dispensed with and the conditions of alienation and misery cannot be abolished within the existing society. While thus closing the door on any rosy belief in easy reforming solutions, Hegel's radical criticism of labor in society does not result in any radical call for activism or rebellion: his insights into modern society call for an integration of this experience through political mediation, not through radical upheavel and disruption.

This vision of the working of modern society comes to Hegel not through any empirical study of social and economic conditions in his contemporary

---

[11] See esp. P. Chamley, *Economie, politique et philosophie chez Steuart et Hegel* (Paris, 1963), as well as his article "Les origines de la pensée économique de Hegel," *Hegel-Studien* III (1965), pp. 225-261. Also Lukács, *op. cit.*, pp. 410-420; Marcuse, *op. cit.*, p. 76 ff; Rosenzweig, *op. cit.*, I, p. 159.

[12] Lukács, *op. cit.*, p. 414.

[13] *Realphilosophie* I, p. 220, Cf. "System der Sittlichkeit," *Schriften zur Politik*, etc., p. 422f.

Germany: these conditions he had analyzed in *The German Constitution,* and his description certainly does not bring forth a vital, active and productive society. Hegel's views on modern society are far more a distillation of the Smithian model, raised to the level of a philosophical paradigm.[14]

Labor to Hegel is the positive outcome of man's confrontation with the natural, external, objective world. The process of labor is an objectification of man's subjective powers, and it is through the instrumentality of work on an object that man, a subject, becomes an objective actuality: "I have done something, I have externalized myself; this negation is positive; externalization (*Entäusserung*) is appropriation." [15]

Hegel has earlier perceived a similar externalization in exchange, where the alienation of one's claims to an object makes one's relation to it actual.[16] Yet in exchange, consciousness still accepts the external world as given, whereas in labor it is creating this world while simultaneously relating to other human beings:

Only here has appetite the right to appear, since it is actual (*wirklich*), i.e. it has itself general, spiritual being. Labor of all for all and the satisfaction of all. Everyone serves the other and sustains him, only here has the individual for the first time an individuated being; before that it has been only abstract and untrue.[17]

Labor is thus by necessity *social* labor; contrary to the atomistic, individualistic view of labor, which sees labor as primary and exchange as secondary and derivative, based on a surplus, labor for Hegel is always premised on a reciprocal relationship, subsuming exchange under its cognitive aspects. No one produces for himself, and all production presupposes the other – hence a basic element of recognition is always immanent in labor.

While the goal of production is recognition through the other, its motive is need. Consciousness, by desiring an object, moves man to create it, to transform need from a subjective craving and appetite into an external object: labor is therefore always intentional, not instinctual; it represents man's power to create his own world.[18] Production is thus a vehicle in

[14] This aspect of Hegel has been realized very early on by Marx in his *Economic-Philosophical Manuscripts* where he says: "Hegel's standpoint is that of modern political economy. He conceives *labor* as the *essence*, the self-confirming essence of man." Yet because Marx bases his resumé of Hegel on the *Phenomenology*, and the *Realphilosophie* remained unknown to him, he ends up with a faulty conclusion: "He (Hegel) observes only the positive side of labor, not its negative side." See K. Marx, *Early Writings*, trans. T. B. Bottomore (London, 1963), p. 203.
[15] *Realphilosophie*, II, p. 218.
[16] *Ibid.*, p. 217.
[17] *Ibid.*, p. 213.
[18] *Realphilosophie* I, p. 236; II, p. 214.

reason's actualization of itself in the world: in a passage which prefigures Hegel's later dictum about the rational and the actual, Hegel remarks that "Reason, after all, can exist only in its work; it comes into being only in its product, apprehends itself immediately as another as well as itself." [19]

There is, however, another link between needs and production, and this one is more problematic. Though every human need is concrete, the totality of needs for which the totality of production is undertaken is abstract and cannot be concretely expressed prior to the process of production and distribution having been completed. Production thus becomes abstract and the division of labor appears related to the needs of production and not to the needs of the producers. Man produces not the objects of his own specific needs, but a general product which he then can exchange for the concrete object or objects of his needs: he produces *commodities,* and the more refined his tastes become, the more objects he desires which he cannot produce himself but can achieve through the production of more objects which he then exchanges. There thus appears a universal dependence of each human being on the universality of the producers and the character of labor undergoes a basic change:

> Because work is being done for the need as an abstract being-for-itself, one also works in an abstract way.... General labor is thus division of labor .... Every individual, as an individual, works for *a* need. The content of his labor (however) transcends *his* need; he works for the satisfaction of many, and so (does) everyone. Everyone satisfies thus the needs of many, and the satisfaction of his many particular needs is the labor of many others. Since his labor is thus this abstraction, he behaves as an abstract self, or according to the way of thingness, not as a comprehensive, rich, all-encompassing spirit, who rules over a wide range and masters it. He has no concrete work: his power is in analysis, in abstraction, in the breaking up of the concrete into many abstract aspects....[20]

The dialectical nature of social labor is thus evident: on one hand, it creates sociability, a universal dependence of each on all, makes man into a universal being – the characteristic of civil society, as later described in the *Philosophy of Right* (# 182-183). On the other hand, this reciprocal satisfaction of needs creates a hiatus between the concrete individual and his particular and concrete needs. By working for all, the individual does not anymore work for himself; and element of distance and a need for mediation is thus thrust between his work and the satisfaction of his needs. Social labor thus necessarily entails alienation:

---

[19] *Realphilosophie* I, p. 233.
[20] *Realphilosophie* II, pp. 214-215.

Man thus satisfies his needs, but, not through the object which is being worked upon by him; by satisfying his needs, it becomes something else. Man does not produce anymore that which he needs, nor does he need anymore than which he produces. Instead of this, the actuality of the satisfaction of his needs becomes merely the possibility of this satisfaction. His work becomes a general, formal, abstract one, single; he limits himself to one of his needs and exchanges this for his other necessities.[21]

The more labor becomes thus divided and specialized, the more commodities can be produced; the more labor becomes removed from the immediate satisfaction of the producer, the more productive it becomes; man thus achieves ever greater comfort at the price of ever greater abstraction and alienation in the process of production itself:

His labor and his possessions are not what they are for him, but what they are for all. The satisfaction of needs is a universal dependence of all on all; there disappears for everyone the security and the knowledge that his work is immediately adequate to his particular needs; *his* particular need becomes universal.[22]

The process of labor – originally man's recognition through the other, intended to create for each his own objective world – becomes a process over which man loses all control and direction. Man is far from being integrated into the objective world through creative consciousness, i.e. labor; the abstract nature of labor, together with the division of labor, make him totally alien to this objective world. Hence Hegel comes to be troubled by the real conditions of factory labor, and his general anthropology of labor becomes social analysis. Quoting Adam Smith, Hegel says:

The particularization of labor multiplies the mass of production; in an English manufacture, 18 people work at the production of a needle; each has his particular and exclusive side of the work to perform; a single person could probably not produce 120 needles, even not one . . . . But the value of labor decreases in the same proportions as the productivity of labor increases. Work becomes thus absolutely more and more dead, it becomes machine-labor, the individual's own skill becomes infinitely limited, and the consciousness of the factory worker is degraded to the utmost level of dullness. The connection between the particular sort of labor and the infinite mass of needs becomes wholly imperceptible, turns into a blind dependence. It thus happens that a far-away operation often affects a whole class of people who have hitherto satisfied their needs through it; all of a sudden it limits (their work), makes it redundant and useless.[23]

This analysis thus makes Hegel into one of the earliest radical critics of the modern industrial system. Hegel goes on to point out the necessary

[21] *Realphilosophie* I, pp. 237-238.
[22] *Ibid.*, p. 238.
[23] *Ibid.*, p. 239.

link between the emergence of machinery and the intensification of alienation and here again Hegel takes a middle position between the idealizers
of the machine and the machine-smashers: while recognizing the alienation caused by the introduction of the machine, it is a necessary element
in the anthropological determination of modern society based on ever-
increasing production. Originally, Hegel contends, tools were nothing else
than the mediation between man and his external world; [24] as such, they
always remain a passive object in the hands of the producer. But,

In the same way, (the worker) becomes through the work of the machine
more and more machine-like, dull, spiritless. The spiritual element, the self-
conscious plentitude of life, becomes an empty activity. The power of the
self resides in rich comprehension: this is being lost. He can leave some work
to the machine; his own doing thus becomes even more formal. His dull
work limits him to one point, and labor is the more perfect, the more onesided
it is . . . . In the machine man abolishes his own formal activity and makes it
work for him. But this deception, which he perpetrates upon nature . . .
takes vengeance on him. The more he takes away from nature, the more he
subjugates her, the baser he becomes himself. By processing nature through
a multitude of machines, he does not abolish the necessity of his own labor;
he only pushes it further on, removes it away from nature and ceases to
relate to it in a live way. Instead, he flees from this negative livingness, and
that work which is left to him becomes itself machine-like. The amount of
labor decreases only for the whole, not for the individual: on the contrary,
it is being increased, since the more mechanized labor becomes, the less
value it possesses, and the more must the individual toil.[25]

We thus have here in one of the more speculative documents of German
idealist philosophy one of the most acute insights into the working of
modern, industrial society: from an *a priori* philosophical anthropology,
Hegel moves on to incorporate the results of political economy into a
philosophical system – an attempt almost identical in its systematic structure with Marx's program forty years later. How many of Marx's later
conclusions are already to be found, explicitly or implicitly in Hegel's
earlier texts, requires however, a separate discussion.

Commodity producing society needs, according to Hegel, also a uni-

---

[24] *Realphilosophie* II, pp. 197-198.
[25] *Realphilosophie* I, pp. 232, 237. The parallels with Marx's description in the
Economic-Philosophical Manuscripts are, of course, striking (*Early Writings*, pp. 120-
134). The major difference, however, has already been pointed out by Lukács: while
to Hegel alienation is a necessary aspect of objectification, Marx believes that alienation
resides not in the process of production, but in its concrete conditions. For Hegel objectification and alienation are identical, for Marx they are separable. Therefore Marx
believes in the possibility of ultimate redemption, whereas for Hegel one will never be
able to dissociate the rose from the cross of the present. Philosophy can only interpret
the world, not change it.

versal, abstract criterion which can mediate between labor and the subject. This is money:

These multiple labors of the needs as things must also realize their concept, their abstraction: their universal concept must also be a thing just like them, but (it must be) a universal, which represents all. *Money* is this materially existing concept, the form of the unity or of the potentiality of all the things relating to needs. Need and labor are thus elevated into this universality, and this creates in a great nation an immense system of communality (*Gemeinschaftlichkeit*) and mutual dependence, a life of death moving within itself (*ein sich in sich bewegendes Leben des Toten*). This system moves hither and thither in a blind and elemental way, and like a wild animal calls for strong permanent control and curbing.[26]

But before Hegel constructs these agencies intended to limit the free play of the forces of the market, he goes into some detail regarding the sociological aspects of commodity-producing society. Aspects of class-domination appear in a very prominent way in Hegel's description when he expresses his awareness of the fact that the wealth of nations can be built only at the expense of the poverty of whole classes: "Factories and manufactures base their existence on the misery (*Elend*) of a class," he remarks.[27] And in another context his description is no less brutal in its candor:

(This power) condemns a multitude to a raw life and to dullness in labor and poverty, so that others could amass fortunes, so that these could be taken away from them.[28]

This sinking into poverty and barbarity is seen by Hegel as being caused by the rapid expansion of the market and of production: social labor not only satisfies needs, but it is constantly creating new needs, tastes and fashions. Again, in a rare insight into the dialectics of ever-changing demand creating pressure for ever-increasing production, Hegel says:

Needs are thus multiplied; each need is being subdivided into many; tastes becomes refined and differentiated. One demands a level of finish which carries the object ever nearer to its use.[29]

Fashion becomes the determinant of production, and Hegel is thus one of the first thinkers who has grasped the immanent logic of constantly

[26] *Realphilosophie* I, pp. 239-240. Cf. II, pp. 215-216. Again the parallel with Marx's fragment on "Money" (*Early Writings*, pp. 189-194), is very close.
[27] *Realphilosophie* II, p. 257. Cf. *ibid.*, p. 232: "A mass of the population is condemned to stupefying, unhealthy and precarious labor in factories, manufactures, mines, etc."
[28] *Ibid.*, p. 238. The last sentence refers already to Hegel's justification of property taxes, and Hegel goes on to say that "the inequality of property causes it to be accepted on the condition that high taxes are imposed."
[29] *Ibid.*, p. 231-232. The slightly censorious tone evokes echoes of Rousseau.

changing fashions and fads and its function within the productive process. The constant disquiet of concrete life in industrial society is here described from the consumer's point of view as well:

But this plurality creates *fashion*, the versatility and freedom in the use of these things. The cut of clothes, the style of furnishing one's home, are nothing permanent. This constant change is essential and rational, far more rational than sticking to one fashion, imagining to find something permanent in such particular forms. The beautiful is not ordered by one fashion; but here we have to do not with free beauty, but with beauty that attracts .... Hence it has accidentality in it.[30]

These fluctuations in taste have a bearing on the basic lack of security which characterizes modern society: whole sectors of the population live by the whim of a changing mode, and Hegel's description of the conditions of life of these classes sinking into poverty is truly amazing when one reflects that Hegel reaches his conclusions through an immanent development of the consequences of the theories of political economy:

Whole branches of industry which supported a large class of people suddenly fold up because of a change in fashion or because the value of their products fell due to new inventions in other countries. Whole masses are abandoned to poverty which cannot help itself. There appears the contrast between vast wealth and vast poverty – a poverty that cannot do anything for itself ....

Wealth, like any other mass, makes itself into a power. Accumulation of wealth takes place partly by chance, partly through the universal mode of production and distribution. Wealth is a point of attraction .... It collects everything around itself – just like a large mass attracts to itself the smaller one. To them that have, shall be given. Acquisitition becomes a many-sided system which develops into areas from which smaller businesses cannot profit. The highest abstraction of labor reaches into the most particular types of labor and thus receives an ever-widening scope. This inequality of wealth and poverty, this need and necessity, turn into the utmost tearing up (*Zerrissenheit*) of the will. an inner indignation (*Empörung*) and hatred.[31]

It is precisely here that any possibility of a radical transformation of society presents itself to Hegel – only to be discarded: this possibility remains an "inner indignation," not an act that has to be externalized. At the height of Hegel's critical awareness of the horrors of industrial society, he

[30] *Ibid.*, p. 232.

[31] *Ibid.*, pp. 232-233. It is extremely interesting to note that the term "inner indignation" (*Empörung*) used here by Hegel is the same he uses in the Addition to Para. 244 of the *Philosophy of Right* where he says that "Poverty in itself does not make man into a rabble; a rabble is created only when there is joined to poverty a disposition of mind, an inner indignation against the rich, against society, against the government, etc." Moreover, the only oblique reference in Marx to Hegel's discussion of poverty in the *Philosophy of Right* is a fleeting hint that *Empörung* is not enough; see K. Marx/F. Engels, *The Holy Family*, trans. R. Dixon (Moscow, 1956), p. 51.

remains quietistic and seeks a solution through integration, not through disruption – an aspect which Lukács tends to overlook.

For the passage that immediately follows this critical analysis of industrial society deals with the emergence of the state as regulating and integrating economic activity within a political framework, transcending the forces of the market. In the course of developing this idea, Hegel adds some further touches to his picture of industrial society when he sees in the state an instrument ensuring economic expansion overseas:

> Government comes unto the scene and has to see to it that every sphere be preserved ... (It has to look for) ways out, for channels to sell the product abroad, though this makes it more difficult, since it is to the detriment of the others. (But) freedom of commerce remains necessary, interference must be as inconspicuous as possible, for this is the sphere of arbitrariness (*Willkür*). The appearance of power must be prevented, and one should not try to save that which cannot be saved, but try to employ the remaining classes in another way. Government is the universal overseer; the individual is buried in the particular. The (particular) occupation will admittedly be abandoned by itself, but with the sacrifice of this generation and an increase in poverty. Poor taxes and institutions are required.[32]

The state thus appears at the moment at which society seems to be heading for disruption and chaos: it is the re-integration of the self into itself as a universal being after economic life has particularized, atomized it and made its activity into an abstraction. The basic scenario of Hobbes is, in a way, being re-enacted here within a context presenting a synthesis of speculative philosophy and political economy: the abstraction of *bellum omnium contra omnes* becomes concrete in terms of human activity and consciousness.

Hence while stressing the minimalist function of the state in those of its activities impinging upon economic life ("freedom of commerce remains necessary, interference must be as inconspicuous as possible. . . . The appearance of power must be prevented"), Hegel can at the same time point to the immanence of political life: "The individual has his supposed right only in the universal. The state is the existence, the power of right, the keeping of contract and . . . the existing unity of the word." [33]
This ambivalent status of the state will later enable Hegel to construct the realms of art, religion and philosophy as spheres transcending the state yet functioning within its context. The state, while incorporating the in-

---

[32] *Realphilosophie* II, p. 233. Lukács misses the whole point about the complex place of the state in Hegel's system when he dismisses this minimalist view of governmental intervention in Hegel as one of his "illusions" (*op. cit.*, p. 423).
[33] *Realphilosophie* II, p. 234.

dividual in a universal unity, does not subsume his activities under its existence. Because on one hand the individual uses the state as an instrument for his own particular ends while on the other the state is the individual's true being, the classical means/ends relationship between individual and state is being transcended:

This unity of individuality and universality exists then in a double way; in the extreme of the universal, which is itself an individuality – as government. This is not an abstraction of the state, but an individuality which has the universal as such as an end, while the other extreme has the individual person as an end.[34]

The general will thus appears in Hegel's system in a radically different way than in Rousseau: Hegel points out in several instances that any social contract theory is a *petitio principi*, because it takes consensus, the readiness to abide by the terms of the contract, for granted. In the same way, as there could be no right in the state of nature, the general will could not be perceived as the constitutive aspect of the body politic.[35] The general will for Hegel is not the premise on which the state is being founded, historically or logically, but the emergent outcome of the lengthy process of *Bildung*, which created through differentiation and opposition the political consciousness out of the diverse elements of man's struggle for recognition.[36] The general will is the will of the individuals made into an object within the institutions of the state:

The general will is the will of all and each . . . . It has first of all to constitute itself as general out of the will of the individuals so that it will appear as the principle and element, but on the other hand it is first and essential. The individuals have to make themselves into a universal through negation of themselves, through externalization and education (*Entäusserung und Bildung*).[37]

This objectification of the individual will as it appears in the general will, in the state, entails the recognition by the individual that what appears as something alien and external – political power – is nothing else than the externalization of his own will. The law is this objectification of the subjective will:

The rule of Law is not meant to be an act of legislating as if the others did not exist: they are there. The relation is the movement of the person educated to obey towards the commonwealth . . . . The second element is the trust that

[34] *Ibid.*, pp. 248-249.
[35] *Ibid.*, pp. 205, 245-247.
[36] On *Bildung* see George A. Kelly, *Idealism, Politics and History* (Cambridge, 1969), pp. 341-348.
[37] *Realphilosophie* II, pp. 244-245.

appears, i.e. that the individual knows himself to be in it as his own essence, that he finds himself preserved in it.[38]

This need for external limitations of the individual's will is the essence of what Hegel calls *Polizei*. The possible misunderstandings connected with this term in the *Philosophy of Right*, emanating as it were from its present usage, can be at least partly cleared up when we recall that for Hegel *Polizei* comes "from Politeia, public life and rule, the action of the whole itself." [39] This public authority is needed since in caring for himself alone and enjoying the quiet bliss of his property rights, the individual may hurt another by simply disregarding the impact that his own actions may have on the life of another. An element of *List der Vernunft* comes into the picture when Hegel describes how the state is willed by the individuals for their own self-preservation and better protection while it also represents an actuality transcending this interest:

> The general *form* is this turning of the individual into a universal and the becoming of the universal. But it is not a blind necessity, but one mediated through knowing. In other words, each is an end to himself, i.e. the end is the motive, each individual is immediately the cause. It is his interest that drives him (to the state), but it is likewise the universal which has validity, is the middle, allies him with his particularity and actuality.[40]

The state is the transcendence of the individual in the universality of the law; the externalization of the will makes the individual into a person because only in this way does he achieve actuality for the other. This universal power is the commonwealth, where the actions of the individual, because they can impinge on the lives of everyone else, achieve objective, universal substance.[41]

The fact that the state is both instrumental and immanent is being represented in the individual by his dual role as a particular being and a universal one. In one of the most pointed expressions which prefigures both his own mature thought as well as Marx's later argument against it, Hegel says that man is both a member of civil society and a citizen of the state and has to strike a balance between these two aspects of his existence:

> Both individualities are the same. The same (individual) takes care of himself and his family, works, signs contracts, etc., and at the same time he also works for the universal and has it as an end. From the first viewpoint he is called *bourgeois*, from the second *citoyen*.[42]

[38] *Ibid.*, p. 248. Cf. the definition of "Right" (p. 206): "Right is the relation of the person to another, the universal element of its free being or the determination and limitation of its empty freedom."

[39] *Ibid.*, p. 259.

[40] *Ibid.*, p. 243.

[41] *Realphilosophie*, I, pp. 232-233; II, pp. 237, 244.

[42] *Realphilosophie* II, p. 249. The French terms appear in Hegel's original German text. For Marx, of course, the splitting of man into *citoyen* and *bourgeois* is the meas-

These two aspects of human activity lead to Hegel's discussion of social classes: the crucial point is, of course, that Hegel does not see the antinomy between man as *bourgeois* and as *citoyen* as something to be overcome in a total, new unity: it is part of the dialectical progress of man towards his self-recognition. This should be kept in mind, since one of the common errors in discussing this problem in Hegel is to be carried away by the apparent similarity between Hegel's discussion of civil society and some aspects of Marx's analysis. The truth of the matter is that Hegel's point of departure is the exact opposite of Marx's. For Marx classes are aggregates formed by types of social labor, linked together by the common relationship of their members to the means of production, seeking a political articulation for their socio-economic interests. The class nature of political power is to Marx a sin against the state's claim for expressing the universal as against the particularism and egotism of civil society. For Hegel, the institutionalization of class relationships into the political structure is the way through which the atomism of civil society is being integrated into a comprehensive totality. The different classes represent to Hegel not only modes of production, but modes of consciousness which are relevant to a society differentiated in its structure according to criteria taken from Hegel's general system. While for Marx classes represent a division of labor that has to be overcome, for Hegel they stand for the integration of this division, regretable, yet necessary, into a meaningful whole. Classes reflect the various stages of consciousness, just as periods in history.[43] For Hegel, classes always remain *estates*, in the sense that they represent a legitimized differentiation (interestingly enough, Hegel uses the term *class* only when referring to those directly involved in labor). Each estate stands for a different mode of consciousness: the principle of immediate trust and obedience is represented in the peasantry; the principle of law and order in the middle classes, and the principle of universality in the bureaucracy, the universal class. Though the principle of classification is similar to that of the *Philosophy of Right*, the internal division of each estate is more complex and represents a slightly more sophisticated awareness of class differentiation than the neat divisions Hegel would adopt later. Furthermore, in the *Realphilosophie* the form of labor performed by each class figures more prominently, and thus the connection between class and the anthropology of labor is brought out much more clearly.

The peasantry is distinguished by being the class of immediate labor,

ure of his alienation in modern, post-1789 society. Cf. "On the Jewish Question," *Early Writings*, pp. 13-31.

[43] *Realphilosophie*, II, p. 253.

whose concrete work relates to a natural object (land) and not to a product. It thus represents a low level of consciousness, not yet differentiated from substantiality. On a social level this reflects itself in the peasantry accepting its work and role as they are without much questioning: the peasantry is the class of immediate trust, unreflective consciousness:

The estate of immediate trust and raw concrete labor is the peasantry . . . . The peasantry is thus this trust lacking in individuality, having its individuality in the unconscious individual, the earth. As for labor, (the peasant's) work does not have the form of abstract labor: he takes care, more or less, of almost all his needs . . . . The inter-relationship between his purpose and its realization is unconscious, natural. He ploughs, sows, but it is God who orders that it will thrive; it is the season and his trust that (cause) that it will become by itself what he had put into the ground. The activity is underground. He pays taxes and tributes because that's how it is; these fields and cottages have been situated in such a way from time immemorial; *that's how it is*, and that's all . . . .
Concrete labor is elemental, substantial subsistence. In war, this estate makes up the raw mass.[44]

When Hegel goes on to the second class, he distinguishes between the burghers (*Bürgerstand*) and the class of businessmen (*Kaufmannstand*). The *Bürgerstand* is made up mainly of artisans, its labor being characterized by adaptation of nature; the business class, on the other hand, is distinguished by its being engaged in exchange. Both the artisans and the businessmen see in law and order the principle of their existence; property, acquisitiveness and social mobility are the pillars of their being. In a striking description of the social ethos of the *Bürgerstand*, Hegel gets at the root of so many of what are unmistakenly middle class values:

(The burgher) knows himself as a property owner, not only because he possesses it, but also because it is his right – so he assumes; he knows himself to be recognized by his particularity. Unlike the peasant, he does not enjoy his glass of beer or wine in a rough fashion, as a way of elevating himself out of his dullness . . . but because (he wants) to show by his suit and the finery of his wife and children that he is as good as the other man and that he has really made it. In this he enjoys himself, his value and his righteousness; for this did he toil and this has he achieved. He enjoys not the pleasures of enjoyment but the joy of his self-esteem.[45]

---

[44] *Ibid.*, pp. 254-255. In the *Philosophy of Right* Hegel includes in the "agricultural class" both the peasantry and the nobility and there thus emerges a slight idealization of the virtues of agricultural life which is totally lacking here. Here it is only the peasantry that is being described, and the similarity to Marx's judgment on the "idiocy of village life" and the basically individualistic, a-social mode of production of the peasantry is again striking.
[45] *Realphilosophie* II, p. 256.

In the business class, on the other hand, a higher degree of abstraction is achieved:

The work of the businessman is pure exchange, neither natural nor artificial production or formation. Exchange is the movement, the spiritual, the means, liberated from utility and need as well as from working, from immediacy . . . .[46]

The mode of existence of the businessman calls forth the emergence of money as a commodity by itself:

The object itself is being divided into two: the particular thing, the object of commerce, and the abstract, money – a great invention. All needs are reduced to this unity. The object of need has become a mere image, unusable. The object is here something that has meaning purely according to its value, not for itself, not in relation to the need.... A person is real to the extent that he has money.... The formal principle of reason is to be found here – it is the abstraction from all particularity, character, historicity, etc. of the individual. The disposition (of the businessman) is this harshness of spirit, wherein the particular, now completely alienated, does not count anymore. (There exist) only strict rights. The bill of exchange must be honored – he himself may be distroyed – his family, welfare, life, etc. may go to pieces – total lack of mercy . . . .[47]

Again, what stands out here is not only the striking similarity with Marx, but the fact that no radical call of action follows this harsh analysis: the nature of modern society is grasped with an amazing lucidity given the period in which these texts were written. But all is being incorporated within the integrative functions of the state. No rebellion, nor deviation.

The integration is carried out through the mediation of the universal class: "The public estate works for the state. . . . Its disposition of mind is the fulfillment of its duty." [48] The business class expresses already a sort of universality – the universality of the market – but it is still abstract. Universality becomes concrete only in the class of public servants who represent "the intervention of the universal into all particularity"; the civil servant is likened to the arteries and the nerves that run through the body; they are not, of course, identical with it.[49]

The universal class is at the apex of the social pyramid not only because of its universal intentionality, but also because it is the only class of society whose objective is knowledge itself, not nature, artefact or abstraction, as is the case with all other classes. The specific academic background of the German bureaucratic tradition is very much in evidence

[46] *Ibid., ibid.*
[47] *Ibid.*, pp. 256-257.
[48] *Ibid.*, p. 259.
[49] *Ibid.*, p. 257.

in this concept of the universal class as an educated estate, including not only civil servants in the narrow sense but also teachers, doctors, lawyers:

> This pure knowledge has to be realized, has to give a content to itself out of itself, a free content, which it at the same time also an uninterested object.... This is science generally. Spirit has here an object with which it deals without relating to appetite and need. It is fulfilled thought, intelligence that knows itself.[50]

This concept of science as non-instrumental knowledge, knowledge knowing itself, then enables Hegel to relate the state to the realms of art, religion and philosophy which are thus beyond objective spirit but need the state for their proper functioning. In the universal class, this is already hinted at, and thus Hegel can close his discussion of the estates and the state and move on to these spheres – exactly as he closes the *Philosophy of Right* moving in this direction.

The discussion of *Kunst, Religion* and *Wissenschaft* is outside the scope of this paper. Suffice it to say that in the *Realphilosophie* just as well as in his later writings, the edifice of the state is nothing else than an infra-structure for absolute spirit – never an end-in-itself.

For the purpose of our discussion, however, a crucial point has to be raised, and this has to do with what appears as a gap between Hegel's discussion of the working of modern society and the kind of integrated solution he envisages for it through the system of estates. Pointing to the French Revolution, Hegel incorporates it here into his system in the same dialectical way in which he deals with it in the *Phenomenology* and elsewhere. It is the integrative side of the revolution which he accepts, while rejecting what he calls its negativity and abstractedness. In a footnote Hegel remarks that the French Revolution did indeed abolish class privileges, but "the abolition of class *differentiation* is mere empty talk."[51]

This is significant, for the society Hegel describes in the *Realphilosophie* is post-1789 society. The aristocracy is not mentioned – contrary to the *Rechtsphilosophie*, where it appears as the upper crust of "the agricultural class." While emphasizing that the privileges of the aristocracy as to taxation, etc. have to be abolished,[52] Hegel sticks to the necessity to mete out different treatment to different classes. He even suggests, for example a difference, more rough and immediate penal code for the peasantry as compared to the middle class; taxes should primarily rest on the burgher class, commercial law should apply in all its severity to the business class

---

[50] *Ibid.*, p. 260.
[51] *Ibid., ibid.*
[52] *Ibid.*, p. 238: "An aristocracy that does not pay taxes runs the great risk of losing violently."

only and even marriage laws should be modified when applied to different estates.[53]

Yet while Hegel thus tries to give to each estate its due place in the hierarchy of consciousness, the system of estates seems to exclude the class of people who are at the root of commodity production. Had Hegel not described the conditions of life of the worker in civil society, it would have been beside the point to ask him for a solution to his problem. But once Hegel did grasp, and with so much rare insight, the social implications of commodity production, the complete lack of this class of people in his integrated system of social estates is a serious defect: for Hegel's social system includes the peasants, the *Bürgerstand* and the *Kaufmannstand*, the civil service: nowhere does the worker appear as being integrated into the social system.

Lukács attributes to the limitations of Hegel's age the fact that he saw in the businessman, rather than the captain of industry, the central figure of commodity producing society. For Lukács this proves that Hegel's views of civil society are yet crude and undeveloped.[54] This criticism seems to make sense, yet one wonders whether it is as cogent as it sounds: at least from our present vantage point we can perhaps see Hegel's description as having more relevance than Lukács credits him with. The captain of industry, the traditional entrepreneur, turned out, after all, to be a passing phenomenon of relatively short duration. With the extension of the market, the traditional industrialist is almost completely disappearing, while it is the businessman who remains at the center of the commodity producing society, though it may be the corporate rather than the traditional private businessman. Here Hegel's insight, basing the nature of modern society on the organization of exchange far more than of pure production, is perhaps more profound than that of Marx (and Lukács).

But Hegel's failure to integrate the worker – whom he had discovered earlier in the manufacture and factory – into his system of estates is a failure of far greater magnitude. It reappears again in the *Philosophy of Right*, where after discussing pauperization and the failure of civil society to integrate the poor into the industrial system, Hegel leaves poverty an open question, without suggesting any solution. Both in the *Realphilosophie* and the *Philosophy of Right*, the worker remains for Hegel in civil society, but not of civil society.

---

[53] *Ibid.*, p. 258. The reference to different marriage laws is probably intended to mean that the system of inheritance, which is part of marriage law, should be different when applied to landed property as against moveable property. In the *Philosophy of Right* Hegel similarly advocates primogeniture for the landed gentry.
[54] Lukács, *op. cit.*, p. 427.

Thus Hegel's imposing synthesis of a radical critique of modern society with a system of integration through consciousness is left with a serious flaw in its center. Hegel's political solution in the *Realphilosophie* is the same as in the *Philosophy of Right*: he sees in the monarch the focal point of subjective liberty and raises it to be the principle of the modern age: in the monarchy, subjectivity is represented and vindicated.[55] Again, there is no way to confront a later, monarchist Hegel with an earlier, radical one: in 1805, as in 1818, monarchy is the form of government integral to modern society according to Hegel.

This monarchy is to Hegel the expression of public opinion, and thus the middle between innovation and preservation. The dialectics of controlled change are never better expressed by Hegel than when he says:

Today, one rules and lives differently in states whose constitution has remained nonetheless the same – and this constitution changes according to the times. Government must not come forward on the side of the past and defend it obstinately; but similarly it should always be the last one to be convinced to introduce changes . . . .[56]

All the quietism of the Preface to the *Philosophy of Right* appears here, and Hegel's inability to jump over Rhodes is, perhaps, after all, at the root of his failure to integrate his rare insights into modern society into a system within which every group or class will be able to find its fulfillment. In this way, Hegel's failure perhaps brings out in paradoxical way his own dictum that when it comes to giving instruction to the world as it ought to be, philosophy always comes on the scene too late. Hegel's great achievement in the *Realphilosophie* – later to be incorporated into the *Philosophy of Right* – was to hold up a mirror to a society in its infancy in which it could see its image as it would look in maturity.

Hegel's achievement has been truly impressive: he can, now, be said to be of the first modern thinkers to articulate the specific difference of contemporary society, and his achievement calls for a re-evaluation of the traditional view of Hegel as a philosopher lost in "abstract" speculations. But the society Hegel so well understood did not have and could not have at that time a solution to the structural problem of poverty, "one of the most disturbing problems which agitate modern society." The problem could be conceived, but not its solution. And if the greyness of the philosopher's mirror failed to show a solution that the greyness of life did not yet bring forth, surely Hegel would be the last one to blame the philosopher.

[55] *Realphilosophie* II, p. 250.
[56] *Ibid.*, p. 251.

COMMENT ON AVINERI'S LABOR, ALIENATION, AND SOCIAL CLASSES IN HEGEL'S *REALPHILOSOPHIE* *

Otto Pöggeler

Professor Avineri has shown in a thorough manner how Hegel's analysis of modern society in *Realphilosophie II* of 1805-6 anticipates essentially the *Rechtsphilosophie* of 1821. To be sure, neither in 1805-6 nor in 1821 did Hegel know the solution to one of the main problems of this modern society, the problem of poverty. Thus, it is incorrect to attribute political radicalism to the author of the *Realphilosophie* and political quietism to the author of the *Rechtsphilosophie*.

I have nothing to add to Professor Avineri's arguments, but I would like to raise an additional question: Is it permissible first to detach from *Realphilosophie II* that outline Hegel developed in the Jena period of the philosophy of law and of the state, and then to insert into that outline additional details or parallels from the *System der Sittlichkeit* of 1803 and the *Realphilosophie* of 1803-4? Is it not rather the case that Hegel's first Jena works display a starting point totally different from that of *Realphilosophie II*?

As Professor Avineri has stressed, Hegel begins with the critique of "positivity." How in western history could religion, but also the constitution of the state, have become "positive?" Positivity, that is, heteronomy or the enslavement by inflexible tradition and unjustified authority, is opposed to morality, self-determination based on freedom. However, Hegel overcomes this opposition in his Frankfurt works. To the opposition between positivity and morality he opposes something else which he calls beauty, love, religious elevation. In beauty, love, religious elevation the infinite shines forth in the finite, and, conversely, finite life discovers itself in, or is lifted up into, the infinite unifying life. The infinite contained in freedom and self-determination is no longer to confront the mere matter of duty as an abstract "you ought"; rather, by way of the institutions of political life and the myths and rites of religion, this infinite is to mediate with itself

* Trans. Keith & Mary Algozin.

everything restricted and finite. For example, the moral-political life is to be able to absorb even narrow bourgeois egoism. In the "spirit of Christianity," therefore, Hegel calls for the "beautiful religion" which no longer flees the world apolitically (as does the orthodox Christian religion, according to Hegel's view at that time); in the Jena essay on natural law he is still calling for the living organization of a people as the "most beautiful form" of moral-political life.

Hegel hoped that the ideal of the Greek polis would be actualized anew by the revolutionary movements of his own time. Yet it is not the case that in his Frankfurt period he fled to unrealistic illusions and to religious mysticism (as Lukács has unjustifiably maintained). Rather, Hegel asked how this ideal could be actualized under modern conditions. Thus, he did not write only political pamphlets; in his commentaries on Kant's *Metaphysik der Sitten* and Steuart's *Political Economy* Hegel also grappled with the tendencies of modernity and with the way these tendencies were theorized in the current *philosophia practica*. For example, he criticized the results of the division of labor as well as the abstract separation of legality and morality and of church and state.

The essay on natural law from the Jena period (1802-3) provides us with a philosophical development of this Hegelian starting point. Here Hegel does not begin with the natural rights which theories of natural law granted to individual men; he criticizes such a starting point as bound to lead to an "atomization" of the moral life. Rather, Hegel begins with "nature" in that sense in which Hölderlin calls the whole of life "nature," and Schelling takes organic nature at peace in itself as the clue to the interpretation of the world. Behind this concept of nature there stands likewise Spinoza's *Deus sive Natura* (that absolute in which everything finite and limited is cancelled). Because it is this "nature" which Hegel sees as actualized in the moral-political life of a people, he can accept the classical political philosophy of a Plato or an Aristotle, and, against the modern theories of natural law which begin with the individual, he can develop the Aristotelian conviction that the people is natural rather than the individual.

The Hegelian philosophy of law and of the state of the first Jena years must derive all determinations of natural rights from that actualization of nature as it occurs in the living whole of a people. The self-intuition and self-conception of "nature" in the moral-political life of a people is to form a "system of morality." If, according to the Spinozism of the time, this living whole is thought of as "power," then phenomena like death, war, conscience, and crime become very significant. The highest task of the individual is to cancel himself and his finitude into the infinite unifying whole of the moral-political life. Only he whose task is philosophizing and political activity, only the noble warrior who risks his life in the struggle, is the authentic moral-political man. Whoever starts from the bourgeois egoism of the individual, from wealth accumulated and goods exchanged, can grasp the sense of life only as mediated by the work of others. If Hegel takes up in this way, in his famous doctrine of the "tragedy of morality," the thematic of the doctrine of the estates, this is because he is still far from putting the formative value of slave labor above the ability of the noble to risk life in the struggle for dominion, his position in the *Phänomenologie des Geistes.*

Hegel could arrive at the position of the *Phänomenologie des Geistes* because he came increasingly to accept both the modern theories of natural law and the modern political economy. Indeed, Hegel discussed the connection between economy and natural law; he sought to show how labor relations demand that economic activities develop laws (especially civil laws) to secure the economic process. But how do labor and law belong to that "nature" which has its authentic actuality in the whole of moral-political life? Hegel posed this question in *Realphilosophie I.* Here he develops first the "ideal" or "formal" capacities which come into being in the actualization of a people. These "capacities" are: language or recollection (that is, the manner in which that which is is represented symbolically, linguistically, for consciousness), then the tool, and thence, labor and law, and finally, possession and family; or more exactly: that moral-political communication as it occurs in the family as the concrete community of love, but also as it occurs in the political struggle for recognition. With the development of these "capacities" there takes place, simultaneously, both the socialization and the individualization of men; the development of these capacities is not the thematic of a philosophy of "subjective" spirit as opposed to "objective" spirit.

However, this acceptance of the theories of natural law and of the modern political economy raises the question: From what unified basis can forms such as labor, property, exchange, law, and reciprocal recognition be developed? In *Realphilosophie II* Hegel presents, as this basis, the "ego" taken as intelligence and will; here, in a first part, there is a preliminary development of "abstract" spirit (the ego as intelligence and will), and then the discussion passes to "actual" spirit. Thus, in *Realphilosophie II,* Hegel no longer begins with "nature," which was thought of, of course, as "power" and spirit; rather, he begins with spirit in its abstractness, the ego as intelligence and will. Thus, he can now accept in a more positive way what some years earlier he had criticized scathingly: the theory of natural law and the practical philosophy of Kant and Fichte. However, now he stretches his insights on the procrustean bed of a systematic which was to find its most rigid expression in the *Enzyklopädie*.

Pursuing this course Hegel became an analyist of modern society and discovered that problem which found no solution either in his philosophy or in reality, the problem of poverty. As Professor Avineri has stressed, with this discovery Hegel's analysis takes on actuality. However, it remains to ask whether the specific starting point of *Realphilosophie I* is not of more contemporary concern than the doctrines of labor, social classes, poverty, and alienation, as these are developed in *Realphilosophie II*, and then in the *Rechtsphilosophie* of 1821. Of course, in a world in which the greater part of humanity is exposed to the scourge of life threatening poverty, what could be of more contemporary concern than the reference to a poverty which arises necessarily from a specific social process? However, there remains the question of how this social process can be changed so that poverty is no longer a necessary result, a question which implies the further question: Which "capacities" are determinitive for the social process? It was this latter question that Hegel posed in a pressing and unresolved form in *Realphilosophie I*. As is well known, Hegel has been reproached for subordinating the sphere of economic production to a political sphere in which man is alienated from himself; so he does not appreciate the emancipating power of the economic-social sphere. On the whole, his grasp of labor, of self-production as the essence of man, is ultimately one-sided, that is, from the side of "theory." If Marx raises such objections, then one must respond to him and to Engels with the question as to whether their grasp of social *praxis*, at least after the *Deutschen Ideologie*, was not onesided, that is, from the side of economic labor and technical production. The question as to how language, tool, family, and political confrontation are "capacities" of social-political life, that is, the basic question of the first Hegelian *Realphilosophie*, is thus still of contemporary importance.

(Heinz Ilting has shown how Hegel let the ancient and contemporary starting points of political philosophy interpenetrate in his Jena drafts: "Hegels Auseinandersetzung mit der aristotelischen Politik," *Philosophisches Jahrbuch*, München, 1963-4, Bd. 71, 38-58. Manfred Riedel has worked out clearly the difference between the starting point of the first so-called *Jena Realphilosophie* and that of *Realphilosophie II*: "Hegels Kritik des Naturrechts," *Hegel Studien*, Bd. 4, Bonn, 1967, 177-204. Jürgen Habermas has attempted to show how a point of departure which grounds *Realphilosophie I* was later given up: "Arbeit und Interaktion; Bemerkungen zu Hegels Jenenser Philosophie des Geistes," *Technik und Wissenschaft als 'Ideologie,'* Frankfurt a.M., 1968, pp. 9-47.)

REMARKS ON THE PAPERS OF AVINERI
AND PÖGGELER

Robert L. Perkins

The paper of Prof. Avineri, Prof. Pöggeler's comment, and the resulting discussion suggested a large number of questions regarding not only Hegel's philosophy but also larger philosophic issues. Among them are:

1. As emphasized by Professor Avineri, mediation does not take place within civil society; alienation is present as one of its permanent characteristics. Does this not require, according to the terms of Hegel's philosophy, that civil society be overcome, discarded? Does not this incompleteness, coupled with Hegel's manifest lack of solution to the problem of poverty, indicate his failure as a social philosopher in the terms of *his own philosophy*, which has as its purpose the systematic inclusion of the totality, which would mean the overcoming of all contradiction and alienation? It is sufficient to order civil society by political means? Granted that such an ordering may be what Hegel intended, can one solve the problems characteristic of civil society extrinsically to civil society? This question is even more exasperating when one recognizes that the political ordering of civil society is purely negative or regulative. When one adds this question to the serious criticism raised by Prof. Avineri of Hegel's lack of inclusion of the worker within one of the *Stände* in his social analysis, one is still more perplexed at the lack of fulfilment of the demand for systematic inclusiveness which Hegel himself raised.

2. The whole discussion of alienation at this symposium produced no unanimity regarding either the origins of this notion in Hegel's philosophy or its meaning. Even the philological points raised were not agreed to by all. This failure of the symposium to reach a conclusion regarding this notion requires that major study be made of the historical origins of the terms and their meanings and that a renewed effort be made to analyze Hegel's own philosophy of alienation using the whole corpus, not just the obvious texts. Perhaps our confusion only reflects an indecisiveness and inconclusiveness on the part of Hegel himself.

3. The question of alienation extends in another direction also. Is alienation a class characteristic or is it universal, i.e. referring to the *Stände* and also to the working class? What are the existential dimensions of alienation set forth in Hegel's philosophy? Is a final solution to the problem possible within the terms of Hegel's philosophy? If the solution to the problem is possible within the terms of his philosophy, is the solution possible within the terms of *Realphilosophie* and/or the *Philosophy of Right,* i.e., within the limits of objective spirit? If the problem of alienation cannot be solved in terms of Hegel's philosophy, what does this fact imply about the ultimate value of his philosophy?

4. Professor Avineri has admirably shown in the space available to him some of the differences between the social conditions existent in Prussia in Hegel's time and some of the structures inferred by his philosophy. However, there did not emerge a complete agreement regarding Hegel's views of *polis*, the French Revolution, Rousseau, etc. The discussion seemed to require a background in social, political, and economic history of which most philosophers loathe to admit the necessity. Should we not rather, as students of Hegel, eschew our professional narrowness and either attempt some of these studies or invite some of our colleagues in other disciplines to engage with us in subsequent symposia?

5. The same type of observation applies in a somewhat different direction. Have we actually found a Hegelian method of dealing with the evils of labor to which the working class has been subjected? At least two respondents to Professor Avineri's paper suggested we indeed have had some success in this matter, and Professor Avineri agreed. Yet there was no unanimity as to the nature of the method or the locale where or the time when this method had been used successfully. Does this disagreement mean that we have not understood Hegel or that we have not understood ourselves and our times? The question of utopianism should be raised here, for it was suggested that the effort to solve the problems of the social system within its own terms has tended historically toward utopianism. Not all discussants would agree that this was the case, and certainly the historical example used by Professor Avineri (that *practices* current in the United States have resulted in the emergence of a corporate state) would seem to be an explicit denial of the necessity of utopian solutions to the problem of the evils of labor visited on the working class and the problem of poverty. Is utopianism necessarily implied by efforts to solve the problems of labor and poverty within the terms of the social system? Has not the prominence of Marxist social philosophy tended in modern times to overemphasize the utopian element in political theory, social theory, and social planning?

II

An interesting set of parallels and comparisons can be made from the references to fashion in Kierkegaard and Hegel. Kierkegaard's views of fashion are found in *Stages on Life's Way* (tr. by W. Lowrie, Princeton: Princeton University Press, 1940) where they are doubly reflected and are subject to the problems of his use of pseudonyms. The tailor in "In Vino Veritas" is one who has established himself as a fashion designer and who used that position and his considerable talent to make fools of his customers. He has complete contempt of women (and their husbands too, if they are also fools) and designs clothes that will make them look as ridiculous as possible. Fashion is also used to indicate class consciousness. The fashion designer also psychoanalyzes the husband and wife in order to express and accentuate the worst aspects of their characters. In this way both the husband and wife are prostituted to the highly intellectualized whim and contempt of the tailor.

As Hegel has pointed out "the immanent logic of constantly changing fashions and fads has its function in the productive process;" Kierkegaard has thought out the immanent morality of an economic order which must seduce the victims to consume artificialities. Kierkegaard's description of the means the tailor used to sell the new fashion is a dramatic moral analysis of the current means of huckstering: creation of artificial need, beguiling, flattery, and class pride to name a few. Kierkegaard emphasized how highly intellectualized the forms of tyranny and alienation are which are expressed in the "rationally" contrived succession of fads. Kierkegaard has also shown the moral degeneration which occurs when one used another: the tailor comes to despise woman and himself. Not only is the female consumer of fashion enslaved by the system, the tailor is also. If anything, he is even more enslaved by the system of artificial need than the woman because he requires her to exploit whereas she does not require him. He as creator of artificial needs is superfluous. This interpretation of the role of fashion in Kierkegaard offers a valuable addition to the Hegelian analysis of fashion and a literary illusion of the omnipotence of the master-slave relation in inauthentic or dehumanized human relations.

III

Although references to existentialism have been remarkably absent from the public deliberations of this symposium, topics relative to it have dominated a number of conversations. Although some have thought this public silence to be a positive gain, others have thought that something was distinctly missing because in a certain sense, as Professor Richard Kroner has suggested, Hegel not Kierkegaard is the real founder of existential philosophy. The organizers of the symposium did make an effort to recruit papers by at least one person who is dedicated to the philosophy of Kierkegaard. This particular student of Kierkegaard felt that the Hegelians should have their day undisturbed by the fundamental epistemological questions Kierkegaard raised regarding the nature of system, logic, empirical knowledge and the place of the *Phenomenology* in reference to the system, etc., etc. Besides these, the purely analytical questions about the use of language raised by Kierkegaard tend to raise the issue of clarity and become argumentative. Best these were unmentioned because as noted above, the students of Hegel themselves confronted the linguistic ambiguity relating to alienation – only to leave it unconcluded.

Most indicative of this omission is the reference Professor Pöggeler made to the three geographical regions. But in addition to the three worlds he mentioned brief reference must be made to this fourth world of the development of Hegel research, that of Kierkegaardian existentialism. Without attempting to construct a bibliography, reference must be made to Niels Thulstrup's *Kierkegaard's forhold til Hegel* (Kobenhavn, 1968). Thulstrup has labored on the Kierkegaard-Hegel relationship for his whole adult life and has offered all the Hegel courses at Kobenhavns Universitet in the last fifteen years. This masterful and exhaustive work deserves to be translated into one or another of the major languages. In addition to this most important piece of research the work of other authors such as Anz, Bense, Schulz, Schweppenhauser and several others has been fruitful not only in revealing the roots of Kierkegaard's thought but also in showing the influence of Hegel on this non-disciple.

HEGEL AND CONTEMPORARY LIBERALISM, ANARCHISM, SOCIALISM: A DEFENSE OF THE *RECHTSPHILOSOPHIE* AGAINST MARX AND HIS CONTEMPORARY FOLLOWERS

James Doull

I

The modern forms of social freedom – liberalism, anarchism, socialism – have as their common principle the moral or subjective will. The institutional existence of this principle is civil society: concrete persons who seek to realize their particularity in the external realm of natural necessity and arbitrary will, but so that their relation to one another is mediated through universal will.[1] This principle and its various forms belong peculiarly to the modern world. The free societies of classical antiquity were founded on a substantial unity where the mediation of conflicting wills did not ultimately fall within the consciousness of their members.[2] Between ancient and modern freedom lies abstract right or "the absolutely free will" as immediate self-relation and opposed to the realm of natural or particular interests in which the will is unfree. Abstract right is peculiarly the principle of medieval society, whose tendency and result was to overcome the separation of rational will from natural interests. The subjective will of modern society can only be understood as this result.[3] For modern freedom is simply abstract personality that has formed the unity of its two worlds in universal self-consciousness and therefore knows natural interests as only apparently falling outside the identity of individual with universal will. The former division between political and purgative virtues has vanished, in that the middle or reflective form of rational will has become the explicit principle of secular activity.[4]

---

[1] *Philosophie des Rechts*, 182.
[2] *Ph. R.*, 273.
[3] *Phänomenologie des Geistes*, ed. Hoffmeister, p. 350 foll.; and "Die Bildung und ihr Reich der Wirklichkeit" in general.
[4] Aquinas, *S. Th.*, I-II, 61, 5; ". . . quaedam sunt virtutes transeuntium et in divinam similitudenem transeuntium, et hae vocantus virtutes "purgatoriae." Ita scilicet quod prudentia omnia mundana divinorum contemplatione despiciat, omnemque animae cogitationum in divina sola dirigat"; etc. cf. Calvin, *Institutio*, III, VII; *e.g.* "Principio igitur in quaerenda vitae praesentis vel commoditate vel tranquillitate, huc nos

This new world appeared both as the renunciation of all particularity of the will in the universal and as the strongest assertion of it in the anarchy of the particular person who claimed for himself the authority of the universal. At first these forms were separate und unmediated. For their unity lay in a secular culture which should not divide reason and nature but express their contradiction. Hence the return from both sides to classical antiquity and a secular culture in which reason and life were still in undivided unity. Not that this culture itself could satisfy but that through it should be found a secular culture where negation of the world was not flight from it.[5]

The development of the new principle took chiefly two forms: Protestant theology and modern philosophy. Both had their source in the world of abstract right and its philosophical expression in Neoplatonism. "The philosophy of the modern age proceeds from the principle which ancient philosophy had reached – the standpoint of actual self-consciousness. It has in general for its principle spirit present to itself. It brings the difference of thought and the existing universe (which was the standpoint of the Middle Ages) to their opposition, and is concerned with the resolution thereof." The form of this new thought is self-consciousness as related to the opposition of thought and being, where the sole interest is to grasp the unity of the opposites at the point of their extremest abstraction. As practical its form is self-consciousness in relation to the opposition of universal and particular will, and what is sought is the concrete unity of the two or the realized good.[6]

Protestant faith is founded on the absolute negation of particular interests except as related to universal self-consciousness. The access of thought to the revealed content is no longer through Hellenic philosophy or the analogy of being but rather through the nothingness of the world as the expression of omnipotent will. For the consciousness of the nothingness of the world is positively the consciousness of it as created or as free infinite will. Self-consciousness is reconciled with the world so far as it has negated the world or its reconciliation is also total alienation. But its secular consciousness is a falling away from the knowledge in which it is reconciled, to the division of consciousness and self-consciousness or to the division between thought and a sensible world. The effort of thought and will is to restore the lost Paradise, but the process and the end are not concretely united.

Scriptura, vocat, ut Domini arbitrio nos nostraque omnia resignantes domandos ac subigendos cordis nostri affectus illi tradamus."
[5] *Geschichte der Philosophie* (1844), 3, p. 196 foll.
[6] *e.g. Gesch. Phil.*, 3, Einleitung.

The philosophy as well as the practical life of the modern age seeks to overcome the subjectivity of its new attitude and know the unity of thought and being in the form of self-consciousness, or the concept. The way to this unity takes two directions according to the nature of the task – a realistic and an idealistic direction. In part there is an endless interest in observing and controlling the particular, an expansion and diversification of science. There is not as in older times a retreat from the technical and economic as banausic and unfree to the freedom of an impractical knowledge of nature. In part philosophy finds its beginning in thought and has for its object the Idea or the infinite purpose and would know the manifold content of experience as having its truth therein. The understanding is the point where both directions meet, as the one seeks law and universality in the sensible and the other raises abstract universality to the Idea by giving it the content of experience. Both directions are therefore inseparable; the difference of empirical and idealistic philosophy is only in where a beginning is consciously made.[7]

The question that occupy the new philosophy are "of an entirely different kind from the interests of ancient philosophy." There is now a consciousness of the opposition between freedom and natural necessity "which was certainly contained in the objects of ancient philosophical thought but had not come to consciousness." In the language of Christian belief this consciousness is the doctrine of the Fall; "To bring forth in thought the believed reconciliation is the universal interest of philosophy." The various systems in their opposition express this movement. The contradiction is resolved, but at first abstractly. Recurring, the opposition is more explicit and complete; and the direction is towards at once the extremest antagonism and concrete resolution.[8]

The organization of society in the modern age proceeds from the same principle. The one direction is the free development of interests and inclinations, therewith an unlimited technical and economic expansion. In this self-interest and the war of each against all has an unrestricted field. But there is against this also the utopian confidence that men can live together in unity of purpose, and the two directions meet in that competition and exploitation is also the presence of the universal in economic life: the technical is science applied and, as production becomes rational, economic life is sundered from the family and has its own laws. Nor is the utopian interest, as once, to permit the best life to those who are capable of virtue, but rather to bring reason also into the external realm of needs

[7] *e.g. Phän.*, Glaube u. reine Einsicht.
[8] *Gesch. Phil.* 3, Einleitung.

and their satisfaction. The movement of society is the tension of these directions; progress is at once the resolution of the contradictions and its more extreme and intense recurrence.[9]

Civil society is the loss or corruption of ethical life. The farther it develops, the deeper is the corruption; until at last not only is the distinction of good and evil obliterated but ultimate evil is declared to be good. The route is the opposite to that of the medieval poet who descended to Hell and ascended thence through Purgatory to the terrestrial Paradise. Here the journey begins in the tranquillity of that garden, descends thence more and more deeply into Hell. The dissolution of the subjective principle in the end is no less complete than of the objective or medieval. The movement of the one was to find self-conscious freedom, of the other to regain objectivity.[10]

Therefore in the course of this modern journey there is an alternation of optimism and doubt, more or less superficial both, and without the extreme confrontation of good and evil of its beginning – but moving towards it. The strife of civil society is resolved implicity in faith and its adequate secular expression in the ethical life of family and state. This resolution does not belong to civil society as such, but to its members so far as also of the state and the religious community. The thought of civil society, its philosophies pious or unpious, existed within this larger circle. Enlightenment would not destroy religion and the state, but make them reasonable. But where the division of civil society reached its extreme, and each side was all but the concrete whole, it could seem to Marxist and Existentialist that the objective authority of state and religion had their source in the subjective will. The Titans occupied Olympus, or thought they did, and declared that we live in a post-Hegelian age.

Their victory went long unnoticed, so long as state and religion maintained their deeper authority. With the mutual destruction of national states in the great wars of the twentieth century, their power was weakened to dissolve civil society and hold it within their objective purpose, and world power passed to the revolutionary societies of the United States and the Soviet Union, which were founded on the supremacy of civil society. Then not only Marxism and Existentialism but also the abstracter philosophies of an earlier period found new life. For in their collapse the national states reverted to the thought of their greater age.

But the principle remains that the philosophies of an age, in their dialec-

---

[9] *Ibid.*
[10] *Ph. R.* 184-187.

tical relation, are a particular solution to the general problem of the modern philosophy. Marxism therefore and Existentialism, as the proper philosophy of the nineteenth century, contain the deepest division of civil society. For in the Kantian philosophy the concept of the moral will came to light, and that the primary opposition in it was of good to evil. In Marxism and Existentialism are therefore resolutions of this opposition, but onesidedly. For the one seeks to bring the original Paradise into economic life, the other to bring idealism ambiguously to earth – to particular individuality – but retreats thence to the substance of the beginning. The truth of both movements is the dissolution of civil society.

The philosophical interest of the present time does not lie any longer in the philosophies of the subjective will. Their common problem was resolved long since in the Hegelian phenomenology. Therewith it became evident that in all this history nothing was known but the relations of consciousness to self-consciousness and in the end the untruth of their division. Philosophers had reasoned about God and nature, about freedom and the state, and much else, but had overlooked that they talked about presupposed concepts none of which they grasped in their philosophies. The true result of modern philosophy was therefore total ignorance. To the more critical spirit of an older philosophy this result had long been known. But then a critical or learned ignorance was the way to a higher knowledge. The ignorance in which the subjective philosophy ends has this further difficulty that is has destroyed *Vorstellung* or imaginative thought as belonging to the reflective attitude of thought to its object. Therefore the new philosophy in its dissolution left no other way open to philosophers than that they should come to know what they were talking about, that is that they should know through concepts.[11]

If the objective immediacy of medieval freedom can be thought overthrown by the iniquities of feudal society, moral or reflective freedom is exposed to a harsher judgment. For the iniquities of modern society are not the work of the natural will but of the perversion of the rational will itself. The moral will can commit even genocide with good conscience. It is long past time that philosophers had passed judgment and had reduced subjective philosophy to its place of a subordinate and superseded moment.[12]

Abstract freedom and morality have their truth in "the idea of freedom as the living good, which has its knowing and willing in self-consciousness and its reality through self-conscious action, while self-consciousness

---

[11] *e.g. Ph. R.* 140.
[12] As is accomplished in *Phän.*, absolutes Wissen.

has in ethical being its substantial foundation and moving purpose – namely the concept of freedom which has become both the existing world and the nature of self-consciousness." In this concept there is realized at once the objectivity of abstract right and the subjective freedom of morality. Natural will has neither a world to itself other than self-conscious freedom, nor is their unity merely reflected through their division and as blind agressive will dissolving at the extreme of its self-assertion into objective freedom. Nature has instead become the nature of self-consciousness (as in the substantial moment of morality), and this nature, of the particularity of the will as human, is also the absolute exclusiveness of individuality. The universal good, as at once the immediate unity of natural and rational and unity restored out of division, is alike the substantial or concrete foundations and the moving purpose in human action. In this idea is united without loss what was sought dividedly in the successive forms of civil society.[13]

The philosophies of moral will, however they be fashioned to a newer taste, are properly only of academic interest. That is, to know what they are is of high importance; as practical, they can in the end only divert attention from what is to be done.[14] For the deeper interest of the young is not in liberalism or socialism of whatever shade, nor in any national tradition, but in the forms of universal spirit. Not a particular relation to European freedom through abstract right or morality is the problem, but that form of freedom altogether. The more strenuously it was sought in morality to resolve the contradiction of avarice and ambition with reason, the more barbarous the resulting forms of society: with the reality of Marxism in Soviet communism and the reality of Existentialism in Nazi Germany the Protestant age came to its end. The young do not live in it any longer. Simultaneously the Catholic tradition, which opposed the Protestant principle during the centuries of its vitality has lost its stability.

The practical interest of the present age is transparently that science and technology be brought under universal will, and that individuals have their particular freedom explicitly and primarily therein – not through the blind conflict of aggressive wills. For the external resolution of the conflict, as in morality, is now the absurdity of total destruction. This is the one interest; the other is the confrontation of European freedom with the immediate and the substantial naturalism of African and Asian races or

[13] *Ph. R.* 142.
[14] *Ph. R.* 140; That philosophers of various schools are preoccupied with language discloses a general consciousness that it is necessary to go beyond reflective thought, and a flight from this recognition.

Neither is accessible to thought save through the Hegelian philosophy.

II

with the substantial transcendence of nature in the Islamic peoples. These are the problems; their solution is the plain condition of human survival. The types of modern social freedom are in the most general consideration, the rights of moral will as these were established historically in civil society against the patriarchal unity of Divine Right monarchy, in which self-conscious freedom is still altogether implicit. The patriarchal state does indeed contain "the true reconciliation" of the natural and the rational will. Ethical life is present, but in the unfree form of unconditional obedience. Subjective freedom is the agency whereby active rational freedom and the participation of all is introduced into the state. It is also the obstacle thereto, in that state power and individual freedom are also antagonistic so long as the state is imperfectly liberated.[15]

The development of freedom appears therefore as the process in which civil society appropriates state power to itself. Such is taken to be the sense of liberal and socialist revolutions. That the ultimate and controlling end is rather the education of civil society to objective freedom is hidden from itself. For in civil society particular interests and their mediation through the universal are external to each other, so that it can apparently be as well said that the state exists for its members as they for the state. "Because of the independence of the two principles" in civil society, their unity is present not as freedom but as the necessity that the particular raise itself to the form of universality, that it seek and gain its stability in that form." [16]

The phenomenology of revolutionary history is less simple than of civil society on the basis of a freed ethical life. For moral freedom appears first in the religious community, and its ideal development as morality proper takes place in relation to religion and state power. When it be said of Hegel that he treats abstractions as though they were real subjects, this is indeed true of the phenomenological attitude and the charge holds as well against his opponents as himself. For it is indifferent from this standpoint whether one says real or economic forces are prior or rather the ideal. The unity of both and thus the subject in truth is only sought in this method. The embodiment of moral will in civil society and the true relation of ideal and real aspects is only known to a deeper inquiry. The

---

[15] *Ph. R.* 185-187.
[16] *Ph. R.* 186.

complexity of the phenomenological history is from its abstractness.[17]

The revolutions of modern society occurred in this total historical and spiritual context. From it may be abstracted however the forms of revolutionary freedom in themselves. As belonging to the history of European states, these forms never had certainly independent existence, and if the American republic severed itself from a particular European connection, its derivation from the general tradition became the more distinct. But the structure of revolutionary societies, if they be considered in themselves, is nothing else than the stages in the evolution of the moral will.[18]

"The moral standpoint is . . . the right of the subjective will," according to which "the will recognizes something and is something only so far as the thing is its own and it is present therein as subjective." In feudal society there is abstract right and there are privileges. In civil society there are properly no privileges in that right is the relation of particular interests to free subjectivity. From this consciousness springs alike all demand that the system of needs and their satisfaction should serve the common liberation of humanity and that each should therein be free to satisfy his personal interest.[19]

For universally the moral world is the concept of freedom or the concrete unity of the rational and the natural will in the form of division or reflection. It is the opposition of self-consciousness to nature and the cancelling of this opposition and the hidden meaning of this mediation is that the Idea is thereby given the form of subjectivity. The activity of the moral individual has for its end the actuality of this form, and by overcoming it to attain concrete or ethical freedom.[20]

The interest of the moral individual is therefore not simply to realize his finite purposes or the satisfaction of work accomplished. Nor is his interest simply in the realm of finite purposes generally. It is rather to know his participation therein as the expression both of his original nature or particularity and as the conformity of this to his rational freedom. Thus there arises ultimately the intensest conflict of his particular will with the universal or of evil with good. For only at the point of their total contradiction is transition possible to concrete unity.[21]

The total movement of moral will has the form of three successive circles. The first is the experience that what is intended by a moral agent is not the immediate end and product of an action but his actuality as uni-

---

[17] *Enc.* 25, note.
[18] For the simple structure of moral will, *Ph. R.* Die Moralität.
[19] *Ph. R.* 107.
[20] *Ph. R.* 141.
[21] *Ph. R.* 112.

versal self-consciousness. To act is to have confined one's will to this particular purpose and to have overcome this confinement in the infinite
reflection of the will into itself in the accomplished work. But this work
and its product or the finite purposiveness of a rational being is, inwardly,
self-related purposiveness; primarily it is the utterance of his freedom.
This inner freedom is made objective through the system of needs and
their satisfaction. (The universal object of work has not as under abstract
right the form merely of wealth but of the concrete reflection of economic
activity into universal self-consciousness.) For therein the individual has
to define his work in relation to the work of others and has thus a general
purpose or sphere of activity. But the truth of this particular form of work
is the connection and necessity of all forms of work in society, and the
truth of this necessity is free subjectivity whose objectivity is then not the
system of needs as such but other persons. In the reflection of the moral
subject into himself out of this objectivity is the knowledge that society is
nothing else than the actuality of free self-consciousness.[22]

To moral right belongs thus the freedom of particular purpose or what
one would do, of private interest in general, and of particular personality
as such. Moral freedom is however, both these existential rights and the
corresponding and opposed rights of subjectivity as rational. Neither
aspect is actual independently of the other. Nor again have the three levels
of moral right independent existence. Therefore moral freedom as real in
civil society is the system of moral rights. The development of civil society is thus that moral right in its totality appear primarily in one of its
aspects or levels.[23]

The ultimate form of moral right or the mutual recognition of free
personality may therefore be immediate or intuitive. It may again be
under the form of abstract universality and division. Finally it may be in
the proper form of free personality itself. This logical succession was also
temporal and appeared historically as:

(1) The British freedom of the seventeenth and eighteenth centuries;

(2) The revolutionary societies of the Enlightenment (American and
French democracy);

(3) The revolutionary ideas and movements that originated in the
German nineteenth century.

---

[22] The three sections of *Ph. R.*, Die Moralität.
[23] *Phän.* gives the development in this concreteness. ("Der Glaube u. die reine
Einsicht" to the end of "Die Moralität").

III

"One could call the English the people of intellectual intuition. They know the rational less in the form of universality than in that of individuality." "The Englishman has the feeling of freedom in the particular; he does not bother himself about the understanding, but on the contrary feels himself the freer the more what he does or can do is against the understanding." The English "appear to constitute the European whose destiny it is, like the class of shopkeepers and artisans in the state, to live always immersed in matter and to have reality and not reason for their principle." [24]

This "intellectual intuition" or the immediacy of concrete personality Hegel found alike in the spiritual intensity of Shakespeare's heroes and in the aristocratic liberalism of eighteenth century England. To this character and its social realization is strongly opposed the abstract intellectuality of the French mind and the radical democracy of the Revolution. That British society could without its ruin absorb universal democracy seemed to Hegel doubtful. For with this came inevitably the demand for a deeper rationality than the British constitution could sustain. It has in a fashion survived both liberal democracy and the more thorough rationality of socialism. Its strength was its concreteness and indifference to thought; revolutionary structures, but not their principles, could subsist within the native freedom without wholly destroying it. [25]

Civil society is overcome in this freedom, if only immediately. For the intuition is that the dividedness of society in its manifold works is dissolved in self-conscious freedom. With this intuition civil society relinquishes its opposition to the state, and finds it an absurdity that public order depends on a contract. Distinctions of class are not overthrown in this freedom, but lose their rigidity. Secularly, as well as in religion, they are known as idle. Neither religion nor historical tradition is opposed; they are venerated and not understood – or even disbelieved. For secular freedom has found a certain completion, and is reconciled to traditional authority.

The state in which this concrete individualism feels itself at home has its incomparable eulogy in Burke's *Reflections on the French Revolution*: as in no other state personal freedom and veneration for tradition subsist harmoniously together. For self-conscious freedom is not universal and looks with abhorrence at rational reform. There is a living reason already

---

[24] *Enc.* (1847), 394, Zusatz; *Phil. d. Geschichte* (1840), p. 507; *Gesch. Phil.* (1844), 3, p. 254.
[25] *Hegel's Political Writings*, tr. Knox, p. 330.

within the state and no need of further revolution: "Each contract of each particular state is but a clause in the great primaeval contract of eternal society, linking lower with higher natures, connecting the visible and the invisible world, according to a fixed compact sanctioned by the inviolable oath which holds all physical and all moral natures, each in their appointed place." [26]

In this freedom is completed the anarchic individualism which sprang from radical Protestanism. For it is the social structure in which arbitrary will and the confusion of selfish interest and inner light are not only brought under law but liberated also to free self-consciousness. The external despotism in which Hobbes saw the only remedy to fanaticism has become educated to inner freedom. But the first correction was through Lockean democracy, in which the "state of nature" was recognized to be not anarchy but civil society implicit. In this democracy universal self-consciousness remains potential, only emerges and is active if the social contract is generally thought to have been broken fundamentally by a tyrannous government. For the moral will knows itself to be the source of the social order, and is the demand that it conform in general to its principle.[27]

The Lockean "state of nature" is civil society implicitly. It is an anarchy in which the distinction of universal law and particular interest is present, but not yet in the form of their opposition. For such in general is the meaning of anarchy, whether in this or another form of society. In the "state of nature" individuals have that freedom which remains with princes in society once constituted. In the Lockean anarchy therefore the relation of the law to particular interests and actions must be thought to have the same externality and immediacy as in society itself. Hobbes knows only the outer aspect of it, and not that it is also inwardly the universality of law and relation to infinite will.[28]

The original Calvinism had enjoined unqualified obedience to magistrates of whatsoever quality they might be. For the divine will appeared in the state through its established rulers; the beginning of justice in its members was the absolute obedience in which the particular will was relinquished. Resistance therefore to tyranny could only rightfully be of duly constituted magistrates to a higher office, not the natural right of the people. Only should the divine law be violated could the people by right disobey in obedience to their divine ruler. Lockean democracy sup-

[26] Burke, *Reflections on the Revolution in France*, Dent, London, 1951, pp. 93-4.
[27] Locke, *Of Civil Government*, ch. XIX.
[28] *O.c.*, Ch. I (*Works*, 1823, V, p. 341, 346).

poses that the distance between divine and natural law has somehow been closed.[29]

The distance has been closed in that natural law itself has come to have a new relation to divine law. For Protestant faith, or at least the metaphysical structure through which it has access to the Christian revelation, is the flight from the world of culture, this both in its medieval from and where an order founded on the reflective (that is, no more on abstract right) relation to self-consciousness is sought in the finite. Protestant faith originates, that is, in a flight also from Renaissance humanism and the restoration of a classical world not yet fallen into the emptiness of abstract right. It has annulled this world – the "true spirit" whose fate was abstract right. Its retreat therefore to faith has the sense that this world is implicitly comprehended in self-consciousness, or the presupposition of the Hellenic world, that there is a nature, is now known as rather the appearance of the world for the self-consciousness whose true object is absolute substance or the unity of thought and being.[30]

Faith itself, however, is not free of that from which it has fled. It is "the immediate and not yet inwardly completed elevation and has its opposite principle through which it is conditioned still in itself, without having become master of it through the mediated movement." It may therefore still take the reason of the world to be the contentless natural law of the Stoics or some variant of the same principle. It has, however, in truth acquired the total content of the world of culture. The object of its thought is this unity in which the seeming stability of the finite has been annihilated. But this is its object immediately and it cannot explicate the content adequately to that unity – which would be in the form of the concept. Therefore its real consciousness, or the world as it is for individuals in their finitude, is alienated from its pure consciousness.[31]

"Driven back (into itself) out of the essenceless, self-dissolving world into itself, spirit is, in truth, in undivided unity alike the absolute movement and negativity of its appearance and its inwardly satisfied essence and its positive rest." But since the relation of the two movements is determined by the underlying alienation, they separate as a doubled consciousness. The one side is "pure insight" or the spiritual process which gathers itself together in self-consciousness. Opposed to it it has "the consciousness of

[29] Calvin, *Institutio*, IV, cap. XX, 29 "Hunc reverentiae atque adeo pietatis affectum debemus ad extremum praefectis nostris omnibus, qualescumque tandem sint."
[30] *Phän.* (Hoffmeister) p. 376 foll.
[31] *Ibid.*, pp. 377, 378.

the positive, the form of objectivity or representation, and it directs itself against this."[32]

To the latter belongs alike the content of the world in the form of pure thought as the emanation out of original unity and return thereto, and as falling within that movement the relation of believing self-consciousness to the real world. In this way "the world of culture" or secular life in general falls within the religious consciousness. Its activity therein is partly according to the spirit of that world; partly, and essentially, it is the abnegation of it as meaningless. Opposed to the realm of eternal rest is a spiritless world of finite existence only to be overcome in a violent and external way. But as the relation of these two worlds, believing self-consciousness has within itself their diremption, or the division in itself between itself as universal and as individual. As the former and as a member of the religious community it is reconciled with the world. The believer as immediate self-consciousness has before him "an uncomprehended sensible world" sundered from the inner world of thought. It is at this point that belief passes into "pure insight" as the infinite negativity in which the self in its immediate or empirical relation to the world is also pure thought. "The concept however, which is the actuality of spirit present to itself, in the believing consciousness remains the inner which is and effects everything but does not come forth." [33]

In this way there takes place in Protestant belief, and especially the Calvinist form of it, a separation of self-conscious thought from the revealed content and thus the transition to a "reasonable Christianity," and then to the Enlightenment. The separation takes place because self-consciousness, although in its negation of the world of culture it had overcome the form of *Vorstellung* or representation, is, as said, still unfree of its external beginning. (That it is implicity beyond language and all reflective thought must be noticed if the subsequent development of phenomenal freedom is at all to be understood.) Logically the development is the same as that by which the Lockean empiricism detached itself from the substance of Descartes or Spinoza, namely by an incompleted reaction of self-consciousness thereto whereby pure thinking took the form of consciousness.[34]

---

[32] *Ibid.*, pp. 378, 379.

[33] *Ibid.*, pp. 380, 381.

[34] *Gesch. Phil.*, 3, p. 375; "So betrachtet, dass der Begriff gegenständliche Wirklichkeit habe, ist die Erfahrung zwar ein notwendiges Moment der Totalität." As against Spinoza the universal tendency of consciousness is now "an den unterschied festzuhalten: Teils um sich, seinem Gegenstande, dem Sein, Natur und Gott, gegenüber, als in sich frei zu bestimmen: teils um in diesem Gegensatze die Einheit zu erkennen, und sie aus ihm hervorzubringen."

More fully, "the immediacy with which the essence is in belief lies in this, that its object is essence or pure thought. This immediacy however, where thinking enters into consciousness or pure consciousness into self-consciousness, has the meaning of an objective being that lies beyond the consciousness of self. It is through this meaning which the immediacy and simplicity of pure thinking obtains in consciousness that the essence of faith falls out of thinking into representation and to a supersensible world which is essentially an other to self-consciousness," and finite self-consciousness, directed to its immediate or sensible world, has the relation thereof to the substance in the form of abstract identity. The Lockean empiricism is both incapable of grasping the concrete structure of consciousness and certain that it has in the abstract identity of thinking the measure of all revelation: God gave man "reason, and with it a law: that could not be otherwise than that which reason should dictate; unless we should think, that a reasonable creature should have an unreasonable law." [35]

Protestant faith, or Catholic, is not simply subject to the structure of the thought that receives its content, but has also negated this limit. Nor is the secular or finite image of faith without this relation. The institutions of Protestant society are therefore also beyond the reflective or moral form of civil society. But for this reason the Protestant state, though in the purer and original form of teaching it has sovereign authority over civil society, is substantial or patriarchical, without developed self-conscious freedom. Therefore, while the Lutheran form of Protestant faith had freed itself from the particularity of its metaphysical form more purely than the Calvinist, its profounder spirituality could only impede the development of secular freedom in civil society and thus the liberation of the state.[36]

Civil society in its Lockean form does not yet have explicitly the moment of free subjectivity. From this its special character and limits are readily understood. The least revolutionary of revolutions, it seeks no more than that society have the form of the moral will. The Lockean man finds interest and truth in the sensible. In action and the exercise of his worldly calling he has also the consciousness of the universal. The turbulence of enthusiasm has been clarified to the light of reason. His outward gaze is thus also reflection into self, though this self-consciousness remains abstract. The end of society is known to be free individuality; of government the limited end of protecting its condition or property. Society has intrinsically its infinite end and government should serve it. Or government

[35] *Phän.*, p. 379, Locke, *The Reasonableness of Christianity*, Works (1823), VII, p. 157.
[36] On differences between the political and social thought of Luther and Calvin, R. Seeberg, *Dogmengeschichte*, Darmstadt, 1959, IV, I, p. 325 foll.; II, p. 617 foll.

becomes properly only administration; nor in this is it to follow a general view but rather take account of particular and contingent evils.[37]

The other side of this radical liberation of private life is that there is no demand that government itself be made popular. For social freedom aims at the liberation of individuals, not the activity of free individuality. Government is thus easily left to a few. Nor do the political representatives of civil society themselves exercise sovereign power, but retain from another concept of government the monarchy. Of this principle indeed no understanding is present, but rather a disposition to favour a republic or commonwealth. For only to concrete personality can heriditary monarchy seem a rational form of government. For then the social contract is known for an unreality and the actual and continuing life of society prior to it.[38]

The fulfilment of this society is that it attain free subjectivity and this according to its special form of immediacy. Philosophically the idealism of Berkeley and then the Humean scepticism are this transition, if they be taken to express dividedly the concrete idealism of the moral will. For the end to which morality moves is to overcome the separation of the particular individual from universal self-consciousness. Partly the resolution is already known to society as the result to which the world of culture attained. Partly the distracted self-consciousness that mastered the world of culture was at the term of its struggle simply "pure insight." The philosophers had brought then to light the logical form through which the externality of work and immediate interest was related to the necessity of the moral law. From the Lockean philosophy and its knowledge that the sensible content is subjective it was a short way to declare self-consciousness the principle. There remained only that this detached idealism take into itself and give universal form to the experience of the "world of culture" – its absolute negation of the externality of universal and particular will.[39]

Therewith ended this first circle. British freedom had its time when all

[37] On the origin of society, *e.g.* "Whenever therefore any number of men are so united into one society, as to quit every one his executive power of the law of nature, and to resign it to the public, there and there only is a political or civil society." (*o.c.* p. 389). A definite social order emerges, a transition from divine to human government. It is not properly a giving up of executive power, the lack of which was a reason for the contract (*ibid.*, pp. 412-413).

[38] "By commonwealth, I must all along be understood to mean, not a democracy, or any form of government, but any independent community" (*o.c.* p. 416); on monarchy, *o.c.* p. 436 foll. As to how the contract appears to a concrete subjectivity, Hume, *Essays* (Oxford, 1966): *Of the Original Contract.*

[39] *Phän.* pp. 385-86; *Gesch. Phil.* 3, p. 440 foll. On the relation of self-consciousness to substance, p. 440: "in der modernen Welt diese absolute substantialität, diese Einheit der Ansicht und des Selbstbewusstseins zum Grunde liegt, dieser Glaube an die Realität überhaupt: so hat hier der Skepticismus die Form, Idealismus zu sein."

learned from it. The conclusion, that the truth of civil society is universal self-consciousness, was taken up by others and made the beginning of a new development.

IV

"Had the forests of Germany still existed, the French Revolution would certainly not have come to life." [40] Free subjectivity is the principle both of American democracy and of the French Enlightenment. In the one case it was carried to its revolutionary conclusion; in the other, from natural advantages, the tension of rich and poor did not reach the extreme opposition which only revolution could resolve. For the revolution sprang from the strongly felt contradiction between the "pursuit of happiness," or the satisfaction of the particular will in general, and the progressive movement or general purpose of society. It came to be known that utility, that is the relation of particular individual or social purposes to the good in general, is in truth destructive of those purposes so far as independent. To say the same in terms now familiar, it came to be known that the technological society was radically unfree and that there was no freedom for individuals save by overcoming it.[41]

By the tensions of rich and poor is not meant principally the struggle for wealth in economic society as such. For individuals in this new form of society have a larger purpose: they seek a satisfactory life in general, and the common interest of society is likewise to achieve a humanly liveable life in this world. Therefore it is not poverty and wealth as such that foment revolution but that life is found totally unsatisfactory.[42]

The first form of civil society was the return to rational self-consciousness and of the realm of particular interests and their satisfaction as immediate. It was possible that self-consciousness simply observe the total process. In that case it did not oppose the ethical life of the state or the religion from which this proceeded. For in the immediate unity of life and self-consciousness, which was the result, these forms also have their existence – but as habit and feeling, not universally. But then rational freedom itself is the immediate unity of self-consciousness with itself, and its right is also immediate or as the right of property. But this right, as now occurring explicitly in moral will, is no longer merely the right of abstract personality to recognition. It is rather the will of society to make equality effective,

[40] *Phil. Gesch.* (1840), p. 106.
[41] The United States was only potentially a state until class conflict should reach the point of contradiction and be resolved (*ibid.*).
[42] *e.g. Ph. R.* 119.

and for moral will in this second form this is properly the one end of its free activity.[43]

Free will is therefore according to its concept intolerant of all particular interests as such. Tradition and privilege are unreason to it. "The English parliament of 1688, imported a man and his wife from Holland, William and Mary, and made them king and queen of England. Having done this, the said parliament made a law to convey the government of the country to the heirs of William and Mary, in the following words: „We, the lords spiritual and temporal, and commons, do, in the name of the people of England, most humbly and faithfully submit ourselves, our heirs, and posterities, to William and Mary, their heirs and posterities, forever." It is not sufficient that we laught at the ignorance of such law-makers; it is necessary that we reprobate their want of principle." [44]

This demand for explicit rationality, whether in jurisprudence, economic life or in the public administration, appears as the principle of utility. It does not seek to impose an extraneous reason but to release the inherent rationality of society or the actual identity of conflicting interests from unreasonable regulation. The liberation of individuals is extended to the whole range of their particular interests. Required of them in return is that the pursuit of their self-interest be enlightened or rational. But this requirement is itself reasonable because the principle of society is now "pure insight" or universal self-consciousness.[45]

There emerges thus a world totally transformed from the old. The interest of the particular individual is now given the form of universality. Primarily in this form or as the demand for happiness is his purpose integrated into the total complex of particular purposes in society, and the object of this universal purpose is the well-being of society in general. A seemingly endless field is opened for the satisfaction alike of particular will and of rational freedom. Society is common work of promoting what is useful to its members singly and collectively.[46]

In this work it is easily overlooked that none achieves what is primarily sought: the actuality of his self-conscious freedom. For the object of enlightened will is the abstraction of the general good outside which falls the particular content of will. What content therefore is given to the good falls to the estimation of particular wills. But whether the purposes in which individuals and groups see the useful and the good to be embodied are in fact realized in the objective conflict of interests and its continuing

---

[43] *e.g. Ph. R.* 208.
[44] Thomas Paine *Works*, ed. Conway, III, pp. 263-64.
[45] *e.g. Ph. R.* 209.
[46] *e.g. Ph. R.* 128; 229.

resolution is altogether contingent. Rather it is inevitable from the essential structure of this society that they be not fulfilled. For the true object and end of this society is nothing else than the actuality of universal right and therefore the negation of particular interests.[47]

Of this society it can truly be said that the state is external to human interests. For there is on the one side an indefinite pluralism that would take to itself in its dividedness to speak for the state. Against this the state proper is another particular will or represents prevalent interests. In the endless extension of desires and the means to their satisfaction in the economic and cultural progress of society – it can appear that its purpose is attained approximately and gradually. It is not indeed supposed that these particular purposes are the end of society, but that they are more widely – and will be universally – shared seems its rational fulfilment.[48]

So long as this appearance stands utilitarian society is not revolutionary. It becomes so when the conflict of interests is clarified to its true form of a contradiction between the total particular interest of individuals or their lives and the system of society. Differently stated, when individuals in the utilitarian society find themselves totally frustrated and the general course of society meaningless, revolution is inevitable.[49]

The revolution repeats in its general structure the awakening of Lockean democracy to free self-consciousness. It repeats it at a deeper level. Universal self-consciousness is here the beginning, and the social structure has its definite form in its relation thereto. The revolution is that freedom in the utilitarian society become actual as thinking self-consciousness. The technological society is the mixed work of reason and liberated self-interest. Its purpose is universal good and that all have their part in it. The will capable of this end is itself universal. As it was there from the first, the revolution may be said only to dissipate the division between individual well-being and the general purposes of society, between reason and self-will. What it discloses is that the two aspects are one concrete reality.[50]

Revolution is immediately absolute freedom. The general will of the Rousseauean state is the immediate negation of the world of utility. The will of that society is therefore the simple, undivided consciousness of the universal end of that society. As the immediate actuality of this end all wills are one, and their one object is to remain in undivided possession of that end. It is an idealism of the rational will, which has this in common with the sensuous idealism of Berkeley that it leaves its objectivity only

[47] *e.g. Ph. R.* 128; *Phän.* 411 foll.
[48] On the realization of the useful, *Phän.* p. 414.
[49] That is, when utility reaches the form of scepticism. *Phän., l.c.*
[50] The transition of utility into universal will as its principle: *ibid.*

formally translated into self-consciousness, and, as at that point in the argument, the true intention is rather to know the concrete unity of personality. But here the sceptical dissolution of the particular is not a detached observation of "pure insight," but rather self-destruction. For the opposition here is of the natural will totally to rational self-consciousness. This opposition was already overcome for individuals in the revolution, and terror is the process in which the concept of the revolution becomes known to revolutionaries. It is the knowledge that the will of individuals in this society is the agency of universal will. In this the utilitarian society is fulfilled, but far otherwise than it had expected. Nor is the conclusion less hard for the revolutionary, who learns that the negation of the hated society which has no place for concrete personality is in truth the negation in himself of its principle.[51]

Of this result it may be said that it is the ground on which the technological society can first begin to be what it supposes itself to be. In themselves its purposes are ambiguously good and evil, nor does its apparent progress lessen but rather intensify the evil, as it exposes its source in benevolence itself or the optimism of the Enlightenment. To itself the modesty that stays with the finite and does the useful, it is rather, objectively considered, limitless will that cannot dominate its works. To the Hellenic society of "true spirit" the correction of Prometheus was from without: the will of Zeus and the consuming vulture. As falling in moral will the reduction of science and technology to human ends is inward, it belongs to the concept of society in this form that it ought to be rather self-destruction than the "destruction" of humanity.[52]

As the older form of social freedom was the secular reflection of Calvinism, so the freedom of Enlightenment derived the structure of its world from Deism. For in that religion is at once the rejection of the concrete content of Christianity by the measure of free self-consciousness and the incapacity to regain a world adequate to the same measure. "Pure insight" directs itself against the representative form of the older religion and itself knows the world only under the same form. The difference is that it is,

---

[51] *Phän.*: Die absolute Freiheit und der Schrecken. Utility and its pluralistic society, so far as taken for primary, are dissipated into nothing: "Das Selbstbewusstsein ist also das reine Wissen von dem Wesen als reinem Wissen. Es ferner als einzelnes Selbst ist nur die Form des Subjekts oder wirklichen Tuns, die von ihm als Form gewusst wird; ebenso ist für es die gegenständliche Wirklichkeit, das Sein, schlechtin selbstlose Form; denn sie wäre das nicht Gewusste; dies Wissen aber weiss das Wissen als das Wesen."

[52] But the limit of this revolution is that the ultimate independence of particular interests has been negated as to its expression, not as to its principle. On which one may consider *Ph. R.* 229.

blindly indeed, constitutive of the form, and therefore implicitly master of it. The metaphysical structure of Deism is in general the same as of the older Protestantism. It is a deeper knowledge of the Cartesian substance, in that it is a reflection out of the immediate knowledge of it in the Lockean philosophy and its successors. The substantial unity of nature and thought is for universal self-consciousness at once the non-subjective and therefore also its relation to subjectivity. As the distinction and unity of these moments the world for universal self-consciousness is both the external totality or the material universe and the inner or essential totality in which the finite is negated. According to this structure the finite is related to universal self-consciousness or infinite self-purpose as means towards it or as useful. Then the knowledge of this world as universal self-consciousness is the reflection out of infinite self-purpose in the form of the immediate unity of ends or as particular will.[53]

Within this general Deistic form fall the several religious attitudes characteristic of Enlightenment according as thought or feeling is taken to be the element where divine and human meet. In America where subjective religion was untrammelled by established churches it exhibited the same pluralism as appears in secular society. At the extreme each man might have his own religion, as secularly his own particular course.[54]

The total structure of moral will in the abstract form of universal self-consciousness shows the three moments:

(a) Deism in its opposition to Trinitarian Christianity;
(b) Emanating therefrom, the utilitarian society of Enlightenment;
(c) The return therefrom to the Deistic principle.

The sense of the conclusion: "As the realm of the real world passes into the realm of faith and insight, so passes absolute freedom from its self-destructive reality into another land of self-conscious spirit, wherein in this unreality spirit is accepted as the truth." That is, the realm of necessity and finite purposes is now founded in a substantial unity that is also free.

---

[53] *Phän.*: Die Wahrheit der Aufklärung.
[54] On Deism *Phil. Rel.* (1840) 3, p. 344 foll. On its result the following: "Dennoch ist auch in dieser letzten Form (sc. that of Enlightenment) eine Versöhnung zu erkennen, diese letzten Erscheinung ist so auch eine Realisierung des Glaubens, Indem nämlich aller Inhalt, alle Wahrheit verkommen ist in dieser sich in sich unendlich wissenden, particularen Subjectivität, so ist damit darin das Princip der subjectiven Freiheit zum Bewusstsein gekommen." (p. 349).
   On religion in United States, *Phil. Gesch.*, p. 105-6; where the incompleteness of the American Revolution is also indicated: "Es finden allerdings rechtliche zustände, ein formelles Rechtsgesetz Statt, aber diese Rechtlichkeit ist ohne Rechtschaffenheit." To make universal right inward and effective was the true meaning of the French Revolution.

The content has the form of the concept, and this is no longer a subjectivity divided from its world.[55]

V

Moral will in its developed form as "the good and conscience" has the same structure in general as in its abstracter forms. The world of Enlightenment and the Revolution ended in the return to substantiality, but now as the identity of self-consciousness and the substance: "Self-consciousness knows duty as the absolute essence; it is bound only by duty, and this substance is its own pure consciousness." But in this identity the object of self-consciousness is "pure knowing, and so purely penetrated by the self it is not object." "But essentially mediation and negativity, it has in its concept relation to otherness and is consciousness." "Because duty constitutes its only essential purpose and object, this otherness is on the one hand a wholly meaningless reality. But because this consciousness is so completely enclosed in itself, it relates itself to this otherness altogether freely and indifferently, and existence is hence on the other hand completely liberated from self-consciousness and equally only related to itself." "It is a world completed to its own individuality, an independent whole with laws of its own, and an independent course and free actualization of them." The objectivity of moral will has come to be the world as life.[56]

The process of return into self-consciousness from this nature is the principle of Marxism. "Communism is the positive cancelling of private property as human self-alienation and therefore as real appropriation of the human essence through and for man. It is therefore the complete and conscious return of man to and for himself as social, i.e. human man – a return which has taken place within the entire wealth of the previous development. This communism is the perfect equality and transition into each other of naturalism and humanism. It is the true man, the true resolution of the strife between existence and essence, between objectivation and free activity, between freedom and necessity, between individual and genus. It is the riddle of history solved and knows itself as this solution." On this beginning hangs the whole of Marxism.[57]

This ultimate solution is a substantial morality in which the realm of necessity is comprehended within free purposive activity. But the inner development of this principle has not taken place, namely of opposition of particular wills to the universal and the resolution of this opposition.

[55] *Phän.*, p. 402.
[56] *Phän.*, pp. 424-25.
[57] Marx, *Ökonomisch – Philosophische Manuskripte, Werke*, Darmstadt, 1962, Vol. 1, pp. 593-4.

Liberated from the economic struggle, men are thought to live in the unbroken unity of generic life. (The existence of this form within the structure of civil society is properly as the substantial or rural class, and Marx's paradise is the tranquillity of such a life no longer enslaved of course to necessary labour.) The struggle of classes in economic society having been overcome, it appears that men can live in harmony. There remains however the original difference of men, the natural will in its distinction from universal will. "The good is the Idea as unity of the concept of the will and the particular will": this is the principle of Marxian communism. But as soon as individuals in this society distinguish themselves from one another and have each his will and interest, a deeper strife begins to appear. For there is now exposed the inner principle of economic conflict: the particular subject as such is here constituted explicitly by his distinction from the universal good. The falling away from substantial unity is no longer clothed in images but occurs in the understanding. "Self-consciousness in the vanity of all otherwise valid determinations and in the pure inwardness of willing is equally the possibility of taking for its principle the absolutely universal or the arbitrary will, its own particularity over the universal, and to realize it through acting – that is, to be evil." [58]

This deeper knowledge of evil did not fall within Marx's view. In revolutionary praxis it cannot lie hidden, and against expectation the harshest and most external means are found necessary in communist societies to repress and discipline the Party itself. Where the state was to be within society, it turns out that it is rather more external, bureaucratic, oppressive than in capitalist countries. It is said then that these societies are rather the corruption of communism. But as Hobbes once commended tyranny to curb the confused conscience of the Puritan saints, so here tyranny must be the only remedy to an intenser confusion.[59]

Marxism is defined by its relation to the *Phenomenology*. As other radical Hegelians of the first years he had a consuming need to seize what concerned him out of the Hegelian argument. In this it was less the inner dialectic of the writings themselves that guided them than the fury of their mutual polemics. Marx might express boundless contempt for Strauss and Bruno Bauer that they onesidedly saw Hegel as a Spinozist or a Fichtean. For, led by Feuerbach, he had moved beyond them to the insight that in the *Phenomenology* both elements are there and that the movement of the argument is their relation and unity. The simple form

[58] *Ph. R.* 129; 139.
[59] In general, despite differences, the criticism of Kantian and Fichtean morality in *Phän.*: Die moralische Weltanschauung apply; namely the confusion that follows from the immediacy of the good.

of phenomenal spirit is the opposition of self-consciousness to absolute substance, whereby is constituted the phenomenal world, and the movement
of self-consciousness to annul the division. In this total movement there is
not properly any moment which can be called the truth of it. Feuerbach
caught hold of the appearance of finite spirit out of the substance and
declared the immediate individual to be the concrete and the subject of
the whole movement. Marx grasped this moment universally as the true
structure of a society of living rational beings, and this as immediate or
substantial. Having thus the concept he sought therewith the form and
direction of his own work, he dismissed the rest of the argument as mystification.[60]

Marxism has then for its object the third form of society in its implicit
form where the particularity of will has not yet been negated in pure self-
consciousness. As no longer subject to blind economic forces, this society
has the proper form of socialism: "through the administration of justice
offences against property or personality are annulled. But right that is
actual in the particular contains both that accidental hindrances to one
or other purpose be removed and untroubled security of person and property be achieved and that the securing of the livelihood and welfare of
each person – that particular welfare be treated and actualized as a
right." [61]

Socialism, however, cannot have its true form until free subjectivity has
established itself in this society. For else it must be extraneous and bureaucratic. Socialism is however properly the freeing of economic activity
from within. It is the work through which the principle of this society –
free humanity – is made actual in the realm of particular interests. The
Hegelian socialism in short is not a flight from the factory or the market-
place to rural simplicity nor does it in general transfer private capital to
the public. It has the deeper purpose of freeing the dividedness and corruption of urban life to self-conscious substantiality – to equalize town and
country life, not by levelling but concretely. It is the transition to a state in
which civil society will be contained, and where substantiality and free
self-consciousness are no longer exclusive but in undivided unity.[62]

It is possible also in this third form of moral will to stay with the moment of difference, the separation of the elements and their formal negation in self-consciousness. This structure to which Hegel gave the name
Verstellung or dissemblance is commonly known as existentialism. It is the

---

[60] Marx, *o.c.*, p. 637 foll.
[61] *Ph. R.*, 230.
[62] *Ph. R.*, 256.

ambiguous will which holds to the existent individual against universal self-consciousness, then abandons this independence before the absolute good. The principle of its actions is and is not the natural will, is and it not the infinite end. The mediation which for Marx is through the world as it is for this standpoint – infinite teleology – this position flees, and seeks the relation of natural and rational will inwardly in feeling and imaginative thought. Therefore also the realm of finite purposes is separated from personal life, is confined within the metaphysics of the understanding, a separation which it is also said should not be.[63]

The tendency of this attitude is easily seen in the larger field of civil society. To Marx, and rightly, the elevation of competition to the form of purpose and a unity of social purposes is seen as the true structure of this society. But negatively there is also present the total conflict of particular personality and economic life. Socialism is in truth this conflict overcome inwardly as well as in the structure of society. But it is easily overlooked that in this society the competitive will is only overcome at the point of its most intense ruthlessness. Out of this is born the corporate spirit, in which existing individuals have a society within society expressive of their particular freedom. The rigidity of corporate will is then broken and united through the agency of the social general will. The existentialist is blind to the mediation of free personality through the system of needs and finite purposes, takes it as immediate and immediately related to the general will.[64]

There results an unmediated fusion of natural will with the universal. Should this will prevail in its conflict with socialistic will and impose its form on society, there appears Nazism and like perversions.[65]

The completion of moral will in its ultimate form is the unity of the two moments that occur independently as communism and existentialism. For the one knows the unity of the existing person and the universal immediately, the other their difference. As in civil society the unity of particular will with general has the meaning that their separation be known as only apparent, so subjectively the hypocrisy of existential will passes into the dissolution of all distinctions in "irony." This last form of moral will consists in this, "that it knows the ethically objective, but not forgetting itself and renouncing itself it does not immerse itself in its seriousness and act from it. Instead, though related to the ethical, it holds itself from it and

[63] *Phän.*, p. 434 foll. The position intended in this paragraph is the existentialism of Kierkegaard or of Heidegger.

[64] *Ph. R.*: the dialectic of *Die Polizei und Korporation.*

[65] The *Rechtsphilosophie* was written to counter such corruptions. *e.g.* Vorrede, p. 6 foll.

knows itself as that which wills and decides, and can just as well will and decide otherwise." "This form is not only the void of all ethicall content of right, duties, laws – evil, and evil complete and universal – but it adds to it the form of a subjective void, to know oneself as contentless void and in this knowing to know oneself as the absolute." [66]

In this knowledge is accomplished the self-destruction of moral will at the point of its complete explication. For morality is the existence of the good as subjectivity. Objectively the good only appears to exist, and "irony" is the adequate insight that this is the case. It is therefore the self-knowledge of morality, that it is empty form which obtrudes itself before the objective.[67]

VI

The resolution of revolutionary will into objective freedom existed in the national states of the nineteenth century. Therefore in the great war of 1914-18, these states exhibited a strength unforeseen by revolutionaries. The resolution was a fact: the *Philosophy of Right* is not about what might be.

But it occured immediately in particular historical communities, was felt but not comprehended. The concept of objective freedom was even lost to philosophers. For with the immediate achievement of freedom, philosophy in a way had finished its work and so disintegrated.[68]

Objective freedom is however, the western spirit universally and its distinction from other universal cultures. That it be known in this form is the only serious philosophical interest of an age which has already known universally, and has rejected the liberal and socialist form of subjective freedom. The better philosophical knowledge of freedom it seemed to Hegel would come to life, when it was needed, among a people founded on universal reason and not bound to a particular history.[69]

---

[66] *Phän.*, pp. 445-472; *Ph. R.*, 140.
[67] The sought integration of good and self-consciousness in morality "ist schon an sich vollbracht, indem eben diese für sich in ihrer Eitelkeit verschwebende Subjektivität der reinen Gewissheit seiner selbst identisch ist mit der abstrakten allgemeinheit des Guten; – die, simit konkrete, Identität des Guten und des subjektiven Willens, die Wahrheit derselben, ist die Sittlichkeit." (*Ph. R.*, 141).
[68] *Ph. R.*, 331: "Das Volk als Staat ist der Geist in seiner substantiellen Vernünftigkeit und unmittelbaren Wirklichkeit;" *o.c.*, 268.
[69] *Aesthetik*, (1843), 3, p. 355. The victory of "Amerikanisches lebendiges Vernünftigkeit über die Einkerkerung in ein ins Unendliche fortgehendes Messen und Partikularisiren" supposes that inwardly Americans would have overcome the abstract, lifeless spirit of the Enlightenment.

COMMENT ON DOULL'S 'HEGEL AND CONTEMPORARY LIBERALISM, ANARCHISM, SOCIALISM'

Shlomo Avineri

First of all, I owe everybody an apology. I did not receive Prof. Doull's paper until I arrived here; and between sessions, dinners and beer I have tried to go very carefully through his paper. I have been tempted to write a 64 page rebuttal of it, but I'm afraid I can't do that. So I shall make a few remarks concerning points on which I disagree with Prof. Doull. Not that I would like to do an anti-Hegel to his 20th century Hegel, because I very much agree with a lot of what he says about Hegel's political philosophy giving us not only insights but far more than that in our modern world. I said earlier in the conference, going perhaps farther than Prof. Doull would agree, that some of the implicit truth of Hegel resides in Marx; and, therefore, I honestly accept the position that so much of the *Philosophy of Right* is terribly relevant to our own age. So the remarks I'm going to make do not mean that I disagree with Prof. Doull's basic thesis. I go along with him quite a way on that. But there are a number of difficulties in his presentation, as I see it, which I just cannot pass over without comment.

First, insofar as Prof. Doull maintains, as he says, that everybody knows that socialism has broken down, this is based on what seems to me to be an uncritical equation of Marxism, or socialism, with the Soviet Union or the experiences of other countries that claim to be Marxist today. I would argue that to try to refute Marxism by trying to show the deficiencies and barbarism of the Soviet Union would be, in all due respect, on the same level as trying to refute Christianity by pointing out the barbarism of Charlemagne. It is on the same level. If we accept equation of the Soviet Union with Marxism, then it seems to me that we are making a historical, a political and a philosophical mistake. This can be very well shown. I'm not going to try to do it here; it would have to be done on the plane of historical research. What can be shown is that most of the barbarisms and inhumanities that we encounter in the Soviet Union have to do far more with 400 years of history of a czarist, bureaucratized, centralized empire that received Christianity first and has Marxism now, and have also to do with an attempt to maintain a political unity against tremendous territorial, ethnic and social odds. Just as czarist Russia cannot be a serious argument against the validity of Christianity, so Soviet Russia cannot be used as an argument against Marxism. I think there is an argument that can be made against Marxism as a social philosophy, but I would very much like to divorce it from the argument against the Soviet Union. I take exception, then, when Prof. Doull says that everybody knows that socialism has broken down. Socialism has not broken down. Whatever happened in the Soviet Union might have broken down, though I think it succeeds very well on the premises of Russian history. That is what Russian history is about.

My second point has to do with Prof. Doull's references to Nazism. Here I am completely puzzled, because on one hand Prof. Doull says (on p. 12)* "with the reality of Marxism in Soviet communism" (I have registered my disagreement with that) "and the reality of Existentialism in Nazi Germany, the Protestant age came to its end." I beg to differ with this very clean cut identification, which Prof. Doull repeated just now in his oral presentation, that the social form of Existentialism is the Nazi state. We have here two statements by Prof. Doull about Nazism, and I can see why Nazism creates a problem here: on the one hand it is said that Nazism is a corruption of socialism, and this was said by Prof. Doull, and then it is said that the social form of Existentialism is a Nazi state. Now, either of those two statements can be correct, but both of them cannot be correct at the same time. It seems to me that the reason why Nazism does provide a problem for Prof. Doull is that Nazism, as well as facism in general, and racism are post-Hegelian developments which cannot so conveniently be subsumed under the Hegelian synthesis. Socialism, liberalism, anarchism may be explicit in Hegel, and on this I would go along with Prof. Doull; but the 19th and 20th centuries brought about a social force and a philosophy which Hegel never anticipated to become paramount, and this is nationalism and its ultimate expression in Nazism. Now, it seems to me that Hegel's main defect in his political philosophy was to view nationalism as some minor type of peculiarism, and to hold, accordingly, that it will be very easily *aufgehoben*, and that it doesn't really pose a threat to his view of rational freedom. On this – to borrow Prof. Dupré's expression – Hegel was dead wrong. The one power which he underestimated, and which became so central and so barbaric in our own time

* See above, p. 229.

is the force of nationalism. And since Nazism is the ultimate barbarity of
nationalism and racism it does not fit into Prof. Doull's system, and therefore it has to be reduced to something else like Existentialism or socialism
in order to be explicated. This seems to me to be a very serious problem
in what otherwise is a very well-rounded presentation claiming that all
the alternatives have been implicit in Hegel. I do not think that all the
alternatives have been implicit in Hegel; there is one at least – nationalism
– which is causing all that much difficulty to our own age.

A further point I would like to make has to do with a distinction which
Prof. Doull in his oral presentation made up to a point, but not as strongly as I would like to make it: the distinction between the French and the
American Revolutions. Let me recall that Hegel said that so long as there
is free land in America, America is still a civil society and not a state. Now,
from what Prof. Doull said a moment ago in his oral presentation I take
it that he perceives the present status of the United States as being that
of an achieved state-stage. Now, following Hegel, I would like to suggest
that America is still not a state but only a civil society; that the way
Americans are viewing their taxation, for example, is still the way proper
to civil society. I mean, if you speak about taxation in terms of "my tax
dollar," this means that you view your relationship to the state on the
plane of civil society. The fact that the only way in which the federal
government can make educational authorities in the South comply with
a Supreme Court decision about integration is by withholding funds
from them means that you have a civil society, not a state: I can use that
sanction with my used car dealer; and this is the sort of thing which is
happening in the United States politically. This really means that on
a very substantial plane America is still not a state. It is a state on one
level alone, the level of its relations with the outside world; and this is
perhaps one of the reasons, if I may suggest, that whenever the U.S.
finds itself in a war it has to be a highly ideological one or it creates a very
difficult internal situation and a kind of internal strife which many other
countries which have waged as brute and as problematic wars have man-
aged to escape. It seems to me this is one of the major differences between
the French Revolution and the American Revolution. For the French
Revolution state power was the guarantor of civil society, and therefore
in order to guarantee civil society you better have to have a strong state
that will be able to guarantee that this civil society in all its plenitude will
be able to function. On the other hand, in the American way, the guarantee for civil society was not political power or federal power but local and
state governments, which again go back to the powers that be of civil

society. Now, this distinction between the American extreme and the French extreme seems to me to have been to a certain degree overlooked by Prof. Doull.

The last point I want to make is, I suppose, a query. There is one passage in Prof. Doull's paper where he gives us an idea of what he would like to see, an idea of his interpretation of the implications of the Hegelian *Rechtsphilosophie* for our modern time. He says "the practical interest of the present age is transparently that science and technology be brought under universal will, and that individuals have their particular freedom explicitly and primarily therein – not through the blind conflict of aggressive wills." (p. 13)* Now I understand this to be Prof. Doull's paradigm of the kind of society he would like to see. But it is my argument that this is precisely what Marxism and socialism are all about. So perhaps he has been speaking socialism all the time without actually realizing it.

* See above, p. 229.

ROUND-TABLE DISCUSSION ON PROBLEMS OF TRANSLATING HEGEL

edited by

Howard P. Kainz

KENLEY DOVE: Let me begin by saying that Professor Pöggeler's presence here has been an invaluable help to me in working out a translation of the *Phenomenology*. As we know, the *Phenomenology* is entitled in the German *Phänomenologie des Geistes* and one has a problem right away in determining how to translate the word *"Geist."* Professor Pöggeler has, in the way of genius, come up with an obvious solution. Sir James Baillie, as you know, translated *Geist* as "Mind." Now there are certain objections to the word "Mind," and these have been voiced so many times that it would be superfluous for me to reiterate them this evening. Others have voiced objections to the other translation which has been used. Professor Findlay, for example, uses the word, "Spirit." Now this is a term that I have been tempted to adopt myself until the ingenious suggestion of Professor Pöggeler, who has said that "Geist" is obviously "Ghost." So the *Phenomenology* becomes the *Phenomenology of Ghost*! Now this struck me immediately as being possibly appropriate, but I would like at this point to throw the discussion open to find out whether or not you thought this was the entirely appropriate translation of *"Geist."*

HOWARD KAINZ: "Ghost" might not be the best selection for a 20th century translation, unless of course, Prof. Dove wants to be a pathfinder.

HENRY HARRIS: I think it would be wiser not to translate it at all, but rather leave it the way *"Dasein"* is left in translation of some contemporary German authors.

KAINZ: I would like to raise one problem about certain terms in the *Phenomenology* that Hegel uses in a technical sense different than the way we use them today. For instance, *"Vernunft," "Verstand," "konkret"* and other such words cause trouble for students of Hegel because they tend to take these words as they are used in common parlance or even in other, non-Hegelian, philosophical contexts. Is there any way to use a different word, or somehow set these expressions off so that we will come to recognize them as the technically different terms?

DOVE: One device is to use capitalization, or figure out some kind of odd term which will upset the reader so that he'll have to think about it. And yet I think there is a real disadvantage with that. The first one I think is suggested by Hegel in his own remarks in the beginning of *The Science of Logic*, where he says that philosophy does not require a special vocabulary of its own but should make use of, if we may coin a phrase, ordinary German. And I think that if it is possible for Hegel to use ordinary German in German it should also be the responsibility of the translator of Hegel into English to use ordinary English, whatever unfortunate contradictions a term may acquire in the meantime, in the translation of Hegel into English. And therefore as a translation of *"Begriff," "Vernunft"* and *"konkret,"* I suggest designating the following paradigms: "concept" and "reason" and "concrete," with the observation that Hegel, as the philosopher of the concrete, shows a very keen sense of what Russell once referred to as the sense of "contextual definition." I don't know if we can say that Hegel and Russell would be entirely in agreement on what "contextual definition" means; but nevertheless it seems to me clear that Hegelian terms have to be understood in the context of Hegelian arguments, and that's something that only Hegel, and not a translator, can provide. I'm open to questions on this; in fact, to me the whole value of a session of this sort is to gain suggestions from others who have tilled in the Hegelian vineyards, and will have useful things which can be, as it were, exploited in the process of editing and translating the Hegelian text. I must confess – and this is not to prejudge or dictate, but simply to confess – that my predilection is to use translations which provide as near equivalents as possible in the English language for the German expressions. In some cases it's more difficult than others, but in case of *"Vernunft", "Begriff,"* and *"konkrete,"* it seems to me that the obvious candidates are those I have listed. Maybe this would be the point to turn to Professor Findlay since I gather, from his remarks in the last few days, that he still has a certain sense of affection for the term which was used in the 19th century as a translation of *"Begriff,"* namely "notion," which had some advantage in that it bore some resemblance to the Greek term, *nous*, and also had the advantage of having been used in the dialogue of Berkeley called the *Siris*.

JOHN FINDLAY: I want to say very strongly that I think there is a tradition in these matters which oughtn't to be lightly disturbed. I've been reading Hegelian works all my life, and I think that there have been conventions set up. Of course, they must be abandoned if they are grossly unsuitable; but I think that we should keep them if they are not grossly unsuitable. Now, for instance, some people have proposed that *"Verstand"* should be translated as "reason"; because "reason" is rather a low-class faculty that we equate essentially with *raisonnement*, whereas it is also being proposed that *"Vernunft"* should be translated "understanding." Now I personally think this is a very bad proposition. I know that the English word, "understanding," has a different sense from the Hegelian and Kantian sense of *"Verstand."* On the other hand, we have established a peculiar contextual sense for *"Verstand"*; and in fact it means something different for Kant and for Hegel. And we should stick to this word. Similarly with *"Vernunft."* Calling it "reason" is not completely satisfactory. On the other hand, this way of translating it has been widely and deeply accepted and I think we should stick to it. Now, I object to "concept"; I think "notion" is better. "Concept," having been proposed in the beginning might have been a good choice; but it hasn't been established in the past. "Notion" is a varied term. It might have been used for *"Vorstellung,"* but it wasn't used in this way. I personally think we should probably stick to "notion." Because "concept" has got quite a different signification in English from *"Begriff."* I mean, the concept is always thought as something rather clear-cut, well-defined, something definable. This is how we naturally think of it; and to talk about the concept doing things, or "instantiating itself," or of a "self-specifying-concept," sounds absolutely *ein Unding*. But I think the "notion" *can* be credited with these powers to discover unfamiliar meanings. I personally believe very strongly in keeping to traditional renderings, for instance *"Anschauung,"* which was rendered "intuition" in translations of Kant. And in translating Husserl's *Kategoriale Anschauung*, I used "Categorial Intuition." Now I know other people use other terms for it but I think this is the accepted version. Many of these things were really devised as Germanic equivalents of Latin terms, so I think we should simply keep these Latin terms since they have been established. I think, for instance, "in-itself" is a better way of talking of *"an sich"* than "implicit" or "in principle" or other terms being used. I think you can get used to using "in-itself" and "for-itself." On the whole, I would say try to use Germanic rather than Latin terms, try to use English terms; but where something has been very well established, I would say that we should not upset the traditional usage.

DOVE: (in response to a question concerning the translation of *Vorstellung, Entfremdung, Entaüsserung*, etc.) Sir James Baillie had a very fecund imagination when it came to translating terms like this; I'm thinking especially of *Entaüsserung*. I've never tabulated the number of renderings he has of the word – sometimes he puts it into Greek, sometimes into Latin or English, sometimes into Germanic English. I do believe that it would be well for a term as technical as that to find a translation as consistent as possible. I don't think it would be wise to mechanically render all the terms of Hegel's technical vocabulary into a precise one-to-one correlation with English, precisely because that might very well hamper the translation. Obviously the matter of which term is important or critical requires judgment; there is no real rule that determines when a term is important and when it is not important. But in regard to terms which strike me as being important ones, I must confess an alternative view. Actually this is a point at which I might very well defer to Professor Pöggeler to ask a question. And the question is suggested by Georg Lukács in his book *Der junge Hegel*, in which he suggests that the term *"Entäusserung"* was originally a translation and indeed not a translation from the Greek, nor a translation from the Latin, but a translation from the English. And the English term which was to have been rendered by *"Entäusserung,"* according to Lukács, who may or may not have been right, was "alienation." But not "alienation" in the Erich Fromm sort of Buddhist sense, but alienation in the 18th century juridical sense, and I must say this makes a certain amount of sense to me. I do not know whether or not it is really true that the term *"Entäusserung"* first made its way into the German language as a technical piece of philosophical vocabulary, in virtue of its having been the translation of the term as it was used by jurisprudential as well as politico-economic writers of the 18th century.

FINDLAY: I think *"Entfremdung"* is the natural translation of alienation. *"Entfremdung"* is the word that is used in all those descriptions of 18th century society, and I think *"Entäusserung"* should be something like "externalization," or something of the sort.

VICTOR GOUREVITCH: In general, should the same English term be used to translate the same German term?

DOVE: In principle it seems to me wise to use the same term whenever possible without introducing artificiality of language; and this should be stressed especially if the terms are technical. The question is which term is technical and which is not, and where to draw the line. That is the problem, and a difficult one, because in philosophy things tend to hang on the small words, a word like *"wir"* in Hegel, *"für uns,"* *"unser"* etc. Now these are words that Baillie (just to name a translator arbitrarily), has treated very arbitrarily. When you have *"wir"* in the text, you might find "we" in the translation, and then again you might not, and this strikes me as being rather inexcusable. Here we have to make a judgment. I personally feel the words *"wir,"* *"unser,"* *"für uns,"* etc. are about as critical as any words – much more critical than long polysyllabic words – typically German words like *"aufheben"* – which are relatively easy to deal with. But the critical words are the small words, the pronouns and what not; and these are the words I would be most keen to render in a way which will be perspicuous to the reader of the English text.

GOUREVITCH: I was just wondering about consistency. It does seem to me that every effort must be made to be studiously consistent rather than to exercise one's judgment. Because such exercise of judgment presupposes an absolutely exhaustive understanding of the text. It seems to me that, with all due respect, you have changed your mind about some interpretations that you made previously. Do you want to be able to rely upon your translation when next you revise your judgment of what it says?

DOVE: For purposes of illustration, I could mention my translation of the Introduction to the *Phenomenology* which appears in the translation of Heidegger's essay on "Hegel's concept of Experience," which I did many years ago. I have used this translation regularly with my students in undergraduate and graduate classes at Yale and, of course, I've made changes in the meantime. I've decided for example that one simply must draw some kind of a distinction which is visible to the English reader between *"erkennen"* and *"wissen,"* and that was not done in the translation as it appears in the Harper and Row version which was published early this year. In the version which I've been using with my students for the last year or so, that distinction has been drawn and presumably the version that I now have will be used in the Introduction that ultimately will be published in the total edition of the *Phenomenology.* This is not to say that, once the total edition is published, that a month or so later or a year or so later, I won't have some sort of new insight, as I'm sure anybody who translated any sort of text will have, and say, "well, I messed up on that." But there are simply some questions that have to be decided, and have to be decided of course with principles of judgment, and judgment – in this connection, I think Kant was absolutely right – has some kind of sense of dependence on experience. In short, we can't use absolute rules. It's not the sort of thing that is susceptible to being computerized. For example, we have a problem of ambiguous reference in German: *"Ihn"* is masculine, and might have a masculine antecedent such as *"Begriff."* Or it might have a masculine antecedent such as *"Gegenstand."* At one point in the Introduction to the *Phenomenology* it has one or the other antecedent; you don't really know, there is no way of telling from the text itself. You can't leave it ambiguous in English. The English language won't allow you that liberty. Now what do you do to decide? Well, if I'm going to decide, I check out every other comparable context in the *Phenomenology.* And in the case I have mentioned, the evidence wasn't conclusive, and I don't think it ever will be conclusive; it is a point of interpretation. So I decided that the sentence in question should read "object as object" rather than "concept as object" (or "Notion as object," as Professor Findlay would prefer to have it).

FINDLAY: I think this is a normal procedure where there is real and serious ambiguity; you simply have a footnote: "or so-and-so." But generally, or very often, the one interpretation is unsuitable: and this would lead you to adopt the alternative translation.

DOVE: There is a genuine ambiguity in the text I mentioned, and I think Professor Findlay's proposal is absolutely right. There should be a footnote. There is not a footnote in the edition as we have it now. I try to avoid academic, scholarly apparatus in this version because, after all, this is not a text of Hegel. Hegel in this connection was serving as a hand-maiden, alas, of Heidegger. In the version of the *Phenomenology* which appears, I'll make the effort to include footnotes to all such ambiguous choices, especially judgments which have been made on the basis of evidence which the computer wouldn't understand.

KAINZ: Does anybody here have an idea of how to translate *"Sache"* or *"die Sache selbst"*?

UNIDENTIFIED: "Subject," or "subject matter." How about something like that?

FINDLAY: I don't think it's suitable in the context where it is used in that passage in the *Phenomenology*.

KAINZ: Again, it is a technical term.

DOVE: Yes, that's the problem, it's a technical term. The term is used again and again, and it's also a term which I think it would be ridiculous not to translate with an eye to the *Logic*, because if the *"Sache"* plays a role in the *Phenomenology*, it plays a still more important role in the *Logic*. The *Phenomenology* is obviously, as Hegel himself defined it, *"Die Wissenschaft der Erfahrung des Bewusstseins."* That title was at one time given to the *Phenomenology* by Hegel, whatever role that title is to play ultimately in the book that Hegel finally published. As Heinz Kimmerle and Otto Pöggeler have commented in their articles in *Hegel-Studien*, this is a difficult question. Nevertheless Hegel at one time thought it appropriate to call the *Phenomenology* the "Science of the Experience of Consciousness." Now, the dialectic which is depicted in the *Phenomenology* is obviously the dialectic of consciousness and its object. The dialectic, if we may call it that, which is developed in the *Logic*, is the development of the *Sache selbst*. Now, apparently *"Sache"* and *"Sache selbst"* play a much more important role in the *Wissenschaft der Logik* than in the *Phenomenology*. In the Logic "*Sache*" is, as it were, right there in the center of attention, while in the *Phenomenology* the "*Sache*" plays a role of being one of those factors which turns out to mediate the dialectic of consciousness as it appears either phenomenally or immanently, over against its object.

FINDLAY: The difficulty of connecting the use of "*Sache*" in the *Phenomenology* with the usage in the *Logic* is that the "*Sache*" as it appears in fact in the *Phenomenology* is a practical concept. It is people who are devoted to the "thing itself," that is, some practical thing. But I don't personally see anything wrong with using the word "thing," because we do use the word this way in English. In this sense, something is "my thing" or "I'm deeply concerned with this thing," that is, some action. Now if you want an equivalent, I think the word "cause" might do, not in the sense of anything which causes, but a cause that I fight for. If I say I'm devoted to the future of the United States, and so on, that is the "*Sache selbst*," this is the thing I'm completely all out for. But I think personally the "thing itself" is the right way of indicating the meaning, perhaps with inverted commas added. It's certainly not "the state of affairs itself" or some of the various things that Baillie proposes, which are grotesqueries.

DOVE: I agree with you completely about Baillie's grotesqueries, but I must disagree with you that the term could be translated in such a way that it could render merely the sense of that which is suggested by "*Das geistige Tierreich*." Because the term appears right away in "Sense Certainty" on the very first page of the *Phenomenology*. "*Sache! Sache ... Ich*, etc."

FINDLAY: This is worth investigating. But I think it has quite a different sense there. I think it has the ordinary, general sense of the "thing itself," any kind of object or any kind of affairs you deal with. That type of thing. But, when you are dealing with the "*Tierreich*," it means a lot of experts or specialists all pretending that their thing is the only thing. The knowledge is the "thing." Anthropology is the "thing"; typology is the "thing"; and so forth.

DOVE: Just let me venture one objection to that. It seems to me that there is at least a connection between Hegel's use of the term "*Sache*" and his use of the term "*Sache selbst*." I discussed this with many German scholars, Professor Pöggeler included, and also Hans Fulda, and I haven't come up with any definite conclusion. Nevertheless there seems to be general agreement that there is some kind of connection. And therefore to render the term in Chapter 5 as if it weren't related to all the other

occurances of *"Sache"* throughout the rest of the *Phenomenology* strikes
me as being a mistake. This would be to abrogate the useful principle
suggested earlier, the one that Victor Gourevitch affirmed so vehemently.
Now, I agree. I think that this term simply must be rendered in a way
which enables the reader to distinguish this as one of the perhaps half
dozen most critical terms of the entire *Phenomenology*. There is also one
point that I must make, about the rendering as "thing." In the *Phenomenology* between pages 297-300*, Hegel distinguishes specifically and
explicitly between *"Ding"* and *"Sache."*

FINDLAY: Yes, but in German *"Ding"* is different from an English
"thing."

DOVE: But how would you render *"Ding"*?

FINDLAY: That's a problem! You put "Thing" with a capital letter or
something like that.

HARRIS: I haven't got any solution. I agree with you about the problem
and I doubt if there is any expression which would effectively work even
for say, 80% of the occurrences. The best I can suggest is "essential thing."
If that won't do, then I think the only solution is going to be to find something that works most of the time and then to insert in parentheses the
word *"Sache"* or *"Sache selbst"* wherever you have to use an alternative.

DOVE: This would be a last resort. May I propose one term? It's a
rather curious one. I have all the occurrences of *"Sache"* designated in one
of my card-files, and there is one rendition that I found not entirely misleading in so far as one recognizes that the term must be defined contextu-
ally; and this is a rendition that I have not used in the translation of
Hegel's Introduction. The term that suggests itself is "situation." Of
course, at first hearing that may seem absurd, and I invite comment on
this.

NATHAN ROTENSTREICH: Why not "case as the case is"?

FINDLAY: Oh no! Not in the *Tierreich*, where it's a devotion to a particular occupation, I mean this cannot be a "case" or a "situation."

(UNIDENTIFIED): One thing that this brings to mind is a consideration
that I think is important and is very frequently used in a good conscience
by good scholars, namely, giving some attention to the book's "market."
I think if I were translating an intricate text in a foreign language I would
give primary consideration to who was going to read my translation. Now
in one sense it doesn't matter too much at all how you translate these "irreducible lumps," if the reader knows the other language, or if you are
writing an edition in which abundant reference may be given to the scho-

---

* Hoffmeister ed.

larly edition. But if you are preparing a college text or a text for graduate students who may not be at home in a foreign language, then I want to raise the question of whether a difference in editorial procedure is 1) permissable and 2) possible.

DOVE: That's Frege's principle, namely, "What difference does it make in practice"?

(Previous speaker): No, what I'm refering to here is whether you think that editorial practice might permit a fully annotated edition, issued jointly with a text where you as translator take one of the options set before you. In other words, if there were a kind of Super Baillie to go with the Baillie that we have, where Baillie had listed his second thoughts.

DOVE: There would be so many. But this raises a question which I would like also to pose at this point. Some students – graduate students, maybe many students – will be using the English text, not so much as a prop, but as a text which they will compare, Loeb-fashion, with the original German. I've talked with the editor of this text as it appears in Harper and Row, about the possibility of issuing a bilingual edition. In many respects it would certainly have a great number of things to recommend it. The one obvious thing to disrecommend it is cost. The *Phenomenology* is not a short book, and while paper is not expensive, it at least turns out to be when publishers get through with it. And that means that for all practical purposes this option must be simply excluded. This raises the question as to how one can work out a version that would be readily comparable with the German text; which is to say how one can work out a cross-reference system. This is no small question. You have the text which was issued in Bamberg in 1807, you have the text which was issued by Lasson, and the Hoffmeister text, and presumably there will be a text issued under the editorship of Professor Pöggeler and his associates for the Hegel *Archiv*. Now, I have a proposal here which I'd like to test since Professor Pöggeler is here, and since I'm on the spot now. I would very much like to use a device like that used in respect to Kant. It seems to me since there are many texts, and these texts may very well continue to be used, we have to make an arbitrary choice – something like the arbitrary choice of primogeniture to assure membership in the Estates in Hegel's *Philosophy of Right*. If you have to make an arbitrary choice, why not base it upon something natural? In that case, the natural thing would be to use the 1807 edition. But it would be stupid to use the 1807 edition if it were not available. Now it's true that with the exception of the version which was reissued in 1907, presumably to commemorate the edition which was published in 1807, no other German text has, so far as I know,

been issued with the 1807 pagination. Now what I'm proposing is that
it would be most advisable that an English translation which tries to be
as responsible as possible should be issued with marginal notations in the
usual way – namely, the way used for the Schmidt edition of Kant, or
the Macqarrie and Robinson edition of Heidegger's *Sein und Zeit* – to
indicate the 1807 pagination. But this would only be reasonable if the
Hegel edition which is forthcoming sometime between now and 2007
were also to indicate the 1807 pagination. I would like to ask you if you
think this would be a good idea.

FINDLAY: There is an alternative to following the original pagination.
In my work on the *Phenomenology*, I take the German text and whatever
the English text is that is being used, and I just number the corresponding
paragraphs in both German and English texts. This is especially useful,
since Baillie sometimes splits a paragraph which is a single long paragraph
in German into multiple paragraphs. I think this is a better way than
pagination.

KAINZ: Should the italics in the German edition be reproduced in English?

DOVE: One thing that should be noted here is that the italics as they
appear in the Hoffmeister edition bear no correspondence to the italics
which appear in the Goebhardt edition which was published in 1807.

OTTO PÖGGELER: The Hoffmeister edition does preserve the italics from
the earlier edition.

FINDLAY: There are two kinds of *kursiv* in German. There is a wide
spacing of a letter so as to make the word a little longer, and in addition
there is the other device of *kursiv*. I usually follow the method of expressing them both by italics. But I think you must express these two types,
you must give an equivalent, because the terms that are written out long
in this way are very crucial.

DOVE: In the Goebhardt edition of 1807, the use of italics is rare. But
spacetype is the common form, and it seems to me that since we're comparing 19th century German usages and 20th century English usages, the
most reasonable course to take would be to express the Goebhardt space
version for emphasis in late 20th century English through the use of
italics.

(UNIDENTIFIED): The use of capitalization is still going on in Hegel
translation. Miller has cut it down rather drastically, but he still retains
capitalization for certain terms. I would prefer to get rid of all of that
apparatus in translation.

FINDLAY: Actually, I'm responsible for the decapitalization in Miller's translation of the *Philosophy of Nature*. Miller absolutely abounded in capitals, and I find that this is a terrible threat to the English; because you find yourself actually forced to write a word which appears in some utterly ordinary context in capitals, because it appeared in capitals somewhere else. You have to write "My wife changed her Mind" in capitals! I should think you would retain capitals with "Notion" because it's, after all, a very technical term. What would the other terms be that would take capitals?

(UNIDENTIFIED): "*Idee*," or Idea?

FINDLAY: Well, "Idea," I think, is legitimate, because "idea" sometimes has connotations of "*Vorstellung*" and so on; and the Idea in the sense of the *Logic* is, after all, a very special idea. But I think you have to use capitalization very sparingly. There is a legitimate use of capitals. Use it sparingly, departing from it when there is any good reason for departing from it. Otherwise the whole thing is spattered, and it all looks terribly un-English and unintelligible.

HARRIS (TO DOVE): What are you going to do with *Vorstellung*, by the way?

DOVE: Well, as those of you who have checked out the translation of the Introduction probably know, I there translate it as "notion." What would you suggest?

FINDLAY: It's quite a good thing, as far as ordinary usage goes; though it's still not in accord with established translation-conventions.

HARRIS: Coming back to the translation of *Begriff* as "Notion," there is a local tradition in the United States for translating *Begriff* as "comprehension."

FINDLAY: How dreadful! I say, I think this is awful. You can't talk of the "comprehension" in nature.

DOVE: I once asked Herbert Marcuse how he would translate *Begriff*. He said that if it were possible, he would render it "comprehension"; but he says it's impossible.

GOUREVITCH: What's wrong with the traditional term, "idea," for "*Vorstellung*"? Because, after all it's what "*Vorstellung*" translates as.

DOVE: Well, once again I would refer to Professor Findlay.

FINDLAY: I think that it would be a *small* "idea."

DOVE: Oh yes, of course, a small idea.

FINDLAY: It wouldn't be bad, but it might be slightly misleading. But, I mean, "representation" is not English; "presentation" isn't English.

DOVE: How do you like the translation "image" for "*Vorstellung*"?

FINDLAY: No. Hegel means "*Vorstellung*" as a kind of low, semi-pictorial type of comprehension.

DOVE: This is exactly what I had in mind in suggesting "image."

FINDLAY: "Image" suggests a technical-psychological meaning only possible in our English-American experience; this is not what *"Vorstellung"* means.

PÖGGELER: How does one translate Reinholz's *Theorie des Vorstellungs Vermögen?*

FINDLAY: I think that one has to translate that as "presentative faculty." I think that when *"Vorstellung"* is used in the technical sense, you've got to use a technical term.

DENIS SAVAGE: The entire *Standard Edition* of Freud – 24 volumes – translated *Vorstellung* as "idea."

FINDLAY: Yes. Well, I think this is the normal translation.

SAVAGE: You can't translate *Vorstellung* as "image."

FINDLAY: Well, somebody's translation of Brentano recently was absolutely ruined by translating "image" and "imagination" for *Vorstellung.* It just didn't work.

KAINZ: If Professor Dove is translating *Begriff* as "concept," "notion" might be used as the ordinary translation of *Vorstellung.*

DOVE: That is the device that I use in the translation of the Introduction. Now, Professor Findlay finds it objectionable.

FINDLAY: I don't think it's very objectionable, but it would disturb me. I mean, it could be used.

DOVE: This is really a question – whether or not one could readily enough get used to certain expressions in context.

FREDERICK WEISS: Really, does it make that much difference in the context? *"Vorstellung"* means that which is literally "put in place before" you. *"Begriff"* is just the opposite in meaning. It's, literally, "to grasp." Now if we translate *Begriff* as "concept" in the ordinary Anglo-Saxon sense of that word, it doesn't do any good. We might as well translate it as "X." It's the meaning that you get, the philosophical interpretation you place on it that is important.

DOVE: In true context.

WEISS: For example, take the word, "Idea," in Hegel as we translate it. People don't understand it because there is an entire philosophy involved in understanding what that word means. What difference does it really make in a sense, what translation we use?

DOVE: That seems a very good question to ask, but translations do not occur *in vacuo.* Translations occur in the tradition of translation and in the tradition of the discussion of the German text and in the tradition of the discussion of the English text which is inspired (or otherwise) by the

German text, and ultimately there is a new translation. A. V. Miller has now done a translation of *The Science of Logic* which is a considerable change from the Johnston-Struthers translation. He is now translating the *Philosophy of Nature*. There will be a revision of the translation of the first part of the *Encyclopedia*, the so-called *Smaller Logic*. And I understand there will also be a translation of the *Zusätze*, and perhaps a revision of the translation of the *Philosophy of the Spirit*, the third part of the *Encyclopedia*. Will that be changed from "mind" to "spirit," Professor Findlay?

FINDLAY: No, it will remain as "Mind," because Knox feels that we shouldn't tamper with the present terminology. And I feel strongly about the excellence of Knox.

DOVE: Is that final? Does Knox have the final say on that?

FINDLAY: No. Lots of people are consulted on it and at last count the decision was in favor of "Mind" at Oxford Press.

DOVE: Maybe if we could arm Professor Findlay with the bastion of the term "Spirit," which seems to me obviously superior in the translation of *"Geist,"* perhaps then some of the experts who consult with the Oxford University Press might be brought to cast a greater weight in the ballot box. Is that conceiveable? Let's have a show of force here.

WEISS: Professor Dove, don't you see how arbitrary that is?

DOVE: Well, not entirely. I admit that I have a strong predilection for "Spirit" as a translation of *Geist*. But more and more people are coming to study Hegel's text these days without the wisdom of Professor Weisses and Harrises and what-not. Maybe it would be useful for these people to have a perspicuous indication that this is, after all, the same term as that important term in Hegel. Let me give you an example. You see, once a gentleman who taught a graduate philosophy course on the *Phenomenology* at the university in New Haven was asked about this distinction. (After all in Baillie's translation of the *Phenomenology*, there is a distinction between the two words: in Chapter Six, he begins translating *"Geist"* as "Spirit" instead of "Mind." Well, one wonders about this.) And so the students innocently enough asked the Professor, what about this distinction between "mind" and "spirit," and the Professor, who never made claim to great, unlimited resources, gave a halfhour lecture on Hegel's distinction between mind and spirit. And then one very timid graduate student, who had, after all, passed the German examination . . . you can fill in the rest of the story.

SHLOMO AVINERI: May I just, for this graduate student, give a conclusive reason why I think "spirit" should be used rather than "mind"? There was a satirical lampoon written in 1832 against Hegel, in which one of Hegel's disciplines is called "*Distillateur zum konkreten Geist.*" Now, this *has* to be "spirit" rather than "mind."

WEISS: Yes, I appreciate that. But Wallace, of course, did use "mind" in his translation of *Geist*; and when you read Hegel and you come to think in terms of Hegel's system you begin to see things. I find "mind" a very rich term. I don't read any of the Anglo-Saxon, Cartesian kind of meanings into it. And besides that, you wouldn't want to treat the Greek "*Nous*" as "spirit." That would be totally misleading. I think that Hegel's "*Geist*" is much closer to the Aristotelian and Greek conception of *Nous*. And you would never want to translate that as "spirit."

DOVE: How would you translate *Geist*, then?

WEISS: As "mind."

FINDLAY: Well "*Nous*" is sometimes translated in German as "*Geist*." *Geistesmetaphysik* could be a book about *Nous*-philosophy.

GOUREVITCH: May I just ask a practical question which was raised earlier, namely, how to make the various translations of the *Phenomenology* hold to one another, to the extent that it's possible. Perhaps it is possible to persuade people who are engaged in the task to put technical terms in the translation in parentheses in the German. This is something which could quickly catch on. One finds in one translation a consistent use of "mind" and in another a consistent use of "spirit"; but the term *Geist* is in parentheses. I know that it's awkward.

DOVE: The practical question we're facing now is whether or not some of this awkwardness could be avoided at least in the forthcoming reissuing of the third part of the *Encyclopedia*. And one of the things I was hoping we might arm Professor Findlay with is arguments in favor of actually tampering with the translation of *Geist*.

FINDLAY: It's too late.

WEISS: Here again, I suppose it's probably a ridiculous suggestion, but I think you could translate the *Philosophie des Geistes* as the *Philosophy of X*, then leave it up to the people who read it to decide what the word means.

DOVE: In Hegel the term "Philosophy" is very problematic, did you know that? He uses the term in various senses. So to be rigorous you'd have to say "the X of X."

HARRIS: I think there is one thing to be said regarding the reaction of Professor Weiss. Although I have no sympathy with his desire to leave traditional patterns of translation undisturbed, at the same time it does seem to me to be going too far to disturb them in a way that would be systematically misleading – for example, to start translating *Vorstellung* by "notion" would so distort the tradition that we've got, that I think it would be dangerous; unless you're convinced that the whole tradition is corrupt.

DOVE: You would pay deference to tradition wherever possible?

HARRIS: Yes, at least where it is not obviously irredeemable.

THE HEGELIANS OF SAINT LOUIS, MISSOURI
AND THEIR INFLUENCE IN THE UNITED STATES

John O. Riedl

The history of the Hegelians of Saint Louis, Missouri, is as much the story of a book as it is of persons and places.[1] The book is a translation into En-

[1] Denton Jacques Snider, *The St. Louis Movement in Philosophy, Literature, Education, Psychology, with Chapters of Autobiography*. St. Louis: Sigma Publishing Company, [1920]. 608 pp. The copy in the library of the Missouri Historical Society, Jefferson Memorial Building, St. Louis, is inscribed: "To the Missouri Historical Society from the author: Denton J. Snider March 27th 1920."
Pp. 27-28:
Accordingly the St. Louis Movement had its start from a philosophic motive, from a system of thought already formulated and organized which we were to master and to apply. Moreover it was a system of idealism, one that put stress upon Idea or Spirit as the primordial creative source of all things. It was a great and necessary discipline which trained us to see underneath the mighty phenomenal occurrences of the passing hour, and to probe to their original starting-point, to their creative essence.

The time was calling loudly for First Principles. The Civil War had just concluded, in which we all had in some way participated, and we were still overwhelmed, even dazed partially by the grand historic appearance. What does it all mean? was quite the universal question. Of course the answer varied in a thousand shapes; there was the political, the religious, the social, the economic, even the wholly selfish and sensual answer. Naturally our set sought in philosophy the solution, that is, in Hegel as taught by our leaders. A great world-historical deed had been done with enormous labor and outer panoramic pageantry. What lay in it for us and for the future? So we began to grope after the everlasting verities, the eternal principles, the pure Essences (*reine Wesenheiten*) as they are called by our philosophic authority. These transcendent energies of man and of the world were said to be collected and ordered in one book – Hegel's Logic. So the St. Louis Movement may be called a child of the period, a peculiar infant indeed, but nevertheless a legitimate birth of the time's spiritual struggle. And this infant seemed to be sent by the time to a worldschool for its discipline.

I may again remark that this pursuit of the Eternal has turned out to have had something eternal in it, at least up to date. The St. Louis Movement retains still a quiet life of its own; it never won an uproarious public existence; it had always to be sought out in its own little nook by those who would know of it and share in its gifts. Just this week for instance (October, 1918,) I have received a letter from an inquirer who wishes to get information about "that original philosophic Club" and its members, mentioning Brockmeyer, Harris, "and yourself." Then he winds up with this expression of opinion: "That is the most remarkable movement known in this country." Not everybody is likely to accede to this view, especially those who have been bred in the home of New England Transcendentalism. But the inquiry, with others of the same sort, may be taken as a sign of a still living interest in the St. Louis Movement after more than five decades.

glish of Georg Wilhelm Friedrich Hegel's (1770-1831) *Larger Logic*.[2]

The central fact about the book is that it was never published. It is a manuscript extant in three copies, one of which is complete. Perhaps twice that number of copies ever existed.

The translator is Henry Conrad Brokmeyer (1826-1906), who had immigrated to the United States at the age of sixteen from his native Prussia, and moved in 1854 to St. Louis, where he practiced law and, as lieutenant-governor of Missouri (1875-1879) was for a time in 1876-1877 acting governor.[3]

The occasion of the translation was the meeting of Brokmeyer with William Torrey Harris (1835-1909) at St. Louis in 1858.[4] Harris was a

---

The St. Louis Movement, although the most significant, is not the oldest evidence of Hegelian studies in the United States. The story of the Ohio Hegelians has been written by Loyd David Easton, *Hegel's First American Followers; The Ohio Hegelians; John B. Stallo, Peter Kaufmann, Moncure Conway, and August Willich with Key Writings*. Athens, Ohio: Ohio University Press, 1966. 353 pp.

The Hegelian interests of Frederick Augustus Rauch (1806-1841), James Murdock (1776-1856), and Orestes Augustus Brownson (1803-1876) were told by Henry A. Pochmann, *German Culture in America: Philosophical and Literary Influences*, 1600-1900. Madison: The University of Wisconsin Press, 1961. Pp. 306, 666; 107-108, 112-114, 561-562; 234-239, 628-631.

[2] *Wissenschaft der Logik*, edited by Leopold Dorotheus von Henning (1791-1866), in volumes III-V (Zweite unveränderte Auflage, 1941) of *Georg Wilhelm Friedrich Hegel's Werke*. 19 volumes in 22, Berlin: Verlag von Duncker und Humblot, 1832-1845

Volume III: Erster Theil: Die objective Logik. Erste Abtheilung: Die Lehre vom Seyn. [pp. 24-452].

Volume IV: Erster Theil: Die objective Logik. Zweite Abtheilung: Die Lehre vom Wesen. [pp. 3-235].

Volume V: Zweiter Theil: Die subjective Logik, oder: Die Lehre vom Begriff. [pp. 3-343].

[3] Biographical details in *Dictionary of American Biography*, II-1, 64-65, s.v. "Brokmeyer, Henry C. (Aug. 12, 1828 – July 26, 1906)," by Ernest Sutherland Bates.

[4] At the time of the meeting Brokmeyer was thirty-two years of age, living intermittently in what he called in his letters, "Backwoods," at Marthasville, Warren County, Missouri. Harris was twenty-three, a teacher and assistant principal in one of the public grammar schools of St. Louis.

George Malcolm Stratton (1865-1957), a former pupil and long a younger colleague of Professor George Holmes Howison (1834-1916) told the story of the meeting, probably as he had heard it from Howison. He set it down in "A Biographical Sketch," in John Wright Buckham (1864-1945) and George Malcolm Stratton, *George Holmes Howison: Philosopher and Teacher*. A selection from his writings with a biographical sketch. Berkeley: University of California Press, 1934. 418 pp. Pp. 51-52:

Harris had left Yale, having been advised near the middle of the course to seek some other place. Wandering to St. Louis, he had taught shorthand, was now in one of the public grammar schools as assistant principal – a young, fair-haired man of delicate skin, talking philosophy in set phrases, almost if not quite unintelligible to others. And he was full to bursting with phrenology and agnosticism.

One evening as he was going home from a meeting in which he had aired his agnostic views, he was followed by Brockmeyer, a rough specimen of a German, who, as Harris mounted his doorstep, laid his hand on Harris's shoulder. Harris turned on him, taking him for a highwayman. He was met with the words: "Ah, don't be

teacher of stenography, educated at Yale College, and had moved to St.
Louis in 1857, living there until 1880. He was United States Commissioner of Education, 1839-1906.[5]

Brokmeyer had become interested in Hegel,[6] as had Walt Whitman

afraid; I am friendly. I've been to the meeting tonight and I've heard your bad talk.
You think you cannot know truth. I have come to convince you that you can, and
to show you how to do it." The two did not part until nearly morning. By that time,
Brockmeyer had shaken Harris's intellectual system, and had persuaded him to
begin the study of German, and, through German, to come to an understanding of
Kant. This was the Brockmeyer whose quasi-translation of the *Phenomenologie* we
have seen feeding the dozen or more hungry souls, of a Sunday afternoon. His violence in the dark of night was the origin of the Kant Club, well established, as has
been said, when Howison came. Brockmeyer, in spite of his roughness, was a man
dominated at times by intellect; when speaking of philosophy, he became as one
transformed, appearing as Howison imagined the poet Schiller must have seemed.
Howison would gaze at Brockmeyer in these flights of his, and wonder how so coarse
a man could possibly be thus changed.
In the preface, page x, there is reference to a manuscript, "St. Louis Reminiscences,"
by Howison. It is a "rough transcript as by a stenographer, which seems never to have
been revised or published," of a paper Howison delivered January 6, 1916. It is
preserved in the University of California Library at Berkeley.
Woodbridge Riley, *American Thought from Puritanism to Pragmation and Beyond.*
New York: Henry Holt and Company, 1915. 438 pp., stated:
To turn to Harris, the second of the triumvirate. Brockmeyer recounts how he met
his foremost disciple at a chance meeting where those present were discussing Oriental theosophy, spiritualism, or something of that sort. The secretary of that meeting,
he narrates, was a young man named Harris, who seemed to me to be the one sane
person of the gathering. After the meeting I accosted him and began to question him
as we walked along. He seemed surprised that such a common workingman, as I
appeared to be, should talk in this way, and we got into a discussion. He made some
quotation from Cousin, and I remarked that Cousin contradicted himself on every
page. On his challenging this statement I accompanied him to his room to prove it
from Cousin's works. This was the beginning of our friendship, and the nucleus of
the group of students that soon gathered together.
    Here was the beginning of the first systematic study of Hegel in the country.
Brockmeyer tells how Harris and two other enthusiastic young men wished him to
cease working in the foundry and give his time to instructing them and to translating
the great works of German thought. But the commencement of the Civil War, of
which the first storm center was Missouri, interfered with this arrangement and broke
up the little band of philosophers.
[5] Biographical details in *Who Was Who in America*, I (1897-1942), 526; *Dictionary
of American Biography*, IV-2, 328-330, *s.v.* "Harris, William Torrey (Sept. 10, 1835-
Nov. 5, 1909)," by Ernest Sutherland Bates. A critical biography has been written by
Kurt Friedrich Leidecker (1902-   ), *Yankee Teacher; The Life of William Torrey
Harris.* New York: Philosophical Library, Inc., 1947. 648 pp.
[6] Brokmeyer's diary, with entries from May 1, 1856 to November 8, 1856, was
published by his son, Eugene C. Brockmeyer (-1951), under the title:
A Mechanic's Diary, by Ex-Gov. Henry C. Brokmeyer Author of "The Errand Boy,"
"A Foggy Night at Newport," "Letters on Goethe's Faust," Translations of Hegel's
"Logic," "Phenomenology" and "Psychology" and Various Political Works. Copy-
right 1910, by E. C. Brockmeyer, Washington D.C. E.C. Brockmeyer, Editor and
Publisher, Washington, D.C. [239 pp.]
The table of contents has the heading, "Why Hegel should be Popular, p. 55." The
entry, on pages 55-56, is as follows:
Pp. 55-56:

(1819-1892),[7] through the ten page selection from the *Philosophy of History* in Frederic Henry Hedge's (1805-1890) *Prose Writers of Germany*.[8] Brokmeyer bought the German text of the *Logic* in the edition of Hen-

July, 11, 1856.

I have recommenced my annual course in Hegel's "Logic." It is a strange book and attractive to me, on account of its noiselessness. Whenever the world within or without commences to brawl as loudly that I cannot hear my own voice, I take a journey into the realm of this primeval solitude. I sometimes think it is a great pity that the man did not live to-day, or at least at a time when the railroad facilities were far enough developed to show him what a book ought to be for man when he travels by steam. As it is, I don't know of a single chapter, page or paragraph that can be read and understood in passing by it at the moderate rate of speed of, say, forty miles an hour, no matter how large the letters might be made, or how long the fence to give room for their display. Yet, even in his day, it was known that a book should be written in such a manner "That he who runs may read," and the circumstances that we do our study, not while running, but while rushing along, leaves us necessarily in a condition the more seriously to regret that he did not comply with the canons of his art, as calculated for his own day and generation. Had he done so, there can be no doubt, when the superior sagacity of ourselves is duly considered, that the increased speed, the haste at which we have arrived, would have been no detriment to the general usefulness of the book. As it is, I fear it never will be of much value as a source of popular entertainment.

I have heard it said that it is owing to the theme, the subject treated, that the work is so obscure; that here are subjects, like the integral and differential calculus, for example, that refuse to be treated in such a way as to become popular reading – or to give up their information to the general public at first glance.

As to that, of course, I do not pretend to judge. But it does seem to me that if there is a theme in nature, art or science that ought to be popular, that ought to be thoroughly, familiar to everybody, it is the one treated in this book; for it treats of nothing but human knowing – knowing, the peculiarity that distinguishes man from the brute. That is the only subject it touches upon, and it treats of that, not in its idiosyncracies, not as it is developed in this or that individual, but as this universal characteristic, as the very essence of all men, as that which makes man what he is – man.

Why, then, is this not the most popular of themes – seeing that each one of us has within himself the entire material treated of?

Or, is it true that we live habitually out of doors and are strangers nowhere so much as in our own house?

The knowing, thought, reason may be occupied with a variety of objects – with objects derived from the senses, from the emotions or from reflection; but in logic it deals with itself, with its own products alone, and the knowing that results, free from all foreign content, is therefore called a "pure" knowing. The products of thought which it investigates, while at first glance they may appear formal and empty, are nevertheless in their totality the ultimate presupposition of every mental operation. They are the products of the human mind, as contradistinguished from the individual mind – of the human mind in its universality. They form the ground work, the foundation of all communication, association and co-operation of man with man; and all the achievements in science and art, whether applied or ideal, are but the tangible and visible results of those invisible powers. They give continuity to human endeavor, and enable the present to strike its roots deep into the spiritual alluvium of the past. To investigate them in their simplicity; to define each in its sphere; to exhibit the law of their genesis, and thus reveal their self-consistent totality – this is the object which the author sought to attain.

[7] Pochmann, *German Culture in America: Philosophical and Literary Influences, 1600-1900*, pp. 467-474; Mody C. Boatright, "Whitman and Hegel," University of Texas Studies in English, IX (July, 1929), 134-150.

[8] Illustrated with portraits. Philadelphia: Carey and Hart, 1847. 567 pp. There were four editions by 1856 by various publishers in Philadelphia and New York.

ning, and on the strength of Hegel's reference [Henning, III, 31] to his previous work on the *Phenomenology of the Spirit*, read it also. Brokmeyer interested Harris in both books and in 1861 the two Hegelian amateurs collaborated in the translation of both. Brokmeyer did the translation; Harris set it down "in phonography," that is, in the new Pitman Short-hand. Harris's shorthand text of the first part of the *Logic*, approximately one-tenth of the work, is preserved in the archives of the Missouri Histori-cal Society.[9] It is the oldest of the three extant manuscripts of Brokmeyer's translation. Harris's shorthand text of the second part of the *Phenomeno-logy*, approximately half of the work, is in the same archives.[10]

A Kant Club was formed in 1858, but the Civil War interrupted the study of Kant and Hegel. The study was resumed in the autumn of 1865. In January, 1866, the St. Louis Philosophical Society was founded, with Brokmeyer president, and Harris secretary.[11] Denton Jaques Snider

---

[9] On pages 1-29 of a bound notebook, 10 1/2″ x 15 1/2″, 44 blue lines to the page, with stamped pagination on both sides of the page. In Harris's script on the first of two end-sheets:
> Hegel's Logic translated into English by H. C. Brokmeyer. Pages 24 to 127 [of the German text]. [In Harris's shorthand:] Written in reporting style by William T. Harris in the year of Our Lord 1861-

[10] On pages 1-141 of a bound notebook, approximately 7-7/8″ x 12-7/8″, linen textured, 41 blue lines to the page, with stamped pagination on both sides of the page. In script on page 1:
> Phenomenology of the Mind Vol. II Page 275 [of the German text] Aug. 4.

And on page 141, part in script, part in shorthand:
> [Page] 591
> End of the Phenomenology –
> Finished August 16 Thursday 1861. 25 minutes to 6 P.M.

Miss Edith Davidson Harris, Daughter of W. T. Harris, listed the item in a detailed memorandum of five typewritten pages, entitled "List of William Torrey Harris Scrap-books, Notebooks, and Letters sent to the Missouri Historical Society by Edith Davidson Harris, October 1943," as follows:
> Hegel's Phenomenology of the Spirit, translated by Henry C. Brokmeyer, August 3rd, 1861 – "In the woods of Marthasville, Warren Co., Mo." "Finished August 16, Thursday, 1861 – 25 minutes to 6 P.M."

The Missouri Historical Society has the detailed memorandum, and much correspond-ence with Miss Harris. She referred to the memorandum in a letter of October 23, 1943. She said that the material was the "first installment," was in a box and a pack-age, and was sent "by express prepaid today." The first installment included the two notebooks with Harris's shorthand text of the two translations, and also many letters of Brokmeyer to Harris from the 1860s to the 1890s.

Several of the early letters of Brokmeyer to Harris referred to the translating of the *Phenomenology*. A letter of June 30, 1861, Backwoods, spoke of the former's coming to town to finish the translation. Evidently Vol. I was done before that date.

[11] Snider, *The St. Louis Movement*, p. 7:
> The foregoing event, which may be regarded as the starting-point of the St. Louis Movement, was the birth of the St. Louis Philosophical Society which took place in January, 1866, after due preliminaries. About a dozen gentlemen assembled in a down-town law-office, according to agreement; out of this number two men stepped forth as the original founders and first members. One of them, the real originator, was chosen President of the Society – Henry C. Brockmeyer, then a practicing lawyer in the city; the other the active organizer, became its Secretary –

(1841-1925), historian of the movement, was one of the original founders and first members. He was at age twenty-five "seemingly the youngest" of the group.

Almost from the beginning a smaller inner circle was formed, with Harris as instructor, to study the *Larger Logic*.[12] It was a revival of the pre-war Kant Club. In subsequent years the club also studied the *Phenomenology of the Spirit*.[13]

William T. Harris, then principal of one of the Public Schools. Each of them spoke briefly his inaugural, emphasizing with enthusiasm the prospect and purposes of the organization; both failed not to flash some prophetic lightning upon our unlit future.

These two men were not only the officers, but were in essence the Society, and remained such. They proved themselves the two philosophers of us all; they might be called Philosophy incarnate; it was their breath of life, but likewise their limit, as time revealed. They turned out very different from each other, not only in their lives but even in their philosophic gift; and yet, as to persistence they were quite alike, inasmuch as both clung to their favorite discipline and its one master till the light of their days went out. They both died, as it were, with their favorite philosopher's favorite book clutched in the still hand.

[12] *Ibid.*, pp. 11-13:

It soon became manifest that there was one book of Hegel which uprose the lofty center round which all the other works of the philosopher, all our studies, in fact all the thought of the All itself gathered – that was Hegel's so-called *Larger Logic*. This was very different from Whately's text-book which I had studied at College, indeed it went quite the reverse of the whole line of treatises on Logic from Aristotle down to the present. This Logic was declared to be the movement of the pure essences of the world, stripped from their outer illusory vesture. Of course I rebounded from it at the start, but I always returned to it as the one fortress of thought to be assaulted and captured for dear life's sake, wherein I was helped often by quick flashes of Brockmeyer's lightning insight. This book has the reputation of being the hardest book in the world, the one least accessible to the ordinary human mind even when academically trained. My wrestle with it was long, intense, and not wholly victorious at the close; still after years of entanglement I pulled through its magic web of abstractions and obstructions, and left them behind me, not lost but transcended.

Now it so happened that an English translation had been made of this book by Brockmeyer about the year 1860, near the beginning of the Civil War. The volume was handed around in writing, copied, discussed, and to a greater or less extent appropriated spiritually. The strange fact is that it was not then printed, and still stays unborn in manuscript after nearly sixty years of waiting. Thus the creative book of the system was never put into English type, and has remained quite inaccessible to the English speaking student. This to my mind has been the chief fatality in the propagation of the work and its doctrines, for it always has had and always will have its distinctive appeal to certain minds and even to certain times.

[13] Stratton, "A Biographical Sketch," in Buckham and Stratton, *George Holmes Howison: Philosopher and Teacher:*
Pp. 49-50:

Within this larger body, however, was a company of the elect, called the Kant Club, of about twelve members, a club formed several years before Howison came; and at once he was taken into it. Its meetings, held on Sunday afternoon at the house of William T. Harris – who was later to be the leading American expositor of Hegel – were occupied with Hegel's *Phenomenology of Spirit*, in what was called an English translation – by courtesy, Howison said; for it could not rightly be regarded as English. The attempt at translation was in manuscript, made by Brockmeyer, a member of the club; and the precious writing was kept under lock and key in a tin box which offered some protection against theft and fire. When the club had as-

Harris took his work as instructor seriously. He copied in longhand the entire text of the *Larger Logic*. It filled three large notebooks,[14] which have

> sembled, the manuscript was brought out from its place of safety, and one of the members read from it aloud, while the rest listened.
>
> The club's tin box was important in another way. At one of the meetings, Harris said: "We are going to have a German philosophical magazine." Howison, surprised, asked who was to give the money for printing it. Harris replied: "We don't propose to print it. We are going to make the papers and read them here, and put them away in the tin box." Into the tin box, then, were poured not only Harris's first papers, later published as his *Contributions to Philosophy*, but also the papers by him and others which grew into the periodical, so honorable a pioneer in its field, The *Journal of Speculative Philosophy*.

Henry A. Pochmann, *New England Transcendentalism and St. Louis Hegelianism; Phases in the History of American Idealism.* Philadelphia: Carl Schurz Memorial Foundation, Inc., 1948. 144 pp.

P. 134, n. 98:

> There appears to be a good deal of confusion regarding whether the Philosophical Society grew out of the Kant Club or the Hegel Club, and whether the Kant Club is not the older of the two. The testimony is not conclusive, but what Harris specifically says in his preface to *Hegel's Logic* about his lectures before the Kant Club during 1877-1887 indicates that it outlived the Hegel Club, and that therefore it was the Hegel Club that became defunct in 1866 when it was merged with the newly organized Philosophical Society. See also D. H. Harris (ed.), *op. cit.*, [*A Brief Report* . . .] 89-93, and William Schuyler, *loc. cit.*, ["German Philosophy in St. Louis"] 82-83.

[14] When Harris was U.S. Commissioner of Education he published an extensive study under the title, *Hegel's Logic. A book on the Genesis of the Categories of the Mind. A Critical Exposition.* Chicago: S. C. Griggs and Company, 1890. 403 pp. He dedicated it as follows:

> To Henry C. Brockmeyer, with grateful recollections of assistance from him in the study of German philosophy, this book is with his permission dedicated.

Harris had written Brokmeyer on October 2, 1890 for the permission. In the preface, pp. v-xvi, to his book, Harris stated:

Pp. xi-xiii:

> In 1866 I for the first time read through Hegel's larger logic, reading it in the English translation that had been made for myself and two other friends (George Stedman and J. H. Watters), by Henry C. Brockmeyer, in 1859 and 1860. I copied the work entire from the manuscript and am sure I read every word of it. But I am equally sure that I did not understand at the most anything beyond the first part of the first volume and could not follow any of the discussions in the second and third volumes, or even remember the words from one page to another. It was all over my head, so to speak. I had of course made myself acquainted with the categories and sub-categories of the work years before through histories of philosophy, and was gradually learning to think something into them; but I could make little of Hegel's deductions or discussions of them. This experience of my own, which lasted for years, is I presume the experience of other students of Hegel and also of students of any system of deep philosophy. One has first to seize its general thought, its trend as a whole, and gradually descend to its details.
>
> The translation which I copied out still exists, but has never been printed, any portion of it. Mr. Brockmeyer, whose acquaintance I had made in 1858, is, and was even at that time, a thinker of the same order of mind as Hegel, and before reading Hegel, except the few pages of Hedge's *German Prose Writers*, had divined Hegel's chief ideas and the position of his system, and informed me on my first acquaintance with him in 1858 that Hegel was the great man among modern philosophers, and that his large logic was the work to get. I sent immediately to Germany for it and it arrived late in the year. Mr. Brockmeyer's deep insights and his poetic power of setting them forth with symbols and imagery furnished me and my friends of those early years all of our outside stimulus in the study of German philosophy. He im-

been lost. Several copies were made of it. The circumstances under which each was made are chapters of the story that recounts the influence of the St. Louis Hegelians.

Harris also began publication of *The Journal of Speculative Philosophy*, the first philosophical periodical in the English language. The first number appeared in January, 1867. It continued its quarterly appearance through 1887, then sporadically through four more numbers ending with that of December, 1893.[15]

II

In 1875 a manuscript of Brokmeyer's translation of the *larger Logic*, comprising twenty-seven sections in large folders, was sent by Harris to Samuel Hopkins Emery, Jr. (1840-1906), at Quincy, Illinois, in response to the latter's request. Miss Sally Williams copied all but the first two sections for him, and he returned the original to Harris in 1876. The letters detailing the transaction are in the archives of the Missouri Historical Society.[16]

The folders were probably three, corresponding to the three volumes which Harris had done in longhand in 1866. Emery had his copy bound in three volumes. The copy has not been located.

Emery had made a fortune in the Comstock Stove Foundry at Quincy. He retired and became interested in philosophy, largely through Harris

pressed us with the practicality of philosophy, inasmuch as he could flash into the questions of the day, or even into the questions of the moment, the highest insight of philosophy and solve their problems. Even the hunting of wild turkeys or squirrels was the occasion for the use of philosophy. Philosophy came to mean with us, therefore, the most practical of all species of knowledge. We used it to solve all problems connected with school-teaching and school management. We studied the "dialectic" of politics and political parties and understood how measures and men might be combined by its light. But our chief application of philosophy was to literature and art. Mr. Denton J. Snider, who entered our circle in 1866, has published his studies on Shakespeare, Goethe and Homer, and Mr. Brockmeyer has printed in the *Journal of Speculative Philosophy* his *Letters on Goethe's Faust*, and these will show sufficiently the spirit and methods of our studies in literature.

[15] Edward Leroy Schaub has an essay, "Harris and the Journal of Speculative Philosophy," pp. 49-67, in a book which he edited, entitled, *William Torrey Harris 1835-1935*. A Collection of Essays, including Papers and Addresses presented in Commemoration of Dr. Harris' Centennial of the St. Louis Meeting of the Western Division of the American Philosophical Society. Chicago: The Open Court Publishing Company, 1936. 136 pp. See the same article with the same title in *The Monist*, XLVI, i (January, 1936), 80-98. See also Frank Luther Mott, *A History of American Magazines, 1865-1885*. Cambridge, Mass.: Harvard University Press, 1957. "Journal of Speculative Philosophy," pp. 385-387.

[16] Included in the first installment of Miss Harris's gift to the Society in October, 1934. On Miss Williams' work as copyist see Paul Russell Anderson's report of personal conversation with her, in his *Platonism in the Midwest*. New York: Columbia University Press, 1963, pp. 146-147.

and *The Journal of Speculative Philosophy*. In the 1870s he started the Plato Club.

In 1879 Emery and his brother-in-law, Edward McClure, also wealthy and retired, went East to study law at Harvard Law School and to participate in the first year of Amos Bronson Alcott's (1799-1888) Concord School of Philosophy.[17] The Faculty at Concord included Emery from Quincy, Harris from St. Louis, Hiram K. Jones (1818-1903) from Jacksonville, Illinois, and Franklin Benjamin Sanborn (1831-1917) [18] from Springfield, Mass.

Emery and McClure took with them on their trip Emery's manuscript of the *Larger Logic*. William James (1842-1910) recorded his encounter of them and their three volumes at a little philosophical club which used to meet every fortnight at the rooms of Thomas Davidson (1840-1900) in Temple Street in Boston. James was mistaken as to the year – he said 1872 instead of 1879 – and he may have been mistaken about the meeting place, but there is no doubt about the identity of the "two young business men from Illinois." [19]

[17] The School ran through nine successive summer sessions from 1879 until the year of Alcott's death in 1888. The lectures for 1882 were published as:
Concord Lectures on Philosophy. Comprising outlines of all the lectures at the Concord Summer School of Philosophy in 1882, with an Historical sketch. Collected and arranged by Raymond L. Bridgman. Revised by the lecturers. Approved by the faculty.
   A. Bronson Alcott, Dean.
   S. H. Emery, Jr., Director.
   F. B. Sanborn, Secretary.
Cambridge, Mass.: Moses King, Publisher, 1883. [168 pp.]
The copy in the library of Illinois College, Jacksonville, Illinois, belonged to Dr. Hiram K. Jones. There is also in the library, under the title, *Concord School of Philosophy, Clippings, etc.*, Jones's collection of 81 pages of newspaper clippings on the subject, dating from July 14, 1879 to August 9, 1883 (?), pasted into a "Variety Scrap Book."
   The lectures for 1885 were issued by Franklin Benjamin Sanborn, editor, *The Life and Genius of Goethe; Lectures at the Concord School of Philosophy*. Boston: Ticknor and Company, 1886. 454 pp.
[18] Biographical details in *Dictionary of American Biography*, VIII-2, 326-327, *s.v.* "Sanborn, Franklin Benjamin (Dec. 15, 1831 – Feb. 24, 1917)," by George Harvey Genzmer. See also Sanborn *Recollections of Seventy Years* 2 volumes, Boston: R. G. Badger, 1909. Volume II: Literary Life.
[19] William James, "Thomas Davidson: A Knight-Errant of the Intellectual Life." First published in *McClure's Magazine* for May, 1905. Reprinted as Chapter V (pp. 73-103) of William James, *Memories and Studies*. London: Longsmans, Green, and Co., 1911. 411 pp.
Pp. 81-82:
   At that time [1873] I saw most of him [Thomas Davidson] at a little philosophical club which used to meet every fortnight at his room in Temple Street in Boston. Of the other members, J. Elliot Cabot and C. C. Everett, are now dead – I will not name the survivors. We never worked out harmonious conclusions. Davidson used to crack the whip of Aristotle over us; and I remember that, whatever topic was formally appointed for the day, we invariably wound up with a quarrel about space and space-perception. The Club had existed before Davidson's advent. The previous year we had gone over a good part of Hegel's larger Logic, under the

III

Dr. Hiram K. Jones, a physician of Jacksonville, Illinois, often came to Quincy, sometimes for weeks at a time, the guest of Matthew B. Denman, a land agent and man of means, and his wife, Sarah (1808-1882). The Denmans had come to Quincy from Philadelphia in 1842. Mrs. Denman was interested in philosophical studies.[20] In 1866 she, with the help of Emery, had founded the Friends in Council.

In March 1878 Emery wrote to Harris that Dr. Jones had been visiting at Quincy for a week and had become interested in Hegel. Subsequently Dr. Jones asked to have a complete transcription of Emery's manuscript of the *Larger Logic* made for him. Emery sent it to him a few months later. The copy, in a fine script and bound in three volumes, is in the library of Illinois College.[21] It is the second oldest manuscript of Brokmeyer's translation that has been located, the only extant copy that is complete. There is no indication in the manuscript who the scribe was, nor when the copy

self-constituted leadership of two young business men from Illinois, who had become enthusiastic Hegelians and, knowing almost no German, had actually possessed themselves of a manuscript translation of the entire three volumes of Logic, made by an extraordinary Pomeranian immigrant, named Brockmeyer. These disciples were leaving business for the law and studying at the Harvard law-school; but they saw the whole universe through Hegelian spectacles, and a more admirable *homo unius libri* than one of them, with his three big folios of Hegelian manuscript, I have never had the good fortune to know.

[20] Pochmann, *German Culture in America*, p. 657, n. 201:
Platonic studies in Jacksonville were reported in detail by Mrs. J. O. King to Mrs. [Sarah] Denman throughout the sixties and seventies. These notes, mainly exegetical of Plato's dialogues, were painstakingly copied by Mrs. Denman. Four volumes of these, covering the years from 1873 to 1879, all in Mrs. Denman's handwriting, still exist and afford ample evidence to show that the ladies of Quincy pursued their philosophical studies seriously.
The volumes are in the possession of the Friends in Council of Quincy, a women's club founded by Mrs. Denman in 1866 with the help and encouragement of Emery. Paul Russell Anderson described Mrs. Denman's notes in detail in his *Platonism in the Midwest*, pp. 135-137. See also his "Quincy, an Outpost of Philosophy," *Journal of the Illinois State Historical Society*, XXXIV, i (March, 1941), 51.
[21] Three volumes elegantly bound in red paper and brown half-leather, gilt title on spine: THE SCIENCE OF LOGIC – Hegel. Most Pages have a small stamp: DAYTON & ARTHUR, Quincy, III. Abstract Legel Cap. No. 16. There are 32 numbered lines to the page, *verso* pages numbered from the bottom. Vol. I, pp. 1-558; Vol. II, pp. 1-299; Vol. III, pp. 5-509.
The first volume agrees in its headings with those in script in the Harris shorthand version of 1861. By counting 4-2/3 pages of the volume to each page of the shorthand, one can immediately spot the place of the heading and expect to find it close by. The 29 pages of the shorthand end on the second line of page 135 of the first volume, with the word "limit." In the shorthand version the word "Grenze" is added in longhand. Both versions contain the "Remarks."
The three volumes of the Jones copy are no doubt a copy of a longhand version made from Harris's shorthand version. The most likely opinion is that the archetypal longhand is also Harris's.

was made. It was presumably made at Quincy, since the paper is from a Quincy firm, and Emery commissioned it.

The Plato Club of Jacksonville had been founded in 1865 and was active until Jones left for Concord in 1879. The American Akademe [22] was organized on July 2, 1883, along the lines of the Concord School of Philosophy, but for the winter months instead of summer. *The Journal of the American Akademe* began publication in 1884, with Alexander Wilder (1823-1908) as editor of the first four volumes, from October, 1884, to July, 1888. After an interruption of two years, two more volumes came out, with Miss Louise M. Fuller as editor. The *Journal* was discontinued with the June, 1892, issue.[23]

IV

About 1882 Meeds Tuthill made a transcript of the *Larger Logic* for the use of the Hegel Club of Chicago. The Club was organized about that time by Rev. Dr. Robert A. Holland, an Episcopalian and most distinguished clergyman of St. Louis. He had gone to Chicago the previous year and had written to Harris at Concord that he proposed "to remove the western headquarters of Hegelian study from St. Louis to Chicago." [24] His interest in the copy of the *Larger Logic* is almost a guarantee that it was taken from Harris's Longhand version. The copy has not been located.

About 1890 Brokmeyer began a revision of his translation of the *Larger Logic*. His letters to Harris are a long account of what he had in mind. He was inclined at one time to do away with Hegel's remarks, because they did not help the reader. Then he decided to add extensive notes of his own. He had his daughter type a clean copy of the revision, but she left it incomplete when she eloped in July, 1894. In a letter of November 26, 1895, he said that he had finished the revision. At the turn of the century, he was again busy with the *Phenomenology of the Spirit*, as letters of May 18, 1899 and February 8, 1902, among others, indicate. At his death in 1906 he was still not satisfied with his translations.[25]

Brokmeyer's son Eugene (-1951) told Henry A. Pochman that

---

[22] *Records of the American Akademe* are preserved in manuscript in the library of Illinois College.
[23] Pochman, *German Culture in America: Philosophical and Literary Influences, 1600-1900*, p. 656, nn. 195, 196.
[24] *Ibid.*, p. 655, n. 188.
[25] Denton Jaques Snider, in his autobiographical work, *A Writer of Books in his Genesis*. St. Louis: Sigma Publishing Co., [1910]. 668 pp., has a section (pp. 363-399) of Chapter Fourth, which is entitled, "IV Brockmeyer's Spiritual Genesis." In it he stated: Pp. 386-387:

when his father was asked on his deathbed what disposition was to be made of the manuscript, he replied,

Just leave it in the attic for the vermin; I have enjoyed every minute of my life devoted to it, in the hope that I might justify my existence by leaving something to posterity worth while, but apparently there is no demand for anything like that at this time.[26]

To honor his memory, his friends made renewed efforts between 1906 and 1909 to have the *Larger Logic* published. To this end they commissioned Louis James Blok (1851-1927) of Chicago to prepare the typescript for publication. He had not completed the work when Harris died in 1909. He worked at it sporadically again in the 1920s until his death in December, 1927.

Here it is in place to give some account of the mentioned philosophical transition of Brockmeyer, who was inclined not to own it, or, perchance, he was not fully conscious of it himself. It undoubtedly occurred through his thinking out and translating Hegel's *Logic* (large edition), about 1859-60. This book became to him, therefore, the greatest of all books, his very Bible; he would read it even during his political career, in order to recover his balance from the ups and downs of life, from the uncertain tetering of party power, and from the high tension of his very excitable emotional nature. It seemed to restore him to a calm endurance and serenity similar to the effect which Spinoza's *Ethics* had upon Goethe, as the latter has described it. And yet in a number of ways Hegel's *Logic* is the opposite of Brockmeyer in character; its passionless manner, wholly unromantic (therein differing from the same author's *Phenomenology*), but chiefly its colossal power of organizing thought, were not his creatively, even if they were his appreciatively. And yet that book was the anchor of his life, which he always flung into the sea of his soul at the height of its oceanic tempests. In his last days I found him reading it still, usually poring over his translation of it, with many retrospective reflections, one of which has stayed in my saddened memory on account of its melancholy implications of a lost career: "If I had my life to live over again, I would devote it exclusively to Hegel – to his explanation and propagation." Still I could never push him to the point of printing his dearest life-work, though he was at that time amply able to bear the expense. Snider, *The St. Louis Movement*, ten years later, stated: P. 13:
   Indeed one is inclined to think that this translation of Hegel's Logic has had a peculiar doom hanging over it from the moment of its first written line. I have watched it more than half a century, now rising to the surface, then sinking out of sight as if under some curse of the malevolent years. Personally I never used it, never needed it, I had the original and could read it more easily than Brockmeyer's English, which on the whole was very literal – so literal that I often had to turn back to the German, in order to understand the English. Here was supposed to be the first duty of the Philosophical Society: to revise and pay for publishing this central work; still we never seriously started. Harris might have printed it in his Journal, but for some reason or other which to this day remains conjectural, he would not. I found Brockmeyer re-translating the original on his return from the indians in the early nineties. And I saw him thumbing over the manuscript only a few days before his death in 1906. It was his one Supreme Book, his Bible; it meant to him more than any other human production, and was probably the source of his great spiritual transformation from social hostility and inner discord and even anarchism, to a reconciliation with his government and indeed with the World-Order, after his two maddened flights from civilization.
[26] *German Culture in America: Philosophical and Literary Influences, 1600-1900*, p. 648, n. 92.

A typed manuscript of the revised version is in the possession of the Missouri Historical Society.[27] It is the translation of all of volume I, and approximately two-thirds of volume II, or a little more than half of the entire *Logic*. The segment of volume II is the original of a carbon copy sent to Block at Chicago on June 10, 1909, except for some pages in carbon copy, the corresponding originals of which were presumably sent.

V

The attempts to publish the *Larger Logic* inevitably led to publishers in Europe.

Logan U. Reavis (1831-1889), manager of *The Inland Magazine*, stated in 1875, in the biographical edition of his *St. Louis, the Future Great City of the World*, that but for the failure of the publishing house

[27] The pages are unbound, in two folders. They are yellow paper, approximately 8-1/4″ x 13-3/4″, without watermark. Beginning with page (101) in the first folder and throughout the second folder, the paper is a cream colored stock of linen texture, approximately 8-1/2″ x 13″, without watermark. Typing is on one side of the page except for two lines on the *verso* of page (54) in the second folder.

Pages in the first folder are numbered (1) to (23) at the bottom center of the page. Then they are numbered (1) to (122) at the top center of the page; pages (2) to (7) of this series are missing.

Pages in the second folder are numbered (1) to (78) at the top center of the page. The heading of the material in the first folder is:

INTRODUCTION
GENERAL COMPREHENSION OF LOGIC

That of the material in the second:

(VOLUME SECOND)
ESSENCE IS THE TRUTH OF BEING

On a red-bordered identification label attached to the brown wrapping of the folder is typed:

HEGEL'S LARGER LOGIC - BROCKMEYER'S TRANSLATION

(Delivered 12/20/1926).

The following is written on a brown cardboard cover
Duplicate
Beginning of Vol. II
p. 1 - 78 -
other copy sent to L J B 6/10 09
[In another hand:]   139 pp. in Volume I
78 pp. in Volume II
April, 1940

The chief characteristics of the headings are that Hegel's 'Remarks' are missing, that the key words are sometimes in a different translation, occasionally a word which is given as an alternative in the Jones copy. For example: On page 4, line 23, of the typescript, "The semblance" is the heading; the corresponding heading in the Jones copy, page 7, line 7, is "The Appearance = (Schein Brockmeyer)." On page 21, line 9, of the typescript, the heading which caused Brockmeyer in the Jones copy to use "differentness" or "difference" as "verschiedenheit marked X," is rendered without comment as "diversity."

in London, Brokmeyer's translation would have formed part of Bohn's Classical Library.[28]

There is reference in a letter of Francis E. Cook to Cleon Forbes, December 11, 1928,[29] about a German publisher who was willing to accept Block's revision for publication, to be printed alongside the German text, but as it was about to go to press Block died (December, 1927) and the publisher terminated the project.

John Henry Muirhead (1855-1940), editor of the Library of Philosophy for the London publishing house of George Allen and Unwin, stated on the occasion of the publication of *Hegel's Science of Logic* in the translation of W. H. Johnston and L. G. Struthers in 1929, that he had also had the option of Brokmeyer's translation.[30]

In the typescript, page (1), lines 1 to 8, of the first folder:

HAGER'S [SIC] LOGIC

The science of logic, subdivides itself generally into
objective and subjective; but, more definitely, it has the three parts
1st. Logic of Being,
2nd. Logic of Essence,
3rd. Logic of the Comprehension

GENERAL SUBDIVISION OF BEING

In the Jones copy, page 38, lines 1 to 9, of volume I:
divided itself into subjective & objective Logic:
still more definitely it has the three parts:
I. The Logic of being
II. The Logic of Essence and
III. The Logic of comprehension
(Objective Logic)
First Book
The doctrine of Being.

The first sheaf of pages, (1) to (23), in the first folder of the typescript correspond to the Jones copy, volume I, pages 1-37. The second sheaf of pages, (1) to (122), correspond to the Jones copy, volume I, pages 38 to 558.

The pages, (1) to (78), in the second folder of the typescript correspond to the Jones copy, volume II, pages 1 to 183, approximately the 23rd line, a score of lines beyond the heading, "A. The law of appearance."

The typescript is undoubtedly the same translation, but in a revised version, with further revisions in pencil. Its probable date is 1894.

[28] A copy of the descriptive volume of Logan U. Reavis, *St. Louis: the Future Great City of the World*. Illustrated with a map. Second Edition. St. Louis: Published by order of the St. Louis Country Court, 1870. 136 pp., is in the Marquette University Library. The biographical edition did not appear until 1875. The reference to Brokmeyer's translation is on page 341.

[29] Published by Charles Milton Perry, editor, *The St. Louis Movement in Philosophy, Some Source Material*, p. 23. See also the letter of David H. Harris to Cleon Forbes, January, 1929, *ibid.*, p. 56.

[30] W. H. Johnston and L. G. Struthers, *Hegel's Science of Logic*. 2 vols., London: George Allen & Unwin, 1929. Muirhead's "Editor's Note" is in the first volume, pages 17-18, both in the London edition and in the edition published at New York by The Macmillan Company. It reads in its entirety as follows:
Pp. 17-18:
It may seem a matter of surprise that the "Larger Logic" which has been described

Muirhead wrote two articles on the spread of Hegelian studies. The first was entitled, "How Hegel came to England." [31] In the second, "How Hegel came to America," he invited Americans to subscribe for the publication of Brokmeyer's translation.[32]

The basic and incontrovertible fact is that in June, 1970, Brokmeyer's translation of Hegel's *Larger Logic* has not been published.

John O. Riedl
26 May 1970.

as the "Bible of Hegelianism" should now, for the first time, more than a century after its publication, be translated into English. It would seem to be a case of the good being the enemy of the better. In 1865 appeared J. Hutchinson Stirling's *Secret of Hegel* in which was included "a translation from the Complete Logic of the whole first section, Quality" and "a Summary of the second section, Quantity." This was followed in 1874 by William Wallace's translation of the "lesser Logic" of the *Encyclopaedia* with the accompanying *Prolegomena* republished in separate volumes in 1892 and 1894 respectively. With these present aids British students, unfamiliar with German, have hitherto been fain to be content. In America the history of the larger Logic has been different through up to the present time, so far as publication is concerned, without more fortunate result. So early as 1858 a group of scholars in St. Louis, Missouri, became acquainted with the book of which Henry C. Brockmeyer, a German who had come while quite a boy to America, executed unaided a complete translation into English. This was copied out by William T. Harris, subjected to revision by some of Brockmeyer's friends, and again before his death revised by Brockmeyer himself, but left by him unpublished.

Some years ago the Editor of the Library of Philosophy was approached by the surviving friends of Henry Brockmeyer with a view to the publication in that series of the translation which he had left. It was to be accompanied with a short biography of the translator, and to partake of the character of a tribute to his memory both as a philosopher and as Governor of the State of Missouri. As it seemed inappropriate to have a volume of this kind included in a series devoted to the pure study of philosophy, it was impossible to accept this offer, and as there seemed no immediate prospect of the American translation coming out, the Editor felt himself free to make an arrangement with the present translators for the publication of a work begun some years before by distinguished Cambridge scholars both of whom have since died. He wishes, however, to dissociate himself from any spirit of rivalry with the American translation. Each must stand on its own merits. Whatever Brockmeyer's may possess, its romantic history and the distinguished names with which it also is associated ought to assure it a welcome on this as well as on the other side of the Atlantic.

[31] *Mind*, XXXVI (October, 1927), 423-447.

[32] *Philosophical Review*, XXXVII, v (May, 1928), 226-240.

P. 236, n. 19:
The fortunes of this translation, which is still in manuscript, would alone be a romantic story. Snider, who was employed upon the revision of it, thought that "the catastrophe of the movement was its failure to make accessible to English readers at the pivotal time the creative book of its system" and that "what is true of St. Louis in this matter is true of the rest of the English-speaking world" (*op. cit.*, p. 327). A translation of the Larger *Logic* is at present being executed by a group of British scholars, but it would be an act of piety on the part of American idealists of whatever shade of opinion to subscribe for the publication of so interesting a relic. It is now in charge of Mr. D. H. Harris, brother of William Torry, in Los Angeles.

BIBLIOGRAPHICAL NOTE

I

For a list of the writings produced by persons in the St. Louis Movement, one would consult the bibliographies of the individual authors. Some help may be found in the following:

Anderson, Paul Russell, *Platonism in the Midwest*. New York: Columbia University Press, 1963. 216 pp. "Writings of Hiram K. Jones," pp. 203-204; "Writings of Thomas M. Johnson," pp. 205-207; published writings of Samuel H. Emery, Jr., pp. 142-145.

Bostwick, Arthur E., "List of Books Written by Denton J. Snider, Litt. D. With Annotations," *St. Louis Public Library Monthly Bulletin*, XXII, v (May, 1924), 102-108.

Buckham, John Wright (1864-1945) and Stratton, George Malcolm (1865-1957), *George Holmes Howison: Philosopher and Teacher*. A selection from his writings with a biographical sketch. Berkeley: University of California Press, 1934. 418 pp. "A list of Howison's published writings," pp. 381-387.

Evans, Henry Ridgely, "A list of the Writings of William Torrey Harris, Chronologically Arranged, with Subject Index, "*Report of the Commissioner of Education for 1907*. Washington, D.C.: United States Bureau of Education, 1908, Chapter II. Reprinted, with corrections and additions by the original compiler, in Charles Milton Perry, *The St. Louis Movement in Philosophy, Some Source Materials*. Norman: University of Oklahoma Press, 1930, pp. 96-148.

Jones, Marc Edmund, *George Sylvester Morris, His Philosophical Career and Theistic Idealism*. New York: Greenwood Press, Publishers, 1968. 430 pp. "The Published Writings of George Sylvester Morris," pp. 413-415; "The Morris Collection at the University of Michigan," p. 415.

Knight, William Angus (1836-1916), editor, *Memorials of Thomas Davidson, the Wandering Scholar*. Boston: Ginn and Company, 1907. 241 pp. "Appendix E: Bibliography of Thomas Davidson's Works," pp. 235-241.

Leidecker, Kurt Friedrich, *Yankee Teacher; the Life of William Torrey Harris*. New York: Philosophical Library, Inc. 1947. 648 pp. "Bibliographical Notes," pp. 619-646.

Perry, Charles Milton, *The St. Louis Movement in Philosophy, Some Source Materials*. Norman: University of Oklahoma Press, 1930. 151 pp. "Works of Members," pp. 84-96.

Wenley, Robert Mark (1861-1929), *The Life and Work of George Sylvester Morris; a Chapter in the History of American Thought in the Nineteenth Century*. New York: The Macmillan Company, 1917. 332 pp. "Writings of G. S. Morris," pp. xi-xv.

II

Early books on Hegel in America include the following, in the order of their first appearance.

Murdock, James (1776-1856), *Sketches of Modern Philosophy Especially Among the Germans*. Hartford: J. C. Wells, 1842. 201 pp. Chapter XI: Hegel's Philosophy, pp. 118-128.

Stallo, John Bernhard (1823-1900), *General Principles of the Philosophy of Nature, With an Outline of Some of Its Recent Developments among the Germans, Embracing the Philosophical Systems of Schelling and Hegel, and Oken's System of Nature.* Boston: W. Crosby and H. P. Nichols, 1848. 520 pp.

Harris, William Torrey (1835-1909), translator, *Hegel's First Principle: An Exposition of Comprehension and Idea (Begriff und Idee).* Accompanied with an Introduction of Explanatory Notes. St. Louis: Printed by G. Knapp and Co., 1869. 82 pp.

Bryant, William McKendree (1843-1909), translator, *The Philosophy of Art; being the Second Part of Hegel's Aesthetik, in which are unfolded historically the three great fundamental phases of the art-activity of the world.* Translated, and accompanied with an introductory essay giving an outline of the entire "Aesthetik." New York: D. Appleton and Company, 1879. 194 pp.

Harris, William Torrey. (1835-1909), *Hegel's Doctrine of Reflection, Being a Paraphrase and a Commentary Interpolated into the Text of the Second Volume of Hegel's Larger Logic, Treating of "Essence."* New York: D. Appleton and Co., 1881. 214 pp.

Kedney, John Steinfort (1819-1911), *Hegel's Aesthetics. A Critical Exposition.* Chicago: S. C. Griggs and Company, 1885. 302 pp.

Morris, George Sylvester (1840-1889), *Hegel's Philosophy of the State and History. An Exposition.* Chicago: S. C. Griggs and Company, 1887. 306 pp. Second Edition, 1892.

Harris, William Torrey (1835-1909), *Hegel's Logic. A Book on the Genesis of the Categories of the Mind. A Critical Exposition.* Chicago: S. C. Griggs and Company, 1890. 403 pp. Second Edition, 1895.

Sterrett, James Macbride (1847-1923), *Studies in Hegel's Philosophy of Religion, with a Chapter on Christian Unity in America.* New York: D. Appleton and Company, 1890. 348 pp.

Burt, Benjamin Chapman (1852-1915), translator, *G. W. F. Hegel's Theory of Right, Duties and Religion.* Translation, with a Supplementary Essay on Hegel's Systems of Ethics and Religion. Ann Arbor, Michigan: The Inland Press, 1892. 69 pp.

Sterrett, James Macbride (1847-1923), *The Ethics of Hegel; Translated Selections from his "Rechtsphilosophie."* With an Introduction. Boston: Ginn and Company, 1893. 216 pp.

Bryant, William McKendree (1843-1909), *Hegel's Educational Ideas.* Chicago: Werner School Book Company, 1896. 214 pp.

Hibben, John Grier (1861-1933), *Hegel's Logic; an Essay in Interpretation.* New York: C. Scribner's Sons. 1902. 313 pp.

Mackintosh, Robert (1858-1933), *Hegel and Hegelianism.* New York: Charles Scribner's Sons, 1903. 301 pp.

Snider, Denton Jacques (1841-1925), *Modern European Philosophy; The History of Modern Philosophy, Psychologically Treated.* St. Louis: Sigma Publishing Co., 1904. 829 pp. Several hundred pages on Hegel.

Adams, George Plimpton (1882-1961), *The Mystical Element in Hegel's Early Theological Writings.* Berkeley: The University Press, 1910. Pp. 67-102. University of California Publications in Philosophy, II, iv. (September 24, 1910).

Cunningham, Gustavus Watts (1881-   ). *Thought and Reality in Hegel's System.* New York: Longmans, Green, and Company, 1910. 151 pp. Cornell Studies in Philosophy, No. 8.

III

Chapters on the St. Louis Movement in some standard histories of American philosophy are useful to consult:

Muelder, Walter G., and Sears, Laurence, *The Development of American Philosophy: A Book of Readings.* Boston: Houghton Mifflin Company, [1940]. 533 pp. Part V: "Idealism from William T. Harris to James E. Creighton," pp. 217-233.

Riley, Isaac Woodbridge (1869-1933), *American Thought from Puritanism to Pragmatism and Beyond.* New York: Henry Holt and Company, 1915.
 . 438 pp. "Modern Idealism – 2. The St. Louis School: William T. Harris," pp. 240-253.

Schneider, Herbert W., *A History of American Philosophy.* Second edition, New York: Columbia University Press, 1963. 590 pp. "Idealistic Democracy," pp. 161-177, "Schools of Idealism," pp. 388-415.

Townsend, Harvey Gates, *Philosophical Ideas in the United States.* New York: American Book Company, 1934. 293 pp. "Chapter VIII: Philosophy in St. Louis," pp. 116-130.

van Becelaere, L., *La Philosophie en Amérique depuis les origines jusqu'à nos jours (1607-1900).* New York: The Eclectic Publishing Co., 1904. 180 pp. Pp. 98-109.

Werkmeister, William Henry, *A History of Philosophical Ideas in America.* New York: The Ronald Press Company, 1949. 599 pp. "Special Conditions at St. Louis – Brokmeyer," pp. 56-59; "Chapter 5, The St. Louis Movement," pp. 73-79.

IV

Following are what for the most part are "secondary" sources of information on the St. Louis Movement. Their common feature is that they are chronicles:

Anderson, Paul Russell, "Hiram K. Jones and Philosophy in Jacksonville," *Journal of the Illinois State Historical Society,* XXXIII, iv (December, 1940), 478-520.

Anderson, Paul Russell, "Quincy, an Outpost of Philosophy," *Journal of the Illinois State Historical Society,* XXXIV, i (March, 1941), 50-83.

Anderson, Paul Russell, *Platonism in the Midwest.* New York: Columbia University Press, 1963. 216 pp.

Dodson, George Rowland, "An Interpretation of the St. Louis Philosophical Movement," *Journal of Philosophy, Psychology. and Scientific Method,* VI (June 24, 1909), 337-345.

Dye, James Wayne, "Denton J. Snider's Interpretation of Hegel," *Modern Schoolman*, XLVII, ii (January, 1970), 153-167.

Easton, Loyd D., *Hegel's First American Followers; The Ohio Hegelians: John B. Stallo, Peter Kaufmann, Moncure Conway, and August Willich, with Key Writings*. Athens, Ohio: Ohio University Press, 1966. 353 pp. "The Later St. Louis Hegelians," pp. 15-19.

Forbes, Cleon, "The St. Louis School of Thought," *Missouri Historical Review*, XXV, i (October 1930), 83-101; ii (January, 1931), 289-303; iii (April, 1931), 461-473; iv (July, 1931), 609-623; XXVI, i (October, 1931), 68-77.

Harmon, Frances Adele (Bolles), *The Social Philosophy of the St. Louis Hegelians*. Thesis (Ph. D.), New York: Columbia University, 1943. 112 pp.

Harris, David H., editor, *A Brief Report of the Meeting Commemorative of the Early Saint Louis Movement in Philosophy, Psychology, Literature, Art and Education, In Honnor of Dr. Denton J. Snider's Eightieth Birthday, Held January 14th and 15th, 1921, At Vandervoort's Music Hall, St. Louis, Missouri*. With Centennial [of State of Missouri]. Appendix and Illustrations, pp. 164-254. [St. Louis]: D. H. Harris, [1921]. 254 pp. Some bibliographies give Los Angeles, 1922, as place and date of publication of what is presumably the same item.

Selected items

Block, Louis James, "The Philosophic Schools of St. Louis, Jacksonville, Concord and Chicago," pp. 13-28.

Harris, Mrs. David H., "The Early St. Louis Movement and the Communal University," pp. 31-47.

Snider, Mrs. Denton Jacques, "Henry C. Brockmeyer's Place in the St. Louis Movement," pp. 51-56.

Chubb, Percival, "Thomas Davidson," pp. 59-66.

Kroeger, E. R., "Adolph Ernst Kroeger," pp. 69-77.

Woerner, William F. "The Early St. Louis Movement, Some of the Early Leaders," pp. 81-86.

Cook, Francis E., "Reflections on the Early Movement," pp. 89-97.

Muirhead, John Henry, "How Hegel came to America," *Philosophical Review*, XXXVII, v (May, 1928), 226-240.

Muirhead, John Henry, *The Platonic Tradition in Anglo-Saxon Philosophy; Studies in the History of Idealism in England and America*. London: G. Allen and Unwin, Ltd., 1931. 446 pp. Part III, Chapter II: "Hegelianism in America," pp. 315-323. This chapter, together with the previous one, are a rearranged reprint, with a few changes, of "How Hegel Came to America."

Perry, Charles Milton, editor, *The St. Louis Movement in Philosophy, Some Source Material*. Norman: University of Oklahoma Press, 1930. 151 pp.

Perry, Charles Milton, "Unknown Quantities in the St. Louis Movement," *Internationale Zeitschrift für Erziehung*, IV (September, 10, 1935), 278-284.

Pochmann, Henry A., *New England Transcendentalism and St. Louis He-*

gelianism; Phases in the History of American Idealism. Philadelphia: Carl
Schurz Memorial Foundation, Inc., 1948. 144 pp.
Pochmann, Henry A., *German Culture in America: Philosophical and Li-
terary Influences, 1600-1900.* Madison: The University of Wisconsin Press,
1961. 865 pp. "The St. Louis Movement," pp. 257-294.
Scharf, J. Thomas, editor, *History of St. Louis, City and County,* from the
Earliest Periods to the Present Day including Biographical Sketches of
Representative Men. 2 vols. illustrated, Philadelphia: Louis H. Everts Co.,
1883.
    Chapter XXXVI: "Culture and Literary Growth in St. Louis," II,
1587-1617.
Schaub, Edward Leroy, editor, *William Torrey Harris 1835-1935.* A Collection of Essays, including Papers and Addresses presented in Commemoration of Dr. Harris' Centennial at the St. Louis Meeting of the Western Division of the American Philosophical Society. Chicago: The Open Court
Publishing Company, 1936. 136 pp.

Selected items

Dodson, George Rowland, "The St. Louis Philosophical Movement," pp.
19-27.
Perry, Charles Milton, "William Torrey Harris and the St. Louis Movement
in Philosophy," pp. 28-48.
Schaub, Edward Leroy, "Harris and the Journal of Speculative Philosophy,"
pp. 49-67.
Townsend, Harvey Gates, "The Political Philosophy of Hegel in a Frontier
Society," pp. 68-80.
Leidecker, Kurt Friedrich, "Harris and Indian Philosophy," pp. 81-122.
N.B.: All these articles, except the first, appear also in *The Monist,* XLVI,
i (January, 1936), 80-153.
Schuyler, William, "German Philosophy in St. Louis," *Bulletin of the Wash-
ington University Association,* no. 2 (April 23, 1904), 62-89.
Schuyler, William, "The St. Louis Philosophical Movement," *Educational
Review,* XXIX, (May, 1905), 450-467. A reprint, "with slight changes,"
of his article entitled, "German Philosophy in St. Louis."
Snider, Denton Jaques, *A Writer of Books in his Genesis.* St. Louis: Sigma
Publishing Co., [1910]. 668 pp.
Snider, Denton Jaques, *The St. Louis Movement in Philosophy, Literature,
Education, Psychology, with Chapters of Autobiography.* St. Louis: Sigma
Publishing Company, [1920]. 608 pp.
Whiting, Lillian, "A Group of St. Louis Idealists," *Theosophical Path,* VII,
v (November, 1914), 356-362. With portrait.

IDEAS AND IDEAL

Nathan Rotenstreich

The broad definition of the idea in Kant's view reads as follows: "I understand by idea a necessary concept of reason to which no corresponding (*kongruierendes*) object can be given in sense-experience (in den Sinnen)." [1] To what extent is the idea a necessary concept of reason? The answer seems to lie in the essence of reason which itself is a system.[2] Since reason is a system, ideas embody its systematic essence. Yet there is no meeting between the system and its ideas, that is to say, between reason and its ideas on the one hand and objects congruous with them and encountered in sensibility on the other. Since there is no correspondence to ideas on the level of sensibility, we are left with concepts only. Thus ideas are but categories extended to the unconditioned,[3] that is to say, categories extended up to the modes of absolute completeness.[4] "The *unconditioned* is always contained in the *absolute totality of the series*." [5] Unconditioned or absolute totality amounts to allness (*omnitudo*) of the reality which is completely determined.[6]

Reason in its systematic essence applies in turn to three relations:

1) the relation to the thinking subject; 2) the relation to the manifold of experiences as objects in the scope of appearances; 3) the relation to all things in general. To some extent it could be said that the third relation is the idea *par excellence*, since it denotes the absolute unity of the conditions of all objects of thought in general. Kant himself designates the third kind of idea as containing "the highest condition," or else as having as its object the being of all beings. Traditionally, it is the knowledge of

---

[1] *Kritik der reinen Vernunft*, B. 384, p. 383; (Kemp-Smith's translation, p. 318). The following references to the *Kritik* will be given by numbers: the first number refers to the "B" edition, the second number to Kemp-Smith's translation.

[2] 766, 592.

[3] 436, 386.

[4] 443, 390.

[5] 444, 391.

[6] 656, 523.

God, or *theologia transcendentalis*.[7] Taking the clue from Kant's presentation of the third category as a kind of synthesis of the two in their respective groups, we may say that the third idea is a kind of synthesis of the two preceding ideas, i.e. the soul and the world, and is thus what we suggested before – the idea *par excellence*; eventually it relates both to the thinking subject and to the sum-total of appearances. This gives the third idea immediately a sort of comprehensive, universal or, let us say, pantheistic nuance. Kant understands pantheism as a conception comprehending the whole of the world as one all-embracing substance, or else viewing the universe as inhering in one subsisting subject as the primary being (*Urwesen*).[8] The third idea occupying this paradigmatic status as an idea has a name of its own: it is an ideal. Our task in the understanding of the view before us, as well as of its traces in Hegel, will be to deal with the details of the notion of ideal.

Speaking about ideas in Plato's sense, Kant says that they are archetypes of the things themselves, and not in the manner categories are keys to possible experiences.[9] Kant uses in this context the German word *Urbild* which is the German rendering of the term *Original*. To be sure, Kant also uses the term *Archetypus*. It is our contention that precisely with reference to the third idea as ideal, Kant retains the Platonic innuendo of *Urbild*, though he does not apply that aspect of the Platonic idea to the two other preceding ideas – of the soul and the world. In the light of the idea of God we view all objects *as if* they drew their origin from such an archetype.[10] The ideal is the *Urbild* of all things which are copies (*ectypa*). They derive from it the material of their possibility; while approximating to it in varying degrees, they always fall short of actually attaining it.[11]

To be sure, Kant carries over the notion of excellence relating to Plato's concept of idea and combines it with the notion of ideas as amounting to a content or to an entity conceived as perfect, supreme or excellent. Ideas, which are in the medieval sense *idealiter in intellectu* become in the modern sense, at least in so far as the term refers to the idea of God, *Urbilder* or *Musterbilder*. The combination of the idea and ideal, expressed in the "ideal" proper, bestows upon the concept of ideal in Kant its particular status. This brings also into prominence its cognitive shortcoming as being only an *Urbild* or *Musterbild* to be copied, but not actually be-

[7] 391, 323.
[8] *Kritik der Urteilskraft*, § 81, § 85.
[9] 370, 311.
[10] 701, 551.
[11] 606, 492; cf. 679, 486.

ing the comprehensive reality. The definition of the ideal is the comprehensive reality, while the function of the ideal is to be a *Musterbild* only of reality. The chasm between the definition and the function has to be investigated now, since it is Hegel's attempt to overcome that chasm.

(2) Kant sometimes uses the word "ideal" in a broad or vague sense as an exemplary content or as an *Urbild* in the sense of excellence. Thus, to adduce only two examples: he speaks about ideals of sensibility, in as much as they are viewed as models, not to be realizable, of possible empirical intuitions.[12] *Mutatis mutandis* he speaks of an ideal of a philosopher, who would personify philosophy as a world concept.[13] Similarly he speaks of the ideal of the human image expressing itself in morality.[14]

In spite of this diffuse employment of the concept of ideal, that very concept has a terminological connotation in Kant's doctrine. To be sure, the nuance of excellence as such is retained in that terminological application: "... the *ideal* seems to be further removed from objective reality even than the idea." [15] Still, Kant goes beyond this aspect of the concept "ideal."

"Reason, in its ideal, aims ... at complete determination in accordance with *a priori* rules. Accordingly it thinks for itself an object which it regards as being completely determinable in accordance with principles." [16] Complete determination is possible only when the to-be-determined thing is placed within the scope of all the possible predicates. Out of that whole we select the respective predicates attributed to a certain limited thing, and negatively – while attributing that predicate we exclude or negate other predicates. The ideal as the system is that totality of the determinations or predicates, from which particular determinations are picked out. The totality precedes here the particularity, or else complete knowledge is achieved when our predications take place against the totality of predicates known, attributed and, by the very same token, excluded. The cognitive ideal as knowledge in its excellence is based on the Spinozian notion of *omnis determinatio est negatio*. To achieve this cognitive ideal presupposes the ideal as a totality of determinations; that totality in turn amounts to the sum-total of predicates.[17] It is in this sense that an ideal cognition starts off from possibility and proceeds to reality, thus overstepping empirical knowledge which, by definition, starts off from data

---

[12] 598, 487.
[13] 866-867, 657-658.
[14] *Kritik der Urteilskraft*, § 17.
[15] 596, 485.
[16] 599, 487.
[17] 600, 488.

and cognizes the data in relations. Understanding is of data, and categories are unifying functions of data; reason is of possibilities, and ideas are principles of knowing those possibilities. The ideal on the pole of cognition is the knowledge of the possibilities, while the ideal on the pole of the contents to be known is the totality of possibilities.

Yet Kant employs an additional description of the precedence of the totality of predicates over any particular and determinate predicate attributed to a thing. He speaks of the material (*Materie*) for all possibility [18] and further: "Reason employs in the complete determination of things a transcendental substrate that contains, as it were, the whole store of material, from which all possible predicates of things must be taken." [19] It is precisely this aspect of the store, substrate or material which leads Kant to assess the concept of the ideal as *omnitudo realitatis*, as being self-enclosed: "an individual object which is completely determined through the mere idea," [20] "the idea, not merely *in concreto*, but *in individuo*, that is, as an individual (*einzelnes*) thing, determinable or even determined by the idea alone." [21]

It is the suggestion of the present paper that Kant oscillates in his exploration – and regulative justification – of the concept of the ideal between two views. The one (a) could be coined the holistic view of the ideal, the ideal being the whole of predicates and possibilities, and thus serving as the formal and material pre-supposition of all propositions. This is so since "all negations . . . are merely limitations of a greater and ultimately of the highest reality." [22] As against this, the ideal has a connotation (b) of a substrate and not of a totality. A substrate is only one layer of the sum-total of reality in the sense usually employed by Kant – as the constant element. Substrate in this sense applies to space and time, to substance as the substrate of that which is real, to all change etc. The conclusion to be drawn from this is that Kant identifies the ideal with substance *qua* ultimate reality. Yet he understands substance as both a totality and as a substrate. He takes over Spinoza's view of substance and still retains the pre-Spinozian view of substance as *hypokeimenon*, or even as the bearer lacking any determination whatsoever.

There is an interesting parallelism in Kant's doctrine between the position of the ideal as the totality of reality, predicates, determinations and possibilities preceding any particulars and the position of the pure intui-

[18] 600, 488.
[19] 603, 490.
[20] 602, 489.
[21] 596, 485.
[22] 606, 492.

tions (*Anschauungen*), i.e. space and time. About space Kant says that it
is represented as an infinite *given* magnitude. Space contains the infinite
number of different possible representations within itself and not under
itself. This comprehensive as opposed to the subordinating character of
space provides for its essence as an *Anschauung* and not as a concept.
As to time, Kant is even more outspoken: "The infinitude of time signifies nothing more than that every determinate magnitude of time is possible only through the limitations of one single time that underlies it." [23]
The holistic character of both space and time emerges clearly from Kant's
presentation. It follows from this that the ideal is on the level of reason,
looked at from the angle of the structure of the relations pertaining between the whole and the parts, what space and time as pure intuitions
are on the level of sensibility or intuition. And again: *vis-à-vis* both space
and time Kant uses not only the holistic language but also the terminology
of the substrate already indicated in the above quotation referring to time
as "underlying" and not only as containing or comprehending. And more
specifically, he speaks about time as a substrate, as the permanent form
of inner intuition,[24] and similarly about space which, as the universal
form of intuition, must be the substrate of all intuitions.[25] Be it as it may,
the ideal and space and time are totalities and just the same substrata.
Kant seems not to be aware of the difference between the two conceptions
or languages – that of "totality" and that of "substrate." To be sure, space
and time are not real totalities, while the ideal is projected as the reality;
space and time are partial wholes, while the ideal is the comprehensive
whole. Space and time are wholes of intuition while the ideal is the whole
of predicates in the conceptual sense of the term. Yet in all these cases,
in spite of the architectonic and topological differences between the levels
of the respective concepts, we may say: wherever Kant employs a concept
which is an ultimate concept in a limited sense or *in toto*, he renders the
concepts as wholes or as totalities and simultaneously applies to these concepts the model of substrate as well.

   This affinity between the structure of space and time and that of the
ideal as a totality may point eventually to the notion that the ideal can be
grasped by a kind of *Anschauung* (intuition) called by Kant *intellectuelle
Anschauung*, that mode of *Anschauung* whose feature is: that it can itself
give the existence of its object. It is a mode of intuition which can belong

[23] 40, 69-70; 48, 75.
[24] 224, 213.
[25] Prolegomena, § 38.

only to the primordial being (*Urwesen*).[25a] This would eventually mean that the type of knowledge characteristic of space and time as pure intuitions applies to the sum-total of predicates and to the *ens realissimum*; though clearly the type is understood in its structure and not in its articulation with reference to sensibility, where precisely space and time are pure intuitions of a sensible and not of an intellectual character.

One of the possible reasons for Kant's oscillation between the holistic interpretation of the ideal and its interpretation as a substrate might be related to the theological meaning bestowed on the ideal. "The concept of such a being is the concept of *God*, taken in the transcendental sense; and the ideal of pure reason is . . . the object of a transcendental *theology*." [26] Since the concept pertains to God, Kant eventually hesitates whether to give God a complete pantheistic interpretation as the totality of reality or an interpretation as a – or the – condition of a reality in terms of a substance separated from the world. To indicate this aspect of separation he possibly employs the term "substrate" which as such denotes separation and not unity. In *"Der einzig mögliche Beweisgrund zu einer Demonstration des Daseins Gottes"* he uses the expression: I am from eternity to eternity, outside me there is nothing, but in so far as it is through me.[27] This expression can be rendered pantheistically as well as theistically. Thus, if this conjecture is plausible, Kant's terminology and phenomenology or description of the concept of ideal has two aspects, the holistic and the substantive one, and the two did not find their adequate synthesis in his presentation. As we shall see, the aspect of substrate is viewed as totally overcome or sublated by Hegel. Hegel's idea is Kant's ideal in its pure version as totality. We move now to the exploration of Hegel's notion of idea, in so far as it is related to Kant's notion of ideal.[28]

(3) Up to this point we deliberately did not address our analysis to the issue which to some extent is deemed central by Kant himself, that is to say the validity of the ideas in general in knowledge and the validity of the ideal in particular in the context of knowledge.

There is no need to dwell on the known facts: there is no corresponding object to the ideas. Ideas are mere creatures of reason.[29] Since ideas do not apply to objects, they apply only to the systematic unity of the mani-

---

[25a] 72, 90. See on Kant the present author's "Bergson and the Transformations of the Notion of Intuition," *Journal of the History of Philosophy*, 1971.

[26] 608, 493.

[27] incl.: *I. Kant's kleinere Schriften zur Ethik und Religionsphilosophie*. Ed. J. H. V. Kirchmann, Zweite Abteilung, Leipzig, (n.d.) p. 114.

[28] On Kant's Dialectic consult the present author's: *Experience and its Systematization, Studies in Kant*, (The Hague, 1965), pp. 59 ff.

[29] 507, 432.

fold of empirical knowledge.[30] Ideas point only to the *continuation* of a possible experience. This validity is called by Kant regulative validity; applied to the idea of God or to the ideal, it is regulative, since it formulates the command of reason, that all connection in the world be viewed in accordance with the principle of a systematic unity.[31] The regulative validity amounts to the regulation of knowledge in its progressive moves.

The meaning of the description seems to be the following one: knowledge proper is concerned with data to be comprehended in relations as established through the functions of understanding, i.e. through the categories and principles. Knowledge, that is to say, empirical knowledge cannot place predicates selected out of the totality of predicates and comprehend things as a limited combination of predicates viewed against their whole. The replacement of relations with predicates is the ideal of knowledge *qua Musterbild* of knowledge, but every empirical knowledge fails to materialize that ideal and essentially falls short of ideal. As long as there is the distinction between data and predicates, or data encountered and predicates selected, the dichotomy between knowledge and the ideal of knowledge is bound to stay. Not to see the ideal character of the ideal – and this to be sure, is here a deliberate play on words – is to make the ideal into a reality. "The ideal . . . is first realized, that is, made into an object, then *hypostatized*, and finally . . . personified." [32] "The concept of the *ens realissimum* is, therefore, the only concept through which a necessary being can be thought. In other words, a supreme being necessarily exists." [33] To hypostatise is to take what exists merely in thought as a real object, existing in the same character outside the thinking subject.[34]

In Kant the identity of reason and reality is a postulate and not an ultimate fact. Hence Hegel took over from Kant the phenomenology of the ideal as the cognitive ideal and by the same token its status as *ens realissimum* and totality. But Hegel takes totality to be actuality proper and criticizes Kant for calling it a regulative principle only, or else considering the ideal as a reality to be a hypostatic entity, and not the real and concrete actuality.

(4) There are obvious differences between Kant's and Hegel's notions of idea. The differences lie mainly in the fact that Hegel abolishes the

---

[30] 699, 550.
[31] 714, 599.
[32] 612, 495; note.
[33] 634, 509.
[34] *Critique of Pure Reason, A* edition, pp. 384-385; Kemp-Smith's translation, p. 395.

distinction between the regulative and the constitutive validity and considers idea to be the totality even beyond the notion of constitutive validity. After all, the constitutive validity in Kant is the validity of concepts *vis-à-vis* data; for Hegel the idea is not the application, be it constitutive in terms of data, or of concepts, but the unification of the subjective and the objective.[35] This difference between Hegel and Kant is expressed in Hegel's criticism of Kant's theory of ideas. In Kant, says Hegel, we encounter the complete emptiness of subjectivity, or the purity of the infinite concept.[36]

The additional point to be mentioned in this context is the following: in Hegel there is *the Idea* and not ideas, as Kant has it – the psychological idea, the cosmological idea and finally the theological idea *qua* ideal in the sense explored before. To be sure, Hegel has the ethical idea etc., but these are embodiments of the idea proper in the process of evolvement of Reason and Spirit. These do not connote partial totalities, since in Hegel there is only one evolving totality gaining in articulation. There is a continuum of wholes and not a coexistence of wholes as Kant has it.[37]

Yet Hegel takes advantage of the terminological distinction between ideas and the ideal; he, too, considers the ideal to be the idea *par exellence*, at least he does so in his early presentation. The ideal, says he, is the idea looked at from the side of existence, but as such conforming with the concept. It is, therefore, the actual in its highest truth. The expression "idea" connotes more the true looked at from the side of the concept.[38] Ideal applies to God as the substantiality or the identical and concrete essence of both nature and spirit.[39]

This is clearly the Kantian terminology transplanted to the plateau of Hegel's doctrine. Hegel retains that terminology in spite of the differences in the conception of Reason (*Vernunft*). For Kant, Reason is mainly the faculty which secures the unity of the rules of understanding under principles.[40] The unity is the unity of principles, and not the unity of Reason and actuality. The assertion of the unity or identity of Reason and actuality amounts in Kant to a hypostatic attitude. For Hegel, Reason is the highest unification of consciousness and self-consciousness, or of

---

[35] Hegel: *Sämtliche Werke* (to be quoted *S.W.*). Ed. Glockner, Stuttgart, Vol. III, p. 116.
[36] *S.W.* I, pp. 326-327.
[37] The view of Hegel as to the distinction between Reason-Idea-Spirit is elaborated by the present author in his forthcoming book: *From Substance to Subject: Studies in Hegel*.
[38] *S.W.* III, p. 163.
[39] *S.W.* VI, p. 302.
[40] 359, 303.
[41] *S.W.* III, pp. 111, 112.

knowledge of an object and knowledge of itself.[41] Where there is identity there can be no hypostasis – this is the first conclusion to be derived from the comparison between Kant and Hegel on the issue of ideas or ideal.

The suggested conjecture about the basic difference between Kant's and Hegel's respective evaluation of ideas put forward here might be summed up in two points:

a. The knowledge about the absolute, says Hegel, is itself absolute.[42] The definition of the absolute is pertinent in this context: the identity of identity and non-identity. This would mean that knowledge as an act and knowledge as grasping of contents are embraced in the scope of the identity and non-identity; there is no room for the assumption of the separation between the knowing subject and the known object. Hence there is no room for what Kant calls "subreption," subreption being the hypostatized consciousness (*apperceptionis substantiatae*).[43] Thus, while Kant clings to a referential view of knowledge, Hegel takes the view that knowledge is a progressive identification of the subject and the object. Kant takes the view that knowledge is the unification of data, while Hegel holds that knowledge is the growing identity of the subject and object, the identity accomplished on the part of the subject.

b. Related to this point is that of the locus of dialectic in the two respective systems. The dialectical illusion in Kant arises from our applying to appearances the idea of absolute totality which holds only as a condition of things in themselves.[44] Again, dialectic is rooted in a kind of subreption, which in this case is perhaps not a hypostasis proper, but still a categorial misplacement, or a kind of categorial mistake. As against this confinement of dialectic to the level of ideas proper, Hegel – criticizing Kant – says explicitly: ". . . the antinomies are not confined to the four special objects taken from cosmology; they appear in all objects of every kind, in all conceptions, notions and Ideas. To be aware of this, and to know objects in this property of theirs, makes a vital part in a philosophical theory . . . true and positive meaning of the antinomies is this: that every actual thing involves a coexistence of opposed elements." [45] The totality as the whole of determinations emerges out of the coexistence of determinations, whereby that coexistence appears as one comprising opposite elements. Here, too, the totality as embodied in the ideal emerges out of previously

---

[42] *S.W.* III, p. 97.
[43] *Critique*, edition A, p. 402 (Kemp-Smith's translation p. 365).
[44] 534, 448.
[45] *Encyclopädie der philosophischen Wissenschaften* 48. The English rendering here is from William Wallace's translation: *The Logic of Hegel*, Oxford, 1939.

established and evolving totalities in Hegel, and is not a leap, or a projection, as is the case in Kant.

Having said this, we still have to maintain the view that the concept of totality as characteristic of Reason is the Kantian legacy inherited by Hegel. Hegel transplants Spinoza's concept of substance to the realm of Reason as established by Kant. The ideal, which in Kant still retains the aspect of a *Musterbild* only, is or becomes actual in Hegel. Thus Hegel moves beyond the distinction between the constitutive and the regulative validity. Totality is more than constitutive, since it no longer holds a functional position. Totality is actuality. Hegel tries to make the Kantian notion of ideal into an actuality. The ideal ceases to be an unattainable. Kant's notion of the idea and, along with that, of the ideal is of a projective character. Hegel's notion of the idea is of an accumulative character. This is expressed, with reference to the move from the particular to the universal pertaining to national minds, as follows: "Their deeds and destinies in their reciprocal relations to one another are the dialectic of these minds, and out of it arises the universal mind, the mind of the world, free from all restriction, producing itself as that which exercises its right. . . . [46] What applies to the rhythm of the emergence of the universal mind out of particular minds applies to the totality in general: it emerges by way of a dialectical continuity out of the finite and particular facets, overcoming them, though retaining them. To this we refer as an accumulation, as against projection applied to Kant.

[46] *Hegel's Philosophy of Right,* Translated with Notes by T. M. Knox, Oxford, 1942, § 340 pp. 215-216.

HEGEL: A BIBLIOGRAPHY OF BOOKS IN ENGLISH, ARRANGED CHRONOLOGICALLY

Frederick G. Weiss

It seems appropriate to find in the published proceedings of a major symposium on The Legacy of Hegel, held in America, and commemorating and celebrating, respectively, his birth and rebirth, a survey of the chief products of Hegelian scholarship which are or have been available in English.

This listing includes books in English by and about Hegel, translations of works into English originally published in other languages, and books which contain or refer to "Hegel" in the title, or which, in the text, substantially and/or originally treat of Hegel's philosophy. It does not include histories of philosophy, or texts containing readings from various philosophers including Hegel. Nor does it list histories of special branches of philosophy which refer to Hegel (such as Bosanquet's *A History of Aesthetic*), or books (such as Findlay's *Language, Mind and Value*) which contain a single article on Hegel previously read at a society meeting or published in a journal.

Numbers of pages in most cases are inclusive of such things as Index and Bibliography when these have page numbers. Full names have for the most part been given, and various editions and reprints are also listed.

1971   Buckley, Michael J., *Motion and Motion's God: Thematic Variations in Aristotle, Cicero, Newton, and Hegel*. Princeton: Princeton University Press, 1971. viii, 287 pp.

Clark, M., *Logic and System. A Study of the Transition from "Vorstellung" to Thought in the Philosophy of Hegel*. The Hague: Martinus Nijhoff, 1971. xiii, 213 pp.

Harris, H. S., *Hegel's Development: Toward the Sunlight (1770-1801)*. Oxford: Oxford University Press, 1971. 550 pp.

Hegel's Philosophy of Mind, being Part Three of the *Encyclopedia of the Philosophical Sciences* (1830), translated by William Wallace, together with the *Zusätze* in Boumann's text (1845), translated by A. V. Miller, with Foreword by J. N. Findlay, F. B. A. Oxford: At the Clarendon Press, 1971. xix, 320 pp.

Lauer, Quentin, *Hegel's Idea of Philosophy*. New York: Fordham University Press, 1971. x, 159 pp.

Pelczynski, Zbigniew A., ed. *Hegel's Political Philosophy: Problems and Perspectives*. Cambridge: At the University Press, 1971. viii, 246 pp.

Steinkraus, Warren E., ed. *New Studies in Hegel's Philosophy*. New York: Holt, Rinehart and Winston, Inc., 1971. vi, 280 pp.

1970   Brazill, William J. *The Young Hegelians.* New Haven and London: Yale University Press, 1970. 305 pp., Bibliographical Essay, Index.

Christensen, Darrel Elvyn, ed. *Hegel and the Philosophy of Religion: The Wofford Symposium.* The Hague: Martinus Nijhoff, 1970. xviii, 300 pp., Index.

Findlay, J. N., *Ascent to the Absolute* (Muirhead Library of Philosophy). London: George Allen & Unwin/New York: Humanities Press, 1970. 271 pp.

Gray, Jesse Glenn, ed. *G. W. F. Hegel On Art, Religion, Philosophy: Introductory Lectures to the Realm of Absolute Spirit,* with an Introduction by the editor titled "Hegel's Understanding of Absolute Spirit." New York: Harper & Row (Harper Torchbooks), 1970. 324 pp., Index.

Hegel's Philosophy of Nature, being Part II of the *Encyclopaedia of the Philosophical Sciences* (1830), translated from Nicolin and Pöggeler's editions (1959), and from the *Zusätze* in Michelet's text (1847), by Arnold Vincent Miller, with Foreword by John Niemeyer Findlay. Oxford: Clarendon Press, 1970. xxv, 450 pp., Index.

Hegel's Philosophy of Nature, edited and translated with an Introduction and explanatory Notes by Michael John Petry. 3 volumes, the first containing Petry's Introduction, Michelet's Foreword (1841), and Hegel's *Mechanics*; vol. 2 *Physics*; vol. 3 *Organics.* London: Allen & Unwin/New York: Humanities Press, 1970. Each volume indexed.

Heidegger, Martin. *Hegel's Concept of Experience,* with a section from Hegel's *Phenomenology of Spirit* in the Kenley Royce Dove translation. New York: Harper & Row/Toronto: Fitzhenry & Whiteside Limited, 1970. 155 pp.

Kaufmann, Walter Arnold, ed. *Hegel's Political Philosophy.* New York: Atherton Press, 1970. 179 pp., Index, Bibliography.

Marx, Karl, *Critique of Hegel's "Philosophy of Right."* Translated by Annette Jolin and Joseph O'Malley, edited with Introduction and Notes by Joseph O'Malley (Cambridge Studies in the History and Theory of Politics). Cambridge: At the University Press, 1970. lxvii, 151 pp.

1969   *Hegel's Science of Logic,* translated [from Lasson's 1923 edition of the *Wissenschaft der Logik*] by Arnold Vincent Miller, with Foreword by John Niemeyer Findlay. London: George Allen & Unwin/New York: Humanities Press, 1969. 844 pp.

Hyppolite, Jean. *Studies on Marx and Hegel,* translated [from *Etudes sur Marx et Hegel,* 1955], with an Introduction "Hegel and Marx on History as Human History," Notes and Bibliography, by John O'Neill. New York: Basic Books, 1969. xxii, 202 pp., Index.

Kelly, George Armstrong. *Idealism, Politics and History: Sources of Hegelian Thought.* Cambridge: Cambridge University Press, 1969. x, 387 pp., Bibliography, Index.

Kojève, Alexandre. *Introduction to the Reading of Hegel, Lectures on the Phenomenology of Spirit Assembled by Raymond Oueneau,* ed. by Allen Bloom; translation (abridged) from the French [2nd edition, 1947, of Kojève's *Introduction à la lecture de Hegel*] by James H. Nichols, Jr. New York: Basic Books, 1969. xiv, 287 pp., including Kojève's Appendix "The Structure of the *Phenomenology of Spirit*," trans. by Kenley and Christa Dove.

McLellan, David. *The Young Hegelians and Karl Marx.* London: Macmillan/New York: F. A. Praeger, 1969. ix, 170 pp., Index.

Soll, Ivan. *An Introduction to Hegel's Metaphysics*, with Foreword by Walter Kaufmann. Chicago: The University of Chicago Press, 1969. xvii, 160 pp., Index, Bibliography, Appendix.

Walsh, William Henry. *Hegelian Ethics.* New York: St. Martin's Press/London: Macmillan, 1969. 84 pp., Bibliography, Notes.

Weiss, Frederick Gustav. *Hegel's Critique of Aristotle's Philosophy of Mind.* Foreword by G. R. G. Mure. The Hague: Martinus Nijhoff, 1969. xxviii, 56 pp., Bibliography.

1968   Mehta, Vrajendra Raj. *Hegel and the Modern State: An Introduction to Hegel's Political Thought.* New Delhi: Associated Publishing House, 1968. 144 pp., Bibliography, Index.

Mueller, Gustav Emil. *Hegel: The Man, His Vision and Work.* [English version of *Hegel: Denkgeschichte eines Lebendigen* (Bern: A. Francke Verlag, 1959,] New York: Pageant Press, Inc., 1968. 451 pp., Appendix (listing Hegel's *Sämtliche Werke*, Stuttgart, hrsg. Glockner), Bibliography, Index.

Wiedmann, Franz. *Hegel: An Illustrated Biography*, translated from the German by Joachim Neugroschel. New York: Pegasus, 1968. 140 pp., Chronology, Notes, Bibliography, Index.

1967   Fackenheim, Emil L. *The Religious Dimension in Hegel's Thought.* Bloomington and London: Indiana University Press, 1967. xiii, 274 pp., Index.

1966   Dupré, Louis. *The Philosophical Foundations of Marxism.* New York: Harcourt, Brace & World, 1966. xiv, 240 pp., Index.

Easton, Loyd David. *Hegel's First American Followers; The Ohio Hegelians: John B. Stallo, Peter Kaufmann, Moncure Conway, and August Willich, with Key Writings.* Athens, Ohio: Ohio University Press, 1966. ix, 353 pp.

Hartmann, Klaus. *Sartre's Ontology; A Study of Being and Nothingness in the Light of Hegel's Logic.* Evanston: Northwestern University Press, 1966. xviii, 166 pp.

1965   Kaufmann, Walter Arnold. *Hegel; Re-interpretation, Texts, and Kaufmann, Walter Arnold. *Hegel; Re-interpretation, Texts, and Commentary.* Garden City, N.Y.: Doubleday and Co., 1965/London: Weidenfeld & Nicolson, 1966. 498 pp., Bibliography, Index. Paperback ed., 2 vols., Anchor Books.

Loewenberg, Jacob. *Hegel's Phenomenology: Dialogues on the Life of Mind.* La Salle, Illinois: The Open Court Publishing Co., 1965. xv, 377 pp., Index.

Mure, Geoffrey Reginald Gilchrist. *The Philosophy of Hegel.* London: Oxford University Press (HUL), 1965. x, 213 pp., Bibliography, Index.

1964 *Hegel's Political Writings*, trans. by Sir Thomas Malcolm Knox, with
an Introductory Essay by Zbigniew Andrzej Pelczynski. Oxford: Clarendon Press, 1964, vii, 335 pp., Index.
Löwith, Karl. *From Hegel to Nietzsche: The Revolution in Nineteenth Century Thought*, trans. from the third revised German edition by David E. Green. New York: Holt, Rinehart and Winston,
1964/London: Constable, 1965. xiii, 464 pp., Bibliography, Notes,
Index. Paperback reprint, Anchor Books, 1967.

1963 Plamenatz, John. *Man and Society*. 2 Volumes. New York: Mc-
Graw-Hill Book Co., 1963. Volume II: Bentham through Marx, chs.
3 & 4: "The Social and Political Philosophy of Hegel."

1962 *Hegel on Tragedy*, edited, with an Introduction, by Anne and Henry
Paolucci. Garden City, N.Y.: Anchor Books, 1962. xxxi, 404 pp.,
Appendix: "Hegel's Theory of Tragedy," by A. C. Bradley, Index.
Kaminsky, Jack. *Hegel on Art. An Interpretation of Hegel's Aesthe-
tics.* New York: State University of New York, 1962. ix, 207 pp.,
Notes, Index.
Travis, Don Carlos, ed. *A Hegel Symposium*. Essays by Carl J. Frie-
drich, Sidney Hook, Helmut Motekat, Gustav E. Mueller, Helmut
Rehder, with an Introduction by the editor. Austin: The University
of Texas, 1962. 139 pp.

1960 Brinkley, Alan B., et al. *Studies in Hegel*. Tulane Studies in Philosophy
Volume IX. New Orleans: Tulane University/The Hague: Martinus
Nijhoff, 1960. 187 pp.
Hegel; Highlights, An Annotated Selection, ed. by Wanda Orynski,
Preface by Kurt F. Leidecker. New York: Philosophical Library,
1960. xvi, 5, 361 pp.

1959 *Hegel, Encyclopaedia of Philosophy*, trans. and annotated by Gustav
Emil Mueller. New York: Philosophical Library, 1959. 287 pp.

1958 Findlay, John Niemeyer. *Hegel: A Re-examination*. London: George
Allen & Unwin/New York: Humanities Press, 1958. Paperback re-
print, Collier Books, 1962. 372 pp., Appendix on "Dialectical Struc-
ture of Hegel's Main Works," Index.
Mure, Geoffrey Reginald Gilchrist. *Retreat From Truth*. Oxford:
Basil Blackwell, 1958. viii, 255 pp., Index.

1953 *The Philosophy of Hegel*, edited, with an Introduction and Notes, by
Carl Joachim Friedrich. New York: Random House, 1953. lxiv, 552
pp., Bibliography.
*Reason in History. A General Introduction to the Philosophy of
History.* G. W. F. Hegel, trans., with a Preface, Introduction, and
Note on the Text, by Robert S. Hartman. Indianapolis: The Bobbs-
Merrill Co., 1953. xlii, 95 pp.

1950 Mure, Geoffrey Reginald Gilchrist. *A Study of Hegel's Logic*. Oxford:
Clarendon Press, 1950. viii, 375 pp., Tables, Index. Reprinted 1959,
1967.

1949 Cairns, Huntington. *Legal Philosophy from Plato to Hegel*. Balti-
more: Johns Hopkins Press, 1949. xv, 583 pp.

1948 *Early Theological Writings*, translated by Sir Thomas Malcolm Knox, with an Introduction and Fragments translated by Richard Kroner. ["With the exception of the speech *On Classical Studies*, the translations have been made from Herman Nohl's *Hegels theologische Jugendschriften (Tübingen*, 1907)"]. Chicago: University of Chicago Press, 1948. xi, 340 pp., Bibliography, Index. Paperback edition with the title: *On Christianity. Early Theological Writings by Friedrich Hegel*. New York: Harper Torchbooks, 1961.

Pochman, Henry August. *New England Transcendentalism and St. Louis Hegelianism; Phases in the History of American Idealism.* Philadelphia: Carl Schurz Memorial Foundation, 1948. 144 pp.

1946   Collingwood, Robin George. *The Idea of History*, ed. and with a Preface by T. M. Knox. Oxford: Clarendon Press, 1946. xxvi, 339 pp., Index. Reprinted 1948, 1949. Paperback reprint, Oxford (GB), 1956, etc.

1945   Collingwood, Robin George. *The Idea of Nature*. Oxford: Clarendon Press, 1945. viii, 183 pp., Index. Prefatory Note by T. M. Knox. Paperback reprint 1960, 1967.

Popper, Karl Raimund. *The Open Society and its Enemies.* 2 vols., vol. 2: *The High Tide of Prophecy: Hegel, Marx, and the Aftermath.* London: G. Routledge & Sons, 1945. U.S. publisher, Princeton U. Press. Reprinted 1947, 1949. 2nd rev. ed., 1952, 3rd rev. ed., 1957, 4th rev. ed., 1962. Paperback reprint, Harper Torchbooks, 1963.

1944   Myers, Henry Alonzo. *The Spinoza-Hegel Paradox. A Study of the Choice Between Traditional Idealism and Systematic Pluralism.* Ithaca. N.Y.: Cornell University Press, 1944. xii, 95 pp.

1942   *Hegel's Philosophy of Right*, translated [from "the work which Hegel published in 1821 under the double title: *Naturrecht und Staatswissenschaft im Grundrisse* and *Grundlinien der Philosophie des Rechts*," with reference also "to the editions of Gans (Berlin, 1833 and 1854 . . .), Bolland (Leyden, 1902), and Lasson (Leipzig, 1921)"] with Notes by Sir Thomas Malcolm Knox. Oxford: Clarendon Press, 1942. xvi, 382 pp., Index. Reprinted 1945 (with corrections), 1949, 1953, 1958. Paperback reprints 1967, 1969.

1941   Gray, Jesse Glenn. *Hegel's Hellenic Ideal*. New York: King's Crown Press (Division of Columbia University Press), 1941. viii, 104 pp., Bibliography, Index. Reprinted (with rev. Bibliography) under the title *Hegel and Greek Thought*, New York: Harper Torchbooks, 1968. 106 pp.

Marcuse, Herbert. *Reason and Revolution, Hegel and the Rise of Social Theory.* London: Oxford University Press, 1941. xii, 431 pp., Bibliography, Index. 2nd edition, with Supplementary Epilogue and Bibliography, New York: Humanities Press/London: Routledge & Kegan Paul, 1954. xii, 439 pp. Reprinted 1958, 1963. Paperback reprint with a new Preface ("A Note on Dialectic"), Boston: Beacon Press, 1960. xvi, 431 pp., Supplement to the Bibliography.

1940   Mure, Geoffrey Reginald Gilchrist. *An Introduction to Hegel*. Oxford: Clarendon Press, 1940. xx, 180 pp., Index. Reprinted 1948, 1959.

1939 Maier, Josef. *On Hegel's Critique of Kant.* New York: Columbia University Press, 1939. viii, 108 pp., Bibliography, Index. Reprinted New York: AMS Press, 1966.

1937 Rāju, Poolla Tirupati. *Thought and Reality; Hegelianism and Advaita* [i.e. the Advaita Vedanta of Sankara Acharya]. Foreword by J. H. Muirhead. London: G. Allen & Unwin, 1937. 285 pp.

1936 Hook, Sidney. *From Hegel to Marx. Studies in the Intellectual Development of Karl Marx.* New York: Reynal & Hitchcock, 1936. 335 pp., Index. Reprinted, New York: Humanities Press, 1950, 1958, 1962.

   Knox, Israel. *The Aesthetic Theories of Kant, Hegel and Schopenhauer.* New York: Columbia University Press, 1936. xi, 219 pp.

1935 Cross, Geoffrey John. *Prologue and Epilogue to Hegel.* Oxford: Pen-in-Hand Publishing Co., 1935. 107 pp.

   Foster, Michael Beresford. *The Political Philosophies of Plato and Hegel.* Oxford: Clarendon Press, 1935. xii, 207 pp., Glossary, Index. Reprinted, New York: Russell & Russell, Inc., 1965.

1932 Lion, Aline. *The Idealist Conception of Religion. Vico, Hegel, Gentile, etc.* Oxford: Clarendon Press, 1932. xvi, 208 pp.

1929 *Hegel's Logic of World and Idea*; being a translation of the second and third parts of the Subjective Logic, with Introduction on "Idealism Limited and Absolute," by Henry Stewart Macran. Oxford: Clarendon Press, 1929. 215 pp.

   Hegel's Science of Logic, trans. by Walter Henry Johnston and Leslie Graham Struthers. With an Introductory Preface by Viscount Haldane of Cloan. ["The greater part of this translation was made from the edition published in 1923 by Felix Meiner, Leipzig, edited by Dr. George Lasson, of Berlin"] 2 vols. London: G. Allen & Unwin/New York: The Macmillan Co., 1929. Reprinted 1951, 1961.

   Hegel Selections, edited, and with an Introduction and Short Bibliography, by Jacob Loewenberg. New York: Charles Scribner's Sons, 1929. xliii, 468 pp. Paperback reprint, 1957, etc.

1927 Haldar, Hiralal. *Neo-Hegelianism.* London: Heath Cranton, Ltd., 1927. vii, 493 pp.

   Sturge, Mary Charlotte. *Opposite Things. A Popular Interpretation of Hegel's Doctrine of the Reconciliation of Opposites.* Bristol: Burleigh, 1927. 110 pp.

1926 Chang, W. S. (I). *The Development, Significance and Some Limitations of Hegel's Ethical Teaching.* Preface by J. A. Smith (Oxford). Shanghai: The Commercial Press, 1926. x, 137 pp.

1925 Cooper, Rebecca. *The Logical Influence of Hegel on Marx,* in University of Washington Publications in the Social Sciences, Vol. 2, No. 2, pp. 85-182. Seattle: University of Washington Press, 1925.

1924 Stace, Walter Terence. *The Philosophy of Hegel: A Systematic Exposition.* London: Macmillan & Co., 1924. x, 526 pp., Index, Diagram of the Hegelian System. Paperback reprint, New York: Dover Publications, 1955, etc.

1921 Reyburn, Hugh Adam. *The Ethical Theory of Hegel. A Study of the*

Philosophy of Right. Oxford: Clarendon Press, 1921. xx, 271 pp., Index. Reprinted 1967.

Sedlák, Francis. *Pure Thought and the Riddle of the Universe.* [The author has "aimed at an original elaboration of the whole subject-matter" of Hegel's *Wissenschaft der Logik.*] Volume 1, *Creation of Heaven and Earth.* London: G. Allen & Unwin, 1921. 390 pp.

1920   *The Philosophy of Fine Art* by G. W. F. Hegel, translated, with notes, by Francis Plumptre Beresford Osmaston. "The first complete translation in English of the three volumes devoted to this subject in the collected edition [ed. H. G. Hotho] (Berlin, 1835)". London: G. Bell, and Sons, Ltd., 1920. Index (vol. 4).

1919   Royce, Josiah. *Lectures on Modern Idealism,* ed. with a Preface by Jacob Loewenberg. New Haven: Yale University Press, 1919. xii, 266 pp., Index. Paperback reprint (fourth printing), with New Foreword by John E. Smith, 1964. xvi, 266 pp., Index.

1916   Flaccus, Louis William. *Artists and Thinkers.* Freeport, N.Y.: Books For Libraries Press, 1916. 200 pp. "Hegel," pp. 104-139. Reprinted 1967.

1915   Croce, Benedetto. *What is Living and What is Dead of the Philosophy of Hegel.* Translated from the original text of the third Italian edition (1912), by Douglas Ainslie. London: Macmillan & Co., 1915. xviii, 217 pp. Reprinted, New York: Russell & Russell, Inc., 1969.

1912   Macran, Henry Stewart. *Hegel's Doctrine of Formal Logic,* being a translation of the first section of the Subjective Logic, with Introduction and Notes. Oxford: Clarendon Press, 1912. 315 pp.

1911   Kelly, Michael (M.A., M.D.). *Hegel's Charlatanism Exposed.* London: George Allen & Co., 1911. 167 pp.

Sedlák, Francis. *A Holiday With A Hegelian, Introducing A Discussion of the Hegelian Philosophy.* London: A. C. Fifield, 1911. 190 pp.

1910   Adams, George Plimpton. *The Mystical Element in Hegel's Early Theological Writings,* in the University of California Publications in Philosophy, Vol. 2, No. 4, pp. 67-102. Berkeley: The University Press, 1910.

Cunningham, Gustavus Watts. *Thought and Reality in Hegel's System.* New York: Longmans, Green & Co., 1910. iv, 151 pp.

Haldar, Hiralal. *Hegelianism and Human Personality.* Calcutta: University Studies, 1910. v, 61 pp.

McTaggart, John McTaggart Ellis. *A Commentary on Hegel's Logic.* Cambridge: Cambridge University Press, 1910. xv, 311 pp. Reprinted New York: Russell & Russell, Inc., 1964.

The Phenomenology of Mind, by G. W. F. Hegel; translated with an Introduction and Notes, by Sir James Black Baillie. 2 vols. London: S. Sonnenschein & Co., Ltd./New York: The Macmillan Co., 1910. 2nd ed., revised and corrected throughout, 1 vol. London: G. Allen & Unwin/New York: The Macmillan Co., 1931. 814 pp., Index. Third impression 1949, 4th 1955. Paperback reprint, with a new Introduction by George Lichtheim, Harper Torchbooks, 1967. xxxv, Bibliography, 814 pp., Index.

1909   Mackenzie, Hettie Millicent. *Hegel's Educational Theory and Practice*, with an Introductory Note by J. S. Mackenzie. London: Swan Sonnenschein & Co., 1909. xxi, 192 pp.

1908   Dresser, Horatio Willis. *The Philosophy of the Spirit*. A Study of the Spiritual Nature of Man and the Presence of God, with a supplementary essay on the Logic of Hegel. New York & London: G. P. Putnam's Sons, 1908. xiv, 545 pp.

1907   Seth, Andrew (Pringle-Pattison). *The Philosophical Radicals, And Other Essays*. With Chapters Reprinted on the Philosophy of Religion in Kant and Hegel. Edinburg & London: William Blackwood & Sons, 1907. x, 336 pp.

1906   *Hegel not Haeckel, or "The Riddle of the Universe" Solved* . . . edited by a student of Hegel. Birmingham: C. Combridge, 1906. 12 pp.

1903   Mackintosh, Robert. *Hegel and Hegelianism*. Edinburg: T. & T. Clark, 1903. viii, 303 pp., Index. Reprinted 1913.

1902   Hibben, John Grier. *Hegel's Logic. An Essay in Interpretation*. New York: C. Scribner's Sons. 1902. x, 313 pp. Appendix: "A Glossary of the More Important Philosophical Terms in Hegel's Logic."

1901   Baillie, Sir James Black. *The Origin and Significance of Hegel's Logic. A General Introduction to Hegel's System*. London: Macmillan & Co., 1901. xviii, 375 pp.

        McTaggart, John McTaggart Ellis. *Studies in Hegelian Cosmology*. Cambridge: Cambridge University Press, 1901. xx, 292 pp. 2nd ed. 1918.

1897   *The Wisdom and Religion of a German Philosopher, Being Selections from the Writings of G. W. F. Hegel*. Collected and edited by Elizabeth Sanderson Haldane. London: K. Paul, Trench, Trübner & Co., Ltd., 1897. x, 1, 138 pp.

1896   Bryant, William McKendree. *Hegel's Educational Ideas*. New York & Chicago: Werner School Book Company, 1896. 214 pp.

        Hegel's Philosophy of Right, trans. by Samuel Walters Dyde. London: G. Bell and Sons, 1896. xxx, 365 pp.

        Lectures on the History of Philosophy, by Georg Wilhelm Friedrich Hegel. Edited and translated from the German [second and amended edition of the *Geschichte der Philosophie* ed. Michelet, 1840, from all available sources including the notes of students] by Elizabeth Sanderson Haldane and Frances H. Simson. In 3 vols., vol. 3. London: K. Paul, Trench, Trübner & Co., Ltd., 1896. viii, 571 pp., Index, Corrigenda for vols. I & II. Reprinted, London: Routledge & Kegan Paul/New York: Humanities Press, 1955, 1963.

        Luqueer, Frederic Ludlow. *Hegel as Educator*. Part I, Hegel's Life; Part II, translations, mainly from Gustav Thaulow's *Hegels Ansichten über Erziehung und Unterricht* (3 vols., 1853-4). New York: Columbia University Press/Macmillan & Co., 1896. x, 185 pp. Reprinted, New York: AMS Press, Inc., 1967.

        McTaggart, John McTaggart Ellis. *Studies in the Hegelian Dialectic*. Cambridge: Cambridge University Press, 1896. xvi, 259 pp. 2nd ed. rev. 1922, xvi, 255 pp. Reprinted, New York: Russell & Russell, Inc., 1964.

1895 *Lectures on the Philosophy of Religion, Together with a Work on the Proofs of the Existence of God, by Georg Wilhelm Friedrich Hegel,* trans. from the 2nd German edition [of Marheineke, 1840] by the Rev. Ebenezer Brown Speirs and Miss J. Burdon Sanderson, the translation edited by Rev. Speirs. 3 vols. London: K. Paul, Trench, Trübner, & Co., 1895. (Index, vol. 3). Reprinted, London: Routledge & Kegan Paul, 1962.

1894 *Hegel's Philosophy of Mind,* translated from *The Encyclopaedia of the Philosophical Sciences* with Five Introductory Essays by William Wallace. Oxford: Clarendon Press, 1894. 320 pp., Index.

Lectures on the History of Philosophy, by Georg Wilhelm Friedrich Hegel. Edited and translated from the German [second and amended edition of the *Geschichte der Philosophie,* ed. Michelet, 1840, from all available sources including the notes of students] by Elizabeth Sanderson Haldane and Frances H. Simson. In 3 vols., vol. 2. London: K. Paul, Trench, Trübner & Co., Ltd., 1894. vi, 453 pp. Reprinted, London: Routledge & Kegan Paul/New York: Humanities Press, 1955, 1963.

Wallace, William. *Prolegomena to the Study of Hegel's Philosophy and Especially of his Logic.* 2nd edition, revised and augmented. Oxford: Clarendon Press, 1894. xix, 477 pp. Reprinted, New York: Russell & Russell, Inc., 1968.

1893 Ritchie, David George. *Darwin and Hegel,* with other philosophical studies. London: Sonnenschein & Co., 1893. xv, 285 pp.

Sterrett, James Macbride. *The Ethics of Hegel.* Translated selections from his *Rechtsphilosophie,* with an Introduction. Boston: Ginn & Co., 1893. xii, 216 pp., Bibliography.

1892 *Lectures on the History of Philosophy,* by Georg Wilhelm Friedrich Hegel. Edited and translated from the German [second and amended edition of the *Geschichte der Philosophie,* ed. Michelet, 1840, from all available sources including the notes of students] by Elizabeth Sanderson Haldane. In 3 vols., vol. 1: London: K. Paul, Trench, Trübner & Co., Ltd., 1892. xvi, 487 pp. Reprinted, London: Routledge & Kegan Paul/New York: Humanities Press, 1955, 1963.

Royce, Josiah. *The Spirit of Modern Philosophy. An Essay in the Form of Lectures.* Boston & New York: Houghton Mifflin Company, 1892. xv, 519 pp., Index. Reprinted 1899. Ch. VII on Hegel; Appendix C on "The Hegelian Theory of Universals."

1890 Harris, William Torrey. *Hegel's Logic. A Book on the Genesis of the Categories of the Mind. A Critical Exposition.* Chicago: S. C. Griggs & Co., 1890. xxx, 403 pp. Second edition, 1895. Reprinted, New York: Kraus Reprint Co., 1970.

Sterrett, James Macbride. *Studies in Hegel's Philosophy of Religion, with a Chapter on Christian Unity in America.* New York: D. Appleton & Co., 1890/London: Swan, Sonnenschein & Co., 1891, xiii, 348 pp.

1887 Morris, George Sylvester. *Hegel's Philosophy of the State and of History.* Chicago: S. C. Griggs & Co., 1887. xiii, 306 pp. 2nd ed., 1892.

Seth, Andrew (Pringle-Pattison). *Hegelianism and Personality*. London: W. Blackwood & Sons, 1887. xi, 230 pp. 2nd edition, Edinburgh: W. Blackwood & Sons, 1893. xv, 242 pp.

1886 *The Introduction to Hegel's Philosophy of Fine Art*, translated from the German, with Notes and a Prefatory Essay "On the True Conception of Another World," by Bernard Bosanquet. London: K. Paul, Trench & Co., 1886. xxxiii, 175 pp. 2nd impression 1905, 211 pp. Reprinted, with a new introduction by M. Moran, 1969.

The Philosophy of Art. An Introduction to the Scientific Study of Aesthetics. By Hegel and C. L. Michelet, translated from the German by William Hastie. Edinburgh: Oliver & Boyd, 1886. xv, 118 pp.

1885 Kedney, John Steinfort. *Hegel's Aesthetics. A Critical Exposition*. Chicago: S. C. Griggs & Co., 1885. xviii, 302 pp. 3rd edition, Chicago: Scott, Foresman & Co., 1897.

1883 Caird, Edward. *Hegel*. Edinburgh & London: William Blackwood & Sons, 1883 etc. viii, 224 pp. Reprinted, Hamden, Conn.: Archon Books, 1968.

1882 Seth, Andrew (Pringle-Pattison). *The Development from Kant to Hegel, with Chapters on the Philosophy of Religion*. London: Williams & Norgate, 1882. iv, 170 pp.

1881 Harris, William Torrey. *Hegel's Doctrine of Reflection*, being a paraphrase and a commentary interpolated into the text of the second volume of Hegel's Larger Logic, treating of "Essence." New York: D. Appleton & Co., 1881. 214 pp.

1879 *The Philosophy of Art*; being the Second Part of Hegel's *Aesthetik*, in which are unfolded historically the three great fundamental phases of the art-activity of the world. Translated, and accompanied with an Introductory Essay giving an outline of the entire *Aesthetik*, by William McKendree Bryant. New York: D. Appleton & Co., 1879. liv, 194 pp.

1874 *The Logic of Hegel, translated from The Encyclopaedia of the Philosophical Sciences, with Prolegomena*, by William Wallace. Oxford: Clarendon Press, 1874. clxxxiv, 332 pp., Index. 2nd edition, revised and augmented [with *Prolegomena* issued in a separate volume, 1894; see above] 1892. xxvi, 439 pp. Reprinted 1904, 1931, 1950.

1873 Stirling, James Hutchison. *Lectures on the Philosophy of Law. Together with Whewell and Hegel, and Hegel and Mr. W. R. Smith*, a vindication in a physico-mathematical regard. London: Longmans, Green & Co., 1873. v, 139 pp.

1869 Harris, William Torrey. *Hegel's First Principle: An Exposition of Comprehension and Idea (Begriff und Idee)*. With an Introduction and explanatory notes. St. Louis: G. Knapp & Co., 1869. 82 pp.

1865 Stirling, James Hutchison. *The Secret of Hegel, Being the Hegelian System in Origin, Principle, Form and Matter*. 2 vols. London: Longman, Green, Longman, Roberts, & Green, 1865. New Edition, Carefully revised (1 vol.), Edinburgh: Oliver & Boyd/London: Simpkin, Marshall & Co., Ltd./New York: G. P. Putnam's Sons, 1898. lxiii, 751 pp. Reprinted, Dubuque, Iowa: Wm. C. Brown Reprint Library, 1967.

1857 *Hegel's Lectures on the Philosophy of History*, translated from the 3rd German edition [ed. by Karl Hegel] by John Sibree. London: H. G. Bohn, 1857 etc., xxxix, 477 pp. Last unrevised edition, London: G. Bell and Sons, 1902. Revised edition, with Prefaces by Charles Hegel and the translator, John Sibree, under the title *The Philosophy of History*, by Georg Wilhelm Friedrich Hegel. New York: The Colonial Press, 1899/New York: Willey Book Co., 1944, xvi, 457 pp. Paperback reprint, with a new Introduction by Carl Joachim Friedrich, New York: Dover Publications, 1956 etc., xvi, 457 pp.

1856 Vera, Augusto. *An Inquiry into Speculative and Experimental Science*, with special reference to Mr. Calderwood and Professor Ferrier's recent publications, and to Hegel's doctrine. London: Longman, 1856.

1855 *The Subjective Logic of Hegel*, translated by H. Sloman and Jean Wallon; revised by a graduate of Oxford. To which are added some remarks by H. S. London: J. Chapman, 1855.

1848 Stallo, John Bernhard. *General Principles of the Philosophy of Nature*: with an outline of some of its recent developments among the Germans, embracing the philosophical systems of Schelling and Hegel, and Oken's system of nature. Boston: W. Crosby and H. P. Nichols, 1848. xii, 520 pp.